*Process, Praxis,
and Transcendence*

SUNY series in the Philosophy of the Social Sciences
Lenore Langsdorf, Editor

Process, Praxis, and Transcendence

James L. Marsh

STATE UNIVERSITY OF NEW YORK PRESS

Published by
State University of New York Press, Albany

© 1999 State University of New York

For information, address State University of New York
Press, State University Plaza, Albany, N.Y. 12246

Production by E. Moore
Marketing by Anne Valentine

Library of Congress Cataloging-in-Publication Data

Marsh, James L.
     Process, praxis, and transcendence / James L. Marsh.
         p.   cm. — (SUNY series in the philosophy of the social
     sciences)
     Includes bibliographical references and index.
     ISBN 0-7914-4073-7 (hardcover : alk. paper). — ISBN 0-7914-4074-5
     (pbk. : alk. paper)
         1. Metaphysics. 2. Religion—Philosophy. 3. Phenomenology.
     4. Existentialism. 5. Imperialism. 6. Liberation theology.
     7. Political science—Philosophy. 8. Liberty. I. Title.
     II. Series.
     B945.M373P76 1999
     191—dc21
                                                                      98-16746
                                                                      CIP

10 9 8 7 6 5 4 3 2 1

To

Thomas Merton and Daniel Berrigan
prophets of resistance and liberation
who have blazed the trail
human and religious
contemplative and active
theoretical and practical
personal and political
            that we
living in the center of the empire
            must walk

꩜

Contents

Preface

At long last, I have come to the end of a journey, a project conceived in September 1981. It would eventually entail the three volumes of *Post-Cartesian Meditations* (PCM; New York: Fordham University Press, 1988), *Critique, Action, and Liberation* (CAL; Albany: SUNY Press, 1994), and the present work. I immediately wrote, in 1981, versions of what would become chapters 5 and 6 of this book.

Initially I intended to write one long book, a twentieth-century *Phenomenology* of spirit, but radicalized by a critique of capitalism and imperialism, radicalized by a reading of *Capital*, both the text and the socio-economic system. Soon, realism overtook me, and a one volume project became three volumes, roughly modeled again on Hegel, the last volume of his *Encyclopedia*. PCM, a phenomenology and hermeneutics of the human subject in the world, corresponds to subjective spirit; CAL, my own version of critical theory, to objective spirit; and this book, *Process, Praxis, and Transcendence*, to absolute spirit. But again, all three volumes are radical and critical in a way that Hegel is not. PCM concludes with a Freudian and neo-Marxist hermeneutics of suspicion, CAL with a critique and overcoming of capitalism and the creation of democratic socialism as a preferable ethical alternative, and this volume with a critique and overcoming of neoimperialism. Hegel's philosophy of world history I also have in mind here, but now radicalized. The parousia has not arrived either intellectually or socially, but needs to be anticipated and created through critique and praxis. Fully adequate dialectical and phenomenological rationality is at odds with and moves to transcend a structurally unjust status quo, not become reconciled with it.

If, as Heidegger has said somewhere, every philosopher has one main idea, then mine, perhaps, is the link between rationality and radicalism in all three volumes. There is not adequate rationality without radicalism; a non-radical rationality, a merely bourgeois rationality, is one that has not gone all the way with questioning, has short-circuited itself, reined itself in, and settled. Radicalism without sufficient rationality, on the other hand, also is problematic; this is one of the main reasons for my thoroughgoing engagement with postmodernism in all three volumes, but especially in CAL. Postmodernism in the works of thinkers like Derrida, Foucault, late Heidegger, Deleuze-Guattari, Lyotard, Baudrillard, and John Caputo has a powerful, insightful, and prophetic critique of capitalist and state socialist modernity. Because the critique of modern, Western rationality is so total, however, these thinkers are unable to ground their critique adequately. As a result and as I argued in CAL, postmodernism becomes a form of ideology, French ideology. It dominantly and reflectively covers up and legitimates late capitalism in its latest phase.

Rather than severing prophetic critique from rationality, therefore, my effort has been to link them in a prophetic, critical rationality or rational, critical prophecy. All of this occurs in a project that, like thinkers such as Ricoeur, Habermas, Lonergan, and David Tracy—all important influences on my thought—strives to be as Hegelian as intellectual honesty allows in the twentieth century. Here is another reason for my energetic engagement with postmodern thought, which tries to limit the purview and validity of rationality too much. The result of my encounter with postmodernism is that modern, Western rationality, while I deny it the right to triumphalistic, overly certain excess, can be a great deal more comprehensive, evidential, systematic, and normatively cogent than postmodernism thinks such rationality has a right to be. My work, then, does not simply reject postmodernism; it has a good deal that is valid to say about such excesses. Its mistake is to think that such excess is essential to Western rationality as such.

The method used throughout these three volumes is "dialectical phenomenology," which has a descriptive moment oriented to describing and arriving at eidetic structures in a lived present of experience, hermeneutical retrieval of the past, and a suspicious critique of psychological and social structures which is committed to a liberating, future praxis. The retrieval and suspicion are directed toward particular structures; the description and eidetic reflection are oriented to universals structuring and giving meaning to experience. There is, therefore, a dialectical interplay between universal and particular in all three volumes: between the phenomenology of the self and reflection on the particular psychological and social unconscious in PCM, between a phenomenology of action and ethical reflection in Part One and interpretation, critique, and overcoming of capitalism in Part Two of CAL, and between a phenomenology of self leading into a processive metaphysics and processive God in Part One; and hermeneutical interpretation and affirmation of a Liberator God linked to a critique and overcoming of neo-imperialism in Part Two of this work. Explanation is not only linked to a hermeneutics of the particular in Part Two, but it also is related to the phenomenology of the self in Part One as its natural metaphysical completion and fulfillment. Description leads into explanation in Part One, and understanding leads into explanation in Part Two in the accounts of Christianity and neoimperialism.

As in PCM and CAL, in this volume in each part there is a movement from cognition as experience, understanding, and judgment to freedom and commitment to action: from the phenomenology of self leading to a metaphysics in the first four chapters of Part One to the self's free relating to God in chapter 5 to the conception of a speculative-political metaphysics in chapter 6, from the affirmation of Jesus Christ as God in chapter 7 and suspicious reflection on such faith in chapter 8 through a hermeneutics of Jesus Christ liberator; intellectual, moral, and religious conversion as radical, political conversion, religious belief and ideology critique, and modernity and religious belief in chapters 9, 10, 11, and 12 respectively to the critique and overcoming of neoimperialism in chapters 13 and 14. Thus, the cognitive, free, acting, socially related, and historical self is the relative "foundation" of both Parts One and Two. I make no apologies about this point. I think postmodernism has shown the invalidity of a totally immediate, apodictic, absolute foundationalism and sense of self, but not mediated, fallibilistic, situated versions of these.

As well, the reader will note parallels between chapters in Part One and Part Two; between the reflection on Kant, Heidegger, and Derrida as questioning the possibility of metaphysics in chapter 1 and interpreting Freud, Nietzsche, and Marx as masters of suspicion in chapter 8, between the speculative-political metaphysics in chapter 6 and religious belief and ideology critique in chapter 11, between freedom's relationship to God in chapter 5, and intellectual, moral, and religious conversion in chapter 10.

This volume, thus, has various relationships with PCM and CAL. In one sense it sublates and builds on them. Thus both personal and social being become just aspects or parts of the being affirmed metaphysically, created and sustained by God, loved redemptively by Jesus Christ, and liberated by a praxis oriented to social, environmental justice. This volume builds on premises and insights from PCM and CAL such as critical, mediated realism, self-appropriation, an ethics of right, morality, and justice, and the critique and overcoming of capitalism. In another sense, this volume expands and generalizes the accounts of PCM and CAL from parts or aspects of being to all of being, from this world as life-world relative to a social self to God and Jesus Christ as ground and savior, from the accounts of personal and historical development in PCM and CAL to development and process as such, and from an interpretation and critique of merely national, Northern capitalism to an interpretation and critique of international capitalism, and from intellectual and moral conversion to religious conversion. Finally, self-appropriation in PCM functions as the basis that is expanded horizontally into an ethics and critical theory of society in CAL and vertically into a metaphysics and philosophy of religion in this work.

Christian theology used in Part Two, foundational in chapter 9 insofar as reflection about whether or not to believe in Jesus Christ occurs and systematic in subsequent chapters insofar as hermeneutical reflection on the Christian message occurs, is simply the hermeneutics of the particular or an aspect of the hermeneutics of the particular, linked to a hermeneutics of international capitalism, that is analogous to similar hermeneutics in PCM and CAL. I refer to my effort in this book as a "philosophy of religion" because the theological moment completes and crowns the philosophical movement of the three volumes. But I would not object if the reader qualifies the description even more: "philosophy of religion-theology."[1]

Even though the book is written with a fallibilistic intent in a pluralistic context of dialogue and scholarly interpretation and critique, I nonetheless have a certain confidence in the method, content, and results. Part of the basis for that confidence is intellectual; a lifetime of reading and reflection and writing has gone into all three volumes. Part of the confidence is also personal and existential. I have tried to live and act out many of the recommendations in this book relating to social change as well as personal, intellectual, ethical, and religious transformation. I have regularly protested, demonstrated, run the risk of arrest, written letters, articles, and books, taught, given talks, spoken at rallies; meditated, prayed, contemplated, worked with and for the poor, homeless, and unemployed. All of these activities and others seem to me to be essential in our socio-historical situation in which the fundamental question is "How does one live as a human being and religious person of conscience within the center of the most virulent empire in the history of humankind?" My answer, theoretical and practical, is a lived resistance to empire and the creation of a positive, human, communal, socialist alternative. Thus, the solution recommended here theoretically has "worked" and is working for me in my life as well; it has practical, existential resonance for me. In a society as unjust, alienating, and dehumanizing as ours is, the most adequate kind of sanity, peace, and happiness open to us is such theoretical and practical resistance and the creation of a positive alternative. Anything else is flight and evasion.

Thus the reader will understand my relentless critique of bourgeois forms of rationality or critical theory such as that of Habermas, which do not go all the way socially or politically, and postmodernists such as Foucault or Derrida who sever rationality from critique too much and thus run the risk of being a safe form of radical theory that turns into, as I argued in CAL, an ideology reflecting, legitimizing, and covering up late capitalism in its latest phase of flexible accumulation, a regimen characterized by the full internationalization of capital, the importance of commodity as image and image as commodity, the dominance of money capital, the attack on the welfare state to the extent that that serves the poor, attacks on labor unions, greater use of part-time labor, more flexible, short range production and marketing of products and less high inventories of goods, and the tendency of firms to farm out work to other, smaller firms.[2]

"Transcendence" in my title refers both to subjective and objective, noetic and noematic aspects. Subjectively it refers to activities of self-transcendence, cognitive, ethical, and metaphysical-religious flowing from and leading to intellectual, moral, and religious conversion. Objectively it refers to the objects of such self-transcendence, being, the right and the good, and God and Christ as related respectively to cognitive, ethical, and metaphysical-religious self-transcendence. What flows from transcendence in both the subjective and objective senses is liberation from social injustice, psychological repression, and sin. Liberation as process is a theoretical-practical praxis of self-transcendence. As goal or object it is the fully liberated person and society. Full self-transcendence and liberation, of course, are radical: intellectual, moral, and religious conversion leading to radical political conversion. This book is an essay, perhaps one of the first to speak in its own voice, in a conceptually systematic and hermeneutical North American philosophy and theology of liberation.[3]

Finally, the reader will understand more fully why I dedicate the book to Daniel Berrigan and Thomas Merton. These two have prophetically illumined the path, contemplative and active, personal and political, human and religious, that I think is necessary to take in the late twentieth century and the beginning of the twenty-first century. Thus theorists such as Husserl, Lonergan, Hegel, and Marx help set the theoretical agenda of these works, and others like Kierkegaard, Berrigan, Merton, and Moltmann help set the practical, existential, political agenda. The reader could do worse than to read this book as a passage between, and back and forth between, these theoretical and practical axes. A fully adequate theory leads to and justifies radical praxis; radical praxis requires rigorous, comprehensive, profound theory.

Finally, last but not least, I wish to express appreciation to my student-typist-colleague, Anne Pomeroy. She has patiently and very competently typed this whole manuscript and given me invaluable input on the content as well. Whatever quality there is in the manuscript would be much less present without her efforts. Nancy McCarthy in the Fordham Office of Research has also generously supplied me funds for word processing, and Sarah Borden has done an excellent job of proofreading.

Part 1

❦

The Self, Being, and God:
Toward a Speculative-Political
Metaphysics

ONE

On the Overcoming of Metaphysics

We need at the very beginning of this book to meet and deal with a challenge to the very foundations of this project. Has not metaphysics, an enterprise attempting to think being and God in a comprehensive, systematic, and rigorous way, been undermined as impossible and illegitimate: impossible because it goes beyond the limits of what we can know, illegitimate because it is an attempt to incorporate, dominate, and repress the other? Kant, Heidegger, and Derrida represent three developing stages of this project of overcoming metaphysics.[1]

The Dialectic of Overcoming Metaphysics

Kant

Kant's *Critique of Pure Reason* is the main source of modern and postmodern critiques of metaphysics. As is well known, this book is an inquiry into the limits of what we can know. Knowledge for Kant lies in the unity of concept and intuition. Intuitions are rooted in sensibility, concepts in understanding. Because science has access to both concepts and intuitions, scientific knowledge can be valid. I can have sensible intuitions that I organize into knowledge of "a chair" with the category of "substance." I can combine intuitions with the category of "cause" to understand the way fire cooks meat.[2]

If correct knowledge has two components, concept and intuition, then metaphysical knowledge can be faulted for having only one, the concept or idea. The three basic metaphysical entities, the external thing, the subject or soul, and God, all reveal themselves to be unknowable noumena, for which we would need an intellectual intuition to know. Since such intuitions are lacking to us and the only intuitions are of sensible particulars rooted in space and time, we have to say that metaphysics as speculative knowledge of noumena is impossible. We are confined to having an objective knowledge of sensible appearances, not things in themselves.[3]

Reinforcing such reflections on knowledge is Kant's conception of the Copernican revolution. Formerly men and women were "realistic" in that knowledge was thought of as conformity to external reality in a passive, unmediated way. As a result of the Copernican revolution of modern science, however, we know now that knowledge occurs through active putting of questions to things. Since, however, it is presumptuous to think that reality should conform to and respond to our questions, we must say that we know only appearances, not reality. Reality would have to be an object of an unmediated, passive intuition, which is not available to us. Objective knowledge is mediated and dependent on us; objective knowledge of reality would have to be of an independent reality present to us in an unmediated way.[4]

What seems apparent, first of all, is an illegitimate dichotomy in Kant between unorganized, brute data and organizing intelligence. Phenomenologically what seems apparent is that I experience and perceive and organize wholes in a context: the brown table in the room, the television set in the corner, or the couch in the living room. Phenomenologically we can describe no such thing as bare, unmediated sense data. Even the "points" or "dots" are seen as "points" or "dots" *in a context*, for example, the white dots on a blackboard.[5]

If Kant's account of the relationship between sensible phenomena and universal categories were true, moreover, there would be nothing in our perceptual experience that could limit or constrain our interpretations of that experience. All interpretations would be equally arbitrary and equally valid. Yet reflection on our experience indicates that some interpretations of our experience are more valid than others. "Couch" is an appropriate designation for this object in my room, "broom" for this implement in the corner. Even Kant at times argues that some categories are applicable in some situations and not in others. "Cause," for example, is applicable in understanding a boat going down a river, not for interpreting a house.[6]

A second related point is that such perceptual wholes appear to us within our experience as distinct from us. The table is "there" in contrast to me "here," is thematic in contrast to my own prethematic awareness of myself as embodied, conscious, intelligent, and intending the object. Its content is independent of me, in the sense that whether I like it or not, choose it or not, it is brown and not red, rectangular rather than circular, rough rather than smooth. The table is detachable from my experience in a way that my own lived body is not. I leave the room and thus leave the table behind, but I cannot leave my body behind. Finally, the table has objective content, verifiable by and accessible to other observers. If I were to say that it was red, circular, or smooth, they would immediately contest this claim.[7]

A further question is the following: is there any reason for distinguishing or separating the thing as present to our own experience, objective, verifiable, from a "thing in itself" as Kant does? If one takes Kant as saying that there are independent things outside experience that nonetheless exist, underlie, and cause phenomena, then the claim is self-contradictory. For I am claiming to know unknowable things in themselves, and I am using categories like "existence" or "substance" or "cause" supposedly applicable to appearances within experience to things outside experience. If we take "noumenon" or "thing in itself" as just limiting concepts, then we need to ask whether they are valid, whether they make sense. They do make a kind of sense, of course; otherwise we would not have been discussing them for three centuries. But is it not a self-contradictory sense? Does it make full, valid sense to talk about a reality totally outside and unrelated to our experience and to things within it? I think not. Moreover, as manifesting ideals of intuitive looking or taking a good look, they are invalid.[8]

Objectively perceivable things intersubjectively available in our experience are the true things in themselves. To say this is not to deny that I can make mistakes; the bent stick in the water turns out to be straight, and the beautiful woman in the department store turns out to be a dummy. But these mistakes are rectified within the course of conscious experience, and a new objectivity emerges, the "straight stick in the water" or the "department store dummy." If we wished, therefore, to save Kant's notion of thing in itself by modifying it to mean "the thing as known through a succession of perceptions that correct one another," exemplified by our corrected perceptions of the "straight stick in the water" and the "department store dummy," this emerges from within knowledge and experience, not outside them.

Where Kant seems to have erred is to have owned up to the fact that there is no unmediated knowledge, but to have held that up to an ideal of immediacy, an immediate, naked intuition of things in themselves. Rather than giving that ideal up in the light of his own quite subtle and enlightening account of human knowledge, he used that ideal to criticize mediated knowledge and find it wanting. But when we honestly, phenomenologically examine the way human beings know, the ideal is itself shown to be unfounded and arbitrary, not able to be grounded in a return to the things in Husserl's sense. Kant's ideal here shows itself to be an example of "philosophizing from on high" in Husserl's sense, using an unwarranted concept of validity that an adequate account of knowledge should force us to renounce. Kant does not have the courage of his convictions and, therefore, remains a disillusioned naive realist or a half-hearted idealist.[9]

Similar reflections occur when we look at Kant's account of the second main noumenon, the soul or self. Rather than being some unknowable entity outside experience, the self is the experienced, conscious agency within experience. Here several points must be made. A) Kant's concept of experience is narrow. Experience is not only of data of sense but also of data of consciousness. When I experience, understand, and judge that the chair is in the room, I am aware not only of the sensible presence of the chair but also of myself as moving around it, looking at it, wondering about it, and using it.[10]

B) Intentionality is operative in at least three senses, empirical, intelligent, and rational. Intentionality includes the object intended, the act of intending, and the self as the agent intending. Correlative to the sensible gestalt are the empirical acts of seeing, touching, moving around, and lifting. Correlative to the meaning and purpose of the chair is the act of understanding it as a chair. Correlative to the reality of the chair is the act of judgment affirming it as real. Underlying and present in each of these acts is the self as their source. I see, I touch, I move around, I lift, I understand, and I judge. Not only is the self an agent and source of acts, but it also unifies them over time. Just as it is the same chair that is seen, touched, lifted, used, understood, and judged, it is the same self who sees, touches, lifts, uses, understands, and judges. This self unifies and synthesizes these activities and contents. Thus, the shape of the chair seen is integrated with the roughness of the chair touched, and they are both aspects of the same chair. Unity in the object presupposes unity in the subject, and this unity is not only thought but also experienced.[11]

C) Just as the concept of the external thing is verified in external data of sense, so the concept of the self is verified in the experience of myself as an experiencing, understanding, and judging subject. Just as the thing is a mediated unity, experienced as given, understood as meaningful, judged as real, so the self is experienced, understood, and judged. I am aware of myself, first of all, or experience myself as experiencing, understanding, and judging. Next I explicitly thematize the meaning of these acts and their relationship to one another. Perceptual experience, for example, of the external thing as sensible gestalt leads into and is presupposed by understanding the intelligible unity understood as an answer to the questions "What is it," "Why is it," or "How is it?" Finally, I not only experience and understand the self, but I also affirm it as real. If I am an intelligible unity characterized by acts of experiencing, understanding, and judging, then I am real as subject. And this reality is verified by having recourse through reflection to data of consciousness.[12]

D) The self, therefore, is not some kind of mystical, transcendental unity that must be thought in order to account for the unity of experience, but cannot itself be experienced and known. Nor is it an unknowable noumenon outside of experience, which can only be deduced as a presupposition of the categorical imperative. Nor is it an unverifiable soul. The self is a unifying and unified agent that is experienced, understood, and judged. It is not known through some kind of inward look or denied as knowable because this look is unavailable or conceptually deduced. E) Kant in his general account of knowledge does not distinguish between understanding as grasp of intelligible syntheses and judgment as positing syntheses to be real. Judgment as an activity is reduced too much to understanding.[13]

As with the external thing, therefore, knowledge of self emerges through experience, understanding, and judgment. What about the third of the problematic noumena, God? Here what has to be resisted is a kind of cryptopositivism in Kant, which I have already criticized and rejected. Reality is not given or presented simply or primarily through sensible experience, but through experience, understanding, and judgment. I experience not just data of sense, but also data of consciousness. Reality is given as known through the act of judgment positing a synthesis. The movement from experience to understanding to judgment, therefore, is a moving beyond the given to fuller and fuller intelligibility. Even within the empirical, constative domain, we affirm as real what is not given in the initial presented data of sense. When I see writing on a blackboard, for example, I can legitimately infer that some person wrote it, even if I never directly see the person to verify this inference.

Moreover, I have shown elsewhere that not only constative but also regulative claims in ethics and expressive claims about feelings are meaningful and valid. "Murder is wrong," for example, is a claim that does not refer to a state of affairs in the world, but it is nonetheless meaningful and valid. Furthermore, we can note a succession of ever higher viewpoints in scientific explanation and explanatory hermeneutics. In PCM I discussed a moment of psychoanalytic explanation concerning a psychological unconscious and a moment of critical sociological explanation concerning the political unconscious of capitalism. In CAL I argued for an explanatory hermeneutics of late capitalism that would flow from and complement immediate phenomenological description and hermeneutical understanding. I not only immediately experience capitalist alienation within the work place but understand and explain such alienation through accounts of surplus value and abstract labor time. Such an explanatory move is analogous to that of the scientist as he moves from experience of falling bodies to conceiving possible hypotheses to explain that experience to working out experiments that would validate or invalidate those hypotheses.[14]

The question that confronts us, therefore, is whether or not there is an explanatory dimension in my attempt to understand the life-world as a whole.

Is there an explanatory dimension in the domain of "absolute spirit" as there is in the domains of subjective and objective spirit? A "yes" answer seems coherent and valid since I am only following the natural bent of my mind to ask and answer all the relevant questions that arise in this domain such as "Why is there something rather than nothing?" or "Is there an intelligible ground for the concrete intelligible unities we experience and for the unity among these intelligibilities?"

A "no" answer, on the other hand, seems to be arbitrary, self-contradictory, or both. It is arbitrary because without reason I stop asking questions at a certain point and rule them out. I admit a legitimate hermeneutical-explanatory dimension in the domains of subjective spirit and objective spirit, but not in that of absolute spirit. Why? No good reason seems to be forthcoming. That the concept of God cannot be verified in data of sense is not an adequate reason for rejecting as invalid such a concept, since we have seen this criterion of meaning and validity to be false. Phenomenology, hermeneutics, ethics, and critical theory all make true valid claims that are not verified in data of sense.

The verifiability criterion seems to imply a reductionism of theory and explanation to the lowest level of physical science. What such reductionism misses is that any higher viewpoint as such has in it aspects that are not in lower viewpoints. Biology has notions of living things not present in physics; psychoanalysis has in it discussions of the psyche not present in biology; phenomenology has in it discussions of freedom and subjectivity not present in psychoanalysis. So also we would expect metaphysics to have a still higher viewpoint not present in phenomenology. One of these is that the notion of God is not present or verifiable directly in experience in the way either a perceived thing or the self is. Such a state of affairs is real and legitimate because that is what helps to constitute metaphysics in its distinctiveness as a higher viewpoint. That God is "transcendent" to the world and to experience means S/He is not present in the way other entities are.

The attempt to deny the legitimacy of the question of God is self-contradictory in the following way. If I posit an entity as really and intelligibly existing and then deny that the conditions and causes exist to explain it, then I am saying effectively that it exists and does not exist. If I see a drawing on the blackboard and deny that someone drew it, I am saying that on the one hand the drawing exists but on the other hand that the causes and conditions necessary to account for its existence do not. Since the causes and conditions do not exist, the drawing does not exist or should not exist; it is, as it were, hanging in mid air without adequate support for its intelligibility and existence. My affirmation of its existence and my unwillingness to affirm a complete explanation for its existence are at odds with one another. I am in contradiction with myself.[15]

As I will argue throughout this book, metaphysical arguments turn on this necessity of complete explanation. If, for example, the existence of things is a fact, and this fact does not find its complete explanation short of affirming God, then God must be affirmed. Metaphysics is simply the final, or if we consider faith and theology, the penultimate flowering of the mind's transcendentally natural bent of questioning: what I describe as the desire to know, which we learn to take quite seriously in the areas of physics, chemistry, biology, psychoanalysis, phenomenology, hermeneutics, and critical theory. Once we finish our inquiry in these areas, however, certain other questions arise: "Why is there something rather than nothing?" or "What explains the intelligibility of the world as a whole?" Again, in calling for the emergence of a higher viewpoint, these questions are analogous to those on other levels. Because data such as slips of the tongue or neurotic symptoms arise that biology cannot explain, psychoanalysis arises as a science.

Just as we do not rule out questions on these levels because they do not conform to the criteria or intelligibilities of previously attained science, so also we should not here. Why should metaphysical questions be reducible in meaning and validity to previous, more limited sciences, any more than critical theory to phenomenology, phenomenology to psychoanalysis, or psychoanalysis to biology? In a way analogous to questions and concepts on other levels, metaphysical questions and notions about being and God are not self-contradictory, are intelligible, and seem to be necessary to explain aspects of our experience that are otherwise inexplicable.

Why is complete explanation necessary? That is a legitimate question that I will not be able to answer fully until later in the book. What I wish to make at least plausible at this point is the claim that in all other domains of human inquiry we regard obscurantism and arbitrariness and self-contradictoriness as undesirable and inauthentic. My project will be to show that antipathy to metaphysics, the refusal to allow ourselves questions beyond this finite world, is similarly obscurantist, self-contradictory, and inauthentic. To take myself fully seriously as human being, knower, chooser, and doer, I need to affirm and choose and love being and God.

If metaphysical questions are legitimate, then attempts to rule them out are arbitrary, obscurantist, and self-contradictory. I arbitrarily cut the process of questioning short at a certain point. In this way I am unfaithful to the mind's and spirit's desire for total, nonarbitrary rigor and explanation. I refuse, in a way that contradicts the imperatives of intelligence and reasonableness, to be fully intelligent and reasonable. Metaphysics and religious belief, contrary to their modern and postmodern critics, are not the negation and sacrifice of reason and freedom but their final fulfillment and flowering.

Heidegger

Late Heidegger was, at least by the early 1930s, shifting from the project of grounding metaphysics to one of overcoming it in works like "What is Metaphysics?" Building on and drawing on Kant's critique of metaphysics, he criticizes not only the possibility but the desirability of metaphysics. Metaphysics is not possible nor desirable because it is a project tending to occlude being, cover it over, dominate it. Metaphysics can have three meanings: the systematic, evidential science of being as such culminating in the knowledge of God; a systematic articulation of the structures of finite being in the world (an example is Sartre's ontology of freedom and thingness in *Being and Nothingness*); and a rational orientation to comprehend the world systematically and evidentially, while rejecting metaphysics in the first and second senses. Habermas's work in *The Theory of Communicative Action* is an example of "metaphysical thinking" in this sense.[16]

I read later Heidegger's critique of metaphysics as focusing on metaphysics in the latter two senses. The legitimacy of Kant's critique is assumed, but what comes into question is the possibility and desirability of metaphysical thinking in the latter two senses. We might say that Heidegger broadens and deepens the critique inaugurated by Kant. The problem is not just with illegitimate "God-talk" or "soul-talk" taking us beyond the limits of reason, but with that reason itself as it operates in all spheres. Later postmodernists such as Derrida and Foucault will take up Heidegger's critique and attempt to bring it to completion. "Philosophy as . . . rigorous . . . science—the dream is over."[17]

In "What is Metaphysics?" Heidegger pursues the question of being differently from his earlier work, in a way that points toward the overcoming of metaphysics. Modern science has forgotten the original task of revealing beings in their essence and has moved into a prediction and control based upon the will to will. In a manner akin to the objectivizing tendencies of modern science, metaphysics has attempted to describe being by reconceptualizing the "is-ness" of what is. In so doing, metaphysics moves everywhere in the truth of being without being able to think adequately or articulate that truth. Because metaphysics forgets its ground by attempting to objectify being, an inquiry into being must overcome metaphysics. Such a thinking, because it transcends the calculative orientation of science to what is expedient and inexpedient, is a sacrifice, an offering of the thinker to being that does not count the cost. The thinker, in trying to reveal being, becomes the guardian of the incalculable truth of being. In opening up to the truth of being, the thinker becomes aware of thinking as a kind of thanking. As Heidegger says in another work, because being is a gift that is most thought-provoking, the "supreme thanks would be thinking."[18]

The move to a thinking beyond metaphysics, then, occurs because later Heidegger begins to see clearly that the end of metaphysics is technology. As later Greek thinkers such as Plato move into a conceptual attempt to think being as form, essence, and structure, being as the incalculable, the mysterious, and ultimate context of contexts recedes. As modern philosophy and science emerge with Descartes and Galileo, this tendency toward thinking as system, as control, as domination increases. Thinking in science and philosophy becomes more and more an attempt to master being. Technology is the final fruit of the history of Western metaphysics. Being has degenerated into the calculable and thinking into mere calculation. "Most thought-provoking about this thought-provoking time is that we are still thinking."[19] In so forgetting both being and thinking, we have moved into a calculative thinking that is murderous, that has killed the truth of being.

With the degeneration of thinking into calculative thinking, thought becomes a representing, an objectifying:

Here to represent (*vor-stellen*) means to bring what is present at hand (*das Vorhandene*) before oneself as something standing over against, to relate it to oneself, to the one representing it, and to force it back into this relationship to oneself as the normative realm.[20]

The dominance of representing and the subject is the essence of modernity.

The fact that what presences—e.g. nature, man, history, language—sets itself forth as the real in its objectness, the fact that as a complement to this science is transformed into theory that entraps the real and secures it in its objectness, would have been as strange to medieval man as it would have been dismaying to Greek thought.[21]

As the dominance of representing emerges, the thinker is replaced by the scholar and the scholar by the researcher. Science as research organizes the world according to a division of labor within the sciences. Historiography, for example, turns history into an object and has more in common with physics than with humanistic science grounded in scholarship. The triumph of research creates a different kind of person, on the move, in a hurry, no longer needing a library at home, negotiating at meetings, collecting information at congresses, contracting for commissions with publishers, who now determine with him which books must be written. The thinker has given way to the academic entrepreneur; he wheels and deals like Donald Trump. Because research is ongoing activity (*Betrieb*), it is always in danger of degenerating into mere "busyness" (*des blossen Betriebs*). The business of America is business or "busyness." Because science as research needs to be organized, systematized, and administered, the modern university arises as the institutional home of research.[22]

With the triumph of the representing subject, our relationship to nature is altered. Nature is no longer a presence to be reverenced but an object to be dominated, no longer a source of inspiration but a means of profit. The triumph of subjectivity leads to an instrumentalizing of nature, which becomes a mere object to be raped and plundered for profit. The hydroelectric plant on the Rhine makes even the Rhine itself appear as something at our command. The Rhine is set into a technological system of means and ends. The plant sets the Rhine to supplying hydraulic pressure, which then sets the turbines turning and generating the electric current for which the long-distance power station and its network of cables are set up to dispatch electricity. The hydroelectric plant is not built into the Rhine River as was the old wooden bridge joining bank to bank for hundreds of years. Rather the river is dammed up into the power plant. If someone were to object to these reflections that the Rhine is still a river that can be viewed contemplatively as part of the landscape, Heidegger's answer is succinct: "In no other way than as an object on call for inspection by a tour group ordered there by the vacation industry."[23]

Heidegger defines his own version of thinking in opposition to technocratic, metaphysical thinking. Metaphysical thinking is conceptual; Heidegger's thinking is nonconceptual. Technocratic thinking is ordered toward domination; *Denken* is inclined to reverent openness toward being. Whereas metaphysical thinking puts questions to the world in a way that allows the world to conform to it, Heidegger's thinking is a receptive listening. Whereas metaphysical thinking is objective, Heidegger's thinking is nonobjective. Metaphysical thinking is methodical and systematic; nonsystematic and nonmethodical approaches characterize thinking. Metaphysical thinking is oriented toward the thematic; the nonthematic context of being is the *telos* of Heidegger's thinking. If metaphysical thinking is so subjective that it does not allow being to reveal itself, Heidegger's thinking is permeated by a care that justice be done to what has presented itself for thinking. If metaphysical thinking is serious, *Denken* is playful, a play that responds in celebration and thankfulness to the world's play. If metaphysical, technocratic thinking is noisy and busy, postmetaphysical thinking is quiet and slow-moving, a saying that is "the ringing of stillness."[24]

To conclude my exposition of Heidegger's thought, let us consider one more example of thinking in his sense. When we sit in a garden and take delight in a blossoming rose, he says, we do not make an object of it in the sense of representing it thematically. When in tacit saying we are enthralled with the lucid red of the rose, this redness is not an object nor even a thing like the blossoming rose. The rose stands in the garden and sways in the wind, but the redness of the rose neither stands in the garden nor sways in the wind.

Nonetheless we can think this "redness" and say it by naming it. "There is accordingly a thinking and a saying that in no manner objectifies or places-over-against."[25]

What are we to think of this very powerful and illuminating attempt to overcome metaphysics and think being? Let us look, first of all, at three initial difficulties. Heidegger's claim about thinking in his sense is that it is non-conceptual. Yet he also claims that we think through language, and language is nothing if not conceptual. Indeed Heidegger's own language seems replete with concepts and universals, "concealment," "unconcealment," "presence," "technology," and so on. Part of the power of the later Heidegger lies in his developing a whole set of new concepts to help us understand our predicament. By "concept" here I mean an articulated, definite intelligible notion with universal applicability to many different situations and instances.

Furthermore, Heidegger's claim is that his own thinking is nonthematic. Yet the experience of thinking as we perform it seems to be one of moving from prethematic to thematic, implicit to explicit, empty to full, vague to definite. For example, the thinker, in contrast to one who does not think in Heidegger's sense, becomes explicitly aware of the danger of technology, the role of tradition and language in thought, and the way in which the rose is not an object. The thinker brings into explicit, thematic focus, perhaps for the first time, what we all experience but have not articulated to ourselves. The role of thinker in the modern era and in all eras, one that Heidegger fulfills preeminently, is to call us to explicit awareness of ourselves and of being. Heidegger's practice, then, and what we experience when we try to follow him on the path of thinking, seem to be in tension with his own account of thinking.

If Heidegger's attempt to think being, therefore, is conceptual and thematic, then his attempt to think being is itself metaphysical, in contradiction to his attempt to overcome metaphysics. Heidegger's is a determinate ontology, expressed in the key words of "es gibt," more oriented to the neutral than the personal, to the Greeks than to the Hebrews, to Nietzsche than to Kierkegaard. As such an ontology, however, it cannot assume the privilege of opposing all other ontologies by confining them inside the bounds of the metaphysical.[26]

After these preliminary considerations, we are now prepared for a more direct phenomenological approach. My basic claim here is that one must distinguish among at least eight kinds of objectivity and objectification. Because these are logically and phenomenologically distinct, it is a mistake to confuse them or to lump them together. Heidegger's rejection of objective, metaphysical knowing rests upon such a confusion.[27]

First, the most fundamental kind of objectivity is perceptual, because all others presume it. To perceive something is to perceive it as distinct from me, emerging from a background. To be aware of the table in my room, for example, is to be aware of it as distinct from me, present in and emerging from the context of the rest of the room, apartment, and so on. I am aware of the table as distinct from me because of the experienced difference between myself and the table. As we saw in discussing Kant, in contrast to my own lived body, which is not detachable from me, the table is detachable from me. In contrast to my own presence "here," the table is over "there." I cannot leave the room without my body, but I can leave the room without the table. Indeed it makes good, ordinary language sense to say that I lost or misplaced or forgot an object such as my pen, but not to say that I lost or misplaced or forgot my body.[28]

A second kind of objectivity is that of the universal known through such disciplines as science, mathematics, formal logic, and philosophy. In contrast to a particular, perceived object, the universal is nonparticular, applicable to many. For example, the particular triangular thing is not the same as the definition of a triangle. In contrast to the imaginableness of the perceived object, the universal is not imaginable. A perceived circle has width in its lines and points, but a conceived circle has no width in its lines and points.[29]

A third kind of objectivity is factual objectivity, that which is present in the "yes" and "no" of judgment. In contrast to the objectivity of the universal, factual objectivity gets at facts. This kind of objectivity gets beyond what is merely true to what in fact is true. The mathematical definition of triangle is true, but that there are particular triangular things is a fact. Factual truth gets us beyond what is merely hypothetical or possible. When the scientist entertains the theory of relativity as a hypothesis, he is considering the merely possible. When he verifies such a hypothesis, then he knows a fact.[30]

A fourth kind of objectivity is thematic. The most obvious example is perception, in which a thematically perceived thing is seen in an implicitly known context. But thematization is present on other levels as well, for example, when I imagine a beautiful woman or remember Velasquez's *Rokeby Venus* at the National Gallery in London or think about a mathematical problem. Indeed thematization is the most universal kind of objectification. Following Gurwitsch, we could say that all levels of conscious experience are characterized by a theme or figure emerging from a background.[31]

A fifth kind of objectivity is that of expression. When I put into words an idea of which I have had only a glimmering or put on canvas a picture only vaguely, inadequately conceived, or compose on the piano a piece of music that was merely inchoate in my mind, then I am objectifying through expression. In a real sense I only fully know what I want to say when I have said it.[32]

A sixth kind of objectification is degradation. When I whistle at a beautiful woman walking down the street or gratuitously insult someone, I am engaging in an alienating kind of objectification. Alienating objectification is one that is inappropriate to the sphere in question. The attempt to quantify or control being technically, objectification of which Heidegger is very critical, is a kind of inappropriate objectification.[33]

A seventh kind of objectification is normative. When I tell a person who has been provoked to "be objective" or "be rational," to give the voice of reason priority over other voices, I am asking that person to be objective in this sense. Normative objectivity is fidelity to the dictates of inquiring intelligence and reasonableness as they are present in different fields of inquiry, for example, consistency, comprehensiveness, and empirical fruitfulness in the physical sciences or emotional expressiveness in the arts. With normative objectivity, the disjunction between objectivity and value breaks down. Norms are values or criteria governing what is to count as true or false, good or bad, beautiful or ugly.[34]

Finally, experiential objectivity is the last kind of objectivity. Experiential objectivity is the given set of data necessary for verifying hypotheses in different areas of inquiry, sensible data in the physical sciences, memories of childhood experience in psychoanalysis, and data of consciousness in phenomenology. If such data are lacking, the hypothesis or insight remains merely a bright idea, possibly true or possibly false.[35]

What should be clear, first of all, is that these kinds of objectivity are distinct. Perceiving a thing is not the same as thinking about a thing scientifically or technically; thinking about a person scientifically or technically is not the same as thinking about or thematizing that person's subjectivity philosophically. When I thematize the character of freedom as *nihilation* in the manner of Sartre, I am thematizing universally but I am not turning freedom into a scientific or perceived object. When I uncover through eidetic reflection the nature of consciousness as temporal, I am reflectively objectifying consciousness as "nothing," but I am not turning it into a perceived or scientifically quantifiable object. Indeed such phenomenological reflection, moving from implicit to explicit, prethematic to thematic, enables us to see clearly and cogently for ourselves what distinguishes us from objects. Claims about freedom and dignity are not only edifying but verifiable.

Again, degrading or alienating consciousness is not the same as thematization. Such alienation, we might say, is a kind of thematization, but not all thematization is degradation. When I compliment a person on her character or work, I am thematizing her, but I am not degrading her nor does she experience it as such. Rather she experiences such a compliment as enhancing and liberating. Indeed at times we want to be objectified. When I go to a psychoanalyst, I wish him to articulate and help me articulate what my neuroses are. When I have a broken leg, I want the doctor to objectify my leg competently. I-thou interaction between doctor and patient nicely complements but is no substitute for such necessary objectification.

With the above points in mind, therefore, we can ask Heidegger whether being is an object. As initially experienced contextually as that from which objects emerge, it is not. But as philosophically articulated in such notions as "the fourfold," "presence," and "unconcealment" arising from concealment, it certainly has to be. Such objectification, however, is not occluding but rather revealing, not alienating but liberating. In moving us from an implicit to an explicit awareness of being, Heidegger thematically helps us to move away from the false objectifications of technocracy present in late capitalism and state socialism.

Heidegger at the very least confuses perceptual, universally scientific, thematic, and alienating objectivity. In making such a point against Heidegger, however, I do not wish to deny that he has a valid critique of claims for total objectification. Because of our rootedness in the world and in language, no objectification can be total. Some partial objectifications, however, can be enlightening and liberating. For these reasons we have to deny Heidegger's equation of alienation with objectification. It is wrong to equate as he does conceptual thinking with domination and metaphysical thinking with technocracy. Objectifying persons and the world is not only unavoidable but at times can reveal and illumine. If the identification of alienation with metaphysical objectification is false, then the way to metaphysics remains open.[36]

This is not to say, however—and here I come to my second, main critical point—that much of later Heidegger's discussion of thinking in relation to being should not be retained, somehow, by philosophy. My strategy here is to deny any sharp cleavage between objective, conceptual thought and *Denken* in the proper sense and to include within conceptual philosophy and metaphysics many of the traits that Heidegger ascribed to thinking. Any philosophical thought worthy of the name, I argue, will be concerned not to impose criteria on the evidence subjectively, to allow being to reveal itself to the thinker, to be passionately grateful for the gift of being vouchsafed to thought. Heidegger's negation of conceptual philosophy enables us to recover certain essential dimensions of philosophy itself, too often left out in overly objectivistic, positivistic versions of philosophy.[37]

Properly conceived, *Denken* is a part of philosophy, at least in the sense of philosophy containing meditative, receptive, and affective dimensions. *Denken* in the sense of a quasi-poetic practice of meditation and contemplation, which can take secular and religious forms, is not and should not be reduced to philosophy. But just by itself, apart from Heidegger's metaphilosophical scaffolding, *Denken* does not imply rejection of philosophy and metaphysics as legitimate enterprises. *Denken* is just one more practice or activity, running alongside of and complementing our philosophical practice. Indeed *Denken* in this sense can aid philosophical reflection, moving it into the depths, helping it to be open and receptive to experience, and enabling it to avoid the superficial, conceptual wrangling that betrays philosophy.

I propose to include elements of *Denken* within philosophy by invoking four transcendental precepts. Corresponding to the level of a descriptive phenomenology attempting to be faithful to the evidence, there is the precept "be attentive." Corresponding to an eidetic, reflective level attempting to rigorously, consistently think and define what it understands, Husserl's distinctness, there is the precept "be intelligent." Corresponding to the reflective marshaling and evaluating of evidence in order to arrive at true eidetic claims, Husserl's clarity, there is the precept "be rational." Corresponding to a chosen openness to being and to tradition exercising a claim over us to be responded to in dialogal openness, there is the precept "be responsible." These transcendental precepts taken together map a movement of knowing from description to understanding to judgment to choice. They are transcendental in a traditional phenomenological sense, because they express an a priori structure of knowing and choosing that philosophy both reflects on and articulates. Because all of the precepts are implemented by and chosen by a freedom open to what is not itself, they are the work of subjectivity. But such subjectivity is not the one-sided, dominating kind of subjectivity rightly criticized by Heidegger but a subjectivity that chooses not to dominate, that wills not to will.[38]

Transcendental method in phenomenology, therefore, is reflection on myself in relation to being as an experiencing, understanding, judging, and choosing subject. For this reason, and this is my third major critical point, I reject the dichotomy between truth and method, the transcendental and the ontological posited not only by Heidegger but Gadamer as well. Truth and being in philosophy become something arrived at through the method of description, eidetic understanding, judgment, and decision.[39]

Fourth, we avoid the one-sidedness of an exclusive reliance either on belonging or on objectifying distanciation. Heidegger reminds us that prior to all explanation and critique is a primordial belonging to tradition and being that cannot and should not be totally conceptualized. It is this belonging that Heidegger refers to when he suggests that we do not objectify or thematize language, but rather that we think out of language. To objectify totally in this sense would be to run the risk of totalitarian arrogance toward experience that would be sheer folly. If I am correct, however, a distanciating objectification is possible that is not only compatible with such belonging but completes it and realizes it. When an author objectifies his meaning in a text, that objectification frees his text from the confining spatial and temporal limits of a merely oral presentation and makes his thought accessible to those in other places and other times.

Finally, my suggested alternative to Heidegger should not be interpreted as an uncritical acceptance of or merely reformist adaptation to modernity. Rather, sharing his critical disillusionment with modernity and desiring to overcome its pathological aspects, I advocate a critique and suspicion based on legitimate objectification. Rather than a *Denken* turned toward the past, I advocate a suspicion oriented toward a present and future, theoretical and practical praxis. Rather than simply rejecting tradition, however, as some in the traditions of Marxism and critical theory are inclined to do, I use it as a source of enlightenment and inspiration, critique and praxis. Such a criticism is one that is redemptive, both critically and hermeneutically, relating to the past not only respectfully but eliciting its utopian potential for the present and the future. Recalling the Rhine the way it was before the onslaught of modern industry can not only enlighten us about the being covered over and destroyed by such industry, but points toward a practice that, by changing the social relations underlying such alienation, would allow being to reveal itself once again.[40]

Part of the tradition that needs to be redeemed is the metaphysical tradition itself. Rather than seeing that as wholly or primarily all of a piece, as Heidegger does, especially in the form that it takes after Descartes, I would see the metaphysical tradition as dialectically at odds with itself. In it is not only the tendency toward a one-sided alienation, objectification, and domination but also a movement toward a critical, self-conscious recovery of self and world at odds with the tendency toward alienation. For these reasons, descriptive, eidetic phenomenology, itself the product of the Enlightenment as Husserl saw in the *Crisis*, can be used as critical fulcrum for transcending modernity in its pathological aspects. His discovery of the life-world, for example, can be used as a ground for criticizing positivism and scientism.[41]

Such transcendence, however, can only take place if eidetic phenomenology is wedded to hermeneutics and suspicion. Indeed if there is a turn toward history even for phenomenology itself, as Husserl saw in the *Crisis*, and a hermeneutics of suspicion must complement a hermeneutics of respect or retrieval, as Gadamer and Ricoeur have both seen, then suspicion and critique are essential for eidetic, descriptive phenomenology itself. Hermeneutics is the crucial middle term between eidetic, descriptive phenomenology and suspicion.[42]

It might be appropriate to conclude my discussion of Heidegger by returning to his examples of nonobjective encounter mentioned in my text; the Rhine, language, and the rose. In contrast to Heidegger's accounts of the Rhine, rose, and jug, I would say that they are present to us objectively in various ways: as perceived, as thematized, as experienced, as judged, as normatively related to me. While agreeing with Heidegger that language is present to us nonobjectively as a sedimented context out of which we think and speak and write, I argue that there are also objective dimensions to language as well. Language is conceptual, is expressed in books and documents, and is thematized by philosophical reflection. Such thematization of the sphere of belonging that is initially preobjective or nonobjective, so important in an era that tends not to recognize these aspects of being, is a task that Heidegger inspires us to take up and pursue, but also one that eventually leads us beyond Heidegger.

Derrida

Derrida sees himself as bringing to a completion Heidegger's overcoming of metaphysics. Heidegger, because he thinks being in terms of presence and truth as a process of moving from concealment to unconcealment or presence, is still caught within the metaphysical tradition. "Heideggerian thought would reinstate rather than destroy the instance of the logos and of the truth of being as 'primum signatum,' the 'transcendental signified' . . ."

This tradition attempts to think being as presence in a way that is logocentric and phonocentric: logocentric in the sense that being manifests and gives rise to an intelligibility that is systematic and evidential, phonocentric in the sense that such a logos gives a priority to voice and speech as loci of full, present self-evidence. "The logos of being, 'Thought obeying the Voice of Being,' is the first and last resource of the sign, of the difference between *signans* and *signatum*."[43]

While admitting that one cannot definitively do without metaphysical concepts, Derrida nonetheless attempts to think beyond them or point beyond them. He does this, first of all, by opposing the notion of *différance* to that of presence. *Différance* indicates that meaning differs from itself and is deferred, never fully present. The meaning of "red," for example, cannot be fully understood without relating to a whole system of color words such as "green," "black," "white," and so on. Moreover, meaning is deferred because of temporality. Any meaning in the present refers to a past that is no longer and a future that is yet to come. Thus, a scientific hypothesis emerges from a whole set of prior perceptions and ideas, and anticipates a future verification rendering it true or false. Because meaning is structured by *différance* in this sense, Derrida claims to have effectively undermined presence and, therefore, metaphysics.[44]

To the concept of phonocentrism Derrida opposes the notion of writing. What he means by this notion is not writing in the normal sense, putting pen to paper in a way that leads to publishable script, but a system of structured significations that informs our speaking and acting in the world. Indeed through a grammatology one can discover a number of such structures as "*différance*" or "supplementarity" that remain more or less hidden from our ordinary consciousness and need to be thematized by postmetaphysical reflection.[45]

To the concept of logocentrism Derrida contrasts the more legitimate notion and practice of deconstruction. Initially concepts in the metaphysical tradition such as "speech" deemed to be central turn out to require apparently more marginal concepts and realities such as "writing." Deconstruction, then, using such concepts as *"différance"* and "writing," aims to subvert the centrality and dominance of the metaphysical tradition. Indeed there is an ethical thrust to Derrida's work that moves to enlist deconstruction on behalf of the marginalized human other, woman, African-American, Latin American peasant, gay, or laborer, done violence to by an unjust socio-economic system. "Not only is there no kingdom of *différance*, but *différance* instigates the subversion of every kingdom."[46]

The first question that arises concerns the apparent self-contradictoriness of Derrida's project. How can one use fruitfully the concepts from an allegedly bankrupt tradition to overcome that tradition? If these concepts are used, why is not this overcoming as bankrupt and invalid as the concepts used? Why is there here not something like the paradox of the broken ladder that Wittgenstein uses at the end of the *Tractatus*, using the ladder of metaphysics to overcome it and then throwing it away as broken, bankrupt, and invalid?[47]

Much ink has been spilled on this issue in the philosophical literature. Many think Derrida gets himself off the self-referential hook by his admitting that he cannot avoid using metaphysical concepts in his enterprise. Why, I would ask, does not that move intensify the contradiction: "I am using the concepts of metaphysics to overcome it, and I admit that I am." Elsewhere, he names the contradiction by talking about the double gesture of staying within the tradition and moving outside it. One way that that talk of double gesture would be noncontradictory would be that he intends the phrase in the dialectical sense of *Aufhebung*: preservation, retention, and transcendence of the tradition. Dialectic, however, is a concept and method of the metaphysical tradition, and most of the time Derrida refers to what he is doing as different from dialectic and is also quite negative about dialectic.[48]

Other strategies of evasion, ways of avoiding the performative hook, are available, which I have considered elsewhere. One is the attempt to evade the charge of performative contradiction by saying that what Derrida's argument amounts to is not an argument in the sense of a set of linked propositions but a gesture or series of gestures, and gestures cannot be self-contradictory. My first response is to say that even though gestures may be one strategy in Derrida's arsenal, present more dominantly in literary works like *Glas* or *The Post Card*, he uses argument massively in more "philosophical" works like *Of Grammatology*, *Margins of Philosophy*, or *Writing and Difference*. It is this presence of a serious, conceptual, argumentative dimension that is insisted upon by some of his more reliable interpreters like Gasche or Norris, who wish to rescue him from the Yale literary critics stressing the more literary, aesthetic, gestural side. To the extent that such argument is present, the issue of performative contradiction remains.[49]

My second response is to say that gesture as such can only manifest difference, not superiority. But the postmodernist means to assert the superiority of his stance over that of metaphysics. Metaphysical presence is inferior to "*différance*," speech is inferior to that of writing, logocentrism is inferior to that of deconstruction. Gesturing, however, just manifests difference, not superiority. Oddly enough the postmodernist recourse to gesture leaves the doing of metaphysics quite in order.[50]

Another common strategy of evasion is the charge of enlightenment blackmail. In accusing the postmodernist of performative self-contradiction, I am employing the standards of validity that he, as someone critical of the metaphysical tradition out of which such standards arise, would not accept. My response is to distinguish between explicit positing and implicit normative presupposing. To explicitly posit the principle of contradiction without argumentation would be an invalid begging of the question. To argue that the postmodernist implicitly presupposes it and other values of communicative rationality in making his claim is not. If postmodernists say to me that Western rationality is logocentric, they presumably mean that claim to be true, comprehensible, sincere, and right in the sense of not violently or manipulatively forcing me to accept it, and noncontradictory. They mean implicitly to deny the contradictory claim that Western rationality is not logocentric. There is an implicit, communicative presupposing of evidential rationality that is at odds with the postmodernist's rejection of it. In other words, the postmodernist's explicit rejection of Western, communicative rationality is performatively self-contradictory. I am not imposing my standards on them; they are using them themselves to make the argument and I am just describing a validity they are already presupposing. If they do not presuppose such validity, their argument falls to the ground.[51]

For this reason, many try to get off the performative hook by resorting to the nonargumentative or supraargumentative, gestural, or aesthetic; here is one reason for the appeal of the aesthetic in the postmodernist discourse as a whole. If this move is made, however, postmodernism has committed its own form of blackmail. It has to presuppose dogmatically the validity of the standpoint from which it speaks. From the point of view of postmodern being or *différance*, neither ontic nor logocentric reason is sufficient or adequate. But what if we denizens of the ontic want reasons, argument, evidence of some kind for moving beyond the mere ontic into the homeland of being and *différance*? Then postmodernism has the option of merely continuing to proclaim prophetically or poetically from on high that we should move to its exalted place, or beginning to discuss, argue, and convince us with reasons. At that point the issue of performative contradiction arises again.

The full dilemma for the postmodernist is one of self-contradiction versus arbitrariness: self-contradiction if one wishes communicatively and argumentatively to redeem the claim that we should transcend Western rationality, arbitrariness if one wishes aesthetically or prophetically or gesturally to assert merely the truth or preferability of its position. In my experience of reading and discussing, there are argumentative and esoteric postmodernists, those who dominantly argue at the price of self-contradiction and those who dominantly assert or suggest at the price of arbitrariness. The postmodern text as a whole moves back and forth inconsistently between these positions, but individual postmodernist thinkers are temperamentally inclined to one or the other position as a general rule. Part of the difficulty in discussions between modernist and postmodernist is this moving back and forth between the terrain of argumentation and that of prophecy. One can learn much from the most insightful in both camps of postmodernism, but both are caught on the horns of a dilemma.[52]

One final strategy of evasion available to Derrideans is the changed Derridean text of the 1980s and 1990s, which, in works like *The Other Heading*, *Limited Inc.*, and *Spectres of Marx*, has become much more positive about certain aspects of the Western tradition, especially in its attention to universal ethical rights, to justice, and to radical social critique indebted to the Marxist tradition. Indeed in *Limited Inc.* he describes himself as always having been a serious philosopher and never having rejected criteria of validity and interpretation and the laws of logic. If so, we are tempted to ask, what happens to the gestural defense of performative contradiction? Is not logical and performative inconsistency a more serious issue than the earlier Derrida and his followers were willing to admit?[53]

Many issues arise here; the main one, I think, is the relationship of the later to the earlier Derridean text. I am inclined to think that there is a postmodern Derrida I of the 1960s and 1970s and a modernist Derrida II of the 1980s and 1990s, reversing Heidegger's trajectory from an early modernism to a later postmodernism. To the extent that the later Derrida is modernist or approximates modernism, uttering the Prufrockian, "That's not what I meant, that's not what I meant at all" to earlier, more extreme interpretations of him, we can ask further questions. If we accept the validity of the later stance, and I confess to finding a great deal of validity in a more obviously philosophical and radical Derrida out of his Marxist closet at last, is not the case against the legitimacy and possibility of metaphysics weakened? Or, if he wishes to be antimetaphysical in all three senses, is there not extreme tension between this position and his chastened Western universalism and radicalism? Are not these metaphysical also? Does not the emergence of a more "sane," "rational," and "responsible" Derrida, whatever be the relationship to his own earlier work, implicitly reopen the case for metaphysics in all three senses?[54]

So the discussion goes! I hope I have done enough to show how difficult it is for the postmodernist to wiggle off the performative hook. Because other possible strategies of evasion remain, of course, the most staunch of postmodernists may not be convinced by what I have tried to do here. What I have tried to do is show the impossibility of making the case, at least the way postmodernists wish to make it, against metaphysics without performative self-contradiction. What that impossibility shows, I think, is a positive necessity: the human vocation to rationality and to metaphysics in all three senses and the full flowering of that rationality. Such a necessity rests upon the universal structure of the human subject as experiencing, understanding, judging, and deciding, as governed by the transcendental precepts, as oriented to communicative action. Deny metaphysics, and you deny or mutilate that rationality. Accept that rationality in its full flowering, and you will be led to metaphysics. My full argument for these claims, of course, has not yet been made; it will emerge throughout Part One.[55]

Self-contradiction, however, is only the first word, not the last word on the postmodern critique of metaphysics. Other issues arise on descriptive and hermeneutical and ethical levels. Here the question is whether postmodernists, in describing Western reason as repressively logocentric, are being just or fair to the different forms of rationality as we experience them, or are they merely giving a one-sided, totalizing claim that does not do justice to modernist difference? I argue that the latter alternative is true.

First, recall what we just did in criticizing Heidegger on objectification. I argued for at least eight kinds of objectification, only one of which is necessarily alienating, oppressive, violent to difference. The other seven forms of objectification are legitimate and illuminating.

Further, we can say that not only are there constative claims about things in the world, but regulative claims about the rightness of moral acts and expressive claims about subjective feelings. "George is now at home" is different from "murder is wrong" is different from "I am glad we passed the exam." These are distinct in type and kind and validity. The first refers to states of affairs in the world in a way that the other two do not; the second obliges me to a course of action in a way that the other two do not.[56]

Next, we can admit that there is a kind of violent or manipulative strategic action that does do violence to difference, and forms of discussion in which the point seems to be to win the argument rather than get at the truth. These are distinct, however, logically and phenomenologically from a form of discussion in which the truth is the primary aim of the discussion, all differences of opinion are welcome, and a patient, open exploration of opinion occurs.[57]

We can note, also, the difference between a just, nonexploitive behavior that recognizes difference and one that does not. For example, if I think that all people as human beings are fundamentally equal, then exclusion of people from political participation in a society because of race or sex or class is unjust. Violence to difference is characteristic of unjust, not just, behavior. Derrida tends, in his earlier phase at least, to lump them together.

Again, Derrida's preference for writing seems to be a one-sided reaction to an equally one-sided emphasis on speech in philosophy, but the full reality, it seems to me, is that of discourse that is a unity of speech and writing, immediate speech acts and unconscious linguistic structures. I can and do engage in communicative speech with others, but that is mediated by different kinds of structure, psychological, linguistic, scientific, social. Phonetic and syntactic structures do genuinely inform my speech as necessary conditions for my activities of communicating, referring, postulating, and asserting. Nonetheless, these activities are not only not denied but are mediated by such conditions. Indeed because linguists can only make the case for phonetic or syntactic structures by such communicative activity, they are in contradiction with themselves if they try to deny the reality and importance of these activities.[58]

A final point concerns the critique of presence itself. Derrida does not adequately distinguish between a critique of naive presence, which is valid, and a critique of mediated presence, which is not. To say that "the trace is not a presence but the simulacrum of a presence that dislocates itself," or that we "cannot think the trace—and, therefore, *différance*—on the basis of the present, or of the presence of the present" is to miss the point that *différance* is known and, therefore, present cognitively: as experienced, as understood, and as affirmed. There is evidence for *différance*, some of which I have articulated, such as the relationship among color words, and evidence implies presence, mediated presence.[59]

On the hermeneutical level—that is, a historical interpretation of modernity and modern philosophy—the problems are similar. Here it seems to me that characterizing modernity as basically logocentric, dominating, pathological, metaphysical in a bad sense, and exterminating difference is to do violence to difference within modernity. As on the descriptive level, the irony is that a philosophy claiming to defend and restore difference ends up repressing difference. Here I am steering between the Scylla of an optimistic Parsonian reading of modernity—every day in every way we are getting better and better—and the Charybdis of a pessimistic postmodern reading. Rather than an uncritical dogmatic, modernist defense of modernity or a rejectionistic, postmodern rendering, I propose a dialectical "yes" and "no." I thus argue that my reading is more comprehensive and more nuanced than either of the other two readings.[60]

Because I have gone into this issue exhaustively in other books, I can afford to be more brief here. I argue that modernity is characterized by a differentiation occurring on a number of different levels. For example, among the spheres of aesthetic, scientific, and moral knowledge—cultural rationalization, or between cultural rationalization and social rationalization, in which purposive rational action, action utilizing technically useful means to achieve goals—is institutionalized in the economy and state, or between a just progressive movement forward in modernity such as democracy, human rights, and the welfare state, and an unjust domination, exploitation, and imperialism. Much about modernity is pathological. I will be arguing, however, that such pathology is criticizable in the name of modernist rationality itself. Violation of democracy, "deterring democracy" in Chomsky's sense, in the first world or third world is criticizable in the light of modernist ideals of democracy that have been to some extent institutionalized.[61]

Postmodernism, then, is self-referentially inconsistent, descriptively inadequate, hermeneutically one-sided, and ethically normless and arbitrary. A final point to be made is that metaphysics finally seems to reassert itself. For underlying the dichotomies, conflicts, and contradictions in the interactions between human beings and nature is a series of "quasi-transcendentals" or "infrastructures" such as "différance," "supplementarity," and "archetrace." These seem to be real, in the sense of being experienced, understood, and affirmed on the basis of evidence, systematic and foundational, in the sense of being the source of the plays of oppositions and differences within ordinary, commonsensical scientific and philosophical discourse. The traditional word for positing entities or intelligibilities that play such a role is "metaphysics," albeit here pluralistic rather than identitarian, a metaphysics of multiple infrastructures not reducible to one another. Metaphysics by any other name is as sweet.[62]

A Provisional Description of Metaphysics and Some of Its Religious-praxical Consequences

What emerges from our brief dialectical discussion is that metaphysics is still possible. The three major critiques of it undertaken by Kant, Heidegger, and Derrida, which are basic, typical, and underlie other critiques, do not finally work or convince.

All of this is not to deny that some forms of metaphysics are problematic. Premodern dogmatic forms of metaphysics, objectivistic or scientistic or logicistic forms of metaphysics or overly certain, dogmatic forms of metaphysics that refuse to own up to a necessary fallibilism in human knowing and doing, need to be criticized. One of the strong points of both Heidegger and Derrida is to insist on such fallibilism and to insist on its incompatibility with metaphysics. I would answer, *some metaphysics*, not metaphysics as such.

A provisional description of the right kind of metaphysics is, first, that it insists on its openness to indeterminacy. Because it intends being, of course, metaphysics has to aim in a sense at understanding being, but I will argue that this intention includes not only the answered but the unanswered questions about being. The attempt to understand everything about everything, perhaps most fully manifest in Hegel, gives way to metaphysics as *heuristic*, as reflecting on our questioning orientation to being. Metaphysics, to borrow from Lonergan, is the integral, heuristic structure of proportionate being. In contrast to Heidegger and Derrida, I argue that starting with the question leads us to metaphysics, not beyond metaphysics.[63]

Because of the heuristic character of metaphysics, because of its openness to the unanswered as well as answered questions, it is necessarily open to mystery. Correlative to the unanswered questions on the reflective level is the felt sense of awe on the level of feeling and spirit before existence and being. Being comes across to me as marvelous, as wonder-full, as astonishing in its negative and positive aspects. We can reclaim here some of late Heidegger's and Marcel's insights about thinking as thanking, as a response to the gift of being offering itself to be thought. Questioning is the piety of thinking.[64]

Unlike Heidegger and Derrida, however, I think this wondering, questioning openness to mystery is compatible with and grounded in the transcendental structure of the human subject as experiencing, understanding, judging, and deciding. As I have already argued, this structure gives rise to four transcendental precepts, "be attentive," "be intelligent," "be reasonable," and "be responsible." In the attentiveness giving rise to openness to insight and evidence and the call to be responsible to the call of the other is an openness to the otherness of being, to its revealing itself to me. There is receptivity of the human subject on all four levels to which an adequate transcendental analysis needs to do justice. We do not, contrary to Heidegger, need to transcend such transcendentality to be properly open to and receptive of being. An overly activist stance toward being is not characteristic of transcendentality as such but of certain one-sided transcendental accounts. Receptivity manifests itself in necessary attentiveness to the splendor of being sensuously giving itself in experience as wonder-full, openness to insights, willingness to be open to and consider all evidence, and obedience on the level of freedom to what reveals itself to be the right thing to do.

Because such a metaphysics is rooted in the exigence of the modern self-knowing subject, it will be critical in several different senses. First of all, this metaphysics will be oriented to judgments grounded in evidence; metaphysical claims that are not so grounded need to be rejected as dogmatic. Such a metaphysics will also respect and recognize the limits of human knowing. No more comprehensiveness, determinacy, or certainty is claimed for it than is possible. Fallibilism is a necessary aspect of such metaphysics. Finally, such a metaphysics will have to give an account of itself in relationship to other forms, empiricist, rationalist, and voluntarist. What makes my version preferable?

The hypothesis that I will be pursuing and trying to demonstrate is that deficient and inadequate forms of metaphysics or antimetaphysics are rooted in inadequate self-knowledge. Empiricism, for example, overemphasizes the moment of immediate experience and does not do justice to understanding, especially its conceptual aspect, and judgment. Rationalism or idealism overemphasizes the moment of understanding and does not do justice to the moments of experience and judgment. Voluntarism, an account of the world like Nietzsche's or Foucault's or Sartre's, overemphasizes the fourth moment of freedom and does not do justice to the moments of cognition.[65]

Because metaphysics is in the mind and because being is known through the intentional activities of mind, the account of being will be more or less, implicitly or explicitly, correlative to the account of knowing. If that is one-sidedly empiricist or rationalist or voluntarist, the account of being, if the philosopher is consistent, will be similarly empiricist, rationalist, or voluntarist. In addition to and complementing the positive account of the relationship of knowing to being is the dialectical account of other positions in relationship to my own. Such an account will be negative and positive, learning from but also criticizing these positions. Thus, I learn from Heidegger's account of thinking as thanking or questioning as the piety of thinking, but have argued that these insights can be recovered and done justice to within metaphysics, not beyond it. A reverential, wondering stance of the thinker before the mystery of being is the appropriate stance for the metaphysician as questioner, as open to being, as a shepherd or guardian of being.

Right away, therefore, we can make a fundamental distinction between position and counter-position that cuts like a knife through the welter of philosophical disagreement. This distinction and its importance flow from what we have said in this chapter. Thus a position occurs when the real is the concrete universe of being and not a subdivision of the "already out there now real," if the subject is known when it affirms itself intelligently and reasonably and not in some prior existential state, and objectivity is a matter of intelligent inquiry and reasonable reflection and not a property of biological extroversion. On the other hand, a philosophical claim will be a counter-position if it contradicts one or more of the basic positions.

In CAL, I expanded this account to include value as well, aesthetic, ethical, political, and religious. Value is either what is authentically experienced, understood, judged, and chosen, or it is something immediately felt or looked at or imposed. The distinction between position and counter-position flows from self-appropriated subjects knowing and choosing themselves. From such self-appropriation results a cognitional theory that is the basis of a philosophy and its expansion into ethics and social theory, metaphysics and philosophy of religion. The cognitional theory is the basis and the other domains the expansion.[66]

We can infer from these claims that counter-positions invite reversal and positions invite development. For counter-positions in cognitional theory or its expansion are at odds with the performance of intelligent inquiry and reasonable reflection. Thus the intelligence and reasonableness of Hume's performance were at odds with the foundational immediacy that he affirmed in sense data. For data of sense, it turns out, are not immediate but mediated, not simply given but interpreted. The red dot I see before me is known as "red" only through a differentiated scheme of colors. "Red," "dot," and "point" are not immediate sense data but genuine universals applicable to many different instances.

If positions are affirmed in cognitional theory or its expansion, then they invite development. Thus a Thomism that correctly affirms the unity of potency, form, and act in being needs to be complemented by and grounded in a cognitional theory that can relate Thomism critically to other accounts of being and knowing. Thomism must become transcendental if it is to become properly methodological and comprehensive, and avoid becoming a lonely island in a sea of controversy.

Derridean insights into difference or *différance* can also be released and reclaimed. Through all three volumes of my project, I have done that. In PCM I argued for the triumph of ambiguity, the rootedness of consciousness in embodiment, language, and tradition, the play of absence and presence, identity and difference on all levels of conscious experience, the reality and importance of the human other, and the existence of a personal and social unconscious. In CAL I argued for openness to the other in communicative action and the ideal speech situation, the ethical necessity to respond to the exploited, marginalized other, woman, black, latino, laborer, poor person, and homosexual, and the reality of unconscious economic and bureaucratic systems. On the levels of subjective and objective spirit, therefore, I have tried to recognize the reality and value of change, difference, otherness, process, and the play of absence and presence. How do I do that on the level of "absolute spirit?"[67]

First, I want to say that being as a whole has to include this processive interplay between absence and presence, identity and difference, permanence and change. Metaphysics tries to think the unity and interplay between subjective and objective spirit. One move that I make here is to agree with Derrida that the Western metaphysical tradition has been guilty at times of overemphasizing presence, identity, and positivity, and has neglected absence, difference, and negativity. Fairness demands that we admit that; fairness demands also that we admit that the Western philosophical, metaphysical tradition has engaged in a self-critique on precisely those issues. Thus, for example, we note a progress from Parmenides' emphasis on being as one and unchangeable to Heraclitus's stress on being as changeable to Plato's imperfect attempt to think the empirical world as an imperfect participation in the unchangeable world of the forms to Aristotle's thinking of the unity of permanence and change, identity and difference, universal and individual. I note also Hegel's attempt to think the unity of identity and difference in his doctrine of the concept and Aquinas's attempt in his doctrine of analogy.

These historical examples again warn us against any simplistic interpretation of the metaphysical tradition as simply logocentric. Rather, what emerges is a criterion of adequacy: the more adequate, truer position in metaphysics will not be one that one-sidedly stresses identity or difference, permanence or change, universal or individual, self or other, but one that thinks them together dialectically and phenomenologically. One common pattern in the history of philosophy is the one-sided affirmation of a trait such as identity followed by its one-sided negation followed by an attempt to think identity and difference together. The history of philosophy, like human and natural history, is dialectical and thus metaphysics as an attempt to think being has to be dialectical.[68]

Antiphilosophical critiques such as those of Heidegger and Derrida can serve this dialectical process, reminding philosophy of a certain one-sidedness and calling on it to think what has been left out or has not been thought adequately. One way that I will attempt to respond positively to the postmodern critique of metaphysics as excluding absence, difference, and otherness is to agree that this claim is somewhat valid for classical forms of theism such as Aquinas and Augustine but not true, or not as true, of the neoclassical theism of Whitehead and Hartshorne. According to these thinkers, change, difference, absence, and otherness are not outside but inside of being and God.

Such a move has certain advantages. First of all, as a comprehensive enterprise, metaphysics should embrace both reflective, critical dimensions of subjective spirit and the political, liberating aspects of objective spirit. Metaphysics is both contemplative and practical, oriented to knowledge for its own sake and to liberation. As such, a process metaphysics does a better job of articulating God's loving relatedness to the world, Her care about and involvement with the world, Her working with all of us as a partner and friend, and God's role as "the fellow sufferer who understands."[69]

Because the world is processive, dialogal, filled with identity and difference, and oriented to liberation, so is God. From the point of view of a process metaphysics oriented to liberation, evil is not a problem to be thought away in some kind of theodicy, but a form of oppression that has to be overcome through the praxis of human beings working with one another and with God. God is not simply or merely supremely perfect dwelling in absolute bliss and unrelated to creatures but intensely involved with the fate of human beings and the earth. The problem, almost insuperable, in classical metaphysics of reconciling divine foreknowledge with human freedom disappears in process metaphysics. God does not know the future any more than human beings do; here we note an absence, a limitation, a receptivity in God that is somewhat responsive to the postmodern critique. God is receptive, can grow, can change, can become even more perfectly God.

Such a conception of God as processive, receptive, and changing is also more compatible than the classical version with a Christianity, my own version of which I argue in Part Two, that affirms a loving, compassionate, suffering, liberating God. How is such a conception of God compatible with the classical notion of God as impassive, perfect, all-knowing, and omnipotent? Here Derrida's critique of presence is right on the money. God is a unity of identity and difference, presence and absence, permanence and change, activity and receptivity.

Because God is receptive, changeable, passionate, and suffering, we think such a notion expresses a "feminine" aspect of God that takes us away from one-sided masculinist notions. Such a notion of God, moreover, liberates us from one-sided notions of God as "Lord," sending down messages and commands from on high to people who are slaves rather than free human beings. It seems that such a notion of God is still prevalent or dominant in the churches, Protestant and Catholic and Jewish, and underlies and legitimates a one-sided, rigid authoritarianism and distrust of freedom. Before such an authority, people are not subjects but objects whose only duty is to obey unquestioningly. "Father knows best."[70]

Liberation, therefore, needs to occur not only outside but inside the church. The notion of God that operates in the church gives rise to and legitimates a practice of governance and preaching that can be and is often and prevalently oppressive, ideological, racist, sexist, classist, and heterosexist. That which should contribute to the process of liberation serves, in contradiction to its own prophetic substance, to repress it. The church is a contradictory unity of premodern and modern, repressive and liberating, dogmatic and enlightened, bourgeois and postbourgeois aspects. A processive conception of God as processive and liberating developed metaphysically and interpreted hermeneutically in the Old and New Testaments is one more resource for analyzing and overcoming the contradictions. To the extent that the church becomes genuinely liberating, then it can become, and we can become with it, a genuine counterweight to the modern fetishes of money, sex, and power. Thus, metaphysics functions as an element of ideology critique inside and outside the church.[71]

Conclusion

Corresponding, then, to transcendentality, the transcendental structure of the human subject, is transcendence in several different senses: the life-world as the surrounding, enveloping context within which I live and move and have my being, the external things within this world, the human other who calls me to ethical responsibility, the poor who motivate me to move into a praxis of justice, being as the totality of that which is, and God as the divine, liberating masculine-feminine other inviting me to self-transcendence. Authenticity lies in self-transcendence. Transcendence as self-transcendence, then, refers to the human subject in community moving to respond to transcendence or "exteriority" in the other senses. Authenticity, we might say in modifying the formula, lies in a self-transcendence moving to the transcendent other of the life-world, thing, person, poor person, being, and God.

The desire to know, our questioning orientation to being, expresses itself in an ever increasing identification with otherness as it is in its otherness. Being as other to me and as including me is the object of the pure desire to know. To experience, understand, judge, choose, and love, in line with the transcendental precepts, is progressively to say "yes" to the other as other, to be converted to the other. We have here a deepening receptivity to the other as other. "Receptivity" and "otherness" are correlative.

Such self-transcendence oriented to transcendence on the cognitional, epistemic, ethical, social, metaphysical, and religious dimensions is what I will be describing, interpreting, defining, and justifying in the course of this book.[72]

༄༅

TWO

Being as Structure and Process

Dialectical Considerations

The history of metaphysics has been plagued by controversies over what being is. Is it the one as Parmenides says, or the forms illuminated by the Good as Plato says, or eternal thought thinking itself as Aristotle says, or absolute spirit as Hegel argues? When one considers the history of metaphysics, it seems like a competing battleground of warring conceptions, which manifest the individual predilections of the thinkers themselves. It is hard not to sympathize with Kant's impatience with all of this, as he contrasts the solid achievements of science with apparently fruitless metaphysical speculations that never get anywhere.[1]

Is there a way of transcending such a situation and putting metaphysics on more solid ground? What if underlying metaphysical accounts on the level of content there were a more formal, second level intention of being that all thinkers have in mind at least implicitly? If so, if we started there with that intention, then we could find some initial common ground on which to resolve disputes. Since the notion of being is in subjects, then an adequate self-knowledge would be essential in order to thematize the notion and move to an adequate metaphysics. Self-appropriation would be an essential presupposition for metaphysics.[2]

Such a self-appropriation has already been performed in PCM. Let us recall the basic argument there. If I experience, understand, judge, and choose, then I am a unified, incarnate subject. Experience, understanding, judging, and deciding have already been defined in chapter 1. To briefly recapitulate, experience is fundamentally awareness of the given in data of sense or data of consciousness, understanding is grasp of the intelligible patterns in the given and answers the questions "What is it?" "Why is it?" or "How is it?," judgment is affirmation or denial of the validity of the conceived intelligible patterns and answers the questions "Is it so?" or "Is it true?," and choice is the free option for one possibility among others—should I go to Canada or New York for vacation?[3]

Let us return to the argument. If I experience, understand, judge, and choose, then I am a unified, incarnate, conscious subject. But I experience, understand, judge, and choose. Therefore I am a unified, incarnate, conscious subject. The syllogism is a conditional syllogism expressing a virtually unconditioned judgment. A virtually unconditioned judgment is one that happens to have its conditions fulfilled. The conditioned, "I am a unified, conscious, incarnate subject," presents no difficulties since it merely expresses what is to be affirmed. The link between conditions and conditioned is materially analytic; if there is knowing and choosing, then these, as I have already shown elsewhere, are unified, conscious, and rooted in an incarnate subject. The problematic area is the fulfillment of the conditions, which fulfillment takes place in the crucible of conscious experience and my reflection upon it.[4]

Now we are ready for a new step in the argument. So far we have been focusing on the self as the noetic pole of my perceiving, understanding, judging, choosing presence in the world. What if we were to turn our attention now to the noematic side, to the reality that is the intended pole of our conscious acts. The phenomenological and hermeneutical traditions, which have nourished me deeply, have various names for this objective pole: "life-world," "world," "being." For now, I will use these terms as roughly synonymous, and will make, when necessary, further revisions later on.

What becomes apparent, first, is that being cannot equal the immediate. The reason is that any given set of data calls forth questions for understanding and judgment. The "real" force of the apple that hits me on the head is not only its immediate aspect as experienced, but its meaning and reality as understood and judged, as subject to verified laws of force. The real poem by Hopkins or Eliot or Berryman is not the poem as simply read and heard, but the poem as understood, affirmed, and appreciated. The real man or woman is not simply this handsome or beautiful creature confronting our senses, but the person as understood, judged, and loved. Feminists not only have valid moral objections to being reduced to objects, things, or sensible appearance, but a cognitive, epistemic one as well. Male chauvinism is based upon a naive view of knowing as taking a good look at a sensible appearance. To the extent that people live up or down to such a model in practice, they miss the real depth or interiority of the person known.[5]

The break with knowing as immediate applies not only to accounts of the external object, but also to accounts of the subject. Any attempt to say that the real subject emerges simply or primarily in a felt existential experience of or look at the subject misses the necessity of understanding, judging, and choosing the subject. As the account of self-affirmation just indicated, the real subject is the subject as experienced, understood, judged, and chosen. Such immediacy is the basis of some attempts within phenomenology and hermeneutics to deny any legitimate explanatory moment in understanding the subject. According to such attempts, such explanation, because it leaves the plane of felt, existential immediacy, cannot give us access to anything real or meaningful in the subject.[6]

I do not wish to deny here that immediacy is an aspect of being and knowing, only that it is the whole story. The force is experienced before it is understood and judged; subjects experience themselves before they come to understand and affirm themselves. Being in the full sense seems to be a "mediated immediacy" and, as we will see, there are one-sided, conceptual, representational accounts of being that overstate its mediated character and understate or leave out its immediate character. The difficulty, however, with different forms of empiricism, positivism, pragmatism, naive realism, personalism, and existentialism is to overstate the moment of immediacy and to reduce or deemphasize or illegitimately subordinate other moments to that.

Postmodern forms of immediacy also need to be criticized: Heidegger's desire, for example, to return to a pre-Socratic sense of being as unconcealment emerging from concealment or Adorno's account of mimesis as immediate, aesthetic relating to people and nature. I am sympathetic to such forms insofar as they express disillusionment with one-sided forms of mediation. But I disagree with them insofar as they confuse one-sided, alienating mediation or objectification with mediation or objectification as such; recall my critique of Heidegger in chapter 1. Moreover, as I have discussed exhaustively elsewhere, such accounts miss the positive role of differentiation in history and being. Such differentiation as a *legitimate* mediation is a forward move. Plato, for example, distinguished between sensible and intellectual knowing and between sensible appearance and form, Aquinas between understanding and judgment, and between essence and existence, and Husserl between philosophy and science and between life-world and quantitative intelligibilities. Differentiation is, all things considered, good; consequently, the attempt to return to an undifferentiated immediacy is problematic and mistaken.[7]

If being does not equal the immediate, then breaking with knowing as looking, as commonsensical and objective in a naive sense, as rooted in and conforming to the natural attitude, is one of the first signs of philosophical awakening. The stance of Archie Bunker has to give way to a more enlightened stance. Once such awakening has occurred, however, and often accompanying it, the resulting reflection can be one-sidedly mediating and reflective. In moving from Archie Bunker's absolutizing of the naive stance within the natural attitude, we must risk an idealism and falling into the apparently bottomless pit of a subjectivity forever cut off from the objective world. At least, that is how it looks to someone like Archie who lives within the natural attitude.

If he knew the history of philosophy, however, Archie might have some ammunition against defenders of critical philosophy. Thus, Plato identifies being with form and minimizes or denies the value of sensible reality, Descartes identifies the real objective world with what can be known about it through science and leaves out the perceived life-world as the ground and context and foundation of science, Hegel identifies being with a minimal conceptual content of "not-nothing," and structuralists and poststructuralists identify fundamental reality and meaning with the hidden structures of language and leave out or minimize as merely derivative or produced effects the realities of concrete human discourse, interaction, and speech.[8]

All of these quite different forms of philosophy have in common an overemphasis on the second moment of cognition—understanding—especially in its conceptual aspects. What they miss, first, is the preconceptual moments even on the level of understanding itself: the initial presentation of data, the questioning directed toward that data, the glimmering of insight into the data, and finally, the definition emerging from that insight. What they miss, second, is the necessary role of immediacy and immediate aspects of reality. Without being hit on the head by the apple, and verifying hypotheses about this experience in experiments with perceivable consequences, the hypotheses conceived on the level of understanding lose their validity. Berkeley and Hume drew this consequence explicitly from Descartes' and Locke's distinction between objective, primary qualities known through science and merely subjective, secondary qualities that are heard or tasted, seen or touched.[9]

What such accounts miss also is the distinction of factuality from such intelligibilities. A scientific intelligibility conceived on the level of understanding is merely possible. Such an intelligibility affirmed or verified is a fact. That my house might or could burn down is a possibility; that my house burned down, as I see when I return home at night, is a fact.

That much philosophy and metaphysics has been caught up in such one-sided mediation is certainly true; indeed Heidegger's reference to modernity as the age of representation or the age of the world picture bears witness to this point. If metaphysics equals representation in this sense, then we certainly need to get beyond it. Lonergan in a way similar to Heidegger sees the whole of modern philosophy as exploring the implications of knowing as looking outward toward sensible givens or inward toward conceptual givens. Knowing as looking is roughly synonymous to representation in Heidegger's sense.

What Lonergan refuses to do, however, is to equate metaphysics with representation in this sense; rather this is simply a bad or inadequate metaphysics.[10]

What Heidegger misses in his critique of metaphysics is the legitimate intention of metaphysics to know being; what he misses also is that knowing being does not necessarily imply making it the object of a concept or definition. Being is not an essence or genus, and thinkers as different as Aristotle or Aquinas or Lonergan have made this point. Being, I argue, initially is a notion oriented to a content and a process, not a concept, thing, or essence. The solution to a bad metaphysics is not overcoming metaphysics, but better, more adequate metaphysics. Overcoming representational thinking does not mean or imply overcoming metaphysics, but simply overcoming bad or inadequate metaphysics.[11]

What does such a dialectical discussion reveal about the notion of being? First and tentatively, and to be developed further and verified in subsequent chapters, beings within the life-world have at least these aspects to them: an aspect of immediate givenness, an aspect of form and structure, and an aspect of actuality present both in activities and factual existence manifest in and functioning as the basis of such activity. Second, being is both one and many: one in the sense that each thing is one actuality, being is a totality of such actualities, known or knowable as such, having in common the fact that they are part of the same life-world and all are immediate, structured actualities; many in the sense that there are these three aspects to being: immediate givenness, structure, and actuality, and in the sense that there are many beings with these aspects. As we proceed in this book, we will discover further dimensions of unity and multiplicity. One touchstone that emerges for an adequate metaphysics is doing justice to both the unity and the multiplicity.

Third, not only is being one and many, but it is also identical and different. I know beings in a context of community through a process of question and answer. I confront objects such as a table or falling body or poem that are different from me. I am not the table or falling body or poem, but I am the same in the sense that we are all immediate, structured actualities acting in the world. Beings also differ from themselves insofar as they change; my going from not perceiving or not knowing the table to perceiving and knowing it makes me different. The table painted a different color or having aged is different from itself. Yet it is the same identical "I" and table at the end of the process of change as at the beginning.

Fourth, being is both present and absent. As what is sought through questioning, being is present to me as this thing questioned, the falling body. Nonetheless, what the question intends is an answer that will emerge sometime, in the next second or next minute or next hour. The questionability of being implies both its futurity, its not-yet being-known or present and its pastness, its already having been known or present. I question this falling body on the basis of presuppositions of past knowledge that are not fully thematized. Both futurity and pastness are aspects of nonpresence interacting with presence; being is a dialectical interplay between presence and absence.[12]

Finally, this dialectical interplay between identity and difference, presence and absence, permanence and change indicates the heuristic character of the notion of being. Being is the object not only of questions I have answered, but of the questions I have not answered. Being is the intelligible, the known/unknown toward which I head in my questioning. Such questioning implies a certain orientation in me, a desire, an eros. I question being because I want to know being, and this desire, when other desires do not interfere with it, is pure. Being in the life-world is the object of the pure desire to know.[13]

The Content of Metaphysics

From Implicit to Explicit Metaphysics

What we have begun to do here dialectically is to effect a breakthrough, envelopment, and confinement. The breakthrough is effected in the appropriation of one's own empirical, intelligent, rational, and rationally self-conscious, free awareness and activities. The envelopment occurs insofar as the protean notion of being is that which we attentively experience, intelligently grasp, and reasonably affirm. The confinement is effected through the dialectical opposition of the twofold notions of the real, the self, objectivity, and value. We achieve, then, a necessity and inclusiveness. One cannot deny the notion of being without implicit or explicit self-contradiction. Any possible claim is included in the range of positions and counter-positions on the issues of being, the self, objectivity, and value.[14]

The unfolding of metaphysics is simply the full, consistent unfolding of my own reality as an empirical, intelligent, and rational knower. If I am self-appropriated, then I see easily that such unfolding cannot be denied without self-contradiction or arbitrariness. If I am not self-appropriated, then I am thrown back into the morass of a polymorphic consciousness and torn between the Scylla of dogmatism and the Charybdis of skepticism, position and counter-position, illusion and truth.

It can seem, therefore, to a person who is not self-appropriated that Kant or Heidegger or Derrida or any of their various offshoots or combinations is right: metaphysics is simply an anachronistic dream of a bygone past that deserves to be left behind. If metaphysics, however, is in the mind as that mind moves from latent to problematic to fully explicit metaphysics and that mind, enfleshed, of course, embodied, and self-appropriated, requires metaphysics as its logical, consistent unfolding and articulation of its own relational dynamism, then persons can turn the tables and claim against Kant,

Heidegger, and Derrida that theirs is the more critical, comprehensive position. Indeed my debate with them in this book, as they emerge from their critiques of other earlier, more dogmatic, less reflective, less critical versions of metaphysics, becomes an instance of the movement from latent to problematic to explicit metaphysics.

Metaphysics, then, is and must be based upon self-appropriation. Accordingly we are now prepared to present an initial definition of metaphysics, again reminding readers that this is initially second-level or second-order, heuristic rather than content-filled. What this content is will be determined by further inquiry. What are the elements of being? Who is right, the Platonist, Aristotelian, Thomist, Hegelian, or Whiteheadian, concerning the account of this content? Is being processive? Is God processive or not? Is God personal or not?

Metaphysics is, first, the conception, affirmation, and implementation of the integral heuristic structure of proportionate being; and, second, and more concretely, the unity of this with the concrete discoveries of common sense and science. The distinction between a narrow and broader conception, while in the spirit of Lonergan's accounts, claims to explicitize a difference that remains somewhat implicit in his account. A heuristic notion is the notion of the unknown content, like the X anticipated in the solution of an algebraic equation, and is determined by anticipating the type of act through which the unknown would become known. A heuristic structure is an ordered set of heuristic notions. Finally, an integral heuristic structure is an ordered set of all heuristic notions.[15]

For example, we define proportionate being as whatever is to be known by experience, understanding, and judgment. The definition does not assign the content of this experience, understanding, and judgment. Nonetheless, it assigns an ordered set of types of acts, and it implies that every proportionate being is to be known through such an ordered set.[16]

If this integral heuristic structure were to be conceived, affirmed, and implemented, then latent metaphysics has become explicit. Latent metaphysics is the unity of empirical, intelligent, and rational consciousness as underlying, penetrating, transforming, and unifying the other departments of knowledge. But an integral heuristic structure of proportionate being performs these offices in an explicit manner. As heuristic, it would underlie all knowledge, in the sense that from it proceed all questions leading to the knowledge of common sense, logic, mathematics, the physical and social sciences, and theology. As the source of the questions, which other departments of knowledge answer, metaphysics would penetrate other fields. As dialectical, it would transform these fields, freeing them from counter-positions and developing positions. As integral, it contains in itself the order that binds other departments into a single, intelligible whole.[17]

What, then, is the nature of the transition from implicit and problematic to explicit metaphysics? In its general form, the transition is a deduction involving a major premise, a set of primary minor premises, and a set of secondary minor premises. The major premise is the isomorphism between the structure of the knowing and the structure of the known. If the knowing consists in a related set of acts, then the known consists in a related set of contents of acts. Consequently, the pattern of the relations among acts is similar in form to the pattern of relations among the contents of the acts. The premise is analytic, an analytic principle rather than an analytic proposition. An analytic principle is true not by definition alone, but follows from a definition as grounded in and emerging from a phenomenology of knowing leading to self-appropriation.[18]

The set of primary minor premises is a series of affirmations of concrete and recurring structures of the knowing, self-affirming subject. The simplest of these structures is that every instance of knowing proportionate being consists of a unification of experiencing, understanding, and judging. It follows from the isomorphism of knowing that every instance of known proportionate being is a parallel unification of a content of experience, a content of understanding, and a content of judgment, or, in terms of our earlier discussion, an element of givenness, an element of form or structure, and an element of act or actuality.

The set of secondary minor premises is supplied by reoriented science and common sense, reoriented according to the distinction between position and counter-position. For example, from the major and primary minor premises is obtained an integrating structure, but from the secondary minor premises is obtained the materials to be integrated. From the major and primary minor premises is obtained a well-defined and definitive set of questions to be answered; from the secondary minor premises is obtained the fact of answers and their frequency. For example, the questions of physical science are those to be answered by experience, understanding, and judgment; the materials have been supplied by Newton's laws and special relativity theory. Another example is the set of questions about social reality coming from cognitional theory, and the set of answers in CAL is my account of social relations under late capitalism. Or another more accessible example is the real Joan to be known through my own experience, understanding, and judgment; who Joan is, whether she is selfish or unselfish, religious or irreligious, just or unjust, smart or dumb, will depend upon what is revealed as I get to know her.[19]

Such an explicit metaphysics is progressive, for results come not from some prior, Platonic contemplative bliss, but from the resourceful reflectiveness of human intelligence in operation. Heuristic notions and structures are known by an analysis of operations with which we have become familiar. Just as other departments of knowledge advance by discovering new methods, so metaphysics advances by adding these new discoveries to its account of the integral, heuristic structure of proportionate being. Here we unfold the full sense of metaphysics as both transcendental and empirical, form and content, a priori and a posteriori, eidetic and pragmatic.[20]

This modification and qualification of Lonergan's account is in keeping with my earlier work in PCM and CAL. In both of these works I argued for dialectical phenomenology as a formal unity of interpretation, description, and critique oriented to a certain noematic content of the life-world available to phenomenological-hermeneutical inquiry and critical social theory. Within both of these noematic accounts, however, there are a priori elements and contingent, empirical content, for example, the character of the perceived object as perspectivally present in a presumptive way and the particular, contingent content of the perceived thing or person; or the noetic-noematic structure of the social world as intersubjective, hermeneutical, mediated by tradition, governed by dialectic between communicative action and strategic action, and ethically structured by criteria of right, morality, and justice; and the hermeneutical-empirical content of capitalism as oriented to and based on class domination, committed to surplus value as its overriding goal, reifying, and exploitative.[21]

Similarly here, we note that the first sense of metaphysics has an a priori structure both in knowing and being; and the second, broader conception links this structure to an a posteriori, contingent, empirical content: physical reality as understood by relativity theory, social reality as understood by critical social theory, and the reality of Joan as known by me in concrete encounters. Corresponding to the subjective, a priori structure of knowing is the objective a priori character of the known, as we will see soon, potency, form, and act. The above examples from PCM and CAL are instances of this interaction of form and content. When I perceive a real thing or I interpret a capitalist social structure, I am experiencing, understanding, and judging it as a real thing or social structure. Natural things and social realities are related implicitly or explicitly to the integral, heuristic structure of proportionate being.[22]

The dependence of metaphysics on science and common sense is not that of a conclusion on premises nor effect on cause, but that of a generating, transforming, and unifying principle upon the materials that it generates, transforms, and unifies. These materials are themselves form and content: the methods of science and common sense as instances of a general heuristic structure and contents discovered by these methods. Metaphysics does not discover or teach or perform science or common sense, but it takes over the results of these efforts, works them into coherence by reversing their counterpositions, and knits them into a unity by discovering in them the extension and concrete prolongation of the integral, heuristic structure that it itself is. Science and common sense are taken over but not uncritically; purified of counter-positions, of extrascientific claims, of uncritical recourse to the "already out there now real," of positivism, of scientism, of commodification.

Metaphysics acts to purify our science and common sense and thus to release them from dogmatism, reveal their limits, and unify them in a broader, more comprehensive whole. We saw an example of this purifying, critical quality of metaphysics in the preceding chapter whereas later in this chapter I use it as an element in ideology critique. The person who has purified and clarified himself through a dialectical phenomenology crowned with metaphysics will be less likely to equate science with the whole of knowledge, to reject common sense and the prescientific life-world because they are not scientifically accessible, to deny his own interiority or subjectivity, to accept a reified, commodified conception of himself—the Fordham or Columbia product, the necessity of selling myself, the emphasis on presenting a pleasing, commodified surface, the tendency to take this surface as the whole story as late capitalism wishes us to do. At the same time, metaphysics, as we will see, can criticize even the critique of ideology. In its rejection of metaphysics, of theism, of religion, is it being fully critical and rational or not?[23]

Is this conception of metaphysics too imperialistic, belying its commitment to fallibilism, indeterminacy and recognition of finitude? I think not, for several reasons. First of all, the unity is one of form, not of content as in more traditional forms of metaphysics. Because the unity is formal, structural, and heuristic, then even in its second, broader sense metaphysics remains open, indeterminate, and incomplete. Unanswered questions about content remain, because the notion of being intends the content of all legitimate questions, answered and unanswered.

Furthermore, even if there is a relative apodicticity on the side of the formal unity rooted in cognitional and ontological structure, because that cannot be denied without self-contradiction, the content from common sense and science is probable, incomplete, and revisable. I note also a reciprocity between metaphysics in the narrow sense and common sense and science. The former unifies, transforms, and purifies the latter, whereas the latter supplies the content that fills out somewhat the heuristic structure. Nonetheless, a relative autonomy is present between metaphysics in the narrow sense and common sense and science.

Finally, metaphysics as integral heuristic structure is relatively stable, for it rests upon the relatively invariant structure of the human mind as experiencing, understanding, and judging. The Aristotelian, Galilean, Newtonian, and Einsteinian accounts of falling bodies are all open to revision because they are determinate accounts. But a merely heuristic notion in not as easily open to revision. One cannot revise the heuristic notion that the nature of a free fall is what is to be known when the free fall is understood correctly, for it is that heuristic notion that is both antecedent to each.

The Elements of Metaphysics

Now we are ready for an important move from the structure of knowing to the structure of the known. If metaphysics is the integral heuristic structure of proportionate being, what are the elements of that structure that would correspond on the noematic side to experience, understanding, and judgment on the noetic side? Up to this point we have already indicated some aspects of the answer. For previously we have referred to an element of givenness, an element of structure, and an element of actuality. And I criticized one-sided accounts of these as excluding or minimizing the others, or reducing the others to one dimension. Thus, empiricism tends to reduce being to what can be known experientially, and idealism tends to reduce being to what can be rationally defined and conceptualized. Critical realism I defended as a more adequate account, because it does justice to the unity, difference, and relationship among these elements.

Also in the previous section I have affirmed isomorphism: the structure of knowing is similar to the structure of the knower. Accordingly, we are prepared to say that corresponding to experience is an intellectually patterned experience of the given potency. The given is known as such in a mediated context of inquiry, in relationship to a question about its form, "What is it?," "Why is it?," or "How is it?"; and about its actuality, "Is it so?" or "Is it true?" Lonergan names the givenness "empirical residue": the individuality, the continuity, the coincidental conjunctions and successions, and the nonsystematic divergence from intelligible norms. The empirical residue is that which confronts me as given, and from which I abstract when I intend or understand form, the definition of the triangle, falling body, or biological species.

Corresponding to understanding is the component in being to be known by answering questions for intelligence, "What is it?," "Why is it?," or "How is it?" Form is what I know when I understand the triangle, falling body, or species, and this is understood in fully explanatory knowledge, the relationship of things to one another. I do not fully know "red" when I am just experiencing it sensuously, but when I understand it in terms of its wave length scientifically. Act is what is known by uttering the virtually unconditioned "yes" or "no" of reasonable judgment. The scientific hypothesis becomes actual or real to me through judgment, as does my correct understanding of a person or a species.[24]

Just as experience, understanding, and judgment constitute a unity, so also do potency, form, and act. One knowing corresponds to one known, but this unit is differentiated into different aspects; once again we see identity and difference as equiprimordial. What is experienced, the free fall or individual animal or woman, is what is understood; what is understood is what is affirmed. These elements are here aspects, not things. One does not know one being by experiencing, a second by understanding, and a third by judging. Rather potency, form, and act are aspects of one being or thing, the falling body, the animal, or woman.[25]

A second major step is to note that there are two major kinds of potency, form, and act: conjugate and central. Conjugate form is what is understood by conjugates—that is, terms defined implicitly by their empirically verified and explanatory relations. Thus, scientific laws governing falling bodies are conjugate forms, the data into which I inquire are potency, and the factuality of the verified law is act. In addition to the relationship of the falling bodies to one another, however, are the bodies themselves as individual entities enduring over time. In addition to the animal interacting with its environment is the animal as a unity-identity-whole. In addition to the relationships between and among men and women giving rise to the explanatory laws of social theory, for example, the general law of capitalist accumulation that, as capitalism develops and becomes more itself, it tends to produce an army of poor and unemployed, or the tendency in capitalism for the rate of profit to fall, are the individual men and women themselves as concrete unities.

Not only are such unities directly knowable, but they are necessary as presuppositions for science. Science advances through the interaction of increasingly accurate descriptions and even more satisfactory explanations of the same objects. Unless the objects are the same, there is no relation between the description and explanation, and no reason why explanation should modify description or description lead to better explanation. But the only object that remains the same is the identical thing or person, for the explanatory conjugates change, and the descriptive or experiential terms undergo modification or rearrangement. So long as science is developing, the notion of an intelligible unity is indispensable.

In their term no less than in their development, scientific conclusions need to be supported by evidence. Evidence emerges in the possibility and actuality of change from data perceived to the final verification of the hypothesis. Without concrete and intelligible unities, there is nothing to change, for change is neither the substitution of one datum for another, nor the replacement of one concept by another. Change is the same concrete unity providing the unity for successively different data; without the unity there is no change, and without change in the knower and the known we lack a notable dimension of evidence.

Moreover, science is applicable to concrete problems, but neither descriptive nor explanatory conjugates can be applied to concrete problems without the explanatory "this," and that demonstrative can only be used insofar as there is a link between concepts and data as individual. Because only the notion of the concrete intelligible unity of data supplies such a link, this notion is necessary for science as applied.

The distinction between central and conjugate forms leads to a distinction between central and conjugate acts. Central act is existence; conjugate act is occurrence or operation. Similarly, the empirical residue divides into conjugate and central potency. If central form is the intelligible unity of data as individual, central potency is identified with the individuality of the empirical residue. On the other hand, conjugate forms are verified in the spatio-temporal continua, conjunctions, and successions. These I will call conjugate potency.

Lonergan gives an example of the distinction between central and conjugate potency, form, and act. Let us suppose, he says, that mass velocity is a notion that survives in a fully explanatory science. Then the mass velocity will be a conjugate act, the mass, defined by its intelligible relationships to other masses, will be a conjugate form, and the space-time continuum will be a conjugate potency. What has the mass will be individual by its central potency, unified by its central form, and existing by its central act.

For the nonscientist a more accessible example might be the loving relationship between John and Jane. John and Jane as individuals have central potency, as structured unities of experiencing, understanding, judging, and deciding, central forms, and as existing, central acts. As possessing capacities to know and love one another, they have conjugate potency; as related to one another in an authentic loving relationship, conjugate form; and as engaging in concrete acts of knowing and loving, conjugate acts.[26]

One advantage of our method of metaphysics is that metaphysical questions can be taken out of the realm of endless speculation and resolved by reflecting on concrete, psychological fact. For example, one question over which much print has been spilled is whether the distinction among the elements is merely notional or real. We can begin to answer such a question by saying that intelligibility is intrinsic to being, for being is the intelligible, the object of the desire to know. Next we must affirm that intelligibilities are of different kinds. Givenness is not form is not act. The data into which I inquire as green are not the same as the form understood as an answer to a question for intelligence, the account of green in terms of wave length; nor is this the same as the actuality known in the "yes" of judgment. Data as green are merely potentially intelligible, as structured they are formally intelligible, and as actual they are actually intelligible.

Correspondingly, just as intelligibility is intrinsic to being, so difference in intelligibility is intrinsic to being. Proportionate being is what is to be known by experience, understanding, and judgment. It is not knowing by experience alone, for such knowledge merely gives us potential intelligibility. We do not know by understanding alone, for that merely gives us bright ideas that may or may not be true. Again judgment cannot occur without previous experience and understanding, without form or hypothesis to be validated, which is itself a product of insight into data. The object of knowing is not only intrinsically intelligible, but it is also a compound of three distinct types of related intelligibility. Once again we see how difference as well as unity is intrinsic to being; proportionate beings are differentiated unities known through a differentiated unity of experience, understanding, and judgment. Difference is intrinsic to knowing and being, but, contra Derrida, I see no reason for making difference more primordial or fundamental than unity and identity. They are equiprimordial.

Accordingly, we see how potency, form, and act are not only the structure in which being is known, but are a structure of being as known, because reality is intrinsically intelligible and intelligibility is of different kinds. Nor are these the only differentiations in being, for we have noted the difference among central and conjugate potency, form, and act. Accordingly, we define the difference between a major and a minor real distinction. A distinction is real if P is, Q is, and P is not Q. A real distinction is major if P is a thing and Q is a thing, minor when P is an element and Q is an element.

I note here again the distinction between positions and counter-positions. If the real is "the already out there now real" or "the already in here now real," then we may be tempted to see intelligibility as extrinsic to being. Because extroversion or introversion of consciousness is prior to asking questions and independent of answers to questions, we might be tempted to deny any real distinction among potency, form, and act. But if the real is the intelligible, if the intelligible is intrinsic to being, and if differences in intelligibility are intrinsic to being, then the elements are real and distinct according to a real, minor distinction.[27]

Being as Processive

Development

At this point we have demonstrated the content and necessity of the metaphysical elements corresponding to cognitional structure; now the task is to demonstrate their meaning and reality as processive. Let us briefly review where we have been in order to determine where we are going. First, we determined the genuine possibility of metaphysics. Next, we affirmed the notion of being as the object of the pure desire to know. Then, we defined metaphysics as the integral, heuristic structure of proportionate being. Finally, we affirmed an isomorphism between knowing and being, and two different kinds of potency, form, and act, central and conjugate.

A further move is to argue that the principal minor premise includes the four methods of possible inquiry, the condition of their use, and the possibility of their integration. The anticipation of a constant system to be discovered yields classical method, most obviously instantiated in Newton's laws or Einstein's theory of relativity; the anticipation that data will not conform to system grounds statistical method, the anticipation that the relations between successive stages of a changing system will not be directly intelligible grounds dialectical method, and the anticipation of an intelligibly related sequence of systems grounds genetic method, our main concern in this chapter. Genetic method has the task of thematizing development.

Data will either conform or not to system, and successive systems will either be related or not in a directly intelligible manner. If data do conform to system, then they can be understood classically; if not, then they can be understood statistically, like the tosses of the coin that turn up heads half of the time. If successive systems are related in a directly intelligible manner, then they can be understood genetically. If not, then they can be understood dialectically. Accordingly, taken together the four methods are relevant to any field of data, do not dictate what the data must be, and are able to cope with data no matter what they may be.[28]

The four methods, then, can be viewed as subheuristic structures within the general heuristic structure of proportionate being. Correspondingly, they allow us to structurally unify our accounts of being. For example, in a universe in which both classical and statistical laws are relevant, the immanent intelligibility of the order of events is that of emergent probability. Emergent probability is the successive realization in accord with successive schedules of probability of a conditional series of schemes of recurrence. This definition needs to be conceptually unpacked.[29]

The notion of a scheme of recurrence is illustrated by a series of events A, B, C, D, . . . such that if A occurs, B occurs; if B occurs, C occurs, and so on. Examples of a scheme of recurrence are the planetary system, the circulation of water on the face of the earth, the nitrogen cycle familiar to biologists, the routines of animal life, and the economic rhythms of production, circulation, and exchange. If an automobile is produced, then it can be sold. If it is sold, then it can be driven and used.

A conditional series of schemes, P, Q, R, occurs when all prior members of the series must function for a later member to become a concrete possibility. Thus, the scheme P can function even though neither Q nor R are functioning, but Q cannot function if P is not already functioning. An illustration is the dietary scheme of animals. All carnivorous animals cannot live off other carnivorous animals. Consequently, a carnivorous dietary scheme presupposes another herbivorous dietary scheme, but there could be herbivorous animals without carnivorous animals. Again plants cannot in general live off animals; the scheme of nourishment involves chemical processes; and that scheme can function apart from the existence of any animals. Finally, chemical cycles are not independent of physical laws, yet inversely the laws of physics can be combined into schemes of recurrence that are independent of chemical processes. A schedule of probabilities articulates the increasingly probable emergence of later schemes as earlier schemes are realized, as well as the probable survival of a present scheme of recurrence.[30]

Development occurs, correspondingly, when different schemes emerge according to schedules of probability: from physical events emerge chemical laws with their corresponding events and things; from effectively functioning chemical laws emerge organic, herbivorous laws and things; from organic laws and things emerge carnivorous animals and the laws of their functioning. Events that are merely coincidental and accidental on a lower scheme of recurrence become essential when organized according to a higher, later scheme or recurrence. Thus, the isolated chemical occurrence becomes part of a chemical scheme of recurrence.[31]

When we understand development scientifically, we note a movement to successively higher viewpoints. Thus, chemical events that cannot be understood according to physical laws can be understood when we move to chemistry as a higher viewpoint. When biological events occur that cannot be understood chemically, we move to biology as a higher viewpoint. When psychic events occur that cannot be understood biologically, then we move to psychology. When events of intellectual cognition and choice occur that cannot be understood psychologically, then we move to philosophy, cognitional theory, and transcendental method. This emergence of successive higher viewpoints grounds the possibility of distinct, autonomous sciences. Physics is not chemistry is not biology is not psychology is not cognitional theory.[32]

Not only is there development of species, in which different kinds of things emerge, but there is also development in individuals. Thus, mewling, puking infants will initially not be able to do mathematics, science, or philosophy until they have learned to do a whole lot of things that are prior: to walk, to talk, to use language, and so on. Such development in the child involves and implies a growing reflexivity and universalization. Thus, using Piaget and Kohlberg, I showed in CAL how moral development moves from responding to particular pleasures and pains to obeying conventional norms to responding to moral principles, in the light of which the previously accepted norms can be modified, transformed, or rejected.[33]

What we begin to sense here both in being and knowing is dynamism, and not dynamism only but upwardly directed dynamism. As the desire to know moves from experience to understanding to judgment, so being moves from potency to form to act. And as intelligence advances from lower viewpoints to higher viewpoints, so being advances from physical levels in which chemical combinations are just a coincidental manifold to a level of chemical laws and things, from there to the level of biological systems, and so on. I will name this upwardly directed dynamism finality.[34]

Such finality is not the working out of a determinate blueprint. Just as cognitional process does not know in advance what the answer to a particular question is, objective process points toward the culmination of a conditioned series of things and schemes of recurrence in accordance with successive schedules of probabilities. Just as knowing is not headed toward a determinate answer, but only toward that which will answer the question framed in an equation containing the unknown X, so proportionate being is not headed to some determinate individual or species or genus. Rather finality goes beyond such determinations. Potency leads to form, but form points beyond itself to act, and act heads beyond itself to coincidental manifolds of acts, and through them to higher forms and higher coincidental manifolds of acts.

Just as cognitional activity is the becoming known of being, so objective process is the becoming of proportionate being. Indeed such cognitional activity is but a part of the universe, but its orientation to being is the instance in which the universal striving toward being becomes conscious and intelligent and reasonable.[35]

Although such dynamism is directed dynamism, I do not deny cataclysm, chance, death, and moral evil, but these are not the whole story. For, in spite of mistakes, human beings do progress. In CAL I showed how in history a limited progress can be affirmed in scientific and moral learning as human history has moved from early, relatively undifferentiated societies to civilizations organized around a state to modern societies with sophisticated science, systems of law, democracy, and respect for human rights. Or, on an individual level, a human being, in spite of slipping, erring, and failing occasionally, can move from being oriented merely to pleasure and pain to responding to conventional norms to responding to universal moral principles. Upwardly directed dynamism, then, proceeds not in a necessitarian manner, but according to schedules of probability.[36]

Is finality real? If I have never moved from question to correct answer and inauthenticity to authenticity, if classical and statistical laws have never been verified, if there is no evidence that species and genera evolve and develop, if human history never shows growth in scientific, moral, and aesthetic learning, then a negative answer makes sense. If, however, evidence exists for yes answers to some or all of these questions, then finality is real. The basis for a "yes" answer is the evidence grounding the virtually unconditioned judgment, "finality is real."

Genetic Method

As classical method heuristically anticipates an unspecified correlation to be specified, the unknown in the equation to be verified, so genetic method finds its heuristic notion in development. In the plant is the single development of the organism, in the animal is the twofold development of the organism and psyche, and in the human being is the threefold development of organism, psyche, and intelligence—freedom.[37]

Development is the linked sequence of higher integrations. In development we note, first of all, a principle of emergence: otherwise coincidental manifolds invite a higher integration effected by higher conjugate forms. Chemical compounds, for example, are higher integrations of otherwise coincidental manifolds of subatomic events. Next we note a principle of correspondence. Significantly different underlying manifolds require different higher integrations. Thus, chemical events require chemical laws. Finally, we note, again, a principle of finality: the underlying manifold is an upwardly directed dynamism oriented to ever-fuller realization of being. Such finality is not merely an a priori demand of intelligence, but is verified in vast ranges and kinds of empirically or hermeneutically known fact—for example, the development of species, the cognitive and moral development of children, and historical development from early, undifferentiated civilizations to differentiated, reflexive modernity.[38]

Again development is marked by increasingly expanding differentiation. Thus, single cells of organisms exhibit quantitative differences in the number of chromosomes, but this differentiation is not comparable to that exhibited in the fuller development of the organism. Men and women of significantly different temperament and character began as infants from patterns of somatic consciousness that are remarkably similar. In early civilizations, as I showed in CAL, we find relatively little differentiation between sense and intellect, individual and society, sacred and secular, philosophy and religion, but in modern societies a great deal of differentiation between these and in other sets of opposites. Thus, we note a differentiation between church and state, science and philosophy, art and morality, and the private and public. History is the progressive differentiation and integration of human consciousness in the world.[39]

In development we note a minor flexibility, in which the same goal is reached through different means. Psychic health can be achieved through spontaneous development or through work with a psychiatrist, material can be taught through Socratic method or lecturing, and the same scientific discovery can be made in different manners, instant, blinding insight or patient, painstaking work done over the course of years. Major flexibility occurs when the ultimate objective shifts. In biology an instance is adjustment to a changed environment, in psychology sublimation, in knowledge a shift from one problem to another.[40]

We can note also in development in general direction, a field, and a mode of operation. The general direction is, as we have seen, from general and indeterminate to specific and differentiated; two children very similar at birth become quite different later on on physical, psychological, intellectual, and moral levels. The general mode of operation is the movement from lower coincidental manifolds to higher integration—for example, the movement from a coincidental manifold of chemical events to chemical laws. The field of development is finality, the upwardly directed dynamism of proportionate being.[41]

If development is higher system on the move, we can distinguish between higher system as integrator and higher system as operator. Higher system as integrator unifies and organizes the underlying manifold. Higher system as operator integrates the underlying manifold so as to call forth by the principle of correspondence and emergence its own replacement by a more specific and effective integrator. One example is the discovery of the constant speed of light, which motivates the movement from Newton's laws to Einsteinian relativity theory. This shift illustrates Kuhn's distinction between normal science, which integrates data and discoveries through the same paradigm, and extraordinary science, which moves to a new paradigm. Another example is Freud's reflection on coincidental data such as slips of the tongue, dreams, and neurotic symptoms, which motivated him to posit the unconscious, super ego, id, and so on. Or again capitalism as alienated integrator and operator points to democratic socialism as a more adequate integrator; or unhappy, inauthentic consciousness to authentic consciousness; or Piaget's distinction between assimilation and adaptation.[42]

Not only can we specify a general heuristic notion of development, but also specific kinds, organic, psychic, and intellectual-moral, each of which exemplifies in its own way the general notion, and the laws and principles of the general notion. Here later stages stand as higher viewpoints to earlier stages, the psychic to the organic, and the intellectual to the psychic. The main difference of genetic method from classical method is that whereas genetic method anticipates sequences in which correlations and regularities change, classical method reduces events to laws. There is not a new law of gravitation for each new century, but organic, psychic, and intellectual development implies a succession of stages; in that succession the previously impossible and improbable becomes actual and real. Now I can speak, write, and walk, but as an infant I could neither speak nor write nor walk.[43]

First, then, I note the development of the cell from underlying sequences of chemical manifolds. Then the cell can either multiply into many cells or grow into a more complex organism. In the latter case we have development from the simple to the complex organism. Study of the organism begins from the thing-for-us, from the organism as available to our senses. A first step is a descriptive differentiation of different parts and, since most of these are inside, this preliminary description involves dissection or anatomy.

A second step consists in the accumulated insights that relate the described parts to organic events, occurrences, and operations. This is a grasp of intelligibilities that are immanent in the several parts, refers each part to what it can do, and, under determinable conditions, will do, and relates the capacity for performance of each part to the capacity for performance of the other parts: physiology follows from anatomy. A third step is to effect the transition from insights that describe parts as organs to insights that grasp conjugate forms systematizing otherwise coincidental manifolds of chemical and physical processes. Here one links physiology with biochemistry and biophysics. Here we grasp the laws of the higher system that accounts for regularities beyond the range of physical and chemical explanation. From these laws is constructed the account of the flexible schemes of recurrence in which the organs function. Finally, the flexible circle of schemes must be coincident with the related set of capacities-for-performance previously grasped in the sensibly presented organs.

The previous steps of anatomy, physiology, and their transformation to the thing itself reveal the aspect of organism as integrator. This higher system as a set of conjugate forms is related to inspected organs as the set of functions grasped by the physiologist in sensible data to the physical, chemical, and cytological manifold as the conjugates implicitly defined by the correlations accounting for additional regularities in the otherwise coincidental manifold, and to immanent and transient activities of the organism in its environment as the ground of the flexible circle of ranges of schemes of recurrence. As growing and developing, a higher system is not only integrator but also operator, and calls forth its own replacement by a more comprehensive integrator.

What illustrates the difference between integrator and operator is the biologist reconstituting the organism by examining the bones. When he reconstitutes the bones as simultaneously interlocking, he understands the system as integrator; when he reconstructs them as successively interlocking, he reconstructs the system as operator. As a dinosaur can be reconstructed from a fossil, so earlier and later stages of the organism can be reconstructed from the fossil.[44]

In the organism both the underlying manifold and higher system are conscious, in the psyche present in animals and human beings the underlying neural and affective manifold is unconscious, but the integration is conscious. In intellectual-moral development both the underlying manifold, the data into which and about which I have insight, and the integration are conscious. The proximate underlying manifold of the psychic manifold are the elements and processes of the nervous system, which involve a core with afferent and efferent branches. The nervous system is at once both a part of the organism and the seat of the manifold of events that have their integrations in conscious per-

ceptions and coordinated responses. Psychic development is higher system on
the move in two different but complementary directions. The lateral movement is an increasing differentiation of psychic events in correspondence with
particular afferent and efferent nerves. The vertical movement is an increasing proficiency in integrated perception and response. The lateral movement
is limited by the multiplicity and diversity of nerve endings. The vertical
movement is limited by the operationally significant set of combinations of
different nerve endings and the existence of higher neural centers in which
such combinations can be integrated.

Study of animal behavior reveals at any given stage of development a
flexible circle of schemes of recurrence. Implicit in such a circle of schemes
are correlations of the classic type, which imply conjugate forms that account
for habitual perceptiveness and modes of aggressive and affective response.
While such study reveals the higher system as integrator at any given stage of
development, comparative study of successive stages of normal and abnormal
successions, of similarities and differences, of successions and different sub-
species, species, and genera, and of the general economy of increasing psychic differentiation reveals the materials to be understood in grasping the
nature of the higher system as operator.[45]

The psyche of the human being, of course, manifests a continually more
complex, differentiated reality. The concept of finality brings under one rubric
Freud's wish fulfillment, the concept of sublimation, and Jung's archetypal
symbols. The unconscious neither means nor wishes in the strict sense of the
term, for these are both conscious activities. Nonetheless, the neural basis is
an upwardly directed dynamism seeking fuller realization on the sensitive
level and on higher artistic, dramatic, philosophical, cultural, and religious
levels. Thus, we see that insight into dream images and associated images and
affects reveals to the psychologist a grasp of the anticipations and virtualities
of higher activities immanent in the underlying unconscious manifold.

The principal illustration of the notion of development, of course, is
human intelligence. A given set of data are understood by insights. As insights
accumulate, further questions arise that direct attention to other data and lead
to the emergence of further insights, and so on. Intelligence as understanding,
formulating, and conceptualizing its understanding of data is the higher system as integrator; intelligence as giving rise to the further question is the
higher system as operator. Insights accumulate into viewpoints, and lower
viewpoints give way to higher viewpoints. In each of the fields of intelligent
inquiry, logic, common sense, empirical science, mathematics, and philosophy, as in organic and psychic development, we note a flexible, linked
sequence of dynamic, higher integrations meeting the tension of increasingly
transformed underlying manifolds through successive applications of the
principles of correspondence and emergence.

As in organic and psychic development, intelligence moves from the undifferentiated and generic to the differentiated and specific. The vague, general questions of the child give way to the specialized, methodologically conscious activities of the logician, the scientist, and the philosopher. We note also an increasing freedom from limitation. Whereas the higher system of the organism or psyche develops in an underlying manifold of physical, chemical, and cytological events subject to their own proper laws, the higher system of intelligence develops not in a material manifold but in a psychic representation of material manifolds. Hence the higher integration of intellectual development is not simply of the person in whom the development occurs, but of the universe. In the human person being as structure and process becomes conscious of itself.

Authenticity

Authenticity or genuineness is an issue I have discussed elsewhere. In PCM authenticity is at one and the same time a condition and fruit of adequate self-appropriation. In CAL authenticity is the fruit of intellectual, moral, and political conversion, and, as such, is essential for adequately doing critical theory. Here I am considering authenticity in relation to metaphysics and to a metaphysical account of being as processive.[46]

In metaphysics, authenticity plays several roles. First, as we have already seen, it is the condition of the possibility of an adequate metaphysics. Furthermore, authenticity is an instance of the finality of proportionate being; it is that finality becoming conscious of itself, not only in my knowing and choosing myself but in my knowing and choosing being. Finally, authenticity is the crown, the flower, the peak of the development of proportionate being, process becoming conscious of itself in relationship to being, comprehensive, reflective, guiding, and directing in a limited sense but in another sense surrendering to and loving the process of proportionate being.

At any given stage of development, the human being is an existing unity differentiated by physical, chemical, organic, psychic, and intellectual conjugates. Each level evolves its own laws, flexible circles of schemes of recurrence, and interlocked set of conjugate forms. The higher of these sets of opposites are integrating higher viewpoints for the lower; the intellectual integrates the psychic, and the psychic the organic. Consequently, I note a law of integration. The initiation of development may be organic, psychic, intellectual, existential, or external, but development remains fragmentary until the principle of correspondence between different levels of development is satisfied. If, for example, the social theory is radical but the life is bourgeois, then there is no correspondence between life and thought. Either the thought will eventually give way to the life and compromise itself, or the life will become radical like the thought. Here is one more reason for claiming that radical political conversion is a condition for doing critical social theory.[47]

Next I note a law of limitation and transcendence; this is a law of tension. On the one hand, the point of departure for development is the human being as is. On the other hand, the direction is toward human beings as they would be and could be. Consequently, a tension arises between facticity and transcendence, "is" and "ought," actuality and possibility. I am called continually to push beyond what I am, but I fear the departure from established routine; the old ways still feel like the best ways. I wish to move beyond the question I have answered to those I have not answered, but I have become accustomed to the security of what I know. I am attracted by the appeal of a more integrated, authentic life, but anxiety arises in the face of the new and of the costs of commitment.

The tension already present in the finality of proportionate being between integrator and operator becomes in the human being a conscious tension. Moreover, I have already noted in the discussion of the counter-positions the tension between the disinterested desire to know and the self as limited, in this time and place, this environment, influenced by this set of dramatic, egoistic, group, and general biases. On the side of the object is the tension between the world of sense known by the human animal and the world of being known by intelligent grasp and reasonable affirmation. On the side of the knowing subject is the tension between the human being as the self-centered center of the world of sense and the other-centered, disinterested operator in the world of being.[48]

Genuineness is simply the admission of that tension into consciousness and, therefore, is a condition of human development. The law of genuineness is conditional and analogous. It is conditional insofar as development occurs only through conscious knowing and choosing. It is analogous insofar as genuineness can take at least two forms. There is the genuineness of the simple soul, like that of Thérèse of Lisieux, in which illusion and pretense have no place. Also possible, however, is genuineness of a more complex and sophisticated kind, like that of a St. Augustine who continually resists the light— "give me chastity and continence, but not yet"—and who is well educated, reflective, and knowledgeable. This kind of genuineness won through a lifetime of self-scrutiny and struggle that expels illusion and pretense seems, and often is, more doubtful and insecure of attainment.[49]

Conclusion

We have taken a decisive step here. Being is shown to be not only structure but also process. Metaphysics has shown itself to be not only an account of structure but an account of process. Thinking structure and process together becomes one of the crucial tasks for a truly comprehensive metaphysics. If some forms of traditional metaphysics overstated the structure and deemphasized process, some postmodern thinkers tend to emphasize process, change, difference in a one-sided way.

One advantage of my account of genetic method is that it can synthesize under one rubric remarkably different phenomena from a wide variety of fields, individual cognitive and moral development, psychoanalysis, evolutionary theory, existential philosophy, history of scientific change, and accounts of historical development. Most of these I have discussed and developed in PCM and CAL. They function, therefore, as instances in which to verify and instantiate my accounts of genetic method. What merely was or seemed to be particular accounts in a particular area, developmental psychology or depth psychology or theory of history, now are generalized and turn out to be instances of finality, the upwardly directed dynamism of proportionate being.[50]

These special fields become particular instances from which we can generalize to a universal cognitional theory and metaphysics. At the same time I note a circle in which the cognitional theory and metaphysics react back on the specific instances, situating them, relating them, setting limits, and normatively criticizing them. What are the limits of an organic or psychic or intellectual model as an account of development? Which viewpoint is higher, more comprehensive, more inclusive? If nature can be said to develop, as I think it does, what are the similarities and differences of this from human development? What are the norms for development and decline?

A confident, yet chastened and fallibilistic, cognitional theory and metaphysics can then approach the questions and supply reasonably precise, determinate answers. They can confidently criticize, for instance, a metaphysics or antimetaphysics that attempts in a reductionistic, scientistic way to explain the world totally in terms of classical laws. Such a critical metaphysics can reject with confidence postmodern rejections of finality and teleology without at the same time giving in to simplistic versions of these. It can steer confidently between the Scylla of asserting that there is no progress in human life and history, and the Charybdis of saying that progress is inevitable or that there is nothing but progress or that theses of progress are incompatible with setbacks, contingencies, and reversals. In a century in which Auschwitz, Dachau, Vietnam, and brutal U.S. intervention in Central America and the Middle East have occurred, genetic method always has to be linked to dialectical method, and metaphysics needs to be sober and clear-eyed, steering between the extremes of asserting too much and too little.

At the same time norms operate in their positive implementation or in their negative avoidance. The transcendental precepts, the validity claims, the desire to know, and the sanction of genuineness all have an impact. Failures in genuineness have their social effects, as I have shown in PCM, CAL, and in the first two chapters of this book, in scientism, positivism, reification, and commodification. If the desire to know does not operate or is insufficiently operative, then different forms of bias, racist, sexist, heterosexist, or classist, take over, and these operate viciously in the current regime of capitalism. If progress generally takes place in the movement from generic and undifferentiated to the specific and differentiated, then failures in differentiation that take the form of falling back to a less differentiated stage or preferring the undifferentiated to the differentiated are a mistake.

Thus, a Heideggerian return to a pre-Socratic nondifferentiation is a mistake, as well as a postmodern de-differentiated account of human cognition, history, and political institutions that misses the legitimate differentiations of modernity and fails to criticize the illegitimate practical, social de-differentiation implied in colonization, reification, and commodification. Capital, in subjecting everything to its sway, obliterates or compromises legitimate modern differentiations that have taken place among the scientific, aesthetic, and moral-political spheres.[51]

At the same time, one-sided rejections of identity are also out of place. The development of personal authenticity is a development in achieving a differentiated oneness with myself, as is psychoanalytic cure on the psychic level—where id was, there ego shall be—and organic development, in which the prehension exercised by each actual occasion unifies the many into a one. The plant integrates the nutrients from the earth, air, and sunlight into one growing unity. The dog synthesizes its perception of data into one pursuit of one downed duck or goose.[52]

This is not all. Metaphysics as political contributes to ideology critique. For as we are invited to worship the immediate commodity fetish, various ideologies of scientism and technocracy function to cover over, express, and legitimize the capital fetish. These ideologies, empiricist in one respect insofar as they bear on and validate their conceptions in immediate sensible data and overlook the experience of the self, are idealistic in another in the sense that they claim that scientific and technological and logical representations mirror reality exhaustively. To see through them as idealistic, therefore, is implicitly and explicitly to criticize them as socially, politically inadequate. The critique of ideology has a metaphysical component, and, as I will show later, a religious component.[53]

Metaphysics as I conceive it, therefore, is both epistemic-cognitive and ethical-political. It involves and implies and builds on both the intellectual conversion argued for in PCM and the moral conversion leading to radical political conversion argued for in CAL. If absolute spirit includes subjective and objective spirit as Hegel says and if the truest account of objective spirit is radical, then metaphysics is and should be radical. If transcendental method is something to be thought as well as chosen authentically, and if capitalism is structurally unjust, then authenticity implies radical political conversion as an aspect of self-transcendence.[54]

Metaphysics has an ethical-political component to it. In this light, I have already argued that an implication of radical political conversion is an orientation to the excluded, marginalized, exploited other: laborer, poor person, African-American, gay, lesbian, homeless. As exploited and left out by the socio-economic system, such a person can have more easily a critical distance on the whole of late capitalism than someone caught up within it and, therefore, a more adequate access to being.[55]

Metaphysics done ideologically and, therefore, more or less falsely is done from the perspective of those within the system and, therefore, favored by it, rewarded by it. Metaphysics done radically and truly will be done by those who are on the margins economically, politically, intellectually, spiritually. That being is "no-thing" is more easily seen by those who are "no-thing," who do not amount to much, who are deprived of commodities, and who, therefore, can more easily see the system as nothing, as illusory, as fetish. Those in the center who live and profit from the ideologies of the thing, of the commodity, are already thinking and living in falsity.

From both epistemic and ethical-political points of view, therefore, metaphysics is done from the point of view of the "exteriority" of the other: nature, the proximate human other, the exploited, oppressed, and marginalized other, being, and God. Poor, exploited human others are privileged epistemically, morally, and ontologically. Epistemically they are privileged because they are more likely to be in the truth, being on the receiving end of injustice; morally because they are on the periphery of a dominating center and we are obligated to a solidarity with them, a philosophically and religiously justified preferential option for the poor; and ontologically because as excluded by philosophies of the center, they call into question their claim to completeness. Only in such a way does a metaphysics having its origin in the West avoid being ethnocentric and Eurocentric.

Understood ethically and politically as well as epistemically and cognitively, therefore, the notion of being can be used to criticize dominant notions of immediacy and representation as ideological, as manifesting and legitimizing in an illusory way the unjust system of exploitation that late capitalism is. The critique of knowing as looking allows us to criticize the society of the spectacle and commodity as immediate looking. The critique of knowing as representation allows us to criticize the various forms of scientism, logicism, and positivism that express and legitimate late capitalism; the reign of the quantified, commodified thing is all there is and all there needs to be. Such ideologies discourage any attempt to transcend such a reign, because such transcendence is unscientific and, therefore, irrational.[56]

An adequate account of self-appropriation allows us to criticize as illegitimate any attempt to reduce the self as subject to the self as they, object, commodity. An adequate account of being, the notion of being, and the life-world allows us to criticize any reduction of being to manipulable, quantified thing. Yet it is this reduction that occurs massively throughout the world as late capitalism exerts its sway in the New World Order. Being is many-splendored, differentiated, complex, two-dimensional or multidimensional; as such it resists reduction to the framework of one-dimensional thought and one-dimensional society.[57]

Because my account of metaphysics is dialectical and phenomenological, I resist the flattening out of being characteristic of capitalism. Reality is and implies dialectical interplay between such opposites as subject and object, "ought" and "is," universal and particular, and quality and quantity. What capitalism, as one-dimensional society giving rise to and in turn reinforced by one-dimensional thought, does is to eliminate the former in these pairs of opposites or reduce the former to the latter. Thus, there is little or no domain of subjectivity, "ought," "universal," or quality to which one could appeal in criticizing this reign of one-dimensionality. The potentially critical, dialectical character of metaphysics gives way to one-dimensional forms of immediacy or representation that reflect, legitimize, and cover up an exploitative, one-dimensional society. Metaphysics as phenomenological and dialectical gives way to metaphysics or antimetaphysics as ideological and obfuscating.

The withdrawal of being, so much commented on by Heidegger, is to a significant extent an ethical-political problem. The question concerning the possibility of metaphysics is not only cognitive and epistemic, but also ethical and political. The question about possibility points to a present and future transformative praxis creating the kind of world and society that would allow being to reveal itself in all of its qualitative, differentiated splendor and mystery.

Drawing on Heidegger again, I could say that as a result being is covered up and covered over in the twentieth century. Being withdraws and conceals itself in the face of two rapacious, technocratic, social systems oriented to profit or domination and exploitation of human beings and nature. In contrast to Heidegger, I do not see the pathology as primarily on the level of absolute spirit or subjective spirit, what being or reason is doing to us, but on the level of objective spirit, what we are doing to being and to human beings. Correspondingly, metaphysics points toward and presumes a more adequate ethical-political solution. Otherwise it remains merely speculative, bourgeois, and one-sidedly contemplative.[58]

Metaphysics, then, points toward ethical revolution and liberation. This, on the other hand, presumes an adequate phenomenology of self, ethics, social theory, and metaphysics. Liberation presumes respectful, reverential, contemplative questioning, questioning that is the piety of thinking, in order to bring into existence social, economic, political structures that take account of that world, respect it, enhance it, and do not do violence to it. Indeed we could say that at a certain point we must move from the stance of the piety of thinking, not giving that up but complementing it, to the impiety of critique and resistance against forms of structural injustice that violate being.

Because more adequate socialistic and communal structures remain mostly in the future, something to be created in the future, our metaphysical contemplation and wisdom can never be simply Hegel's owl of Minerva that peacefully surveys the scene at dusk, but demands, even as contemplative, a creative novelty and emergent future allowing the splendor of being, of nature, of human beings, and of God to manifest itself ever more fully. And this novelty would not stop when socialism is attained in principle, but would go on more fruitfully and less exploitively with regard to nature and human beings. This manifestation, as I have argued in PCM and CAL, demands and requires radical transformative praxis, a praxis that itself proceeds from, serves, and is ordered to contemplative revelation and disclosure. A fully adequate metaphysics, because it values creative novelty, is revolutionary.[59]

⤳⤳⤳

THREE

The Idea of God

In discussing the question of God, I confront two different questions, the practical question and the speculative question. The practical question deals with the compatibility and relevance of God to human freedom and human praxis. The speculative question deals with affirming the existence of God philosophically. In this chapter I will deal with the speculative question first and in so doing develop a conception of God that relates to the issues of compatibility and relevance as well as to existence. In the next chapter, I will move to reflection on the existence of God, and in the chapter after that confront the issues of compatibility and relevance.[1]

The Idea of God: Dialectical Considerations

The existential and Marxist debate concerning God is not primarily speculative but bears on the idea of God. The issue is not so much whether God's existence can be rationally proved, but whether and how God relates to human freedom. Is belief in God as omniscient and all-powerful compatible with human freedom, or is there a basic antagonism between God and human beings? Is God relevant to human freedom, essential to human beings becoming free, or is God an outmoded luxury, an anachronism unnecessary to reflective, self-aware, responsible, twentieth-century human beings?

The atheistic wing of existentialism, thinkers such as Nietzsche and

Sartre, unequivocally affirms the absolute incompatibility between God and human beings and the utter irrelevance of God to human beings. Nietzsche triumphantly announces the death of God and the birth of a new kind of person, one who will no longer receive values from without, but create values. Nietzsche's overman is one who has the courage to affirm himself, his own sensuality, intelligence, and freedom, and to leave the false consolations of persons infected with slave morality, taught for centuries by Christianity to despise their senses, distrust their intelligence, and flee responsibility.

The essence of religious alienation for Nietzsche is the reception of values from without and resulting hatred of oneself. Over the grave of God new persons can now march, who do not need God because they are sufficient unto themselves, and who do not need another world because they have learned to love the earth. "Once the sin against God was the greatest sin; but God died, and those sinners died with Him. To sin against the earth is now the most dreadful thing."[2]

Jean Paul Sartre continues to explore the consequences of Nietzsche's atheistic stance. Freedom for Sartre is absolute and total:

> Either man is wholly determined (which is inadmissible, especially because a determined consciousness—i.e. a consciousness externally motivated—becomes itself pure exteriority and ceases to be consciousness) or else man is wholly free.[3]

Freedom, therefore, is totally independent and unreceptive. For to be determined from without is to be unconscious, like a thing. Since I am conscious and since denial of such a basic phenomenon is absurd, I am totally free.

This indeterminate, unreceptive character of freedom renders genuine mutuality between persons impossible. Since receptivity is incompatible with freedom, receptivity to another person is the degradation of freedom. When a person on the stairs looks at me as I am looking through a keyhole, I feel my freedom drain out of me—I become an object before the hostile gaze of the other person. The only way I can regain the initiative is to stare back and thus assert myself over the other. The essence of intersubjectivity for Sartre is conflict—either domination or submission, sadism or masochism, triumphant independence or abject dependence.[4]

The seeds are thus planted for Sartre's atheism. If dependence on the other is incompatible with freedom, then dependence on God is the denial of freedom. If freedom degrades itself by trusting openness to the finite look of the other, then openness to the infinite look of God would be infinitely destructive of freedom. If existence precedes essence in the sense that human beings freely create their own identity, then human beings cannot have received their essence from God. A human being is not like a paper cutter, the idea of which existed in the mind of its creator. To think of persons in this way is to degrade them to the status of a thing and overlook the distinctiveness of freedom, which is to create values and to be a lived tension between facticity and possibility, past and future.[5]

The thing is simply what it is and cannot be otherwise. Persons are what they are not and are not what they are. They are what they are not in the sense that they live certain possibilities that have not been realized. They may be conventional doctors now, but they are always aware of the possibility of rejecting this choice and becoming something else, social workers, teachers, bums. Human beings also are not what they are in the sense that they are not totally identified with what they are. There is always the dim awareness of possibility, making it impossible for them to be totally secure in what they are. Because of such awareness, present and past choices can be overturned in the future.[6]

God is incompatible with this paradox of human freedom. To exist harmoniously with God persons would have to be unparadoxical things, passive, totally identified with what they are, and totally dependent for their identity on an essence received from without.

Such is the very powerful atheistic challenge to theism from the viewpoint of practical reason. Nonetheless, what I will develop in the rest of the book should enable us to see the questionableness of such a stance on the issue of God. For such a stance rests upon two presuppositions: the notion of closed, totally autonomous freedom and the notion of an essentially conflictual intersubjectivity. If, however, these two presuppositions are false, then such atheism falls to the ground.

As I have already shown elsewhere, the presuppositions are false. In the chapter on freedom in PCM, I showed that a notion of strict indeterminacy and independence of the other is not only self-contradictory, but contrary to experience. For in arguing for indeterminism over determinism, Sartre implicitly asserts a bond between freedom and reason. In arguing that freedom is essentially negative, desirous of being God, temporal, and conscious, Sartre posits a structure in freedom. Also in asserting the preferability of good faith over bad faith, Sartre implicitly owns up to the motivated, receptive character of freedom. Freedom, in being aware of qualities in things or in being affected by the gaze of the other, shows itself to be limited and open to the world, not unlimited and shut up in itself.

If freedom is essentially motivated, receptive, and limited, then it is also social and open to the other. Sartre, when he tries to convince us of the truth of his claims through appeal to four validity claims, implicitly is presupposing the possibility of such openness. For Sartre is not trying to manipulate us or dominate us, but to convince us of the truth rationally. Such an effort presupposes the possibility of one freedom affecting another freedom beneficially. Appeal is not coercion, nor is dialogue manipulation.

Also in the discussion of ethics and justice we discovered that human beings are essentially ends in themselves in a community of ends, needing one another, desiring one another, loving one another. A receptive freedom is essentially receptive in many ways: in physical nurturance, education, culture, economics, and politics. There is no necessary incompatibility, therefore, between or among freedoms.

Since the Sartrean model of freedom and intersubjectivity is flawed, his case for atheism also is flawed. However, there is a sense in which his argument challenges us to reconceive the notion of God. The God who is incompatible with human freedom is a traditional, classical notion of God: unchangeable, perfect, unrelated to the world, able to foresee all future acts, capable of dominating human free acts. Such a God, I would argue, is indeed incompatible with human freedom and should be rejected.

First of all, there is an odd incompatibility between such a God and a world conceived as processive, developing, creative. In such a world such a God becomes a curious anomaly, an exception to the general rule.

Moreover, such a God is not only an exception, but nonsensical. For what kind of sense does it make to say that God knows and loves the world but is unrelated to it? What kind of sense does it make to say that God does not know or respond to, or allow God to be internally moved by changes in the conditions of creatures, from good to bad or bad to good? Either God is really related to the world and, therefore, is able to be changed by it and respond to it, or God is not. But if the latter is the case, God is not God in any recognizable or acceptable sense, one who can love and know and be sympathetic to the plight of creatures.

Not only is the classical notion of God oddly exceptional and nonsensical, but it is also irrelevant to human striving in the world. Human praxis attempts to create a world through its efforts; yet such striving does not affect God in divine, eternal, unchangeable blessedness. Belief in such a God has often led believers to belittle human praxis as unimportant, as a mere prelude to gaining heaven. Such an attitude toward the world is incompatible with serious science, philosophy, or social action, which presuppose in their striving that their efforts are important and do make a difference.

Moreover, such a classical notion of God cannot handle successfully the problem of divine foreknowledge and human freedom. For, according to the traditional conception, there is nothing God does not know, not even the future. Yet if God knows the future, human actions must be predetermined and freedom must be illusory. On the other hand, if freedom is real, then God cannot know the future—God cannot be God. Through a different route we have returned to Sartre's dilemma.[7]

Finally, such a traditional notion of God cannot handle the problem of evil, a problem that is really a mystery in Marcel's sense, that has perplexed traditional theism. For, as Hume puts the question, God is supposed to be both omnipotent and good. If God is omnipotent and events such as Auschwitz and Dachau and Vietnam occur, how can God be good? If God is good and such events occur, how can God be omnipotent? The mystery of evil cannot be illumined adequately in classical theistic terms.[8]

Is there any way out of these dilemmas and perplexities? There is one conception of God that can lead us out, and that is the processive conception as enunciated and argued for by thinkers such as Whitehead, Hartshorne, and, in his own way, Hegel. Such a conception, for example, posits that God changes and, therefore, is not an anomaly in a processive world. Not only does such a God change, but God is really related to the world in knowledge and love. God is, as Whitehead says, "the fellow sufferer who understands."[9] The processive notion, more than any other, is able to make sense out of the religious intuitions of many religions that God is love.[10]

I do not mean to imply here that God is totally changeable and that none of the traditional attributes remain. Rather, I am performing an *Aufhebung* here of traditional theism, not only negating, but preserving valid aspects in a new synthesis. God is changeable in one of the divine aspects, but unchangeable in another, the primordial nature. As existing in Godself, God is unchangeable; as related to the world, God is changeable. God preserves moral integrity and holiness through all changes, just as good persons will preserve their basic integrity through various experiences and their basic cognitional structure through all experiences.

Traditionally there has been a preference in theodicy and indeed in metaphysics for one attribute in different sets of attributes, permanence as opposed to change, independence as opposed to dependence, absoluteness as opposed to relativity, necessity as opposed to contingency. In reality and in God the latter pole of such pairs has often been regarded as secondary or illusory.

However, what has been discovered over and over again in this book is the necessary mediation between such opposites, what has been formulated by Hartshorne as "the logic of ultimate contrasts."[11] Briefly stating it, we can say that each opposite depends for its meaning on the other: no necessity without contingency, independence without dependence, and so on. Such a relation applies not only to the relation between God and the world but to God in Godself.

To take one set of these opposites, the absolute-relative, we can say that what has been emphasized in discussions of God is the absolute pole. What process philosophy recommends is that this pole is just an aspect, not the whole story. Taking the absolute as the totality, we end up with a curiously one-sided, masculine notion of God that is logically inadequate, evidentially insufficient, and existentially irrelevant.

However, according to the process conception, God is not only absolute but supremely relative, present to all beings in the intimacy of their experience, and, therefore, capable of being affected by them. Such divine relativity is eminently divine in that all other beings are only relative to some, not all, other beings. Such divine relativity, I would suggest, accords better with what has been developed in this book and what we experience as desirable. What I have argued for in this book is a moral ideal of sympathy and dialogal openness; one is more perfect insofar as one is more open and more receptive. To affirm such a conception and to affirm a God who is perfect because he is absolute is to be in flat contradiction with oneself. It corresponds more with both philosophy and experience to say that one is more perfect insofar as one is less closed up in oneself, less self-seeking, less hardened. Disposability, to use a concept of Marcel's, should be present both in human beings and God.[12]

A similar point could be made about another set of contraries, independence and dependence. We have seen that Sartrean independence as that is maintained phenomenologically is erroneous and that there is a kind of dependence on the world and other human beings that is not only inevitable but fruitful. We have seen that bourgeois independence is not only self-contradictory but unjust and undesirable, and points toward ethical, socialist community as a higher viewpoint. This is not to say that there is no place for independence; one's perfection as a human being is achieved when one can maintain moral integrity and identity in a multiplicity of situations. Nonetheless, such maintenance of identity should be complemented by openness to the other, not closedness. What is true of human beings is also true of God. Because God is God, God is more dependent, not less, more open, not less, more receptive, not less.[13]

A similar point can be made about necessity and contingency. As supremely moral and existing, God is necessary; as aesthetic and actual, God is contingent. What it is God knows and how much aesthetic enjoyment God receives from the world depends upon what we do and what we make of the world. A thousand year reich gives God less enjoyment than the reign of a just, equitable society, Auschwitz and Dachau less enjoyment than Selma and Birmingham in the civil rights struggle, Hitler and Stalin less enjoyment than Martin Luther King and Dorothy Day. For these reasons human praxis building a world is not irrelevant to God nor God to it as in the classical conception. God and world form one whole in which each influences the other.[14]

Such capacity to receive implies that God is not omniscient in the traditional sense. God is omniscient in the only meaningful sense—that is, God knows all that exists but not what will exist. What will happen tomorrow is news to God as it is to us. For this reason the problem of divine foreknowledge and human freedom dissolves. If we are active at all, and our whole analysis of praxis and freedom indicates that we are very active, then God to that extent is extremely passive in relation to us. The notion of an active receptivity and disposability applies more to God than to us. God creates us, but in a very real sense we create God as well.[15]

For similar, related reasons the mystery of evil is illumined. For God, although good, is not omnipotent in that God could or would prevent the exercise of human freedom. Auschwitz, Dachau, and Vietnam are tragedies that, for God, are unavoidable.[16]

Now one could object to such a conception of God, and I would remind the reader that it is still a conception that we are dealing with here, not a verified, affirmed truth, that I have resolved the above dilemmas only by weakening the concept of God to such an extent that God is no longer recognizable as God, no longer omniscient, omnipotent, eternal, unchangeable, and so on. I would respond, first of all, by saying that these properties are retained as abstract aspects, but not the total, concrete reality. God as a concrete reality is both unchangeable and changeable, eternal and temporal, necessary and contingent, independent and dependent, powerful and limited in power, knowledgeable about the present and ignorant of the future.

Second, such a conception of God implies a strict difference between God and everything else. For example, as I have already shown, God is supremely relative whereas everything else is only partially so. God knows and loves everything that is, whereas all other knowers know only imperfectly. Finally, God is unique in that God is not surpassable by others, but only by Godself.[17]

The process conception of God, therefore, is logical and relevant to the ongoing human attempt to build a world. It also does far more justice, as I will show more fully later, to the Old and New Testaments. There are many symbols and expressions in scripture about a loving, sympathetic, crucified God that would have to remain mere metaphors if the classical conception were accepted. If, as I have already argued, metaphor is referential, then these scriptural expressions have to be taken far more seriously than classical theodicy has done.

Finally, one could object that such a conception of God weakens the notion of God's providence. However, I would argue that we are forced merely to redefine what such providence means. God's influence on the world is dialogal and persuasive, not dictatorial and totalitarian. In this way God guides the world toward its end and sets limits within which human beings encounter one another. What God cannot and will not do, however, is take away human freedom or prevent human beings from experiencing the consequences of their acts. To do more would be to treat us as children, and such treatment would be incompatible with the life of responsible freedom to which God is calling us. Process philosophy, more than any other, affirms a creative, emergent, free novelty as the joint work of God and humankind. The dialogal, intersubjective model employed throughout this work has its fullest, most comprehensive meaning and expression here. On the level of philosophical theology as on the levels of eidetic, hermeneutical, phenomenology, and critical social theory, dialectical phenomenology is a philosophy of freedom and liberation.[18]

What has emerged, therefore, in our discussion is a conception of God as dialogal, responsive, sympathetic, changeable, infinitely knowing and loving. What grounds the emergence of such a conception is the awareness of ourselves as knowing and loving selves in community. Extrapolating from such an awareness we can form a conception of God as an unrestricted act of understanding and love.

With such conceptions of God and human freedom, we can see where the reality can be supremely relevant to human freedom and praxis. For only with such a conception and belief can we be confident that our actions will have any lasting effect and make any ultimate sense. If the point of praxis is to make a difference, then it is better to make a permanent difference than merely a transitory difference. Freedom as projecting the idea of an infinite good always desires what is more perfect and, therefore, intends permanence and immortality. Not only does freedom in individual or collective praxis contribute to the infinite, eternal life of God, but also to itself as a vocation to live with God. Freedom in creating a world creates itself.

Such a life of praxis with God cannot help but inspire greater confidence and hope. Rather than working in the darkness of finite interiority with no confidence in the ultimate meaningfulness of the world or my work, I work alongside others with God to create a world. Rather than living in Godself in infinite bliss in divine indifference to what I am doing, God is infinitely interested and concerned with what I am doing. The search for truth and justice, rather than being just a human project I take upon myself, becomes a carrying out of God's will.

The Positive Content of the Idea of God

Dialectically we have concluded that an adequate notion of God must include both traditional attributes such as necessity and eternity, and nontraditional attributes such as contingency and changeableness. Such an idea seems to dissolve the main objections presented by thinkers such as Nietzsche and Sartre against the strictly classical conception of a God who imposes blueprints on us, and, therefore, effectively negates freedom, a dominating, as opposed to a liberating, God. Thus far, then, the processive idea of God seems to be superior to both the atheistic and classical conceptions.

What we have to do now is to articulate positively and descriptively the content of the notion of God and ground it critically. In this sense I am following our general sense of scientific, cognitional, and metaphysical method that insists on a distinction between questions for understanding and questions for reflection, between asking what something is and asking whether it is.

Transcendence

The question with which I am concerned in the next two chapters is whether transcendent being exists and can be known. Consequently, we need to determine what transcendence is. First of all, it is not that which lies beyond immediate looking and, therefore, is problematic. For we have already rejected the account of looking as an account of knowing and, therefore, the notion of transcendence that it implies. Another sense of transcendence is "going beyond." We move beyond data of sense through questions for intelligence, beyond mere bright ideas to grasp the virtually unconditioned in judgment, and beyond mere knowing to what is chosen and loved.

A tension arises in me between the questions I have answered and those I have not, between the limited attainment and the unlimited desire. Its existence seems undeniable, for even the questioning of its existence reveals its presence insofar as the question manifests the desire to know and its objective as unrestricted. For its objective is being, and being is the real, and outside of being there is nothing. If I wished to posit an X outside being, that X itself turns out to be a being, and, therefore, inside being. If I wish to question whether my desire to know is limited, the very questioning reveals a transcendence of that limit. To question a limit is already to anticipate a possible "beyond," and this "beyond" is itself anticipated and projected by the desire to know.[19] Only the content of an unrestricted act of understanding can be the idea of being, for it is only on this supposition of an unrestricted act of understanding that understands everything about everything that we can have an idea of being.

Such an idea of being is absolutely transcendent, because it is the content of an unrestricted act of understanding present neither in our external nor in our internal experience. Such an idea is projected legitimately on the basis of our experience of knowing and the desire to know, but it takes us beyond all human achievement and assigns the ultimate limit to the process of going beyond.[20]

The Idea of Being

An idea is the content of an act of understanding. Such content is familiar to us insofar as we have appropriated our own knowing. Thus, the definitions of a triangle or a free fall or the theory of relativity are contents of an act of understanding. Such an act, however, is restricted insofar as it can be mistaken, further relevant questions can arise, and further, more correct definitions can emerge.

Because being is the objective of the unrestricted desire to know, the idea of being is the content of an unrestricted act of understanding. Because apart from being there is nothing, the idea of being is the content of an act of understanding that leaves nothing to be understood. Because being is completely universal and concrete, the idea of being is the content of understanding that understands everything about everything. I am not denying here, however, that even in God further understanding can and does occur. Because God is processive, understanding can develop insofar as natural events and human decisions occur that sadden God or make God unhappy. God has no further questions about all that is as that has occurred up to the present, but God does have questions about the future.[21]

The Idea of God

The one unrestricted act and idea is the primary intelligible in contrast to the world as the secondary intelligible. For if there is an unrestricted act of understanding, then there is a primary intelligible; this is what we mean by "God."

Because the act is unrestricted, it is infallible, in contrast to our own knowing. In contrast to classical theism, such infallibility is compatible with God being open and receptive to the world as it changes and develops and, consequently, comes to understand more or differently as that world changes, declines, or develops. What God understands, God understands infallibly, but what God understands changes.

Because what is known by correct and true understanding is being, so the primary intelligible is the primary being, and the primary being is spiritual in the full sense of the identity of the intelligent and the intelligible. Furthermore, God is perfect in a neoclassical sense, unsurpassable by others but surpassable by Godself insofar as God's understanding changes and develops and increases in aesthetic satisfaction through receptivity to the world.

Because the good is identical with the intelligible, the primary intelligible is the primary good. As the perfection of the spiritual requires that the intelligible be intelligent, so this perfection requires that affirmable truth be affirmed and lovable good be loved. Because the primary intelligible also is the primary truth and primary good, in a completely perfect spiritual being the primary intelligible is identical not only with an unrestricted act of understanding but a completely perfect act of affirming the primary truth and a completely perfect act of loving the primary good. God is an unrestricted act of understanding, affirmation, and love.

The primary intelligible is self-explanatory. For if it were not, it would be incomplete in intelligibility, and such incompleteness is incompatible with an unrestricted act of understanding. Not only is God self-explanatory, but God is explanatory of the world as efficient cause, as creator. For if God's causality presupposed some matter and was limited to fashioning and ordering it, then the matter would be unexplained and what is unexplained does not pertain to being, because being is the intelligible, nothing more and nothing less, and consequently the alleged matter would be nothing. Such creation of being also implies conservation. If a fire warms a steak, the steak only remains warm as long as the fire sustains it as hot. Similarly, if the creator is the only adequate cause of existence, then the creator is the only adequate cause of conservation in existence. Just as an adequate cause of a painting on the wall of a cave can only be a being whose nature it is to be intelligent and thus to produce a painting with intelligible pattern, so also the adequate cause of existence can only be a being whose nature it is to exist, and that being is God. If God's being were not identical with God's existence, then God would be contingent, and so would not be God.[22]

Because the world is created and known and loved as good, then God must be free. If God were not free, then the world would be necessary, not contingent.

Furthermore, if God chose to create the world, then that choice was contingent, not necessary. Consequently, God is not merely necessary because God is self-explanatory, but contingent in God's consequent nature. God is a union of necessity and contingency, not merely necessary nor merely contingent. And this contingency is present not merely in the decision to create the world, but in the continuous relating to the world knowingly and lovingly as that changes and develops.

If God is a necessary efficient and conserving cause of the world and the beings in it, God is also its final cause. For God is the source of the emergent probability of the world as the upwardly directed dynamism of proportionate being, and knows, wills, and chooses the pattern and its effective realization. To the extent that realization occurs, God knows it, loves it, and is made happy by it and retains the knowledge and love of that realization forever. We could say that the ultimate purpose of world process is the happiness of God and the happiness of the world as God comes to know and love the world in its greater realization and liberation, and as the world comes to know and love God.

Moreover, God is the all-knowing, exemplary cause. For God is the idea of being in both its primary and secondary components and, therefore, grasps the world as an intelligible order of emergent probability. Because this pattern is generic and structural, there is room within it for the relatively independent action of secondary causes, to which God then reacts and incorporates into God's idea of the universe as it is and as it should be according to God's will.

But this will acts on the world not coercively, but dialogally in attempting to guide it to full liberation and justice and happiness.[23]

We may say also that God is omnipotent in a neoclassical, not a classical sense. In a neoclassical sense this claim means that a supreme social agent can do much for the universe, but God cannot and does not and will not do everything. God cannot and does not and will not do for subhuman agents what they can and will do only for themselves. God rules the universe not as a tyrant but as a supremely sympathetic, feeling, loving father and mother setting up conditions for its optimal unfolding, influencing it, soliciting it, motivating it, but not dominating it. Because creatures and human beings can respond in different ways that are not predetermined, we could say that providential power and chance, power and freedom are inseparable from one another and imply one another.[24]

Consequently, the mystery of evil is significantly illumined under the neoclassical view, for this mystery is theorized on the assumption of power in the illegitimate sense that excludes or minimizes freedom and chance. If, however, chance is built into the world and it runs according to emergent probability blending classical and statistical laws, then floods, earthquakes, and other chance events contradict neither the goodness nor the power of God. They do not contradict God's goodness because God wills our well-being in a world shot through with indeterminacy, chance, and contingency, which God cannot and will not abolish. Such events do not contradict the power of God because this power does what it can do as universally, providentially concerned with the least hair on the head of every creature, but this power cannot and will not do everything, prevent everything, or control everything. The power of God is the power of understanding, sympathy, and love ruling and soliciting and appealing to the world through these, not the edicts of a tyrant.

Similarly, human, moral evil is not willed by God, God is not malicious. Moral evil proceeds from individual and collective human choice that violates the imperatives of the desire to know, transcendental precepts, validity claims, and criteria of right, morality, and justice. God wishes these to be observed and achieved as real and good, but God will not force us to observe them. To do so would be to deny the kind of freedom God has placed in human beings, and the kind of indeterminacy and creative novelty God has put in the world as a whole; and such denial would imply that God is self-contradictory.[25]

Because God is an unrestricted act of understanding and love, God is omniscient in a neoclassical, not a classical, sense. Consequently, the problems of divine foreknowledge and human freedom dissolve. God infallibly understands everything that is, but the future is not yet and, therefore, is not known by God. Present, real acts in nature and human beings are not determined by God, because of what we have already said about power. Future free acts also are not determined and are not known. Ignorance about the future is one indicator of the finitude of God; God is not simply finite and not simply infinite but a unity of finite and infinite.[26]

Consequently, we could say also that God is supremely independent and dependent. God blends these apparently opposite attributes within Godself. God is independent and necessary and uncaused in God's primordial and relational being, because no influence from the world is able to force God to cease being good, wise, and loving. God is supremely dependent insofar as God is supremely open to receiving everything from the world and from creatures, knowing and loving and sympathizing with every creature for its own sake down to the last detail or hair of its being.

Because God is God, God is absolute in one sense, relative in another. God is absolute in the sense of being wise and good and omniscient and perfect, but relative in the sense of being related to all that is, and here even in a way that surpasses human creatures. For we are characterized by an ability to relate to only a few things, and even these imperfectly. But God relates to everything totally and with perfect sympathy and love. We can affirm, then, dual transcendence in God, God is both supremely absolute and supremely relative, and both of these attributes distinguish God from finite creatures.[27]

Such a combination of opposites should not seem altogether odd to us. For as transcendentally structured unities of experience, understanding, judgment, and decision, we are in the world as unchangeable. Yet as interacting with the world, we respond to it differently in different contexts.

Again we may consider the relative permanence and unchangeableness of a person of character buffeted by fortune and misfortune, prosperity and adversity, happiness and unhappiness. Just as such a character is compatible, however, with being supremely open and responsive to different circumstances and situations, so also the unchangeableness and permanence of God is compatible with supreme relativity and changeableness. Indeed, just as a person of some moral character who is too inflexible and rigid in different circumstances is less preferable than somebody with moral character who is flexible and responsive, so also a God who is supremely absolute and unchangeable is less perfect than one who combines absoluteness and relativity, permanence and change, independence and dependence, activity and receptivity.[28]

All of the foregoing implies that God is supremely social. Here again God functions as the completion, ground, and flowering of a metaphysics that is social from the bottom up. The human being is in the life-world, related to it, involved in tradition and history, essentially social and oriented to others through communication grounded in validity claims, governed by the ethical norms of right, morality, and justice, and oriented to love for the world, others, and God as the flowering of human freedom. God as social, as involved with the world, as related to it through sympathetic, loving prehension, as working with it praxically to liberate it from unhappiness and injustice, therefore, is more adequate than God as merely in Godself independent, unchangeable, and absolute. God does have these attributes, of course, but they are linked to sociality and relativity, just as human beings are transcendentally structured in themselves is related to the world socially.

Classical theism, then, because it wishes to say that God knows and loves the world and yet is really unrelated to it, is in contradiction with itself. To know and love the world implies being receptive to it, and such receptivity implies contingency, change, and real relatedness. A neoclassical conception of God overcomes this contradiction and moves to a broader, richer, more profound conception of God.

Does such a conception deny or minimize mystery in God? Here I wish to distinguish among three positions: one that says we can know nothing of God, one that says that we can know everything, and one that says that we can know something but not everything—my position. I would argue that affirming dual transcendence in God enhances God's mystery. Not only do we affirm traditional attributes such as omniscience, necessity, infinity, albeit redefined in a neoclassical direction, but we affirm other attributes such as relativity or "surrelativity." God is supremely present, loving, and sympathetic to each of God's creatures, wishing its well-being, happy when it succeeds, unhappy when it fails, suffering when it suffers. In a way that anticipates our discussion of particular religious revelation, we could say that the meaning of life is divine love: loving God for God's own sake with my whole heart and whole soul and being loved by God, and my love translating into loving others as myself, as God loves them. My metaphysics affirms a supremely personalistic universe. Love of God is the flowering of the fourth level of freedom. This love takes the form, we only see more fully later, of disposability and creative fidelity.[29]

Let us try to be more precise, then, about this sense of mystery in God. First, God as an unrestricted act of understanding and love is genuinely transcendent, present neither in my inner nor outer experience. Furthermore, if God is an unrestricted act of understanding and love, mine is not. While having some knowledge of God, I have still more questions about the content of God's divine life and God's relationship to the world. If it is true that I do not have exhaustive knowledge even of one individual thing or person, it is also true to say that I do not have exhaustive knowledge of God's knowledge and love of that creature. That lack of knowledge rooted in my own questioning grounds the experience of mystery giving rise to awe, reverence, and worship on an emotional, existential level, reverent awe before benevolent mystery. Rightly done, metaphysics, in its beginning and end, increases our sense of mystery. There is an initial wonder giving rise to questioning, and a subsequent wonder that succeeds questioning.

Finally, a processive conception of God allows us to distinguish between the abstract attributes attributed to the primordial nature and those attributed to the consequent such as sensitivity and love. We can know that these attributes are present in God, but how they relate to the day-in and day-out life of the consequent nature, confronting, knowing, and benevolently loving the world in all of its detail and complexity, remains mysterious to us. God as processive actuality adds a dimension of mystery not present in the classical conception. A neoclassical conception of God, therefore, accounts better than classical theism for the difference between what can be known about God abstractly and what remains to be known through concrete religious tradition, revelation, and experience.

We can know, therefore, that God as the primary intelligible knows God and loves God with an infinite knowledge and love, but how God does so remains shrouded in mystery. When the mystery reveals more of itself in historical revelation, then we can know more, for example, of the trinitarian nature of God.

God as transcending our full knowledge, therefore, even though we know something about God, reveals God as worthy of awe, wonder, and worship. In this sense God as wonder-full, worthy of admiration as benevolent, gracious mystery, completes and crowns our experience of the life-world and being as wonder-full and mysterious. "The world is charged with the grandeur of God; It will flame out like shining from shook foil."[30] Being as the object of the desire to know is being as the object of questioning wonder that does not know everything, even about finite being. God as the unrestricted act of knowledge and love crowns this reverent, respectful, questioning wonder, and allows us to move from knowledge to commitment and love, appreciative abandonment to benevolent, loving mystery.

Such a claim should not fully surprise us. For in the intimate knowledge of friendship and romantic love, we experience the simultaneous knowledge and the sense of mystery about the person. Such simultaneity is not present all of the time, of course, because some relationships become or remain superficial, oriented more to vital pleasure or functional satisfaction. In such relationships "I-Thou" gives way to "I-it." But in relationships where the partners maintain a genuine, reverential presence to one another, knowledge deepens the mystery and vice versa. If we can make this claim about human relationships, then so also with our knowledge and love of God.[31]

A related objection is that all of this emphasis on God as relative, changeable, and loving seems to make God too warm, fuzzy, "touchy-feely." What happens to the sense of God as inscrutable *mysterium tremendum* inspiring fear in God's believers and rendering angry judgment toward the world when it departs from God's will. I think the neoclassical conception retains that sense as *part*, not the whole story about God, in its emphasis on the primordial nature. But the neoclassical account links God as *mysterium tremendum* to God as benevolent, gracious presence in a way that is more adequate and comprehensive than either the classical or the excessively humanistic version.

Furthermore, because God is both intelligent and good, God is also just and demands justice from us. God is a God of justice and, therefore, condemns unjust regimes that are racist, sexist, heterosexist, and classist. Here I am beginning to link a processive conception of God with liberation philosophy and theology. God is loving but is also just and thunders in the skies about injustice inflicted every year upon millions of human beings through unemployment, homelessness, starvation, hunger, terror, repression, and war.

My move to a processive God is conceptually necessary and rigorous, motivated by a sense of the contradictions and inadequacies in the classical account. To the extent that the classical account is one-sided in its stress on God as in Godself, powerful, inscrutable, omnipotent, and omniscient, then my account may still not seem to stress these elements enough. But then the argument between the classicist and me returns us to the question of the relative adequacy of our accounts. Here I think, fallibilistically, that neoclassicism has all the better of the argument.

A final consequence of my approach is that we have a metaphysical basis for grounding feminist insights into God. For if attributes like omnipotence, necessity, and omniscience manifest a "masculine" side of God, attributes like dependence, relativity, and receptivity manifest a "feminine" side of God. God, of course, in Godself is neither male nor female, because God is spirit, but does contain in Godself and blend in Godself "masculine" and "feminine" attributes. I am using "masculine" and "feminine" here not in any essentialist sense but only to refer to the meanings of these terms as they have evolved in contemporary Western culture. Traditional philosophy and theology have overstated and overemphasized the masculine side and ignored or minimized the feminine side of God, thus leaving us with a one-sided account of God even as spirit.[32]

One concrete result in the churches, as I will develop more fully in Part Two of this work, has been uncritical power worship. God as Caesar becomes the object of religious worship, and this version of God translates into a religious authority that is often paternalistic, oppressive, and distrustful of human freedom. The result has been different forms of injustice in the church, one of which has been sexism, and its alliance in ideology and in reality with secular, unjust regimes, which are racist, sexist, heterosexist, and classist. Religion, rather than functioning to liberate us from injustice, supports it and legitimates it. Women, already regarded as second-class citizens within secular society, are also second-class citizens within the church because of an overly "masculinist" conception of God that grounds and legitimates injustice. Once again we see the ethical, political implications of metaphysics.[33]

Conclusion

The reader should be beginning to sense the ultimate metaphysical conclusion to my argument with and against postmodernism as that has developed throughout this book and the two volumes that precede it in the trilogy. Simply put, I do justice to discovery of difference by affirming difference of God in a way that makes it equiprimordial with identity. God as primordial nature is identity; God as consequent nature is different, receptive, changeable, contingent. Summing up, then, I have inscribed difference in our metaphysics in the following ways: in the knower as a unity of experiencing, understanding, judgment, and decision; in proportionate being as a unity of potency, form, and act; in the life-world as ultimate horizon and context within which different things and persons emerge and different levels of interaction obtain, perceptual, scientific, aesthetic, ethical-political, and religious; within language as differential structure; and finally, within God as a unity of primordial and consequent nature. Because difference is inscribed within metaphysics, there is no need to overcome metaphysics in order to affirm difference.

Because difference is inscribed within metaphysics, we find no need to overcome metaphysics in order to affirm difference, only to overcome a less adequate form of metaphysics in favor of a more adequate version. Moreover, God is preserved as different, as transcendent, as other, as mysterious in my account, but not as absolutely other, completely unrelated to my desire to know and love. This conception of God makes no more sense than the notion of a thing or a human being as noumenally, absolutely other, for if I know the other exists, then there is evidence for such otherness that can be articulated. Otherwise what is arbitrarily asserted can be rationally questioned and denied. Because such difference and otherness can be recovered, theorized, and affirmed as different and other within metaphysics, we do not need to go outside of metaphysics, as post-modernists claim, to recover difference and otherness.

We have thus developed a conception of God as an act of unrestricted understanding and love, processive, surrelative, dependent and independent, changing and permanent, contingent and necessary. But does God exist? Is God merely a bright idea? To answer this question is the purpose of my next chapter.

FOUR

The Reality of God

At this point we have come to a new stage of inquiry. For if we know that the metaphysics of proportionate being is actual, that being is composed of the metaphysical elements of potency, form, act, and dynamically oriented to ever-higher viewpoints, and that the notion of God can be conceived without nonsense and self-contradiction, we still have not answered the question, "Does God exist?" That is the task of this chapter.

Dialectical Considerations

Within many circles of philosophy, especially continental philosophy, the very idea of a rationally grounded affirmation of God, of an argument for the existence of God, is scandalous. For it seems to be presumptuous for mere human reason to arrive at the reality of God, to deduce or infer somehow this reality and to claim to know that reality. Whether one is influenced by existentialists such as Kierkegaard, positivists such as Carnap, or critical philosophers such as Kant, the very idea seems preposterous.

The very air we breathe today seems to be and is hostile to metaphysics. That is the reason that we have conducted our inquiry in a series of carefully thought out steps. Thus, in chapter 1 I demonstrated the possibility of metaphysics and showed that the denial is based on inadequate self-knowledge leading to and grounded in dogmatism and obscurantism. In chapter 2 I showed that in our practice of inquiry is the notion of being, and that we cannot deny this notion without self-contradiction; how the structure of proportionate being is linked to experience, understanding, and judgment by isomorphism, and that being is dynamic and processive system on the move. Finally, I showed in chapter 3 how the notion of God can be extrapolated from the notion of being.

The human being, then, is naturally and spontaneously metaphysical and religious. If I can ask questions in a way that is structured by experience, understanding, and judgment, then that praxis of asking questions implies the notion of being. If I have the notion of being, then I can know proportionate being as a unity of potency, form, and act. If I can know proportionate being as a unity of potency, form , and act, then I can know through genetic method being as dynamic and processive. If I can know being as structured and processive, then I can conceive the notion of God as the possible ground of such being.

By *modus ponens*, then, I can say, "If A, then B, . . ." all the way up to the idea of God. If I deny that I have the idea of God, then, by *modus tollens*, I go all the way down. If A, then B; not B, therefore not A. I end up having to deny that I am a knower. I cannot deny that I am metaphysical and religious without denying that I question and that I am a knower.

Metaphysics as I have described it thus far rests, then, on self-appropriation as that has occurred not only in the first five chapters of this book, but also in PCM and CAL. Reflecting on the question of God comes at the end, or close to the end, of a long process of inquiry. Only at the end of such a process does it make sense to ask and answer the questions about being and God. Self-appropriation is a necessary condition for such inquiry.

Moreover self-appropriation leads to and implies intellectual and moral conversion. Only if I in transcendental method have experienced, understood, judged, and chosen myself in relation to being am I intellectually converted. Only then can I say and mean and ground fully, as a consequence of such self-affirmation, that being is intelligible. If being is not intelligible but something else, if intellectual conversion has not occurred, then metaphysics in a fully adequate, critical, defensible sense is impossible and the affirmation of God is impossible.

If, however, I am a questioning knower, if I operate according to the notion of being, then I have to refuse all obscurantism and dogmatism. I cannot and should not simply close off or reject certain questions because they are inconvenient or go counter to certain dominant positivist or postmodern fashions. The desire to know impels me to be faithful to it; to do less is to be inauthentic. Where does the spirit of questioning lead me if I am totally faithful to it, if I do not arbitrarily stop questioning at a certain point? Is it possible that the refusal of God's existence is based upon a denial or short-circuit-ing or limiting of this spirit of questioning that is either arbitrary or self-contradictory?

Modern secular society, as we have seen, is a soil in which the sacred does not easily take root or grow. To modern, secular men and women, tough-minded, empirical, living on the surface of themselves, reified, commodified, objectified, the questions of being and God seem empty. We are sympathetic to thinkers as different as Marcel and Heidegger, therefore, who affirm the need for a philosophical reflection that shakes up this secularism, challenges it, shows its limitations. Such reflection excavates, in a sense, a place for being and the sacred. Such reflection, grounded in intellectual and moral conversion, shows that human beings are not just surface but also depth, not just body but also spirit, not just object but also subject, not just commodities but also dignified human beings with an ethical, political, and metaphysical destiny.[1]

The soil in which modern atheism and agnosticism grow is alienation. The very social alienation manifested in reification, individualism, and scientism, which I criticized phenomenologically-hermeneutically in PCM and ethically-politically in CAL is itself, perhaps, the greatest obstacle to metaphysics, affirmation of God, and belief in God.[2] What philosophical reflection does, and what I have tried to do in the first five chapters, is to till, and to stimulate the reader to till, a different kind of soil, one that is deeper, more personalistic, more reflective, more variegated. With such tilling it seems to me, an openness can emerge to the questions about being and God. What if full self-knowledge leads me to being and God as the full manifestations and implications of such self-knowledge in relation to the world? What if I cannot understand and know and love myself without fully knowing, understanding, and loving being and God? What if denial of these leads to and implies denial or mutilation of self, because I do not go all the way with questioning and, therefore, end up being inauthentic? Why, on the other hand, should the deliverances and prejudices of an alienated, reified, commodified consciousness be normative or have the last word? Is not that consciousness already too mutilated, too dogmatic, too sunk in the life of the crowd to be taken seriously or be credible?

The so-called argument for the existence of God, therefore, is not just conceptual and ratiocinative but intellectualistic and existential, based upon and flowing from self-appropriation, intellectual conversion, and moral conversion. Moreover, and here I am following Lonergan's lead in his later work, such an argument looks forward to, anticipates, and is ultimately in the context of religious conversion, falling in love with God, religious belief. Here I am not denying the validity of the argument as a philosophical argument, but am arguing that it makes sense fully and adequately only in such a context, which I articulate in Part Two. Unless I am at least open to such falling in love and belief, unless I have at least minimal good will rooted in transcendental method (remember transcendental method is the choice of myself as an experiencing, understanding, judging, and deciding subject in relation to being), self-appropriation, and intellectual and moral conversion, I will be fighting myself and the argument and the desire to know, because I do not wish to go where they seem to lead. Better it is to return to Heidegger's definition of authenticity and postmodernism and various other kinds of postmodernism, which let me off the intellectual, ethical, metaphysical, and religious hook.

There is, then a broad, comprehensive hermeneutical circle in this book that includes the transcendental, universal as well as the particular, historical dimension in Part Two. My own circle has as a real starting point my situation as a believer, a Christian, and a radical liberationist. What happens, as we move through reflecting on the possibility of metaphysics, the notion of being, intellectual and moral conversion, the metaphysics of proportionate being, the idea of God, the affirmation of God, belief in Christ, hermeneutics of suspicion, and the commitment to Jesus Christ, Liberator, is a testing, refining, and deepening of these initial beliefs and commitments. Perhaps they will not stand up to critical scrutiny. Perhaps atheism is the better course. Perhaps God is just a projection of need.

What is happening and will continue to happen in this book, therefore, is a movement from relatively immediate belief and commitment through a process of mediate testing to a mediated immediacy of renewed immediacy and commitment, a second naivete or second Copernican revolution. Arguments for the existence of God, are, therefore, contextualized; they have their own relative validity and cogency, but they do not mean anything, or at least not very much or insufficiently much, without this prior, present, and posterior personal, existential, and social context. They are a part, not the whole, and, therefore, need to be grounded in and illumine and serve that whole. Without that whole, without the prior beliefs and commitments or at least the openness to belief, without the process of intellectual, moral, and religious conversion leading to radical political conversion, without the religious experience, one aspect of the second naivete, that flows from belief and falling in love with God, an argument for the existence of God, means relatively little.

But have I so relativized and contextualized the argument that it is no longer relevant? Why argue at all? One way of answering this question is to say that argument completes and renders clear, explicit, and evidential my process of knowing. If the process of coming to know is one of moving from the implicit to the explicit, then argument is an essential way to do that in the intellectual pattern of experience and in others as well, in more informal ways. Argument expresses the transcendental structure of the mind as it moves from question to insight to definition to reflecting on the unconditioned to judging that the unconditioned is or is not present to linking different understandings and judgments in the series. Argument most adequately understood is simply this series.

Moreover, argument as I intend it and use it here functions as a form of indirect communication appealing to the reason and freedom of the person as a subject, not forcing him or compelling him as an object. Argument in indirect communication encourages a double reflection, not only on the content presented but on myself as related to that content. "How does this content square with my own process of self-appropriation?" Argument as indirect communication says, "Here are my reasons or evidence for holding what I hold to be true. What do you think?" Argument functions as an "appeal" to the reason and freedom of the other to "do something" with it, to respond, to think, to understand, to judge, to accept or reject, to choose to follow up on implications, to respond to me with question or insight or another argument that, as a part of our conversation, agrees, qualifies, or disagrees. Argument as I intend it and use it here is not a last word closing off the conversation; it is a first or a next word opening it up.

We need to see the argument for the existence of God as contextualized, rooted, grounded in the overflowing mystery of a natural and human life-world that is simultaneously scientific and prescientific, subjective and objective, personal and intersubjective. Only if human life or philosophy have already opened me up to the mystery of life, can I be open to the mystery of being and God as manifested through this life. If the life-world is so covered over and functionalized that it banishes mystery, then the mystery of being and God cannot be manifested or take root.

Let us dwell a bit on this point. In what way is the life-world mysterious? First of all, it is present to me as the nonthematic and prethematic context in which I live and move and have my being. I am sitting here writing now, but I am aware of the surrounding environment of my room, apartment building, and out-of-doors as the sun streams through the window, and sounds are audible from the street. Furthermore, I have valid perceptions; I see the sparrow, I hear the rain fall, I feel the snow against my face. Moreover, aesthetic awareness and moral perception reveal to me the inexhaustibility and mystery in a leaf, a sunset, or a beloved other human being. I am also somewhat mysterious to myself insofar as I have not fully understood my life history, my relationships with people, my sexuality, and my transcendental subjectivity; I know myself somewhat but not fully.

Finally, on the side of subjectivity, my desire to know as unrestricted makes me aware of the difference between questions I have asked and those I have answered, and the emotional-spiritual effect in me is, or should be, awe and wonder before the mystery. If I am integrated authentically, then, by the principles of correspondence and integration, awe and wonder should be simultaneously emotional, intellectual, and spiritual. "Spiritual" here refers to the fourth level of freedom insofar as that consents to be open to, choose, and love the depths in myself, others, being, and God—silent, reverent awe before the mystery.[3]

Such is the alternative soil which a reflective, phenomenologically, hermeneutically, critically, and transcendentally oriented philosophy would till, a philosophy that now sees itself as mirroring the mystery, serving it, being thankful for it—thinking as thanking. And what better way to be thankful than to think the mystery, articulate it, reveal it. The human being as philosopher in this sense is the guardian or shepherd of being.[4]

Nonetheless, out of the dominant, reified, alienated soil are objections that grow from it and nourish it. And these have to be considered on their own terms; it would be too simplistic philosophically to reduce these objections to alienation and be done with them. Moreover, even if it is the reified, alienated soil that nourishes them and gives them weight, people of good will raise such objections. Positivism, for example, wishes to confine questions to what can be empirically verified in data of sense, but positivism, as I have argued elsewhere, is already self-contradictory. The principle of verifiability, which states that all meaningful statements are either analytic or descriptions of actual or possible empirical states of affairs, is neither analytic nor a description of such states of affairs. It is not analytic because we can putatively conceive other meaningful statements, aesthetic, ethical, political, and metaphysical, that are not either analytic or synthetic in the above senses. It is not a description of states of affairs, because it is a prescription; it states what would obtain if rational, meaningful discourse goes on, not what in fact does obtain. Indeed what does obtain in the life-world are various kinds of meaning, commonsensical, aesthetic, political, philosophical, and religious, which contradict the principle of verifiability.[5]

The principle of verifiability is not itself verifiable. Moreover, we have already seen earlier the difference between two senses of science: science as positive science oriented to data of sense and philosophy as generalized empirical method reflecting on data of consciousness. Such a broader conception of science implies a broader conception of experience; it is not simply data of sense but also data of consciousness. I see the table, touch it, lift it, understand it, judge it, but I am aware of myself in my acts of seeing, touching, lifting, understanding, and judging.

Finally, the positivist confuses the notions of verification and experience. If the theory of relativity, however, is verified, it is not experienced as such. All that is experienced is a collection of sensible contents. It is not experience but critical reflection that asks whether the data corresponds to the theory sufficiently for the theory to be affirmed. It is not experience but judgment that reflectively grasps the virtually unconditioned: that the conditions necessary to ground the theory as probably true obtain.[6]

Logical positivism, then, is more or less committed to the counter-positions on being, knowledge, self-knowledge, and value, because logical positivism does not break with the thesis that knowing is looking. Because it does not break with knowing as looking, it identifies the real not with being as the object of the pure desire to know but being as sensibly, sensuously looked at. Since this is an incorrect account even of how we know proportionate being, it cannot be taken as a telling objection against knowing transcendent being. We see again how important intellectual conversion based on self-appropriation is. And we see one example and verifying instance of the general claim that atheism rests upon inadequate self-knowledge.[7]

Nonetheless, questions and suspicions persist. Perhaps with Kant we are tempted to say that God as the object of a metaphysical proof rests upon a transcendental illusion. But our argument is based upon the pure desire to know in light of which we distinguish between truth and illusion. Nor can the pure desire to know be an illusion, for it exists, and it spontaneously transcends the limits that positivists and Kantians wish to set up.[8]

Moreover, we have seen in chapter 1 that this talk of a transcendental illusion is based upon an untenable distinction between phenomenon and noumenon that is self-contradictory, on a narrow conception of experience that confines it to sensible data, on an illegitimate conflating of understanding and judgment, and on a questionable limiting of the unconditioned to the merely regulative, not constitutive. Furthermore, drawing on our just concluded reflection on positivism, we note a crypto-positivistic tendency in Kant to confuse verification and legitimate judgment with sensible experience. Kant is a disillusioned positivist, smart enough to know that knowing as looking does not give us knowledge of real being, but not smart enough to know that genuine knowing does not equal looking. Kant incompletely and inadequately breaks with the account of knowing as looking.[9]

If, however, the unconditioned is constitutive and not merely regulative in our knowledge of external things, people, and ourselves, then the question arises about whether these beings as mere matters of fact that happen to occur require further explanation. If so, then the possibility and necessity of affirming transcendent being emerges. If not, then we are caught in the contradiction of affirming that being is intelligible and saying at the same time that things merely exist as mere matters of fact hanging in mid air with no adequate explanation of what or how they exist. At least some aspects of being are not intelligible, and consequently, being both is and is not intelligible. I will develop this point more fully in the next section.

Similar kinds of things can be said of discussions of God such as Jean-Luc Marion's based upon postmodernism and especially Derrida. For Marion affirms a God who is pure giving and, therefore, beyond metaphysics as ontotheology, as philosophy of being. But our conception of God is initially that of an unrestricted act of understanding and love, prior to conceiving God as being but not excluding that affirmation, because outside of being is nothing. Marion's argument may have some kind of legitimacy against a traditional Thomistic or classical conception of God, but not ours, which stresses that God is processive and affirms God's being as manifested through God's understanding and love. Indeed Hartshorne answers this point squarely insofar as for him attributes like necessary existence and permanence and identity are just abstract aspects of God. The full reality of God is a unity of primordial and consequent natures, permanence and change, being and activity, being manifesting itself through understanding, loving activity, and receiving from the world in the same activity. God is relationship through and through.

In fact, we find that, paradoxically, Marion insufficiently affirms difference in God. For in stressing that God is pure giving, he gives in to the worst aspects of classical metaphysics, which denies that change and receptivity and suffering and contingency are in God. Paradoxically the postmodern conception of God does less justice to difference in God than my modern, metaphysical, neoclassical conception.[10]

Finally, we need to consider the ontological argument, which moves from the idea of God to the existence of God. But conceptions of God are no more than analytic propositions, true by definition alone, and analytic propositions can only become analytic principles implying existence if we can affirm God in reflecting on a judgment of fact. We can show that conceiving God as perfect is contradictory to conceiving God as not existing but this is a contradiction only between analytic propositions. Such a rejection of the ontological argument is consistent with our conception of metaphysical method, which distinguishes among experience, understanding, and judgment, and argues that existence is correlative to judgment. Conception alone on the level of understanding does not give us existence, only a conception of existence.

Nonetheless, this reply may seem too quick and too simplistic. For what defenders of the ontological argument insist on is that God is sui generis; the idea of God as an unrestricted act of understanding is the idea of a necessary God, whose nonexistence is nonconceivable and who is perfect because necessary existence is better than conceivable nonexistence. If God's non-existence were conceivable, then the idea of God would be contradictory; God would be both necessary and conceivably nonexistent—that is, contingent. Therefore, it may be that the idea of God is a notion that is, as stated in a proposition, both an analytic proposition and an analytic principle. A notion that may seem to be merely an analytic proposition turns out to be an analytic principle sui generis.

I respond that if God exists, God exists necessarily. But whether God exists cannot be determined by concepts alone. A distinction must be made between *de dictu* and *de re*, conceptual and ontological necessity. Consequently, it is not a contradiction, as defenders of the ontological argument maintain it is, to say, "If God exists, God exists necessarily." The reason is that the conditional phrase refers to an epistemic condition and contingency, and the main clause refers to an ontological necessity present in the idea of God and truly present in God ontologically if God exists. The sentence, therefore, is not contradictory.[11]

The Affirmation of God

Preliminary Considerations

What I have done in the dialectical section is to show how the absence of being and God is rooted in an alienated, reified soil, and the way the leading forms of atheism, agnosticism, and antimetaphysical approaches emerge from and nourish that soil. I have tried in the spirit of dialectical phenomenology to combine argumentative rigor with existential, phenomenological, hermeneutical insightfulness and revelatory power, avoiding the extremes of mere poetic dwelling and mere sterile argumentation. The best philosophies, it seems to me, combine rigor with insight and revelatory power, and therefore avoid the extremes.[12]

What has emerged is the untenability of the main alternatives to affirming the existence of God metaphysically, and at least the plausibility of such an affirmation. The alternatives were shown to be rooted in the counter-positions and, therefore, to be based on inadequate self-knowledge. I am now in a position to develop what an adequate expression of such self-knowledge would be. What are its ultimate implications?

Once again I insist that my "argument" for the existence of God is, as an argument, only a conceptual expression of self-knowledge and self-appropriation, leading to intellectual, moral, and, as we will see later, religious conversion. Concepts, propositions, and arguments that link concepts and propositions are only expressions of direct and reflective understanding, which in turn is rooted in a prior questioning receptively open to the world in reverence, wonder, and awe, questioning as the piety of thinking. I have no intention, therefore, of browbeating the reader, of forcing the reader argumentatively into accepting my position. What I am offering is a series of marks on paper containing possible insights, judgments, and arguments that can aid readers in their own self-appropriation and following out its implications. My intention here is to engage readers in the spirit of Gadamerian dialogue in a play of questions and answers in which my text brings them into question and they in turn bring it into question.[13]

Another way of putting the above point is to say that a valid "argument" will not be just conceptual and judgmental but will express my receptive fidelity on each level of cognition, experience, understanding, and judgment, and this fidelity has both objective and subjective aspects. The objective aspect is fidelity to what is revealed at each stage of cognition, the perceptual gestalt on the level of sensible perception, the received insight on the level of direct understanding, and the disclosed evidence on the level of reflective understanding. Subjective is my fidelity to the desire to know as that moves me from experience to understanding to judgment. There is an a priori, transcendental aspect; the desire is the source of the notion of being and the transcendental precepts, but that always interacts with an a posteriori aspect that is received, that is other, that I do not create. This union of objective and subjective, a posteriori and a priori, is another way in which the active-passive unity of authentic knowing manifests itself.

If we reflect on the intersubjective, communicative context in which knowing takes place, we note the same kind of unity. Argument is part of a larger conversation, a play of question and answer, in which many preconceptual and postconceptual and propositional elements such as prejudice, feeling, presuppositions, and spontaneously held values come into play. If the conversation is authentic and not simply an attempt by one or more parties to "win" the argument, then we note a necessary openness to the views of the other, a willingness to have myself brought into question by the other, and a willingness to change my mind if the evidence demands it. At the same time I also have the right to bring the other into question, to test the opinions and to evaluate the evidence that the other presents. Here again is union of activity and passivity, question and answer, listening and offering opinions.[14]

This union of activity and passivity has been present throughout my three volumes. For example, in my account of perception, my discussion of knowing and loving other persons, the hermeneutical play of question and answer in interpreting a text, a similar play of question and answer in communicative action, fidelity to the ethical norms of right, morality, and justice, and my openness to the excluded, marginalized, exploited other. Part of the offense that postmodernists and some phenomenologists and hermeneuticists take at argument is in not seeing it as part of a broader context of understanding and conversation. Sometimes, the *way* people argue and discuss gives some legitimacy to the offense, but those offended are reacting to a caricature rather than the full, true reality.

Another way of putting this point is to distinguish between logic and method. Logic is the conceptual unification of a set or a system of propositions and is static. Method refers not only and not primarily to the conceptual products of cognition, but to the underlying acts from which they proceed. Transcendental method, then, focuses on the acts of experiencing, understanding, judging, and deciding from which explicitly conceptual products emerge. Method, moreover, is dynamic. It refers not just to one system, logical or otherwise, but to the epistemic or ontological movements from one system to another.

Thus, philosophical method moves in my three volumes from phenomenology-hermeneutics to critical theory to metaphysics-philosophy of religion, and in this work from cognitional theory to the metaphysics of proportionate being to the metaphysics of transcendent being. The logical cogency of my approach is not denied, but it is relativized. It is less fundamental than the acts of knowing from which it proceeds, and it is part of a logical whole of knowledge and conversation that is dynamic, developing, existential, dialectical, and a unity of preconceptual and conceptual. It makes all the difference in the world, therefore, whether one sees proof and argument as proceeding primarily from logic or method.[15]

If what I have said about argument is plausible and true, then my account should apply to discussions of the existence of God. Such arguments are not necessarily and do not have to be an expression of my own will to power aggressively blackmailing and forcing people to affirm and believe almost against their wills, but invitations to follow through completely on the implications of self-appropriation as I and we see it. If knowing is a unity of experience, understanding, and judgment, if the notion of being is operative truly in my knowing, if being is the intelligible, if proportionate being is a unity of potency, form, and act, if the notion of God emerges as an extrapolation of the unrestricted desire to know in a way that makes sense and is not self-contradictory, then further implications are present. Do I need to affirm the existence of God as the ultimate consequence and final explication of fidelity to being and the desire to know or not? Is theism or atheism or agnosticism the most honest, compelling choice?

Causality

At this point, the existence of God is a hypothesis like any other. I hope that I have convinced the reader to see it as at least a plausible hypothesis. In order to evaluate the hypothesis, we first need to consider the nature of causality. As I understand it here, causality is simply the objective, real counterpoint or correlative to questions raised by the desire to know. Because questions are of various kinds, we can distinguish among different causes and kinds of causes.

The basic division is that between internal and external causes. Internal causes are the conjugate and central potency, form, and act already discussed. External causes are efficient, final, and exemplary, and can be considered in three manners—namely, in concrete instances, in principle, and in the fullness that results from applying the principles. In a concrete instance, a community needs to build a new symphony hall. Here the final cause is the purpose or use to which the hall is put, the exemplary cause is the architectural model of the hall, and the efficient cause is the people building the hall. But if we are to avoid anthropomorphism, we must ask whether such causality is rooted in a deeper principle allowing us to say that it is generally valid.[16]

First of all, being is the intelligible and nothing but that. The notion of being is of that which can be intelligently grasped and reasonably affirmed. On the other hand, what is apart from being is nothing, and so apart from intelligibility is nothing. Consequently, to talk about mere matters of fact that admit of no full explanation is to talk about nothing. If existence is a mere matter of fact, then it is nothing. If it is a mere matter of fact that classical and statistical laws obtain, that finality is present in the upwardly directed dynamism of proportionate being, and that genetic method gives us a correct account of emergent probability, then the knowing and the known are nothing.

If this sounds harsh, we can only recall the results of our reflections up to this point. To deny the equation of being and intelligibility is to revert to the counter-positions, in which we refuse to identify the real with being, confuse objectivity with extroversion, and offer mere sensible experiencing as a model of knowing. But counter-positions tend to reverse themselves once they are intelligently grasped and reasonably affirmed. Since the claim cannot be avoided by an intelligent and reasonable subject, the reversal cannot be avoided. And since the reversal cannot be avoided, we are right back to affirming that being is the intelligible, apart from being there is nothing, and mere matters of fact with no full explanation are nothing.[17]

This argument may seem too quick and pat and dismissive, so let us dwell on the point for a moment. What I am arguing is that denial of the full intelligibility of being is logically and self-referentially contradictory. It logically contradicts claims made in chapter 2 equating being with intelligibility. It performatively contradicts my spontaneous orientation toward what can be intelligently grasped and reasonably affirmed. We note also something arbitrary about such contradiction and denial. I enter a classroom, and I find a poem written on the board. I ask, "Who wrote that?" and somebody says, "No one wrote that. There is no need for explanation here." Why do we spontaneously resist such a response? Another example: we enter the classroom and the chairs are rearranged in a way that displeases me. I ask for the reason or final cause of such rearrangement and for the efficient cause, and somebody says, "There is no reason for the new arrangement, and no one did it." Is this response plausible?

One could say, of course, that asking for reasons and causes is cultural, something learned in our Western context. That claim is true in one sense; modern, Western society has educated us and encouraged us to think scientifically and metaphysically, but is such education an educing of something that is already in us a priori or not? Certain beliefs, such as belief in Santa Claus, drop out as we mature, but belief in the legitimacy of causal explanation is not one of these. All or most cultures, not simply in the West, seem to have accepted the legitimacy of science, such that even the metaphysical skeptic in the West or East can inquire socio-scientifically about the causes of our odd Western belief in science and causality. Moreover, note the experience, understanding, and judgment involved in the claim, "Belief in causality is merely Western and originates in the West." Once again, a counter-position, once it claims to be intelligent and reasonable, reverses itself. Causality is asserted in the process of denying it.

Maybe, the skeptic might say, being is partially intelligible. It is not totally unintelligible, because that is obviously self-contradictory, difficult to sustain, and contradicted empirically by any successful scientific experiment or human interaction. But maybe being is partially, not totally, intelligible. Such a claim implies that in proportionate being there are aspects that are intelligible, such as the conjugate forms discovered by science, and those that are not, like existence. But if so, we have slid back into a counter-position again, for we have at least some aspects of being that lie outside the realm of intelligibility. We are refusing to identify the intelligible with being. Moreover, once again there is a problem of arbitrariness as well as self-contradiction. Why affirm the legitimacy of seeking intelligibility for some aspects of being and not others? Why stop the questioning short?

A person could reply that some of the unintelligible aspects are those relating to evil and chance. Here I think the neoclassical, processive conception of God sheds light on this great and, perhaps, main obstacle to affirming the existence of God while not totally removing the mystery of evil. For chance is simply the result of individual things and persons acting "freely" and "indeterminately" in relation to scientific law and probability. We do not need God to explain chance events like earthquakes any more than we need God to explain the evil resulting from the wrong use of human freedom. Individual things and human beings are fully capable of explaining such realities.

If an earthquake or tornado or flood occurs, for example, scientists can and do inquire into the peculiar set of atmospheric conditions, state of the earth, and weather that brought about the events in question. A chance event is not an uncaused event; it is one that goes beyond and escapes normal causality. Indeed science is becoming so adept that it can often predict and warn us about earthquakes and tornados and floods. What seems to be an exception to my claim that being is totally intelligible confirms this thesis.

Moreover, for at least some kinds of chance or evil, we note something negative and lacking about them, an absence of intelligibility. And lack of intelligibility does not need explanation, any more than the tendency of a body to stay in motion needs a positive causal explanation. The insight here, as Lonergan tells us, is inverse; there is nothing to be understood.[18]

Now, of course, if we see chance and evil in another sense as parts or aspects of a universe governed by emergent probability, then they become parts of that whole and in that sense require explanation. Here the question reappears. Is emergent probability just a matter of fact, or is it intelligible? If the former, then as a mere matter of fact it is nothing. If the latter, then it requires complete explanation.

Defenders of partial intelligibility could defend themselves against arbitrariness by saying that the question about complete intelligibility is a bad question. But then we have to ask for the justification for this claim. The question about complete intelligibility, one form of which is "Why is there something rather than nothing?," is not meaningless or self-contradictory. Moreover, it cannot be rejected because of positivism or Kantianism or postmodernism, for we have seen how limited and mistaken such perspectives are. Moreover, to deny the question as legitimate would seem to contradict the affirmation already made concerning the notion of being as intelligible. We either have to move to a metaphysics of transcendent being or remain in logical and performative contradiction.

The metaphysics of transcendent being arises to resolve these contradictions. In this sense, it is a higher viewpoint in relation to common sense, science, and nonmetaphysical philosophy, in a way that chemistry is a higher viewpoint in relation to physics or biology is a higher viewpoint in relation to chemistry. In each case the higher viewpoint arises to explain data and to answer questions that the lower viewpoint is incapable of explaining and answering.

To ascend from the lower viewpoint to a higher viewpoint all the way up the ladder of knowledge and then to deny the legitimacy of the metaphysics of transcendent being seems to be a curious exception to this general way of proceeding. At this point we become curiously reductionistic in a way that violates our whole previous way of proceeding. We reject metaphysical questions because they are not answerable through using normal common sense, science, or philosophy. Why not reject biology because it is not chemistry, or empirical psychology because it is not biology, or transcendental philosophy because it is not psychology, because it focuses on data of consciousness rather than simply data of sense? Why not become consistently reductionistic?

A new method arises because the old methods were not capable of explaining the data and answering the questions that stimulated new methods. It is as much of a mistake to impose the methods of empirical science and premetaphysical philosophy on metaphysics or to reject metaphysics because it does not conform to these methods as it is to impose the method of physics on chemistry or biology, or to reject these sciences because they are not physics. The method of explanation by external, metaphysical causes arises because the other methods of interpretation and explanation simply in terms of immanence within proportionate being prove to be insufficient.

The argument that emerges, then, is disjunctive. Either being is partially intelligible, fully unintelligible, or fully intelligible. It is not totally unintelligible nor partially intelligible for reasons that we have already seen. Consequently, we must affirm total intelligibility. Either proportionate being is fully intelligible, or it is nothing. It is not nothing, for we have already affirmed ourselves and the world as real. Therefore, being is fully intelligible.

Let me now return to the main thread of our argument. First, I have argued that being is intelligible. Second, if being is intelligible, it is fully intelligible. Third, we cannot confine human knowledge within the domain of proportionate being without confining it to mere matters of fact without explanation and, therefore, implying that it is nothing. Either proportionate being is real and intelligible, or it is nothing. If it is real, then proportionate being requires transcendent being if we are not to fall into the counter-positions.

We do not know until we judge, and our judgment rests upon a grasp of the virtually unconditioned, a conditioned that happens to have its conditions fulfilled. Thus, every judgment raises a further question; it reveals a conditioned that happens to be fulfilled, but why is it fulfilled? As long as we remain within proportionate being, the question is not answered fully, for every other being within proportionate being is virtually unconditioned.

This is the structure of the argument, and it can be given as many applications as there are distinct features of proportionate being. Existence, for example, is something for which neither empirical science nor methodologically restricted philosophy can account for. "Why is there something rather than nothing?" Statistical laws can assign the frequencies with which things exist and account for numbers of different kinds of things, but the number of existents is one thing and their existence is another. In particular cases, the scientist can deduce one existent from another, but in those cases he cannot account for the existence of the others to which he appeals for his premises. Philosophy can show that it is self-contradictory to deny that I exist, as I did in the discussion of the notion of being, but it is one thing to demonstrate the fact of my existence and another thing to account for that fact. Indeed what a fully lucid philosophy shows is that proportionate being cannot account for existence.

Not only existence but also the structure of the universe remains, as long as we stay within the domain of proportionate being, a mere matter of fact. Classical laws are not what must be; they are empirical, what in fact is so. Genetic operators enjoy a major and minor flexibility, and so in each case are in fact what is so. Explanatory genera and species are not necessary, but are more or less successful solutions to contingent problems set by contingent situations. The course of generalized emergent probability is one among a number of possible courses, and the actual course is contingent, what happens to be or occur as a matter of fact.[19]

If being is intelligible, therefore, and mere matters of fact are nothing, and remaining within proportionate being is to remain within mere matters of fact, then we conclude negatively that knowledge of transcendent being cannot be excluded. Positively we need to ask what constitutes our knowledge of transcendent being.

In the fourth place, our transcendent being must be sufficiently necessary to account for matters of fact. I am not denying, as classical theists are wont to do, contingency in every respect, for that is in the consequent nature of God. Indeed even its contingency is part of the explanation for proportionate being, for God's loving, intelligent decision to create and sustain the universe in being and well-being functions as a large part of the explanation. As such, transcendent being, in addition to being self-explanatory, is capable of grounding the explanation for everything else.

If transcendent being is self-explanatory and explanatory of everything else to the extent required, then we avoid the problem of an infinite regress. For such a regress of conditioned causes still leaves the whole series a mere matter of fact and, therefore, nothing. If there are conditioned beings, there are fulfilling conditions, and no conditions are fulfilled simply at random. Chance is present in the universe, but not pure chance or pure chaos. Conditions are fulfilled, therefore, according to some exemplar, and we must posit an exemplary cause that would account for the pattern within which conditions are fulfilled.

Because being is intelligible, it is good. As potentially intelligible, it is manifold, and this manifold is good insofar as it stands under an intelligible structure, a good of order. Since possible orders are many, and the universe has one order, then this order must be a value and its selection due to rational choice. Such a choice cannot be necessary, because otherwise the universe itself would be necessary. The choice cannot be arbitrary, because what results arbitrarily is a mere matter of fact without any possible explanation. What is neither arbitrary nor necessary, yet intelligible and a value, is what proceeds from the reasonable choice of a rational consciousness.

The final cause as the ground of value overcomes contingency at its deepest level. Being cannot be arbitrary, and contingent being must be a reasonably realized possibility. Its possibility lies in its exemplary cause, its realization in the efficient cause, and its reasonableness in its final cause. Without such reasonableness, the universe would be arbitrary and would be apart from being, what is apart from being is not possible, and what is not possible cannot be realized. Transcendent being as efficient, exemplary, and final cause must be affirmed if we are to avoid saying that proportionate being is a mere matter of fact and, therefore, nothing. The ultimate consequence of philosophical self-affirmation, therefore, is transcendent being.

We have moved, then, from instances of external causality to their validity in principle as accounts of the universe as a whole to their full realization in the affirmation of transcendent being. But have we avoided anthropomorphism? It may not seem to be so, since our transcendent being is an unconditioned, intelligent, rational, and loving consciousness who grounds the universe intelligently and freely in the same way that human beings ground their actions and products. On the one hand, what is strictly anthropomorphic is not a pure, intelligent, infinite unconditioned rational consciousness, but one that is limited, finite, and is in tension with other desires. On the other hand, insofar as I consider solely human beings as intelligent, rational, and free, I consider what is most intimate to the universe and its ultimate ground. For the universe and its ultimate ground can be nothing other than the objective of the pure desire to know.[20]

The Reality of God

I have affirmed the reality of transcendent being as the final stage of our discussion of causality. Here it is only necessary to draw out the full implications of this argument, make it more explicit, formalize it, and make it more rigorous.

The reader at this point should have the gist of what I wish to say. The affirmation of God is necessary as a consequence of authentic self-affirmation. If I do not affirm God, then proportionate being is a matter of fact. If proportionate being is a mere matter of fact, then it is nothing. If it is nothing, that contradicts my affirmation of being as real and implies a disjunction between the real and the intelligible. To posit this disjunction is to fall into the counter-positions and, therefore, to be in contradiction with authentic self-affirmation. This way of arguing is *modus tollens*. If I affirm myself authentically, then I must affirm God. But I do not affirm God. Therefore, I do not affirm myself authentically or I contradict such self-affirmation.

Modus ponens, of course, is another version of the same argument. If I affirm myself authentically, then I must affirm God. But I affirm myself authentically. Therefore, I affirm God. The minor premise simply affirms what I argued for in chapter 2, in which I experienced, understood, judged, and chose myself as an experiencing, understanding, judging, and deciding subject in relationship to being. Such an affirmation has as a consequence the acceptance of the positions and the rejection of the counter-positions.

The major premise takes the form of a series of conditional claims that we have already argued for throughout this book. If I exist, judge, and choose myself authentically, then the notion of being exists in me not only as implicitly operative but as explicitly articulated and owned up to. If the notion of being is so articulated and owned up to, then we can affirm proportionate being as structure and process, as an instantiation and partial realization of the notion of being. If proportionate being exists, the idea of God can be conceived as an unrestricted act of understanding that can be a possible explanation of proportionate being. If proportionate being is intelligible and is not a mere matter of fact, then we must affirm God's existence.

Here I stress again that as an argument it is part of a broader cognitional and existential movement, having its roots in wonder—why is there something rather than nothing—rooted in my receptivity to the world as perceived, intelligible, and rational, and expressing my understanding and judgment of that world as real and fully intelligible. Wonder and argument, then, are mediated by perception, understanding, and judgment as activities.

Why is there something rather than nothing? Like Heidegger, we ask this question in a reverent, awe-filled wonder before the mystery of a rose, a sunset, or a beautiful, deep human being. Being attentive means being open to being in this sense. Unlike Heidegger, to adequately answer this question, we are led to affirm the existence of God as an unrestricted act of understanding and love. We have thus far developed two arguments, conditional *modus tollens* and conditional *modus ponens*, to make this affirmation. A third very effective form is Lonergan's. If the real is completely intelligible, God exists. But the real is completely intelligible. Therefore, God exists.

The minor premise is, as we have just seen, an explication of self-affirmation. For being is the object of the pure desire to know and, therefore, is intelligible. If the real is intelligible, then it is completely intelligible, for outside being there is nothing and partial intelligibility is, as we have seen, a contradictory half-way house. Anything affirmed must, therefore, have its adequate explanation either in itself or in something else.

Let us move, then, to the major premise. If the real is completely intelligible, then complete intelligibility exists. If complete intelligibility exists, then the idea of being exists. If the idea of being exists, then God exists.

Let us consider each of these subpremises in turn. First, if the real is completely intelligible, then complete intelligibility exists. If it did not, if it were merely a bright idea or mere possibility, then the adequate explanation for proportionate being would not exist and being would not be completely intelligible.

If complete intelligibility exists, then the idea of God exists. For intelligibility is either material or spiritual or abstract. It is material in the objects of the physical sciences, spiritual when identical with understanding, and abstract in concepts of unities, laws, and ideal frequencies. But abstract intelligibility is incomplete by itself, since it is an expression of material intelligibility. Again, spiritual intelligibility is incomplete as long as it can still inquire into what is, insofar as it does not understand everything about everything. And material intelligibility is incomplete insofar as it is contingent and cannot be reflective and cannot know itself. Consequently, the only feasible candidate for complete intelligibility is an unrestricted act of understanding that understands everything about everything.

Finally, if the idea of being exists, then God exists. For if the idea of being exists, then at least its primary component exists, and this we have seen to possess the attributes of God.[21]

The implications of such an argument at the final stage of explicating my authentic self-understanding are enormous. First, if the argument is correct, then at my deepest and most fundamental level, I am a desire to know and love God. At my deepest, therefore, as we shall see more fully in Part Two, I am an openness to a possible religious revelation of God. The fullest, most honest, most rational, most authentic way to live life is to live it theistically, not atheistically or agnostically. Both atheism and agnosticism, and in this book I claim to have reflected on the most fundamental and most important forms of these, rest upon different versions of obscurantism, dogmatism, and self-contradiction that betray the desire to know.

Perhaps, a critic might argue, my argument is based on wish fulfillment. I want God to exist because God satisfies my need for meaning and intelligibility. To paraphrase Nietzsche, God makes me happy, therefore God exists. But my argument is not based on just any desire or any wish, but on the desire to know itself, which functions as critic of illegitimate wishing, desiring, and projecting. The very source of criticism, to which Nietzsche appeals in criticizing wish fulfillment, is the desire to know, upon which my argument is based. How can that desire itself be the source of illegitimate wishes and projections? Once again we need to distinguish rigorously between the desire to know and other desires that may be in tension with it and can be the source of illusion.[22]

What is clear here, then, is that I have articulated the basic premise upon which all or most arguments for the existence of God are based: that being is intelligible and, therefore, completely intelligible. For the most part in the past, this premise has remained more or less implicit and ungrounded. I, however, have led up to our argument by grounding this premise in the cognitive and existential self-appropriation of ourselves as knowers. This premise, therefore, is not automatically or dogmatically presumed, but rigorously justified and grounded in self-appropriation.

The move to affirming God occurs as the last step in a series of steps: existential-phenomenological description, articulation, and choice of the self as a knower, chooser, and lover; the notion of being leading to the claim that being is intelligible, the metaphysics of proportionate being, the notion of God, and the argument for the existence of God. One of the main reasons that such arguments have been unconvincing in the past is that these prior steps have not been articulated. As a result metaphysically grounded theism remains "a lonely island in an ocean of controversy," unable to account adequately for itself and for its superiority to and relation to other positions.

If, however, people are not aware of themselves as subjects, if they are aware of themselves superficially primarily as objects, commodities, producers, and consumers of commodities, if being is an empty word to them, then God will be an empty word. Self-blind, person-blind, being-blind, and God-blind, such persons confidently proceed on their path in the supposedly happy secular society, ignorant of themselves, alienated from themselves, and cut off from the life-world, other people, being, and God. "There are more things in heaven and earth, Horatio. . . ."[23]

Consequently, the issue becomes at the same time very personal and yet very rigorous, objective, and universal. "Who am I?," the most personal and fundamental of philosophical questions, leads to the questions about being and God. I have already affirmed that my knowing in the world seems to make sense, that moral striving seems to make sense, that work to liberate the oppressed makes sense. But once again as finite, contingent actions, they are just matters of fact. Why does my knowing seem to have a natural isomorphism with being? Why is moral striving preferable to self-indulgence? Why be moral? Why strive for justice? Either these very exalted human activities are just isolated facts in an otherwise absurd world or they are themselves fully intelligible in a fully intelligible universe. That in me which is most meaningful and valuable is either ultimately absurd or it is not.

As with transcendental method, in which I choose myself as an experiencing, understanding, judging, and choosing subject in relationship to being, so here on the issue of transcendent being my freedom has come into play. I have to choose to go all the way with intellectual conversion, to be open to what it implies, and to be "disposable" to the appeal of complete intelligibility and divine transcendence.[24]

Rigor and universality are also present, for I am arguing something universal and explanatory and compelling for all knowers if they are intellectually converted and intellectually honest. In this sense the link between God and the universe of proportionate being is an analytic principle. It cannot be denied, once I am intellectually converted, without performative self-contradiction and logical contradiction.

Performative self-contradiction has been a form of argument and way of philosophizing that has been present in all three volumes; in my arguments with postmodernists and for self-appropriation in PCM, in my argument for the moral principle of generic consistency in CAL, and now in my argument for the existence of God. It is misinterpreting this argument to see it as mere conceptual or logical word play; rather it bears on the deepest issues in a human life of authenticity and genuineness as they manifest themselves cognitively, ethically, and metaphysically. To be performatively consonant with myself and with my life-world is a fundamental demand of such authenticity. In this sense personal, existential self-knowledge and universal rigor and necessity go together or not at all.

Conclusion

Because of my desire to know and love, I am a natural desire to see and love God; here lies the root of the legitimacy not only of contemplation but of the action that flows from it in service and love. For that reason I will argue in Part Two of this work that we are transcendentally open to a possible religious revelation. If there is no transcendental openness, why would and how would a religious revelation mean anything to us? Why would it not be "a tale told by an idiot, full of sound and fury, signifying nothing?"[25] A God answering to no human need, capacity, or desire, even transcendental versions of these, is a meaningless, irrelevant God.

If I affirm God as an unrestricted act of understanding and love, then conformity between knowing and doing or choosing demands that I commit myself to and love this unrestricted act. I am looking for someone in whom I can trust absolutely and whom I can love absolutely, without reserve or restriction. Short of such correlation between my transcendental activities and God, why would He be any more important to me than a baseball game or a hamburger at Macdonalds? Why is God more intelligible and valuable and worth loving than these? If there is little or nothing in me and in my conscious intentionality to which God responds or corresponds, there is no way of answering these questions.

We see, then, that thinking as questioning functions within the horizon of God. To question anything is to question within a horizon of intelligibility, the notion of being leading to the idea of God. But this horizon of intelligibility presumes God as the efficient, exemplary, and final cause and condition of its possibility. As long as I have not fully consented in freedom to the transcendental movement of my questioning, then this horizon remains more or less unthematized and implicit. Once I do consent, however, then thinking becomes a kind of love, a kind of thinking as thanking, a gift of myself to being and God. To refuse to own up to such being and God-directedness is to be at odds with myself as thinking and choosing and willing and loving. I deny that God is the condition of the possibility of the horizon of intelligibility which makes thinking possible at all. Thinking that fully owns up to itself as thinking and thanking is God-directed, God-intoxicated, an initial falling in love with God.

Once I choose to go all the way with experiencing and understanding and judging and choosing, with thinking and loving, then a formerly all or mostly secular world becomes luminous. The world, which seemed to be merely an arena for common sense manipulation or scientific prediction and control, becomes itself a manifestation of God, a mirroring of transcendent mystery. If as a believer I begin my questioning with a belief in God as the foundation of the luminosity and mystery and intelligibility of the world, now that hermeneutical starting point begins to be verified and confirmed. That which is initially a strong belief becomes a transcendental necessity. It becomes literally the metaphysical air without which I cannot breathe or think or choose or love. Transcendental mystery is not antithetical to thinking but the very milieu in which it functions. To deny such a horizon is to deny myself.

༄༅

FIVE

Freedom, Receptivity, and God

As we have seen, much of the modern and contemporary debate about God is not speculative and metaphysical, but practical and existential. The issue is not whether God can be proven argumentatively but whether God is compatible with and relevant to human freedom. As we have also seen, a "no" answer rests upon inadequate conceptions both of God and human freedom. God is conceived as totally transcendent and unrelated to the world, unreceptive, and unchangeable. Human freedom is conceived as totally indeterminate, closed, and independent of its other.

In prior books and somewhat in this book I have criticized this conception of human freedom extensively. I showed, in PCM, against Sartre, that freedom, rather than being a disjunction between such opposites as passivity and activity, positive and negative, determination and indetermination, self and other, is in reality a lived unity of such opposites.

Moreover, such an actively receptive freedom and free intersubjectivity presupposes and leads to and is linked to other forms in other levels and patterns of experience. Perceptual experience, for example, in which I actively and receptively see the duck-rabbit figure as a duck or a rabbit, is one example. Aesthetic experience, in which I attend to the meaning of a work of art, is another. Intellectual inquiry, in which I operate out of a questioning, receptive openness to being—"be attentive"—is another. Hermeneutical openness to tradition, in which I must be receptive and suspicious, and moral experience, in which I must be responsive to the call of the other manifesting obligation and in various forms of injustice and marginalization, is another. Religious experience in reading, meditation, prayer, and contemplation, about which we will reflect in the second part of this chapter and in the second part of this book, is another. Human beings in the world, therefore, as described, reflected upon, interpreted, and criticized, are active-receptive on many, indeed on all, levels of their being. Bad or inadequate phenomenology or existentialism reduces such dialectical reciprocity to an either-or dichotomy.[1]

Description

Freedom and Receptivity

I take it as established, therefore, in this work and in prior works, that freedom is receptively active and that it can be receptively open to its human and natural other in a fruitful way. In this section, drawing heavily on Marcel as well as my own prior work, I move from the fact of this dialectical interplay to a further development of its content and to the implications of this for the relationship to God. If freedom is basically receptive and active, open to its natural and human other, then is God compatible with and relevant to such freedom? Freedom is incompatible with receptivity if receptivity is conceived materialistically—to be receptive is to be like a piece of wax receiving a seal. Receptivity in this erroneous sense is a purely passive sensible suffering, whereas activity is a totally spontaneous, constructive movement of the spirit. Activity and passivity are disjoined in an either-or manner.

True receptivity is something else entirely. One illuminating example of it is hospitality, receiving somebody into one's home. Here there is an element of creation in that the host makes the person feel at home by creating a warm, congenial atmosphere. To receive in this sense is not to passively undergo or suffer; here the false disjunction between activity and passivity is overcome. True receptivity is creative in that it is an opening of oneself to the other, a presence to the other, a gift of oneself. Even on the very lowest level of sensation, this active quality is present. Since the coherence of a fact is conferred on it by the understanding self, there is no strictly external, objective fact.[2]

To perceive a table in a room, for instance, is to actively make that the figure or theme of my attention. I can attend to something else, a book, a person or the landscape outside my window. In that case what was formerly figure slides into the background and a new figure emerges. This is a meaningful gestalt, actively understood and interpreted. What I perceive is not simply a mass of disconnected sensations, but a meaningful unity, a "book" or a "person." Such active interpretation, however, is not creation. When I look at the table, its color or shape or size is experienced as there independent of me. It is not due to me that the table is a table, black, rectangular, and so on. Meaning is discovered and actively revealed by perception, not created.

The deepest need of human beings is to be receptive in this sense. Beyond the lowest level of perception or feeling, however, this need can be either ignored or fulfilled. When a person chooses to be receptive, disposability (*disponibilité*) is present. To be disposable is to be open to what is deepest and most unique in the other: nature, art, people, God. When I meet a person on a train, for instance, he is at first a "her" or "him," someone in the third person. We talk about the weather, the war, the economy, but I feel as though I am filling out a questionnaire. However it can happen that the walls break down, we discover an experience we have both shared, and a unity is established between the other person and me. The other person ceases to be "her" or "him," and becomes "thou." The disposable person is one who is continually, actively open to the possibility of such a relationship.[3]

When such an encounter occurs, the other person helps me to discover myself; my defenses and the other's break down. I communicate effectively with myself only insofar as I communicate with the other. Marcel in this context refers to one of his plays, *Quartet in F Sharp*. In this play, Clair is married to Roger, her second husband and the brother of Stephane, whom she had divorced because he was unfaithful. Through her husband, Clair is led to ask herself whether it was not her first husband whom she still loved. Thus Clair, through the loving honesty of her husband, understands herself better and becomes freer. She realizes her freedom, not in spite of the other, but through the other:

> However, it may also turn out that submerging oneself suddenly in the life of another person and being forced to see things through his eyes, is the only way of eliminating the self-obsession from which one has sought to free oneself.[4]

Such openness to the other is not abject capitulation; to see it as such is to confuse coercion and appeal. I do not resign myself into the hands of the other as a slave, nor does the other coerce me into a course of action. Rather through her or his eyes, I am able to see possibilities in myself and my situation that I would not have seen otherwise. In dialogue with me the other person helps me to articulate and choose these possibilities. One's stance toward me is that of appeal—she or he offers me a point of view that I can accept or reject.[5]

The stance of disposability, however, is not inevitable or necessary; I can be so encumbered with myself that I am not open to the other—I am indisposable. Such indisposability seems to be rooted in the attitude of having, because I consider myself and everything around me as a possession that I am afraid of losing. I am basically in competition with other human beings. If he or she has more, then I have less, and vice versa. I construe my life as something quantifiable, like a sum of money that I might lose. Capitalism is not only socially unjust, but also degrades our life with others; "having" is rooted in capitalism.[6]

In such an unjust society, disposability toward the other takes the form of an openness to the other, a willingness to hear the other's voice, a responsibility to and for the other. Such disposability can take the form either of receptivity toward somebody who, like me, is within our socio-economic system, well fed, well educated, well taken care of, relatively well off. Or disposability can take the form of an ethical responsibility to and for the sake of the exploited, marginalized, excluded other: black, laboring, feminine, gay, lesbian, poor, homeless, hungry. In a structurally unjust society, as capitalism is, both forms of disposability are essential for an adequate human, ethical, metaphysical, religious stance.

Self-preoccupation, however, makes it impossible for me to properly sympathize with the victim of injustice or tragedy. The person appeals to my sympathy, but I am unable to offer any but the usual stock replies, formulas that sound as though they are being read out of a catalogue. I am so preoccupied with myself that I am unable to be present to the other person.[7]

Another example of the indisposable person is the poser, the person whose attention to others is motivated by a desire for their good opinion. Self-preoccupation here takes the form of playing to the gallery, of not being open to the other person for his or her own sake, but only insofar as he or she thinks well of oneself. What posers want from others is their favorable opinion of themselves, because their ego is something they have. They are, therefore, continually on the lookout for anything that would threaten it or enhance it. By themselves, they are nothing; only through the good opinion of others are they something.[8]

Such relationship to others always involves manipulating them to obtain a desired effect. On the other hand, a person with genuine disposability treats others as an end in themselves. Disposability is essentially connected with admiration. I meet a person, I grow to know her or him. I come to love and admire her or him. Such admiration tears me away from myself and yet restores me to myself. When I go to the symphony and hear Stravinsky's *Rite of Spring*, I am deeply moved. My mind and feelings are ecstatically outside myself and focused on the work—its beauty, its complexity, its strange, unusual rhythms. I respond to the work with gratitude and praise, and exalt in the fact that such a work and such a composer exist.[9]

Here we are a long way from the either-or dilemmas of Nietzsche and Sartre. Here the self is not degraded but rather fulfilled by admiration:

To affirm: admiration is a humiliating state, is the same as to treat the subject as a power existing for itself and taking itself as a center. To proclaim on the other hand, that it is an exalted state is to start from the inverse notion that the proper function of the subject is to emerge from itself and realize itself primarily in the gift of oneself and in the various forms of creativity.[10]

Self-love and love of the other are, therefore, inseparable. To properly love oneself is to continually transcend oneself. Such transcendence is not a denial of limits and of the necessity of being incarnate in a situation, but it never settles down and remains satisfied with any particular work or achievement. The form that such self-transcendence takes is *creative fidelity*. Here we again relate two apparently contradictory notions. Is not creativity production and, therefore, the opposite of any conformity to values received from without? Certainly this is the way Nietzsche understood it. The overman is the one who obeys only himself, not a moral law imposed by God.[11]

My reply is that such opposition between heteronomy and autonomy is false. That which is essential to all creation, even artistic creation, is a placing oneself at the disposal of something outside oneself, something that in one sense depends upon the other for its existence, but which in another sense transcends the other. To create is to *respond to*; it will seem to the artist that sometimes he or she invents, sometimes discovers. There is no clear line of demarcation between the two. Cézanne in developing his new sense of space, Matisse in his fauvist conception of color, and Picasso in cubist distortions of the object all are faithful to certain visions of the world and of painting. Here is the way we really see the world—here is what painting should really be. Artists are continually nourished by the world and by the very things they are trying to create.[12]

Even the most abstract of painters utilizes shapes, colors, and lines drawn from the external world. Even the most creative and independent of artists is influenced by other artists and other styles. Picasso's cubism is a discovery born out of his own creative response to the world and the influence of Monet and Cézanne. Because of such receptivity to the world, Picasso's *Portrait of Ambroise Vollard* seems to reveal the personality of the subject, as much or more than a more "realistic" portrait.

Creativity and fidelity are thus inseparable. Fidelity is the opposite of inert conformism, because there is the continual effort to free oneself from dead habit and routine, and to be present to the world in a fresh and responsive manner. Fidelity is inseparable from recollection, a detachment from superficial aspects and concerns, and presence to what is deepest in oneself and the world. To respond fully to a painting, a piece of music, or another person, such recollection is demanded. Otherwise human beings remain imprisoned in the "interesting"; they are like tourists who pass through a city, see all there is to see in a few hours or a few days, and then move on.

This attitude, rooted in the commodification and reification proper to capitalism in which I am tempted to identify with what I am superficially, contrasts with the recollected contemplative presence and appreciation of a person who has lived in the city for many years. Such recollection is paradoxical in that persons enter into their own depths in order to get out of themselves.[13]

Not all human beings have the talent and inclination to be artists, but all do have a vocation to be themselves, to be persons. Being a person, however, is both to accept oneself and to create oneself. A person has a certain temperament, definite inclinations, specific talents. It is up to him or her to discover what these are and not to betray them. To discover what they are is to discover what they can be, and what they can be in the most profound sense is a presence and gift to the world. Such presence and such giving are creative and the opposite of any complacency, because complacency implies a subtle degradation to the realm of having. The self is regarded as a thing, with a definite set of properties, possessions, and achievements to its credit. Actually, however, the self is a gift, a seed to be cultivated, not a possession to be locked up and guarded. Being a person, in the authentic sense, is creatively to respond to a call.[14]

Because such is the case, at a certain level of existence the opposition between heteronomy and autonomy no longer applies. In the realm of having, autonomy means "I want to run my own life." I treat my life and that of others as something to be administered, over which I exercise control. Here there is opposition between heteronomy and autonomy. In the realm of being, however, the inexhaustible concrete that cannot be adequately described or understood by objective scientific thought or common sense, such oppositions disappear. The more I enter into an activity with the whole of myself, the less legitimate it is to say I am autonomous in the strict sense, because I am responding to an appeal from outside myself. Thus, the philosopher is less autonomous than the scientist and the scientist less autonomous than the technician. Such nonautonomy, however, is not heteronomy either; where the self is degraded or alienated, but freedom in the highest sense of the word: a noncoerced response and commitment to being, proceeding out of one's deepest self.[15]

Such is the freedom of the philosopher. Marcel describes philosophy as secondary reflection on mystery. Secondary reflection binds together opposites, such as self and other, activity and passivity, creativity and fidelity, which abstract, primary reflection has split asunder. A mystery is that in which I find myself involved, whose essence is not to be completely before me. A mystery is not a problem in which the pertinent data are external to the enquirer. Scientific research is concerned with problems—scientists in dealing with the meaning of a free fall prescind from their own subjectivity and attend only to what can be verified in the objective data. In a mystery, however, the distinction between what is in me and what is before me loses its meaning. To think philosophically about the question of freedom, for instance, or the mystery of evil involves reflection on my own experience of freedom or evil. Also a mystery, as opposed to a problem, is not solved once and for all, because a mystery is inexhaustible.[16]

To reflect on mystery implies a certain capacity and attitude on the part of the philosopher. Just as there can be no authentic music where there is no ear for hearing, so also there can be no philosophy worthy of the name without a certain "ear" for experience. This sensitivity takes the form of a "wonder that tends to become a disquiet." A person with a philosophical mind will not simply accept the fact that reality appears meaningful in an ordered succession of moments. They will ask themselves whether this order is not a form of appearance for something that could appear quite otherwise.[17]

The stance of the philosopher, therefore, is that of the questioning explorer who is continually restricting the scope of what is taken for granted. The explorer is like the child in that there is this impatient curiosity where discovery is sought for its own sake. Only as long as this wondering, questioning stance persists is a person a philosopher in any genuine sense:

> Whoever philosophizes *hic et nunc*, is, it may be said, a prey of reality: he will never become completely accustomed to the fact of existing; existence is inseparable from a certain astonishment.[18]

Philosophy, therefore, is a reflective form of creative fidelity, a disciplined listening to being. That admiration, essential to disposability, takes, for the philosopher, the form of wonder.

Nor do philosophers think for themselves alone. Their vocation is to recall human beings to a sense of themselves as persons and to an awareness of being, a sense that is continually in danger of being betrayed and lost. In modern technological society, the human being is a function, a worker, producer, or consumer existing only as a means to the gross national product. Nature is a system of objects to be dominated and exploited for the sake of profit. Because modern life is progressively impoverished, the task of the philosopher is to recall human beings to a sense of the sacred in themselves and the world.[19]

There is thus a continuity in me between my most basic level of perception or feeling and my highest, most creative activities. Even on the very lowest level of perception, activity is present in that I open myself to the world, interpret it, and attend to this or that aspect of it. Even on the very highest creative levels, a receptivity is present that should be acknowledged. Thus, although "receptivity" has a wide range of possible meanings, from perceptual openness to the gift of self, it is never purely passive. Freedom is authentic when I respect and live according to this basic receptivity in myself—freedom is disposability or creative fidelity.[20]

Receptivity and God

Creative fidelity to another person is the model according to which we conceive the God-human relationship. Faith is fidelity, and faith in God is fidelity to an absolute "thou." Just as a finite person is not adequately known when he or she is treated as a "he" or "she," so God is debased when treated as a cause with a set of objective attributes. Because God is not a cause moving human freedom from without, but rather a person appealing to human freedom, finite human freedom is compatible with God's existence.[21]

God is relevant to human freedom as well, because I experience myself as an exigence for transcendence, for the answer to the question "What am I?" If I am a member of a political party or any other organization, I become aware of the fact that the party cannot answer the question. To resign my fate into the hands of the party, a group of persons neither infallible nor omniscient, is the height of irresponsibility. Nor can another human person give me the ultimate answer; how should I ascribe to the other person a privilege I deny myself. Moreover, it is I who confer on the other this property of revealing me to myself; I judge the competence of the judge. At this point the question changes into an appeal to someone who knows me and evaluates me, someone within me more intimate to me than I am to myself. Just as in the "we" relationship between two human beings, the either-or dichotomy between myself and God is overcome.[22]

My own freedom is experienced and known as a gift from God, and God is present as a person who wants me to be free. God is inviting me and appealing to me to be free and to accept my freedom as a gift from God. To reject God is to use this very gift of freedom to betray God and thus myself, to shut myself off from God and become radically indisposable.[23]

How do we know all this? Where is the evidence for such claims? Prayer is one crucial datum for the philosopher of religion, because in prayer the human being experiences the presence of God. Openness to God in unrestricted questioning is another. Careful phenomenological reflection on religious experience is thus the source of our claims about the God-human relationship. In such experiences, we see the final flowering of that wondering, admiring, open disposability already discussed—to question, to understand and affirm God, to commit myself lovingly to God, and to pray is to admire and say yes to God with an attitude of adoration. The whole of the spiritual life may be thought of as "the sum of activities by which we try to reduce in ourselves the part played by nondisposability."[24]

Such humility is not humiliation, any more than admiration is a humiliating state. What the believer feels is a deep need for dedication to God, and such a gift of self is ultimate fulfillment. Such consecration is not experienced as something external to self or imposed on the self, as Sartre thinks. Freedom is the capacity to be disposable, and the most consecrated people are the most disposable, the most free. The spirit of prayer might be negatively defined as the rejection of a temptation of being shut in on oneself in pride or despair. Positively it is a receptive disposition toward everything that detaches a person from self and from blindness to personal failings.[25]

Such a consecration to God helps to ground fidelity to another finite person. For without such a ground, finite fidelity seems very tenuous indeed. To marry someone, for instance, is to promise that I will always love her and be committed to her. Yet is this promise not presumptuous, given my changeable emotional state? How do I know I will not be disappointed in her to the extent that she seems not to be the person I married? However, the more my consciousness is settled on God, the less conceivable such disappointment will be. If it does occur, it will only be an indication of my own inadequacy. Hence a fidelity that seems precarious when it is centered only on another human being becomes unshakable when it is centered on God. I do not count on myself and my own limited resources, but on God.[26]

Creative fidelity, as I will show more fully in Part Two, is inseparable, therefore, from hope, a hope unconditionally centered on God. An invalid who says to himself, "Everything is lost if I do not get well," has a conditional hope. If the requisite conditions are not fulfilled, despair is the result. To believe and hope in God, however, is to lay down no conditions. Even if the invalid does not get well, he can still hope for the strength and encouragement to live a useful, productive life:

> We can, on the other hand, conceive, at least theoretically, of the inner disposition of one who, setting no condition or limit and abandoning himself in absolute confidence, would thus transcend all possible disappointment and would experience a security of his being, or in his being, which is contrary to the radical insecurity of *Having*.[27]

Such absolute hope, then, seems necessary if the drive toward disposability and creative fidelity is not to wither and die. Such is the hope of patriots who refuse to despair of the liberation of their native land. They refuse to admit that the darkness that has fallen on their country is definitive or final; such an admission would seem to them a betrayal. It is not that they cannot believe in the death of their country, but rather that they do not consider themselves to have the right to believe it. To despair is to be disloyal; to hope, on the other hand, helps create the conditions for the eventual liberation of the country. To hope is to be creatively faithful. When patriots hope, they strengthen a certain bond relating them to the matter in question, a bond that seems religious in essence.[28]

Yet, a critical reader might ask, how do I know that there is a God in whom to hope? How do I know that faith in God is not just a subjective sentiment, with no objective referent? When I make the appeal to an absolute person in order to answer the question "What am I?," how do I know there is someone there?

Marcel's answer to this question, which arises again and again in his works, is threefold. First of all, a careful phenomenology of religious experience indicates that it is intentional, that the consciousness of believers is centered on that which is not themselves. To talk about belief in God as a mere subjective sentiment is, therefore, to give a distorted description of that experience. Believers experience prayer as a relation to a transcendent mystery not reducible to their own subjective states. I will develop this point more in Part Two.[29]

Maybe, however, believers are deluded. Perhaps even though their experience is not purely subjective, that experience itself is misleading, because there is no objective evidence for the existence of God. At this point, Marcel's second reply is that any demand for such evidence is to turn a mystery into a problem and thus to make a "category mistake." The demand for empirical evidence is inappropriate in the realm of mystery. The transcendent is by definition "metaproblematic," beyond the realm of possible experience and, therefore, not subject to empirical verification. Just as the experience of the body or of freedom should not be reduced to a problem, neither should the belief in God.[30]

One might still want to object that surely empirical evidence of the sort that science gives is not the only kind of evidence. Marcel through secondary reflection on mystery gives all sorts of evidence to support his claims about freedom, intersubjectivity, and disposability. Might there not be a similar kind of evidence for the existence of God? Is there not, for instance, the possibility of a nonproblematic, metaphysical proof for the existence of God?

Marcel, while not ruling out such a possibility, suggests that such a proof presupposes a prior openness to the possibility of God's existence. One can prove the existence of God to a person only if he or she wants to go in that direction. Without such openness, proof is unpersuasive and with such openness, it is not strictly necessary. Not only can proof not be substituted for belief, but proof presupposes belief, the prior affirmation of a whole set of spiritual values. It is the presence or lack of this prior openness or disposability that is the real issue.

As my prior chapters indicate, I am in agreement with Marcel's claims up to a point; proofs for the existence of God mean nothing without a prior openness and context. Nonetheless, with such conditions present, evidential, metaphysical affirmation of God makes a difference. I am certain in a way that I was not before and drawing on sources of evidence that I did not have before, that God exists; such certainty is in the mode of an analytic principle. God's existence cannot be denied without logical and self-contradiction.[31]

Conclusion

The practical question about God's relation to human freedom is the issue between Nietzsche and Sartre, on the one hand, and myself, on the other. God is compatible with human freedom, for me, because God is conceived as an absolute "thou," not an objective cause, and because human freedom is essentially disposability, open and receptive to the other. God is relevant to human freedom because God is more intimate to me than I am to myself, because God can reveal to me possibilities about myself and the world that I can then accept or reject. If the other is essential for self-knowledge in the finite sphere, then the absolute other is essential for the deepest self-knowledge. Also, God is essential as the ground of that hope without which creative fidelity would die.

The most fundamental question, therefore, of the atheism-theism debate is the nature of freedom. If freedom is conceived in an "either-or" manner as totally subjective, independent, and closed in upon itself, then there is an essential antagonism between human beings and God. If freedom is conceived in a "both-and" fashion as both independent and dependent, active and receptive, personally responsible and yet open to the other, then there is not antagonism, but rather fruitful interaction. Such free relating to God and others on the fourth level does not deny cognition, but does sublate it. Falling in love with God in a spirit of disposability, creative fidelity, and adoration is both where such cognition begins, at least in the sense of an openness to go where a reverant, respectful, receptive questioning leads, and where such cognition leads.[32]

SIX

తుసిఖ

Toward a Speculative-Political Metaphysics

At this point I am ready to conclude Part One of this book devoted to a phenomenological, metaphysical, and political approach to being and God. In the first four chapters, as is appropriate, my approach was primarily cognitive; in the last chapter I moved into reflecting on the fourth level of freedom in relationship to God. All the way through Part One I have been reflecting on the political aspects and implications of metaphysics. Now I am ready to draw these reflections together in a more unified, organized way by first reflecting on the interplay between Whitehead and Marx, and then moving to a descriptive articulation of metaphysics.

In this chapter I extend freedom into the political realm, but not in such a way as to leave the cognitive or volitional relationship to being and God behind. Rather speculative-political metaphysics sublates these ideas and realities, and incorporates them into a larger whole and in doing so brings out the political character of metaphysics, implicitly present but often unthematized in philosophy so as to give the impression that "real metaphysics" or "real philosophy" is apolitical and does not dirty its hands with issues of alienation, social injustice, and praxis. The ideological implications of such a stance are obvious. So-called "real metaphysics" can leave an unjust social order uncriticized, and so indirectly and implicitly justify that social order. As nonengaged, apolitical metaphysician, I can withdraw from the messy world of praxis and move into my own speculative world of contemplative bliss. Such contemplation, which may have some validity depending on what is contemplated, what is experienced, understood, and affirmed, is nonetheless one-sided in relation to a more adequate model of contemplative speculation that leads into critique and praxis, grounds them, points toward them, and is complemented by them.

As a result of what we do in this chapter, we are better prepared to undertake Part Two of our endeavor, which will affirm the unity of a contemplative and political approach to God and Christ. Jesus Christ, liberator, emerges as the most adequate interpretation of Christianity in the late twentieth and early twenty-first century. The transition is not from a purely apolitical metaphysics to a socially and politically liberatory religious belief and practice, but from a speculative-political metaphysics to a contemplative-practical Christian faith and practice.

I need to say a few words about my use of Whitehead and Marx in relation to my own systematic theory. That relationship is one of influence, sublation, and expansion. Influence occurs insofar as Whitehead and Marx fundamentally affect and determine my own thought; no thought is completely original. Sublation occurs insofar as Whiteheadian and Marxian insights are incorporated into my own theory. Expansion occurs insofar as such thinkers contribute to a widening of purview and scope, the expansion of metaphysics into a more fully adequate processive account of being and God in the case of Whitehead, and the expansion of phenomenology and hermeneutics into radical social theory in the case of Marx.

With regard to Marx, this triple relationship of influence, sublation, and expansion has already significantly occurred in PCM and CAL.[1] What remains in Part Two is, using Marx and other sources, to expand my interpretation and critique of capitalism into a theory of neoimperialism and liberation in the center of the empire, the North. With regard to Whitehead some influence, sublation, and expansion has occurred, for example, my discussion in earlier chapters of being and God as relational and processive, but more needs to take place in this chapter. In this chapter, therefore, more than with Marx, there is the introduction, development, and incorporation of insights from Whitehead hitherto not articulated or articulated inadequately.

My encounter with Whitehead, therefore, in this chapter has five aspects. First, I use concepts developed by him that are basically synonymous with or overlap with concepts already developed by me. "Occasion" or "event," for example, are basically synonymous with "operation" on the conjugate level, and "eternal object" with "form" on the level of understanding. Second, I use terms that refer to realities already affirmed by me but bring out aspects of these hitherto not discussed or adverted to; thus "prehension" and "feeling" refer to the relational aspects of conjugate acts; and "concrescence" refers to the terminal phase of a process of becoming. Third, in the last, descriptive part of my essay I will reflect on Whitehead's troublesome "atomism," and rejection of substance and substantial self in relation to my own theory. Fourth, I will show how Whitehead's metaphysics requires a radical social theory rooted in and deriving its basic inspiration from Marx. Fifth, I will show how a radical social theory needs a process metaphysics initially developed in earlier chapters and filled out in this chapter.

A person might wonder about the relevance of comparing Whitehead and Marx. Are they not so dissimilar as to make any comparison simply a pedantic exercise of interest only to scholars? A first way of countering such an objection is to note that Ernst Bloch, a very important thinker within the Marxist tradition, grounded his social theory in a process metaphysics. A second reply is to note that some scholars have already discussed the way in which Whitehead can illumine and overcome some difficulties within Marxist theory. A third answer is to suggest that on the current philosophical scene there is already too much isolation, and that, therefore, a reflection on affinities between two major philosophical options can be beneficial. This is what the first part of our dialectical section will address. A fourth answer to the objection of irrelevance is that, as I will show in the second part of our dialectical section, the two thinkers can mutually fructify each other. As our essay progresses through dialectics, description, and conclusion, where we discuss the possibility of a political metaphysics, the ideas of Whitehead and Marx progessively gear into one another and become internal to one another.[2]

Dialectical Considerations

Process in Whitehead and Marx

The central controlling category of our analysis in this part of the chapter is that of process—both Whitehead and Marx are process thinkers. One operates on the level of metaphysics, the other on the level of social theory. For Whitehead, the world is a developing, dynamic world in which objective actual entities are continually absorbed in the histories of new actual entities creating themselves. Even God is not immune from this process of self-creation, for God's consequent nature is a result of the interaction of Godself and the world.[3]

For Marx, history is a decisive category, because there is development, change, revolution. In *The German Ideology*, he describes Western history as a movement from the ancient, communal era through the Greeks and feudalism to modern industrial capitalism. In the *Grundrisse*, he has a threefold scheme of historical development. Prior to capitalism human beings were immediately related to the earth and to each other and use-value, a good satisfying a real, concrete, human need, was more important than exchange-value, the value of the product as measured in money. When capitalism emerges, it ruptures this immediate unity. Exchange-value begins to dominate over use-value. Even though a development in productive forces and in self-consciousness occurs, men and women are separated from themselves and from the earth. Communism, full economic, social, and political democracy, will be and should be a third stage in human history, in which use-value again reigns over exchange-value. Also, human community emerges once again, and capitalism's genuine gains in productivity and consciousness are integrated within a nonalienated social context.[4]

Exploring this central notion of process more fully, we see further that for Whitehead and Marx it involves a unity of individual and universal, private and public. For Whitehead, the process of a new concrescence starts with the prehension of a complex network of actual entities standing in various forms of natural and social relation to each other in the real, public world. Conversely, the process terminates in the private, individual satisfaction of the new actual occasion. All origination of feeling is private, but what is private pervades and expresses itself in the public world. "The theory of prehensions is founded upon the doctrine that there are no concrete facts which are merely public, or merely private."[5]

Similarly Marx rejects an isolated interiority cut off from the world and argues that true interiority is essentially social. The language that I use, the motivations that drive me, and the goals that I pursue, even when I am performing a private activity, are fundamentally social. "But also when I am active scientifically, etc.—when I am engaged in activity which I can seldom perform in direct community with others—then I am social, because I am active as a man."[6]

For both thinkers, a concern for freedom rides in tandem with an affirmation of individuality. In Whitehead, it is the individual satisfaction of the individual actual entity that is the goal of the process of that entity—its "subjective aim." In Marx, the goal of history is a "rich, many-sided individuality" that should and would emerge in a postcapitalist, communist society. Both thinkers reject a false individualism cut off from the public and the social. Whitehead renounces the one-sided "subjectivist principle," which denies an internal relation of the individual to society, in favor of a "reformed subjectivist principle" that affirms such dependence. Marx rejects a bourgeois individualism that denies internal, social dependence for a postbourgeois individuality, in which the individual flowers in a context of genuine community.[7]

Both philosophies are philosophies of freedom. Whitehead's individual actual occasion is one that freely determines itself and creates something new. The goal of this process is the free emergence of each individual actual occasion as a free response to the world and God. Marx's postbourgeois individual is one who is able to develop freely in a community of ends, relating to others as ends in themselves in a nonexploitive economic and political context. Both Whitehead and Marx, however, reject a freedom that is total, unin-fluenced and unlimited by the environment. Respectively, they tell us that "it is to be noticed that 'decided' conditions are never such as to banish freedom. They only qualify it." "Men make their own history, but they do not make it just as they please; they do not make it under circumstances chosen by them-selves but under circumstances directly encountered, given, and transmitted from the past."[8]

Because freedom is essentially influenced by the environment, freedom is also essentially motivated. Process for Whitehead moves from many to one, from prehension of a multiplicity of past objectifications and future possibil-ities to one definite decision. Out of many possible sites for a vacation, I choose one; out of many possible women to marry, I decide on one. Similarly for Marx the decision of workers to revolt is based upon real motivations aris-ing from their real situation, in which they are alienated from the object pro-duced, the act of production, species life, and other men. Very low wages, unenjoyable work, bad working conditions, and an antagonistic relationship to employers all contribute to workers' awareness of being unhappy, split off from themselves, at odds with themselves.[9]

Despite the causal influence of the environment, Whitehead and Marx are both philosophers of creativity: "the universe is thus a creative advance into novelty."[10] For Whitehead, this novelty of an actual occasion resides in its prehensions of its past actual world, its subjective form, subjective aim, and its satisfaction. Even though they may have some data in common, no two actual occasions have exactly the same data of feeling. The subjective form of feeling is also different. Even when two actual occasions prehend data that are similar, the ways they prehend those data are different; Einstein and Rem-brandt will relate to the same sunset very differently. Two occasions will dif-fer also in their subjective aims; knowing the sunset scientifically is different from painting. Finally, the attainment of the subjective aim is novel. The structural relationship among the prehended data, the subjective form, and the attainment of the subjective aim constitutes the individuality of the actual occasion.[11]

The function of reason for Whitehead is to promote the art of life, to help each individual actual occasion and the totality of actual occasions reach the maximum possible satisfaction. To promote the art of life is to promote a threefold urge: (1) to live, (2) to live well, (3) to live better. The art of life is first to be alive, second to be alive in a satisfactory way, and third to require an increase in satisfaction. The primary function of reason is, therefore, to direct an approach to the physical and social environment. The life of reason, therefore, essentially contributes to and is part of a praxis, the art of life. Even speculative reason is oriented to criticizing, elaborating, and distinguishing the goals of life, in order that human beings may live well and live better.[12]

For Marx as well, men and women create themselves through praxis. Rather than conforming to a static, preexisting essence, human beings create their essence through interacting in the world. Labor as one form of praxis acts on a material cause, materials of production, to incarnate in that material a structure, a formal cause, in order to produce a final result, envisaged as a final cause. For example, workers in an automobile factory will work with steel to produce an automobile of a certain make and design, a two-door sedan or a sports car or a large, four-door luxury model.

In such labor, workers create not only objects, but also themselves as producers and consumers. As capitalism develops, the needs of production and consumption require an expansion of existing consumption, creation of new needs by propagating existing ones in a wider circle, and production of new needs and creation of new use-values. The result is the cultivation of all the qualities of a social human being as rich as possible in needs "for, in order to take gratification in a many-sided way, he must be capable of many pleasures [*genußfähig*], hence, cultured to a high degree."[13]

Both Whitehead and Marx are nonreductively "materialist" in the sense of insisting on the importance of the embodiment or incarnation. For Whitehead, it is personal embodiment that allows us to experience most adequately the dependence of presentational immediacy on causal efficacy in relating to the world. Contrary to Hume, I can say "the flash made me blink," because I feel such efficacy in my body. Perception is not confined to presentational immediacy. For Marx as well, human beings are natural beings, incarnate, in the world. For this reason, work as a form of expressing and realizing one's incarnate self in the world is all-important for Marx. For this reason also, the quality of the relationship between man and woman is a crucial determinant of how advanced the civilization is:

> In this relationship, therefore, is *sensuously manifested*, reduced to an observable *fact*, the extent to which the human essence has become nature to man, or to which nature to him has become the human essence of man. From this relationship one can therefore judge man's whole level of development . . . the relation of man to woman is *the most natural* relation of human being to human being.[14]

In both thinkers, objectification is essential to process. For Whitehead, as Christian puts it, "Objectification is the way an actual occasion transcends itself . . . and enters the experience of other occasions."[15] Once an actual entity moves to a definite, determinate satisfaction, it becomes objective, public fact, and can enter as a datum into the concrescence of other actual entities. When something happens to you and makes you feel angry, I can relate to your anger as a datum and respond in a certain way—indifferently, critically, or sympathetically. Your anger becomes an essential part of my experience, and I take it up into my own in a certain way, with a certain subjective form. If, therefore, Whitehead's doctrines of individuality and creativity help to account for the social transcendence of one occasion over another, his doctrine of objectification helps to account for the social continuity between one occasion and another.

For Marx as well, objectification is fundamental to the process of self-creation. As we have already seen, essential to labor as one kind of praxis is the public externalizing of an idea in the mind of the worker. Ideally, when labor is not alienated, there is continuity and unity among the causes involved in objectification—formal, material, efficient, final, instrumental. In capitalism, however, these causes are split off from one another, internal from external, efficient from final, formal from instrumental. Work, rather than being an expression of workers in which they discover themselves and grow, becomes mindless and trivial. In the name of efficiency oriented to profit, the mind of the work is transferred to the capitalist manager or machine.

Rather than the machine being an instrument of workers, which they use to express themselves, workers become appendages to the machine. That which should be the means becomes the end, and the end becomes the means. Individual and collective enjoyment of work and self-discovery in work is subordinated to efficiency and profit. Capitalism for Marx is an absurd, upside-down world in which the less important takes precedence over the more important, the means over the end, the lowest over the highest. For these reasons, there is all the difference in the world between legitimate objectification, essential for the self-realization of human beings, and alienation, present in irrational societies such as those that are capitalist. A confusion between objectification and alienation occurs not only in Hegel, but also in some contemporary versions of existentialism and phenomenology.[16]

Because both Whitehead and Marx affirm a purposive, forward movement in process and history, human life for them is value-laden—the aesthetic is an essential category for both thinkers. For Whitehead the whole point of a process of concrescence is the final felt satisfaction attained by the actual entity and, through it, by God. There is no prehension of the world as devoid of values, and that an idea be interesting, is more important than it be true. In the supplemental stage of a concrescence, which intervenes between the initial responsive stage and that of its satisfaction, there is an ineluctable aesthetic dimension. "The second stage is governed by the private ideal, gradually shaped in the process itself; whereby the many feelings derivatively felt as alien, are transformed into a unity of aesthetic appreciation immediately felt as private."[17]

For Marx as well, the aesthetic is fundamental to an integrated, non-alienated social existence. Because of the alienation endemic to capitalist society, however, such a satisfactory aesthetic relationship of human beings to the world is often not forthcoming. The senses caught up in crude, practical needs have only a restricted scope. For example, such a person is interested only in the content, not the form of food—the way it is cooked, the way it is served. A dealer in minerals can be so preoccupied with profit that he can see only their financial value—not their beauty. Because labor is alienated, the human senses and mind are not educated to appreciate the world aesthetically, noninstrumentally. A crude human ear not educated to appreciate music will not appreciate Bach or Stravinksy or Bartok; a crude human eye not educated in painting will be bored by a Picasso, a Renoir, or a Kandinsky. Such crudity is grounded in the capitalist equation of being with having. "Private property has made us so stupid and one-sided that an object is only *ours* when we have it—when it exists for us as capital, or when it is directly possessed, eaten, drunk, worn, inhabited, etc.—in short, when it is used by us."[18]

Marx argues for communism as a negation of capitalist private property and, therefore, the overcoming of the antithesis of mind and body, spiritualism and materialism, subjectivism and objectivism. If private property grounds the crude, utilitarian approach to nature and other persons, communism grounds an aesthetic, noninstrumental appreciative response. In communism, the opposition between a sophistication of needs on the one hand, confined to those who have money, and a bestial barbarization on the other, present in most of the population who do not have money, would cease. Money would not be the primary determinant of success and value. Rather, political power would go hand in hand with a political savoir faire, aesthetic education with talent and sensitivity, and so on.[19]

For Whitehead and Marx internal relations are necessary to explain process and history. Whitehead affirms the principle of relativity, which denies the possibility of complete abstraction and complete transcendence. That is to say, as noted above, no entity exists or can be considered in complete isolation from all other entities. Accordingly, philosophy is a reflection on the modes of togetherness of actual entities. The most fundamental mode is causal objectification, in which a past actual entity enters into the constitution of another actual entity in the process of becoming. If A prehends X, then X is in A objectively as a datum of physical feeling and effectively as internally affecting the constitution of A. A's experience is different from what it would have been without X. The prehension makes an essential difference to A in that A becomes specifically like X in some way. The subjective form of A relating to X conforms to the subjective form of X. I perceive the anger of X, or I allow myself to be influenced by one of X's ideas, or I delight in X's beauty.[20]

As Ollman has demonstrated, internal relations are basic to Marxist thought. Particular historical epochs are gestalts with internally related elements or aspects. In capitalism, for example, the concepts of capital and labor are not understandable without each other. Capital as self-augmenting value (value here is defined as the worth of a product measured in money and grounded in labor time) is impossible without the labor that is the source of that value. Similarly labor in this society could not be labor without the means of production, and instruments and materials of production supplied by capital. Labor and capital, then, are internally related parts of the social whole that is capitalism.[21]

Finally, Whitehead and Marx are both dialectical thinkers. Dialectic is understood here as a process in which opposites initially opposed to each other in thought or in reality come to be united with one another. Philosophy for Whitehead is a reflective overcoming of one-sidedness in which opposites which seem mutually inconsistent—such as discipline and freedom, permanence and flux, unity and multiplicity, order and novelty, God and the world—are seen to internally imply one another. Such a dialectical approach not only is theoretically more adequate than its contrary, but also has practical results. The difference between an approach to education that relates discipline to novelty and one that does not is striking in its effects upon teachers and students. Also, the difference between an artistic academicism present in nineteenth-century France and the revolt of Manet and Matisse, Cézanne and Picasso, who built upon the past but went beyond it as well, is significant.[22]

For Marx as well, dialectic is not only form but also content, not only method but also the way the world is. As I have already indicated, the movement from precapitalistic times through capitalism to communism is a movement from a one-sided immediacy through a one-sided mediation to a unity of mediation and immediacy. In this movement, opposites cut off from one another in capitalism, such as subject and object, individual and community, and mind and body, find a new unity in communism. Communism would retain capitalistic gains in productivity and self-consciousness but would reject the one-sided, alienated context in which those gains took place. Communism would represent a new, mediated immediacy in which human beings relate to one another in community, use-value is again preeminent over exchange-value, and human enjoyment in work is the goal of work.[23]

Complementarity between Whitehead and Marx

In this part of the dialectical section, I wish to look at some of the different ways in which the two thinkers complement each other. In general, the hypothesis I shall develop here is that Whitehead's is a metaphysics in search of an adequate social theory, and Marx's is a social theory in search of a metaphysics. Whitehead, then, metaphysically grounds Marx, and Marx completes and fills out Whitehead in the social arena. Whitehead's, then, is the general theory of which Marx would be a particular instance, and Marx saves White-head from becoming, after a certain point, a comforting, class-based ideology. Whitehead generalizes Marx, and Marx critically redeems Whitehead.

I propose to develop and validate in a partial, schematic way this hypothesis by looking at two ways in which Whitehead complements Marx metaphysically and two in which Marx complements Whitehead socially. First, on the issue of God, Whitehead would say that there is in Marx a false dichotomy between God and world, divine influence on the world and human freedom. Also if process, even in a historical, Marxist sense is going to occur, there has to be a God as the source of the initial possibility, as the source of order, because of God's prehending relevant possibilities, and as the ground of the givenness of the past.[24]

Such a God is, as I have already indicated, a processive God, not moving the world through domination or power, but through love. "God is the great companion—the fellow sufferer who understands."[25] Because God is processive, changeable, and dialogal, God is compatible, *contra* Marx,[26] with human freedom and creativity. The incompatibility between God and human freedom is perhaps true of the immutable, all-knowing God of classical Christian theism, but not of a processive God. Moreover, if Whitehead and I in chapters 3 and 4 are correct, such a God is not only compatible with human freedom and creativity, but essential for them. Also, with a processive God, human praxis is not a superfluous luxury for a God already complete and happy in Godself, but actually contributes to the building up of God.

The second way in which Whitehead complements Marx is by supplying an ontological ground for a critique of a one-dimensional, positivistic, technocratic society. As capitalism develops and matures, technology becomes essential for increased efficiency and profit, and moreover, moves into the social and political spheres in the form of advertising, state administration of the economy, and propaganda. Politics, rather than being a matter of dialogue between people and president, becomes a matter of "selling the president." Technology and science become the kinds of rationality most appropriate for twentieth-century industrial society in both West and East, reflecting that society and legitimizing it. If science is equated with rationality, however, then it becomes difficult to mount an ethical, political argument for transcending capitalism or state socialism. Democracy becomes whatever the current practice is, and justice essentially mirrors the status quo. If scientific description of fact exhausts the definition of rationality, then any argument for transcending the social status quo is irrational.[27]

Marx uses anthropological, moral constants, such as human beings as ends in themselves in a community of ends or the notion of justice implying equal access of all to the means of production.[28] But these remain undeveloped and are lost in the onslaught of positivism and positivistic Marxism in the early twentieth century. The triumph of positivism and the resulting under-mining of the very possibility of critical dialectic leads to a crisis of founda-tions in Marxism. To what criteria do we appeal in saying that we should tran-scend capitalism, and is such transcendence rational?[29]

Whitehead can strengthen the foundations for critique with his notion of the eternal object or universal ingressing into each actual occasion.[30] As a result, we do not adequately describe an occasion when we list simply its fac-tual, particular, empirical elements. The occasion is a union of particular and universal, normative and factual, possible and actual, ideal and real. The actual occasion points beyond itself to other possibly more adequate instanti-ations of the universal. If capitalist society approximates "justice" in some respects because of the legal, formal, democratic political equality enshrined in our institutions, it is possible that economic democracy, democratic owner-ship of the means of the production, would be a more adequate form of jus-tice. Capitalistic justice does not necessarily equal justice in the full sense. Whitehead thus enables us to ground a two-dimensional logic at odds with and able to criticize the one-dimensional logic of late capitalism or state socialism.

For Whitehead the organic level of being, which includes human beings, is basically creative of novelty, whereas the nonorganic or preorganic level is more repetitious and reproductive, only minimally creative of novelty. The human tendency is to create a surplus, which in capitalism takes the form of surplus value or surplus labor time appropriated by the capitalist. The human laborers, therefore, who merely receive wages necessary to reproduce their own labor power from week to week, necessary labor power, are reduced more and more to a level of inorganic life in contradiction to their nature as living, reflective, creative human beings. Capitalist appropriation of surplus labor time over and above necessary labor time for the benefit of the capital-ist is not only morally unjust but metaphysically offensive. The creative enjoyment of novelty, which should characterize the human race as a whole, is reserved for the capitalist few. The mass of humankind is reduced to a sub-human, preorganic, repetitive level manifesting itself in boring, mindless work, empty leisure, reduction of the worker to an appendage of the machine, unhealthy working conditions, technocratic homogeneity and suppression of quality, unemployment, poverty, homelessness, disease, and death. Capitalism as a reduction of living to dead labor, of the organic to the inorganic, is an economy, polity, and culture of death, phenomenologically dehumanizing, ethically wrong, and metaphysically offensive.[31]

In justifying such a critical function for metaphysics, I do not mean to imply that it is a substitute for a fully worked out ethics or social theory, only that it fruitfully complements and helps ground and complete such a theory. Indeed, Whitehead himself points out the necessity for metaphysical clarity in doing ethics when, in Part I of *Adventures of Ideas*, he analyzes several possible interpretations of Bentham's utilitarianism. Nor is it correct to suggest that, because metaphysics deals with universal and necessary concepts valid for all ages and epochs, such a metaphysics is necessarily irrelevant to contingent ethical and political issues involving human choice. For the point is that human beings can attempt to flee such necessities through their use of freedom. Even though, for example, human life is essentially social, I can attempt to flee that reality through belief in the "subjectivist principle" or "the bourgeois individual," isolated, independent, self-sufficient.

The falseness of such stances becomes evident when the free attempt to deny certain realities ends up affirming them. In this way the necessity of such realities emerges. A contradiction occurs between explicit claim and implicit performance. For example, the affirmation of the bourgeois individual, followed through to the end, implies an internal, essential, relationship to society. The capitalist entrepreneur is only possible because of a historical separation of labor from means of production, accumulation of means of production and money in the hands of the capitalist, and a group of laborers working for him to produce surplus value. Because the bourgeois entrepreneur is essentially related to society in these ways, the attempt to deny such a relationship is self-contradictory. Freedom and necessity here are not mutually exclusive, but rather require one another.[32]

Marx also complements Whitehead in at least two ways. First of all, Whitehead is correct in moving from the subjectivist principle to a reformed subjectivist principle. What Marx would insist on, further, is the socio-economic basis for such concepts. For him, the subjectivist principle ultimately derives from the bourgeois ego, operating in apparent independence and freedom from history and society, but actually profoundly dependent on such society and history. As I have just shown, capitalist entrepreneurs emerge from a social history and require labor to achieve their ends. Even though the total independence of individuals from society is illusory, nonetheless capitalist society systematically produces the appearance of this independence.[33]

A second way in which Marx complements Whitehead is by showing the socio-economic roots of the phenomena theoretically criticized by Whitehead, for example, the one-sided scientism and rejection of secondary qualities Whitehead criticizes as the "fallacy of misplaced concreteness."[34] If such scientism is, as I have already indicated, rooted in capitalism as a form of life, the theoretical critique of scientism must move to a practical critique of the society that brings it forth. We have to see the theoretical one-dimensionality so justly criticized by Whitehead as rooted in the lived, practical one-dimensionality of late capitalism.

Also, Whitehead is very critical of the way people are dehumanized in their work, private lives, and education.[35] If Whitehead is, as I have already suggested, a philosopher of freedom, then consistency and comprehensiveness demand that he be critical of the conditions that breed alienation or unfreedom. The question that Marx would ask Whitehead is whether freedom can be fully realized in a capitalist, class society, which Whitehead seems to endorse in books such as *The Aims of Education*. If there is a contradiction between Whitehead's affirmation of freedom and his acceptance of capitalism, then is there not a danger of his philosophy becoming, after a certain point, excessively contemplative, insufficiently related in a critical, practical manner to a status quo dedicated in principle to undermining Whitehead's ideals?

To develop this point a bit further, I see Whitehead arguing for education as a rhythmic process moving from romance through precision to generalization—education is education for freedom. We see him criticizing current educational practice for being too dedicated to precision and neglecting romance and generalization. What Marx would add is that such focus on precision is no accident. In a society dedicated to and built upon a stultifying division of labor oriented to profit, it is important that students become used to such division of labor and to unenjoyable work. In a society built upon class domination, it is essential that schools be places where students become accustomed to discipline, to hierarchy, to following orders, to being "good" and "obedient," to not thinking for themselves. In such a society, education is less for freedom than for conformity, less for generalizing and seeing the big picture than for keeping one's nose to the grindstone and not asking inconvenient, unpleasant, unsettling questions.

Finally, if science and technology are ideologies justifying and reflecting late capitalism, it is clear why this definition of reason begins to predominate in schools, not only in what is taught and emphasized—computer literacy as opposed to poetry, science as opposed to philosophy—but in the way decisions are made and students are evaluated. If technique, science and technology oriented to commodious living, is the common sense of the contemporary era, then the task of schools in a capitalist, class society is to reflect and legitimate that common sense. Too much Whiteheadian freedom is not good for the system.[36]

Description of a Speculative-Political Metaphysics

As we have seen, both Whitehead and Marx are philosophers of praxis. What emerges, then, as a possibility in reflecting on their similarities and differences is that of a political metaphysics. Such a metaphysics has several different aspects. First, it is a metaphysics of freedom, dedicated to the liberation of individuals and groups from unnecessary, repressive, social constraints.

Furthermore, such a metaphysics avoids both the extremes of a one-sided focus on practice to the exclusion of theory and a one-sided academic contemplation unrelated to political, social critique. There is a legitimate, contemplative moment in such a metaphysics, of knowledge for its own sake with as much speculative breadth and sweep as possible, but such contemplation is essentially related to and inclusive of praxis.

Such a metaphysics is critical of all theoretical and practical reductionism, especially the theoretical and practical one-dimensionality dominant in late industrial society and the reduction of all workers and many other people to a preorganic, noncreative level. To such one-dimensionality a political metaphysics proposes a two-dimensional logic and ontology dedicated to understanding, criticizing, and transcending the contemporary status quo. In its insistence on the essential, dialectical reciprocity between private and public, individual and society, such a metaphysics also gives us an ontological basis for criticizing the one-sided individualism of capitalism and the one-sided collectivism of state socialism. If the individual is not fully an individual in an atomized, utilitarian, capitalist society, then neither is that community really true which represses or ignores individual, aesthetic satisfaction, sacrificing it as a mere means to some imagined, future, social bliss. The idea of the unity between individual and society, then, functions not merely contemplatively in my metaphysics, but critically, pointing toward a transcendence of societies that do not adequately embody this ideal.

Such a metaphysics is processive, and "process" functions as a critical category. If the world is basically processive, then no historical epoch is necessarily a final, permanent parousia, satisfying all human aspirations. Capitalism, then, because it had a historical beginning, can also have a historical end. Such a metaphysics would pivot among or move among three different poles: the personal, self-knowing and self-choosing human subject; the social world, and God. There would be reciprocity between and among these poles. For example, self-knowledge would expand into a social theory and metaphysics. On the other hand, the metaphysics includes self and social world as parts or aspects of itself. The freedom of the human person, the freedom of the social world, the freedom of God—such are the three poles within which such a metaphysics would live, move, and have its being.

Finally, speculative-political metaphysics is an expansion of cognitional-transcendental theory, is grounded in such theory, sublates both cognitional-transcendental theory and critical theory as parts, is generally and ultimately explanatory, and is ideological-critical. Just as critical theory may be seen as a horizontal expansion of cognitional-transcendental theory into critical, social theory, from subjective, human being to social being, metaphysics may be seen as the vertical expansion of such theory. At the same time metaphysics is descriptively, epistemically, and critically grounded in such cognitional-transcendental theory. We have seen the working out of this grounding and expansion in the first five chapters of this book in reflecting on the notion of being, in the contrast between positions and counter-positions, in affirming an isomorphism between knowing and being, in conceiving and affirming God as an unrestricted act of understanding and love, and in describing the relationship of freedom to God.[37]

Metaphysics, on the other hand, sublates cognitional, transcendental, hermeneutical theory and critical theory as parts of a more comprehensive whole. As such, it can correct a certain one-sided emphasis on human subjective and social being in the first two parts; prehuman and subhuman nature comes into full view as an important part of being. Human beings are now seen in their relationship not only to a transcendent God but also to an immanent nature from which they emerge in an evolutionary manner. My lived body, affirmed in PCM and CAL, is also my immersion in nature. My lived body has not only epistemic and cognitional significance, as that which grounds knowledge, decision, and praxis, and critical-theoretical significance, as that which bears the brunt of capitalist and state-socialist exploitation, domination, and alienation, but also is metaphysical as my immersion in the whole of nature.[38]

As a result, metaphysics can react back on cognitional-transcendental and critical theory, and remind them of certain possible overemphases or exclusions and correct these. It can remind a subject-based cognitional-phenomenological theory of the immersion of the person in the lived body and nature, and it can insist against critical theory that a recommended socialism be an ecological socialism giving the environmental degradation caused by unjust social systems its full due and attention. Such a metaphysics reminds us in a speculative and poetic celebration of nature that "There lives the dearest freshness deep down things" and that "The world is charged with the grandeur of God." Such a metaphysics in its insistence on the reality and importance of being and God can resist the possible attempts of cognitional or critical theory to absolutize themselves in an ontological and aesthetic blindness and to divinize capitalism or state socialism into a kind of fetish, the capital fetish or state socialist fetish; only being is being and only God is God.[39]

In a fully adequate metaphysics, nature, human beings, being, and God must be distinguished and related to one another. Nature is the natural home of human beings in which they live, move, and have their being and are at the same time created by God and subject to an evolutionary process sustained by God. Human beings are rooted in nature and oriented to being and God. Being is the whole of which human personal being and social being are parts, and God is the ultimate ground of being as a whole and in its parts. This general, explanatory function contrasts with the particular explanations of the personal unconscious in relation to personal, subjective human being in PCM and the social unconscious in relation to human social being in PCM and CAL. Metaphysics, by making human beings a part within a more comprehensive whole and relativizing their importance in relationship to God, retains a valid humanism, but ultimately limits it in relation to the whole of being and God.[40]

As a result, the other done justice to in metaphysics is not just the human and divine other, but also the other of nature. Nature is itself the other that is done violence to by an exploitative capitalism that is equally exploitative of human beings. Responsibility and disposability, therefore, mean listening to the voice of nature as well as that of the human and divine other. Exteriority, therefore, is many-leveled: nature, human beings, human beings as poor, dominated, exploited, marginalized, the life-world, being, and God. Metaphysical reflection will be liberating and not dominating to the extent that it listens to and responds to the call of these others.

The ideology critique practiced by critical social theory is subsumed in and receives new content from speculative-political metaphysics. Because such metaphysics affirms a fundamental interiority and depth to human beings, it criticizes the reduction of human beings to a reified, commodified surface. Because such metaphysics affirms qualitatively distinct levels of being, it criticizes the reductionism present in scientism, positivism, and technocracy. Because my metaphysics affirms the basic social character of individuality, it rejects the capitalist elimination of or minimizing of the social and the state socialist rejection of or minimizing of the individual. Because such metaphysics affirms creative novelty throughout being, it rejects all reductionism to a preorganic or mechanical thinglike level. Finally, because metaphysics is speculative as well as practico-critical, it affirms a contemplative moment in knowing and living that is "useless," valuable in itself, and that criticizes implicitly or explicitly the capitalist reduction of meaning to utility; everything, even the most sacred of activities, is a mere means to money.[41]

We need to discuss somewhat at the conclusion of this section the troubling relation of Whitehead's event pluralism and rejection of substance and substantial self from the perspective of my theory already developed in the first five chapters. Obviously, my emphasis on self-appropriation running all the way through PCM, CAL, and this volume seems to be at odds with Whitehead's rejection of substance and substantial self, and my stress in these same volumes on the gestalt character of perception, on the internal relationship of experience, understanding, judgment, and decision to each other and to their correlatives in the social world, and my affirmation of the way that aspects of capitalism such as capital and labor, surplus value and labor, and capitalism and science imply one another would seem to be at odds with Whitehead's atomism of events.[42]

My own inclination is to view both of these disagreements as, up to a point at least, more apparent than real. If one, for example, rejects as I do the notion of substance and self as "the already out there now real" or "in there real" available to an immediate inward or outward look, and affirms the notion of the thing as an intelligible, unity-identity-who and the self as a personal, reflexive, conscious version of that, then my conception of thing and self overlaps with and is similar to Whitehead's notions of "society" and "personal society."[43] Both of these are intelligible patterns of relations between and among events, and, therefore, what Whitehead and I reject legitimately at one level, he and I recover at another level. Also, as I have already argued in chapter 2, thing and self in this more mediated sense are not opposed to change but are required by it to ground it and explain it. For the most part, therefore, the difference between us is more verbal than real.

What I would emphasize more than Whitehead does is that thing and self in the above, legitimate senses are not only temporal but also spatial, not only diachronic but also synchronic, not only horizontal but also vertical. I am as a self, for example, not only a temporal unity of past, present, and future stretched out temporally, but at any given time a structural whole, vertically organizing physical, chemical, organic, psychological, and intentional conjugate potencies, forms, and acts, all of which are unified and sublated in a central potency, form, and act.

Such a horizontal and vertical unity give an intelligible unity and coherence to a multiplicity of successively or simultaneously occurring events or occasions that are necessary to explain becoming; otherwise we have substitution or instantaneous creation, not change. Such a unity is necessary also as a source of operations; otherwise we do not have an adequate account of freedom and self-determination. Events do not just pop out of nowhere but proceed from something or somebody who is acting. When you and I are speaking together, I am aware that my act of speaking proceeds from "me" here rooted in my own lived body, and your speaking proceeds from your own lived body "there." We need a phenomenology of agency here that complements Whitehead's insights into society and personal society as forms of intelligible unity and coherence.

Such an account of thing and self on a central level grounding the conjugate level seems to be necessary to account for the reality of capacity. That a plant is able to grow, Fido to run, and a person to speak presupposes capacities to do that are resident in a plant, dog, or person. Moreover, after performing an activity many times, I develop a capacity, a habit or virtue, to do it well; I can think profoundly or write clearly or speak articulately. These capacities and virtues exist and are real even if their acts are not occurring. Also there is in me not just one but many capacities and virtues. What distinguishes and accounts for my capacities and virtues in contrast to yours "there"? Only the thing and person as real and conscious unity-identity-wholes can explain both the reality and unity-coherence between real and different loci of such capacities and virtues. If these are real and really unified here and different from you "there," then a real central act and form must be affirmed to account for their reality and intelligibility. Reality cannot be resident in nothing; intelligibility cannot proceed from unintelligibility or chaos.

Moreover, if capacity and virtue are grounded in real things and if acts proceed from and depend on capacities and virtues, then conjugate act depends on and proceeds from central form and act. Capacities and virtues become the middle term between central form and act and conjugate act or occasion. Finally, because these all exist and occur in a spatial context discussed previously as empirical residue, extension, and coincidental manifold, then conjugate act implies central potency as well as central form and act. Events and occasions are only adequately accounted for and explained—and for Whitehead as well as for us being is intelligible—in unified central potency, form, and act.[44]

The priority given to events and occasions in Whitehead's philosophy has to be, therefore, qualified. In order of discovery, events certainly come first. I discover what kind of person or thing something is by the way it acts. But *ontologically* the thing or person comes first. There has to be an agent in order for a thing to act, and a certain kind of agent in order for certain kinds of action to occur. *Teleologically*, agent and event interact. The event proceeds from the agent, but the event helps the agent develop and become a different kind of agent. Dialectical interplay, therefore, between agent and event is the final, maximal, teleological story, sublating but not denying epistemic and ontological priorities.

What about Whiteheadian "atomism" or event pluralism? Again, the disagreement here is more verbal than real. Already in the first chapters influenced by Lonergan and Whitehead, I have developed my own version of such pluralism. Different things and different kinds and persons interact with one another through different kinds of operations, and such operations are free in the minimal sense of not being reducible to their prior conditions and causes, and maximally in persons to the extent that some of their acts result from motivated decisions, choosing one project from among a multiplicity of competing projects. Also in chapter 3 I affirmed the reality and importance of both internal and external relationships.

If I have affirmed internal relationships, so also, as we have already seen, does Whitehead.[45] X, as prehended by and objectified in A, internally affects A. Moreover, in chapter 3 I have affirmed the reality of external relationships. Love may be necessary and essential to me as a human being, but that I love John or Mary, Jack or Jill, is external and contingent. Event pluralism operates insofar as I affirm numerically and, at times, qualitatively distinct acts. Experience is not understanding is not judgment is not decision.

Experience, understanding, judgment, and decision are related structurally and essentially, but are external and contingent existentially. Experience can occur, but it is not necessarily followed by insight or the correct insight; understanding can occur, but may remain a bright idea calling for but not completed by judgment. Judgment can occur, but may not lead to the requisite decision. I can remain a perpetual Hamlet, judging that I should kill Claudius, but not being able to do so.

Moreover, the Whiteheadian notion of concrescence, in which a preceding actual occasion is objectified in a subsequent actual occasion, generalizes to the whole of reality what I mean by sublation on an intentional, human level. Understanding builds on and retains but goes beyond experience; judgment builds on and retains but goes beyond understanding; decision builds on and retains but goes beyond judgment. I agree with Whitehead's generalizing of this idea to the whole of reality as processive. Each concrescence, as we have seen, manifests a limited sense of freedom in the sense of being novel and irreducible to previous causes and conditions. Human freedom, on the other hand, and human, free acts as motivated, conscious, reflective, and responsible are qualitatively different from this generic freedom, even though at the same time as concrescences they are instances of it.

In PCM I insisted on the way in which any quality in a perceived thing is perceivable only against a background and in relationship to other qualities. In this respect, figure is essentially related to background; at the same time what the particular quality is at any given time and in any given time is contingent. It could be red or orange, blue or green, black or white. Here there is some overlap with the Whiteheadian distinction between presentational immediacy emphasized by Hume and Locke and causal efficacy as implying a background from which quality emerges.[46]

What my approach, finally, can do for Whitehead is to relate his account methodologically to cognitional theory in a way that he does not and as I have tried to do in part, to show, for example, how occasion is related to judgment and eternal object to understanding. Moreover, I may distinguish more sharply between central and conjugate levels than Whitehead and relate them more adequately. Finally, because of the critical modernist character of my metaphysics, self-appropriation is more central to my approach than to Whitehead's. What Whitehead, and Hartshorne as well, contribute to my account is to develop the processive, social, relational character of being and God.

Conclusion

At this point I have completed a trajectory that begins by reflecting on the possibility of metaphysics and the notion of being, continues through reflecting on being as structure and as process, develops by conceiving and affirming a processive God as an unrestricted act of understanding and love, and concludes by articulating freedom's relationship to God and a speculative-political metaphysics. Self-affirmation and self-choice of myself as a knower, chooser, and lover have thus unfolded their implications in relationship to being, God, and praxis.

I am now prepared to develop the particular hermeneutical implications of this project in an interpretation of a particular religious belief, Christianity, and a particular socio-economic system, national-international capitalism. More precisely, Part Two will be devoted to unfolding the critical, hermeneutical, and praxical relationship between Christianity and capitalism. This hermeneutics builds on and presupposes what I have done here. If God exists as a processive, unrestricted act of understanding and love, has God been revealed historically? If so, what is the most adequate interpretation of that revelation? What is the most adequate way to believe in and live out one's religious belief in relation to national and international capitalism?[47]

Part 2

೧೧೧

*Liberation in the
Center and Periphery:
Jesus Christ and the
New World Order*

❧❧❧

SEVEN

The Christ Event:
Hearing the Word

Dialectical Considerations

As I begin Part Two, let me review what I have accomplished so far. I have established the possibility of metaphysics, developed a metaphysics of proportionate being as both structure and process, affirmed a processive God, established the compatibility and relevance of God to human freedom, and argued for the legitimacy of a political metaphysics.

An implication of Part One is that the human being, as a natural desire to see God, is open to a possible religious revelation. Such a revelation is neither necessary nor inevitable, but is possible and contingent. If such a revelation were to occur, it would be an expression of God's loving freedom in the world to which human beings could also respond lovingly and freely. The human being as naturally, essentially metaphysical and religious is a lived openness to such a revelation. This openness can either be owned up to and accepted or denied and covered over by flight into the superficial living encouraged by the commodity form.

Because God is free in relation to the world, such a revelation would be free, contingent, loving. If such a revelation were to occur, the appropriate response by human beings would also be free and loving. Such freedom and love on the part of the human being is the final flowering of the love and disposability already operative in metaphysics. In authentic intellectual and moral conversion I choose to go where my questioning leads and not cut it off arbitrarily at a certain point. Already in such authentic questioning is a choice, commitment, and, therefore, love. Transcendental method, we have seen, is the experiencing, understanding, judging, and choosing of myself as experiencing, understanding, judging, and deciding in relation to being.[1]

If doing is to conform to knowing, then, we can say that my commitments and my love should conform to the order of love as articulated so far. I can conform or not conform. I can refuse to be a receptive openness to being and God, and close myself up in pride and self-assertion, or I can choose to conform to and respond to this order of love. If I do so, then I become actually what I am potentially and essentially. I am that individual "who stands in free love before the God of a possible revelation." I am attentive to the speech or silence of God to the extent that I have opened myself in free love to the message of the speech or silence of God, if God chooses not to be revealed further. I can hear the message of a free God only if I have not restricted already by a perverted or limited freedom the horizon of being, if I have not removed in advance by a lack of openness the possibility of God addressing me.[2]

Metaphysics is hard work. What contributes to making it hard is not merely something material and empirical, but something intellectual and spiritual: the necessity of overcoming bias in myself, of not restricting the horizon of legitimate questions, of overcoming counter-positions and moving to positions, of following up on the implications of authentic self-transcendence, of living up to intellectual, moral, and, as we shall soon see, religious conversion. Metaphysics, if it is to be done well, requires a kind of intellectual and spiritual asceticism, a work of will as well as knowledge, of love as well as intellectual cogency, of commitment as well as rigor. It is as rigorous, if not more rigorous, than the physical and social sciences. We have seen that God is affirmed in relation to being in an analytic principle and cannot be denied without logical and performative self-contradiction. But because more is at stake in metaphysical inquiry—namely, the life of the self—more effort is demanded of us in this domain than in the domain of common sense, science, and mathematics.[3]

Following Marcel, we could say that positive science is in the domain of "problem," in which we reflect on data outside the self and the self is not included in the data. Philosophy as phenomenology, critical theory, and metaphysics is reflection on "mystery," in which the self becomes at least a part of the data reflected on. Involved, then, in any philosophical question, especially that concerning the affirmation of God or religious revelation from God, is my own openness or lack of openness to such an affirmation or revelation, and the authenticity or inauthenticity of my own self-knowledge and self-transcendence.[4]

If readers have followed and assented to and committed themselves so far to what I have said, then they have committed themselves to being open in this sense. Metaphysics in the sense I am doing it here prepares the way for and clears the path for such a revelation, but it is not that revelation, nor is it the theological reflection that follows upon such a revelation. Metaphysics as knowing prepares the way for and gives way to the faith that "is the knowledge born of religious love." Just as the fourth level generally sublates cognition, so also here. I note a necessary self-limiting of metaphysics here, a necessary humility and admission that there are domains beyond it. A metaphysics that was arrogant and overreaching would be a betrayal of itself, antimetaphysical, because it is not based on what is real.[5]

If the further revelation were to occur, that would be a legitimate transcendence of metaphysics, in a certain way a modernist "overcoming" of metaphysics. Postmodernists are correct in noting the necessity and legitimacy of transcending rationality, and, with it, metaphysics. They just locate the source and object of such transcendence in the wrong place, and they transcend wrongly and inconsistently in a logical and performative way. In my sublation of metaphysics, on the other hand, I do not deny the necessity or legitimacy or validity of metaphysics, nor do I locate the source or object of such transcendence completely beyond reason. God as the source of further revelation is an act of unrestricted understanding and love who completes and fulfills my search for meaning. God is not beyond the horizon of being, but within it.

Where would such a revelation occur? When and where is its locus? Already to have asked the question in this way is to have answered it. For a revelation to occur it would have to be a free act of God at a certain time and place in history. Because the human being is the kind of being that knows through encounter of sensible, perceived things and persons and language and communication between and among persons, the revelation would have to appear sensibly, publicly, and socially within history. Because the human being is *incarnate* spirit, the revelation would have to be incarnate within history. To the extent that this revelation is an expression of God's life and intelligibility and meaning, it is a word of God, not necessarily verbal but tangible, sensible, and meaningful. For human beings to encounter it adequately, they would have to become receptive, disposable hearers of the word.[6]

Why would or could or should such a revelation occur? Why would it be important to human beings if it did occur? It seems to me that there are at least two possible answers to such a question, one positive and the other negative. The positive answer is the desirability of further communication between God and human beings. God wishes to be better known to creatures whom God knows and loves, and human beings wish to know more intimately and deeply the God whom they love and seek.

The negative reason is the problem of evil as it occurs on a human level. Here what first manifests itself is the gap between essential and effective freedom. As I have already shown in PCM, people are essentially free in that they have the capacity to choose between and among alternatives, commit themselves, love and intervene effectively in the world, and change that world. But essential freedom is one thing and effective freedom is another. Effective freedom is the actual conformity between human knowing and doing on individual and social levels. How much and how often and how generally do human beings in their lives and actions actually live up to the dictates of inquiring intelligence and reasonableness?[7]

Here the answer is complex and nuanced. It is true that there have been individuals who were quite moral and even saintly. It is true also that groups of people have acted morally and have achieved gains in social justice. We note, for example, the civil rights, feminist, environmental, antinuclear, and antiwar movements that have occured in the last thirty to forty years in the United States and western Europe.

More prevalent and more general, however, is human moral impotence both on individual and social levels. We only have to live in the world and to be awake to notice how often the human individuals we encounter in that world, and I myself as well, go against the light and manifest various kinds of pettiness, egoism, selfishness, envy, and cruelty. Murder, rape, theft, adultery, and dishonesty are very frequent and very common in all cultures, East and West. On a social, institutional level, I have already noted and will continue to note the prevalence of racism, sexism, classism, and heterosexism. Later on I will show more fully how the problem of unjust capitalistic neoimperialism is now worldwide in a way that none of us can avoid.

Even though the problem is socially expressed, it seems to have its primary roots in the human individual. Nor do we have to look far to see why. For in addition to the pure desire to love and commit myself, there are also different kinds of bias: dramatic bias urging me to play a social role cutting me off from my deepest self, egoistic bias inclining me to prefer my own good before the legitimate good of the other, group bias that expresses itself in the different practices and institutions of racism, sexism, classism, and heterosexism, and general bias that leads me to prefer the tangible, short-range, immediate solution to the less tangible, long-range, more permanent solution.

To the extent that such human biases rule human choice more than the desire to know, then choices made by individuals add up to and coalesce into a way of life in the community. This way of life solidifies into institutions and spreads to other parts of the world, and these corrupt, unjust institutions in turn react back on and educate people in their individual choices. To the extent that I am raised, brought up, and educated in a society that is structurally unjust, racist, sexist, classist, heterosexist, imperialist, I am formed by such institutions and educated by them. I begin to take it as self-evident that men are better than women, whites smarter than blacks, heterosexuals more moral than homosexuals, the rich more industrious than the poor, and the North more civilized than the South. My everyday life becomes a lived form of capitalist common sense in which having is preferred to being and making money to creating justice or making love.

To the extent that individuals and groups grow up in a certain unjust mileau and make choices that reinforce and reflect that mileau, then their willingness to be persuaded by reason lessens. A dilemma develops insofar as one sees that individuals and groups need to be persuaded to follow the dictates of the desire to know rather than bias. But what if one is not open to persuasion? What if the bad will underlying the lack of openness to persuasion has become habitual in individuals, groups, and a whole society?[8]

Confronted with such a problem, Marcuse posited a benevolent, leftist despotism that would force people to be free. Such a solution is ethically problematic insofar as it violates the precepts of right, morality, and justice that must be institutionalized in a fully liberated society. It is politically problematic insofar as it just substitutes one form of alienation for another. In addition to a general social-economic alienation in which people are seduced into following norms that divide them from their deepest selves, a political alienation arises in which a coercive state forces people to do what they do not wish to do. The problem of evil is not so much solved as displaced.[9]

The problem will not be solved merely by a correct philosophy, for a correct philosophy will be but one of many, will appeal to and be understood only by a select few, and will not be received favorably in a society that is already in a lived way committed to the counter-positions and dominated by them. Nor will the problem be solved by mere social revolution, for though moral impotence expresses itself in a social surd, its roots are elsewhere. If these have not been dealt with, one unjust system will simply be replaced by another. Liberation is individual as well as social, and addresses primarily the socially related individual's lack of willingness to be persuaded, his or her own tendency to go against the light.

The solution has to be a higher integration of human living, because the problem is radical and permanent, and it is independent of underlying physical, chemical, organic, and psychic manifolds. The problem is not met simply by revolutionary change nor by human discovery nor by the forced implementation of human discovery. The solution has to meet people where they are in their limitation and transcendence; it has to work through and not deny human intelligence and reasonableness and freedom. While it may not eliminate either development or tension, it must replace incapacity by capacity for sustained development. Only a higher solution can meet such requirements, for only such an integration leaves underlying manifolds in their autonomy and yet introduces a higher systematization into their nonsystematic coincidences.

What we need, therefore, is a further manifestation of finality, of emergent probability, of the upwardly directed dynamism of proportionate being in relation to transcendent being. Whether such a manifestation has occurred is an empirical-hermeneutic question, a question of fact. It is to that issue that I will turn in Part Two.[10]

The Content of the Solution

Its Heuristic Structure

I have been reflecting on the possibility that would be both the positive completion of the human being's natural desire to know, love, and see God, and a higher viewpoint on the fact of evil. Because the fact of evil is a general, statistical law, it is not necessary. Because it is not necessary, essential freedom is not denied and some range of effective freedom is both possible and actual. But nonetheless, moral impotence rooted in a widespread bad will, lack of openness to and fidelity to the desire to know, is deep, general, and far-reaching. Consequently, a solution will have to be similarly deep, general, and far-reaching.

In the first place, the solution will be one, for there is one God, one world order, and one problem of evil that is both individual and social. Moreover, because the problem affects all human beings in all places and times and classes and groups, the solution will similarly be universally accessible and permanent. Such a solution will be a harmonious continuation of the natural order of the universe, because it is a higher viewpoint that does not destroy but preserves what it integrates. Such a solution will not consist of new central forms of a new genus and species, because the solution is for human beings and has to be addressed to human beings. The solution will consist of new conjugate forms in human intellect, will, and sensitivity. For the problem lies in the lack of habitual good will, and consequently, the solution will be in providing intellect, will, and sensitivity with forms or habits that enable the human being to overcome evil. Because the problem comes from nature, these forms will be in some sense supernatural.

Since the solution is a harmonious continuation of the actual order of the universe and since that order involves the successive emergence of higher integrations that systematize nonsystematic residues on lower levels, the relatively supernatural conjugate forms will constitute a new and higher integration of human activity unifying and controlling elements that would otherwise remain nonsystematic. Because human beings and the world are processive and developing, these forms will pertain to higher systems on the move and will be capable of some adaptation and development. Since higher integrations leave intact the nature of the underlying manifold and since the human being is intelligent, rational, and free, it follows that the solution will come to human beings through their knowledge, consent, and cooperation.

We need to further specify the relevant conjugate forms. It seems, first of all, that the appropriate willingness will be some form of love or charity. For good will follows intellect, and as intellect knows the reality of God and other people, good will wills the good of God and other people. But such willing the good is love. Such a good will can contribute to the solution of social evil, insofar as it adopts a dialectical method that parallels the dialectical method of intellect. The dialectical method of intellect consists in grasping that the social surd neither is intelligible nor should be treated as intelligible; the dialectical method of will is to return good for evil. For only insofar as human beings are willing to meet evil with good, to love their enemies, and to pray for those who injure them is the social surd a potential good. Consequently, the love of God as it embraces this actual world and responds to it, and human beings' love for God and for the world to the extent that they embrace the solution, are forms of self-sacrificing love.

Such self-sacrificing love of God and neighbor is repentant. Though human self-consciousness develops and becomes good, it has in the past been less good and perhaps evil. Rational self-consciousness, then, self-consciousness on the fourth, moral level, properly repents when it regards the evil that it did not will but nonetheless committed and the good that it willed but did not perform. Such repentance becomes repentance over sin and rises above the limited viewpoint of ethics insofar as sin is revealed to be a revolt against God. Repentance becomes sorrow insofar as a relation between stages in one's life is transformed into a personal relation to the one loved above all.

Such good will is, moreover, joyful. For it is love of God above all and love is joy, and it knows more about God and deeper knowledge of the beloved brings joy. Contributing to that joy is the hopefulness in the light of which the intervention of God in human life and history counters the despair that seems to attend all merely human affairs. Such a hope is not presumptuous, because the fulfillment of the conditions for the emergence of a truly rational order lies not with human beings but with God. The conjugate form of a confident hope aiding and reinforcing the desire to know is a hope that God will bring the human intellect and will to a knowledge and love of the unrestricted act of understanding and love, and provide an effective solution to the problem of evil.

Moreover, we can affirm not only a conjugate form of love and one of hope, but also one relating to the human intellect. Since love and hope follow on knowledge, then there will be communicated an additional knowledge of God in Godself and in relation to the world. Moreover, since an immanently generated knowledge based on evidence will be communicable only to a few, at best, and since some of God's self-revelation cannot be immediately generated even by the educated, the knowledge communicated, if it is to be universal and permanent, will be one of faith or belief. I believe in the testimony of God and of others who bear direct witness to God.[11]

At this point, however, difficulties arise, for we can legitimately inquire whether belief is something to which human beings trying to be intelligent and reasonable about their lives should commit themselves. Is not the dawn of modernity, signaled by Descartes, Kant, and others, an invitation to see for myself and to critique uncritically inherited beliefs?

Nonetheless, I have already criticized Descartes in PCM on various levels and for various reasons. One of these is his general difficulty in recognizing the social character of knowledge and its rootedness in tradition; one aspect of this social character is the necessity of collaboration in various departments of human knowledge. Human beings learn not just by personally understanding and verifying every judgment that they hold to be true. Rather they learn through a complex interplay of belief and personal insight and judgment, which operates everywhere, especially and in a most noteworthy manner, in science. Science progresses by scientists taking over from the past belief claims verified by other scientists, conceiving and verifying their own hypotheses, and communicating them to the wider scientific community, at which point they become beliefs.[12]

Such a process of collaboration is widespread, it occurs in all departments of knowledge, it is inevitable if I wish to get anywhere in increasing and broadening my knowledge, and the alternative to such collaboration seems to be a relative ignorance, a perpetual starting over. Consequently, it seems legitimate to affirm in general the value of belief. One can, then, move from affirming the value of belief in general to a reflective act of understanding that, in virtue of particular judgments, grasps as virtually unconditioned the value of deciding to believe one particular proposition, to the consequent judgment of value to the decision to believe that is the act of belief. Note that the virtually unconditioned grasped here is not evidence for the proposition that is believed, but the value of deciding to believe some particular proposition.

If the reflective act is to occur, there must be a conditioned, a link between the conditioned and its conditions, and the fulfillment of the conditions. The conditioned is the value of deciding to believe a particular proposition. The link between the conditioned and conditions is that if the proposition is to be grasped as unconditioned in a manner that satisfies the criterion of truth, then there is value in believing it. Finally, the conditions are fulfilled if the proposition to be believed has been communicated accurately from its source, and the source uttering the proposition uttered it as true, uttered it truthfully, and was not mistaken.

For example, if a good friend tells me that he saw my wife coming out of a motel room with another man, I would be inclined to believe him if I regarded him as trustworthy and as having my best interests at heart and did genuinely see what he claimed to see—for example, that he was close enough not to mistake my wife for another woman. Whether the motel encounter was one of romantic, sexual encounter remains, of course, to be determined by further investigation, but at least I believe what my friend has told me.

There are many differences, of course, in the ways belief is arrived at. It can occur through a personal encounter with the person believed or through a series of intermediaries. I can rely on my personal knowledge of someone's character or on the testimony of others whose character and ability I know. Or one can appeal to general laws operative in human collaboration that tends over the long run to ferret out error and to discern and confirm the truth. Whatever the procedure, the only general rule is to be intelligent and reasonable in arriving at the virtually unconditioned judgment that it is good to believe this particular person.

Not only can legitimate beliefs occur, but illegitimate beliefs can be rooted out. Here the way to proceed is not through some Cartesian systematic doubt and rehabilitation of all beliefs, but through being intelligent and reasonable in my believing and in my criticism of belief. In the case of my wife's possible infidelity, for example, I may discover that my friend, like "honest" Iago in relation to Othello, had it in for me. Or I might discover through various kinds of direct and indirect checks that my friend was mistaken—for example, my wife was somewhere else at the time and could not have been at the motel. Or I question my wife, and she convinces me that she was at the motel for a business meeting or she was counseling a friend, a friend whose wife had left him and who had taken a room at the motel.

The critical modernist turn, in philosophy and hermeneutics, does not repudiate belief but does encourage the tendency to move from uncritical to critical belief. Like Gadamer, I accept hermeneutically the role of "prejudice," or presuppositions that I have not examined critically but just assume and take over, and of belief as one form of prejudice. But I insist on the possibility and necessity of criticizing belief and sources of belief. In such criticism I do not do away with belief—scientists, for example, need in general to trust the past results of others that they take over, but I may learn to distrust some sources of belief and critically trust others. If my friend turns out to be a contemporary Iago, then I will no longer believe him in the future.

I do not claim to convert totally claims believed in into personally understood and verified virtually unconditioned judgments, but I do claim the legitimacy and necessity of becoming critical about belief and forms of belief. Religious belief and Christianity as a form of religious belief can be criticized and justified in the above sense.[13]

Consequently, if faith is one of the conjugate forms of the solution to the problem of evil, then the solution will be a new and higher collaboration of human beings in the pursuit of truth, analogous to but differing from the collaborations of common sense, physical and social sciences, history, artistic and literary criticism, and philosophy. Because the solution is continuous with the natural order, it will involve a collaboration maintained by truthfulness, accuracy, and immanently generated knowledge. Because the solution is a higher integration, it will be a newer and higher collaboration. Because it is a solution to the problem of error and sin, the new and higher collaboration will provide an antidote to the errors to which human beings are inclined. Because it is a transcendent solution, it will be a collaboration between human beings and God. In such a collaboration God is the initiator and principle agent.

Because such faith is a transcendent belief operative within a new and higher collaboration of human beings with God, the act of faith will be an assent to truths transmitted through the collaboration, and such faith will be motivated by humans' reliance on the truthfulness of God. The act of faith will include not only belief in truths inaccessible to human reason, but also an affirmation of truths accessible to reason such as human beings' spiritual nature, our capacity to know being, our freedom, our responsibility, our sinfulness, and God's nature and existence. Truths accessible to human reason are included not because ordinary human collaboration cannot arrive at them, but because it fails to achieve unanimity about them. Our acknowledgment of the solution will be intelligent and reasonable to the extent that we grasp the problem of evil and our inability to cope with it, divine wisdom's awareness of many solutions, and its implementation of one of them that has all the earmarks of our heuristic structure.

Moreover, human beings will be intelligent and reasonable insofar as our acceptance of the solution reveals as unconditioned the value of deciding to assent to the truths of the new and higher collaboration because of the initiating and preserving truthfulness of God. For from the grasp of the unconditioned will follow with rational necessity a judgment on the value of deciding to assent, a decision to assent, and the act of assent itself. Such a decision to assent and the assent itself will be a "leap of faith," but unlike the way Kierkegaard talks at times, it will be a motivated leap based on a rationally motivated decision based on evidence.[14]

Again, because faith is the knowledge born of religious love, such an assent will be on the fourth level of freedom, decision, commitment, love, "falling in love with God." Because it involves and implies a loving relationship with God, the leap of faith has all the risks of a loving relationship with a human being. My friend who told me about my wife could have been mistaken, or could have bad will toward me. The decision to marry can be rational in the sense that it is based on evidence of the potential spouse's good qualities, abilities, compatibility, and love of me, but it is still a leap because it is a promise and commitment for the future and I can be mistaken about myself or her. Because the relationship with God is one of love, its point is primarily on the fourth level affecting my antecedent willingness to be reasonable and responsible. Knowledge and faith lead up to such a commitment, are sublated by it, and are effects of it. Insistence on the rationality of faith and the evidence grounding it and leading up to it does not minimize or deny the risk. What such an insistence does is to link or mediate rationality with faith and commitment, and to avoid any "either-or" separation of the two.[15]

Since the solution is a harmonious continuation of the actual order of the universe, human beings will not only acknowledge and accept the solution, but will collaborate with it. Consequently, because the solution is universal and accessible, there will be collaboration that consists in making known to others the good news of the solution and its nature. Because the solution is permanent, there will be the collaboration that consists in transmitting it from one generation to the next. Because the solution is universal and because it must be expressed in many different contexts, there will be collaboration consisting in recasting the solution into equivalent expressions for different times, places, classes, and cultures.

Nonetheless, because evil is expressed in injustice and because the solution is concerned to remedy evil and, therefore, injustice, the solution will be especially concerned with the victims of injustice, the poor, the oppressed, the hungry, and the homeless. Because the solution to the problem of evil respects human freedom and leaves it intact, we can expect that human beings' collaboration will be marked by differences having their roots in individual, dramatic, group, and general bias. The overcoming of self in charity will be replaced or compromised at times by an excessive egoism and lust for power, the witness to the truth of God will be compromised by a desire to look good, the universality of the message will be distorted by racism, sexism, classism, and heterosexism, and the commitment to the long-range, spiritual, and permanent will be overturned by a praxis that is short-ranged, materialistic, and superficial. The lust for power will be in tension with the commitment to the kingdom of God as expressed in the solution, and concern for the poor and oppressed will be replaced by courting of the rich and powerful. Nonetheless, because the solution and the collaboration is of God, God will continue to be present in it, and God's light and truth and love are there to be called upon at all times and to be cues to criticize and overcome the aberrations occurring within the collaboration itself.

Because the human being lives on both a sensible and intellectual level, because the human being has an orientation to mystery as expressed in symbols, and because the whole person should be addressed by the solution, it will be something that not only renovates will and enlightens intellect, but also is mysteriously expressed in symbol. Because mystery is a permanent need of human intersubjectivity and sensitivity, while myth is an aberration, the solution as sensible must be not fiction but fact, not a fictional story but a narrative history, which will include the sensible data that are correlative to human beings' sensitive nature and that will command their attention, arrest their imagination, stimulate their intelligence, strengthen their will, control their aggressiveness, and intimate to the level of sense its own finality, its own yearning for God.

Finally, because the solution is supernatural with a force and vivacity and power and significance of its own, it will introduce another tension into the human being. Now there will be a tension not only between sense and intellect, but also between natural and supernatural. Just as the tension between intellect and sense can be lived fruitfully, so also can the tension between natural and supernatural. Because such fruitfulness is not inevitable, however, there will arise the temptation to assert a humanism that is religious in name only or to move into a one-sided supernaturalism that merely escapes or one-sidedly negates the natural, human world. Both of these ways of living the tension are inauthentic in contrast to the authentic sublation of natural by supernatural, in which the former is retained but no longer absolute. Rather I come to the conclusion that to be merely humanistic is not enough, that being a human being in the full sense requires more than that, and that the proper terminus of the human desire to know and love is a religious revelation that is both desirable in itself and that functions as a solution to the problem of evil that human beings cannot solve by themselves. To be natural in the fully adequate sense is to be supernatural.[16]

The Reality of the Solution

Thus far I have been considering the solution as hypothesis, as heuristic structure. But has it occurred in history? Many, of course, claim that it has in one of the several forms of Christianity. For many there is no doubt that they have found the God for whom their souls long, and they are trying now merely to bring forth the fruits of their faith, hope, and charity, with which they have been endowed through their commitment to Christ. They claim to have already discovered the deep happiness and joy which the further revelation of the Trinity, the Incarnation, Crucifixion, Resurrection, and Eucharist have brought to them. In their daily encounter with God in the mysteries, in prayer, in ritual, and ordinary life, they have already encountered the beneficent mystery that surpasses all understanding and yet fulfills understanding. In their preference for the poor with whom they live daily, they already embody and respond to and live out the universality of the solution and function as implicit or explicit protests against a merely bourgeois Christianity, a

Christianity of the middle and upper classes. They claim to embody in themselves that self-sacrificing love that returns good for evil and that expresses God's self-donating love for the world.

One initial way of arguing, then, would be to say that Christianity instantiates all of the heuristic structure laid out in the first part of this chapter. The preceding paragraphs make this point in a general, summary fashion. Rather than leading the reader through the identification of Christianity with the heuristic structure point by point, which not only readers but also myself would find boring and which they can do for themselves, I prefer to undertake a more urgent task. For this is a philosophical work and, in this part especially, a work in philosophy of religion. I cannot, therefore, simply presume the legitimacy of the Christian faith or assume too easily that it fulfills the requirements laid down by the heuristic structure. Rather, we must lead up to faith in Christianity, reflect upon it, "justify it" to the extent that is possible. Why is Christianity the solution to the problem of evil? Why is it a revelation of God? How do we know that it has occurred historically?

I have in mind an ideal reader, who has followed me and agreed with me all the way through Part One and through PCM and CAL, who has affirmed the existence of God, and who is at least open to the further possible revelation of God and to a solution to the problem of evil. Such a person is already in love with God in a certain limited sense spelled out in previous chapters and is, therefore, open to going where further questions will lead. She or he is not captivated by the counter-positions, by positivism, by neo-Kantianism, by postmodernism, or by a stiff-necked humanism that refuses to bow its head before or worship or admire anything beyond itself.

Nor is such a person bothered by the fact that faith plays an essential role in such a revelation and such a solution. For such a person realizes already that faith plays a major role in all or most departments of human life, in common sense, in the physical and social sciences, in historical study, in personal commitments, in falling in love and committing oneself to other human beings, to a social movement, to a friend, a lover, or a spouse. The task is not to renounce faith or to convert it into directly verifiable judgments in a Cartesian manner, but, as much as is possible and necessary, to move from a precritical to a critical faith, from a first to a second naivete. Human life is saturated with prejudice and by faith as one form of it, and the task is not to renounce prejudice or to liberate ourselves from it, but to become more critical and reflective about it. One of the differences between a simplistic and a chastened modernism lies in this relationship between critical enlightenment and belief, either-or for the former, both-and for the latter.

The relationship runs both ways. As we have seen, enlightenment purifies and criticizes belief, but belief also nourishes and enriches, and gives substance and content to enlightenment. Ricoeur's way of putting this point is to say that the symbol gives rise to thought, and thought never exhausts the symbol. When I give myself hermeneutically to a text or symbol or narrative, aesthetic, historical, philosophical, or religious, that giving of myself leads to recovery of myself enriched by a content that is initially alien. Even in confronting philosophical texts, like those of Kant or Hegel or Marx, there is an initial "belief" or "trust" in the authority of the text, in its capacity to enlighten me and to bring me into question. And those texts or symbols or narratives can serve as positive resources for bringing into question an oppressive, unjust present. Plato's Parable of the Cave, for example, in the *Republic* can aid us in showing how capitalism is a twentieth-century cave from which we have to liberate ourselves.[17]

My ideal reader, therefore, has already affirmed the first claim in the movement already sketched, the legitimacy of belief in general. What about the other steps, the reflectively unconditioned grasp of the value of believing a particular proposition uttered by a particular person, the judgment of value, the decision, and the assent that is the act of faith? Here I stress that the process of coming to believe and commit self to Christ is evidential in a real but limited sense. There is evidence relevant to well-founded belief, but this nonetheless remains belief, leads up to and flows from a commitment on the fourth level, and does not exclude risk. The decision to believe is a leap, but it is a motivated leap. The evidence, then, relevant to belief is already present in an evidential and existential manner to a person who is intellectually and morally converted, theistic in a philosophical sense, and open to religious conversion.

One possible path to tread, then, is to reflect upon the reflective grasp of the value of deciding to believe Christ's testimony and that of his disciples in the New Testament that he is God and that, therefore, he should be believed because what he says is true. If we assent to the value of believing that what the human being Jesus says or implies about himself and lives out in his life is true, that he is God, then the further acts, the judgment of will, the decision, and the assent follow rather easily.

But why should we believe that Christ as manifested in the New Testament and traditions of Christianity—Protestant, Catholic, and Orthodox—and, based upon these, prayer and mystical experience, is God? Why is not all of this illusory? Here one way of proceeding would be to ascertain the historicity of the New Testament: show that those who wrote it were those who claimed to write it and to whom it has been attributed, that they were trustworthy witnesses, and that they accurately reported what they witnessed. The massive research into the New Testament in the last century has rather solidly established this fact.[18]

Second, if the New Testament is historically accurate, reliable, and trustworthy, then it makes sense to say that there was a human being, Jesus, who really did exist and who said and acted out and was subjected to the things recorded in the New Testament. This claim follows from the first. If the New Testament is generally true and reliable, then it would seem that we would need to affirm the existence of its central referent, Jesus.

Next, we can ask whether Jesus is sent by God, at the very least is a prophet of God. Here we need to reflect not only on numerous miracles such as the raising of Lazarus from the dead and numerous references to his mission as divinely appointed, but on the general moral physiognomy of his life. Here we can note a certain *coincidentia oppositorum*, unity of opposites, such as justice and mercy, solitude and community, willingness to eat and drink with pleasure and insistence on self-denial. This unity of opposites manifests a certain sanity and balance in the human being Jesus that makes him trustworthy as a human being. Such sanity is present in the way he forgives in the face of the Pharisees the woman caught in adultery (John 8:1–11), in his claim that the Sabbath is made for human beings rather than human beings for the Sabbath (Mark 2:23–28), and in his claim, upon hearing from a woman that the womb was blessed that bore him, says, "Rather blessed are those who hear the word of God and achieve it" (Luke 11:27–28).[19]

Such sanity and balance incline us to trust and believe Jesus in actions and claims expressing and articulating his being sent as a prophet of God. Either, we are inclined to say, he is sane and wise and, therefore, must be believed, or he is insane in making claims about his divine sending. Yet how can he be so wise and so apparently perfect in the human living of his life and claim to be sent by God, if the claims are not true and if he is filled with delusions of grandeur? If, on the other hand, the claims are not true and are deluded, then how could he be so wise and balanced?

If Jesus is genuinely sent by God, then he turns out to be God. Such was the conclusion the community drew after Jesus' resurrection from the tomb, attested to not only by the empty tomb but also by numerous appearances and sightings of Jesus. As recorded in the New Testament, the post-Easter community took Jesus' resurrection as a confirmation of his divine mission and as an expression of his divinity. Consequently, more and more phrases and titles expressing or implying divinity appear in the New Testament from this post-Easter period such as "God," "Son of God," "Lord," "Savior," and "Messiah." These are ascribed by Jesus Christ to himself or by his disciples to refer to him. Paul, for example uses "Lord" 230 times in his writing. Jesus speaks of God as "Father" and as "The Father" 73 times in a way that bespeaks an intimacy and familiarity not normal in the average human being. Again, "Abba, Father," is used by Jesus in a way that is unique to him, as in the prayer in Gethsemane, "Abba, Father, all things are possible in you; take this cup from me. Yet not my will, but yours" (Mark 14:36).[20]

One has to be careful here. Historical-critical studies of the New Testament in the last hundred years or so have warned us that not every saying attributed to Christ was necessarily uttered by him; such a saying could simply be an expression of the way the believing community understood Christ and the way he generally understood himself. Some sayings and events are, however, historically accurate, and those that are not are genuinely trustworthy in expressing Jesus' self-understanding and the way he was understood by the evangelists and the Christian community. Thus, the infancy narrative in Luke says, "today there has been born to you in the city of David a Savior who is Christ the Lord" (Luke 2:11). Paul says (Hebrews 1:10–12):

> At the beginning, O Lord, you established the earth and the heavens and the works of your hands. They will perish, but you remain; and they will all grow old like a garment. You will roll them up like a cloak, and like a garment they will be changed. But you are the same, and your years will have no end.

Christ says of himself, anticipating the last Judgment:

> Then the righteous will answer and say, "Lord, when did we see you hungry or thirsty or a stranger or naked or ill or in prison, and did not minister to your needs?" He will answer, "Amen, I say to you, what you did not for one of these least ones, you did not do for me, and thus will all go off to eternal punishment, but the righteous to eternal life." (Matthew 26:44–46)

Or the blind men say to Jesus, "'Lord, let our eyes be opened.' Immediately they received sight, and followed him" (Matthew 20:33–34).

Here it is important to advert not only to passages in the New Testament that assert or imply divinity and are admittedly few and are late, but that do make patent and unequivocal what is latent in the whole. For example, Jesus forgives sins, as only God can do (Matthew 9:1–8); he feeds the people in a desert place, as God did their fathers in the wilderness (John 6:1–15); he rules the sea, like the Lord described by the psalmist (Matthew 8:23–27; Mark 4:31–41); he gives life to the dead as the Father does (John 11:1–44); he proclaims a new law and inaugurates a new covenant (Matthew 5:12–21). He has knowledge of God unique among human beings (Matthew 12:25–27); he expels demons with the finger of God (Matthew 12:22–32); the prophetic day of the Lord is his day (Mark 1:1–12); and prophetic preparation of the way of the Lord is preparation of the way for him (Matthew 3:1–17). To know him is to know the Father (John 4:7); all that belongs to the Father belongs to him (John 4:35); he is the equal of the Father (John 5:18). He is associated with God in the work of creation (John 1:1–15); and he is the word who was with

God in the beginning (John 1:1–2). He is Emmanuel, which means "God with us" (Matthew 1:23); and he is the beloved son in whom God is well pleased (Matthew 1:17).

He teaches with authority (Matthew 5:21–48), and reveals himself as Lord on the day of judgment (Matthew 7:12–23), heals the sick (Matthew 8:1–17), and is proclaimed by Peter, after walking on the water, as the Son of God (Matthew 14:33). At last judgment he judges the righteous and unrighteous as only God can do (Matthew 26:31–46). He is the bridegroom in whose presence it does not make sense to fast but to celebrate (Mark 2:18–22), he is the Son of Man who is Lord of the Sabbath (Mark 2:23–28), and he clears the temple of money changers, referring to it as "my house" (Mark 11:15–18). No one knows the Son but the Father and who the Father is but the Son (Luke 10:22), Christ is in the Father and the Father is in him (John 14:11) and "before Abraham was I am" (John 9:38) and "When you lift up the Son of man, then you will realize that I am" (John 8:28). "The Father and I are one" (John 10:30).

Like all kinds of historical evidence and testimony, then, the New Testament is hermeneutically mediated. There is no "already out there now real" here any more than there is anywhere else. As hermeneutically mediated, what comes across accordingly is the presence of a person, human and divine, who combines in himself apparently opposite traits such as so-called "masculine" and so-called "feminine" qualities. Here I am not using essentialist language in discussing "masculine" and feminine," but only using these concepts as they have evolved historically to describe certain collections of traits.

Christ, of course, is masculine and often manifests a very masculine strength as in his driving the money changers out of the temple (Matthew 21:12–14) or in his denunciation of the scribes and Pharisees (Matthew 16:5–12), but he also manifests a surprising "feminine" gentleness and meekness and humility as in his blessing of children (Matthew 19:13–15) or in his riding into Jerusalem on a donkey (Matthew 21:1–11). Sometimes such attributes enter into Jesus' self-description, as when he compares his mission to that of a mother hen gathering and protecting her chickens under her wing (Luke 13:34–35).

As I argued in Part One, God embodies the best of "masculine" and "feminine" qualities. Such a recognition of this point more than occasionally comes out in the Old and New Testaments, as when God is compared to a woman in childbirth (Isaiah 42:14), the divine love is that of a woman for her children (Isaiah 49:15), God wishes to comfort suffering people like a mother (Isaiah 66:13), God conceives and begets the chosen people (Numbers 11:12; Deuteronomy 32:18), the Spirit descends upon Jesus in the form of a dove (Luke 4:18), Jesus talks about the necessity of being born of the Spirit (John 3:4), and Spirit acts as sophia-Spirit, as a bakerwoman kneading the leaven of kindness and truth into the thick dough of the world until the whole dough arises (Matthew 13:33). Also after the birth of the New Testament in the history of Christianity, God is often referred to as feminine by thinkers and mystics such as St. Bernard of Clairvaux and Julian of Norwich. Thus, in the Christian tradition itself are resources for overcoming a one-sided sexism both within the church and outside it.[21]

Finally, Jesus Christ, in the pages of the New Testament, confronts the possible believer with a personal existential question and decision, "Whom do you say I am?" On the one hand, the most comprehensive and consistent answer respecting the massive amount of evidence that I have indicated and outlined is that he is true man and true God. A rejection of his claim to divinity, on the other hand, seems to be less comprehensive in ignoring or not doing justice to the evidence for divinity, arbitrary in accepting the New Testament up to the point where belief in his divinity is called for, and inconsistent with my original admission of the historicity and trustworthiness of the New Testament. In tension with these claims, I would have to say that at a certain point Jesus Christ and his apostles and the evangelists and the Christian community were massively mistaken and deluded.

If, on the other hand, the New Testament really is historically valid, as true and accurate as any secular historical document of that period according to Schillebeeckx, if Jesus was eminently human and sane, then I must accept him as sent by God and as divine. If, however, he is sent by God and his own self-understanding and that of the Christian community is that he is divine and if his mission and self-understanding is confirmed by God's raising him from the dead, then it seems imperative to believe that Jesus Christ is both man and God. Either Jesus is God or, even as man, he is insane and deluded. But he is not insane and deluded. Therefore. . . .

Such is some of the reflection that my ideal reader might go through in moving to belief in Christ. Again I stress that this is not the only path such reflection can take. Such reflection could take as focus and starting point the reality of the church or one of its saints. Rather than being noematically and objectively focused on the historicity of the New Testament and of Jesus Christ as manifest therein, such reflection could be more subjectively and noetically focused on an encounter with Christ in prayer. Christ appeals to the believer or would-be believer as the ultimate meaning in her life, as that being and person that will totally satisfy passion for the infinite, and who will bring, in Kierkegaard's words, the aesthetic in line with the ethical and sublate them both in religious faith. As a believer or would-be believer, in reflecting and praying I experience personally and subjectively Christ as the fulfillment of my desire to know and love God, and as the solution to my own problem of evil as I am individually and also socially related to late capitalist society. Christ appears as he who saves me as I lose myself in his love.[22]

There are different modes and kinds and levels of evidence, objective and subjective, mediated and relatively unmediated as in prayer and mystical experience, historical and experiential. Even a reflection more explicitly objective and historical, as the above has been, is linked necessarily to a subjective desire to know and love and achieve salvation. I am interested in the historicity of the New Testament and in the historical Christ, human and divine, because I am in the process of discovering and choosing him as what my infinite passion seeks, as the meaning of my life. Even a relatively subjective faith finally needs to focus itself on the historical Jesus and Christ.

In a related way we could say that the faith of our ideal reader become believer includes and relates to the initial historical existence of Christ and the apostles, the postresurrection faith of the early community of Christians out of which emerged the New Testament, the further theological development up through the twentieth century including people like St. Augustine, Aquinas, Rahner, and Lonergan, the lives and testimony of mystics like St. Bernard of Clairvaux, St. Teresa of Avila, St. John of the Cross, and St. Thérèse of Lisieux, the contemporary witness of Christians like Daniel Berrigan, Dietrich Bonhoeffer, and Martin Luther King, and my own relatively immediate (but still highly historically, hermeneutically, and theologically mediated) response to God and Christ and the events of everyday life. All of these different aspects become a part of a past tradition leading into a living present and emerging future. That present is relatively unmediated, but still highly mediated, a second naivete if you like. My faith has passed through the dark night of doubt, philosophical reflection, historical critical interpretation and criticism, and, in the next chapter, suspicion to reach such a second naivete.

My faith is a belief in the living present and God present to me in contemporary events, people, and prayer, but is mediated by a tradition going all the way back to the historical Jesus. That past is not simply past but is phenomenologically and hermeneutically related to an ongoing present and emerging future. As a human being I am dynamically temporal in my intentionality, open to a past that nourishes me, a present that engages me, and a future that calls to me. Past, present, and future are distinct but related aspects of one historical consciousness in which I experience and interpret and know the historical Jesus as one with the Christ in whom I believe in the present.[23]

As rooted in tradition, my faith relates to and becomes part of a narrative or story. I can believe in Jesus Christ as human and divine because my existence is essentially and necessarily historical, hermeneutical, and therefore, narratival. As a narrative, the Christian faith can be related to, initially, naively, prethematically, and dogmatically, then move into the night of criticism, doubt, and suspicion, and then become the object of a second naivete, a postcritical hermeneutical-explanatory faith that is no longer naive about the historical character of its object, its mediated status, and the risk associated with belief. The "fact" of the historical Jesus is not something to which access is granted in a form of scientific looking that is value-free, but is mediated by symbol, story, and narrative.[24]

In any event, once I make in this objective-subjective context the virtually unconditioned judgment that Christ should be believed because he is God, then the decision to believe follows and the act of assent in faith occurs. I believe in Christ with the faith that is knowledge born of religious love. If I make this movement of faith and commitment fully, then I fall in love with God in a real, full sense. I undergo religious conversion, and such falling in love retains and at the same time sublates other finite loves. They become linked to my love of God and expressions of it, and my love of God contributes to making my love of other human beings more unselfish, more generous, more discerning, more self-forgetful.

In contrast to Kierkegaard and Bultmann, then, who deny or minimize the value of the historical Jesus contrasted to the Jesus of faith, I wish to argue that the former as manifested in the New Testament and apostolic witness is a necessary but not sufficient condition for the latter. If I am to believe and commit myself to the Christ event as the saving event, then that must have a basis in real, historical existence and fact. Otherwise there is no real basis for revelation or saying that it occurred, and in the absence of such a basis, faith seems to be mere arbitrary fiat. On the other hand, even though the two ultimately refer to the same divine-human reality, there is at least a difference of aspect between the historical Jesus and the Jesus of faith. I would locate this difference most fundamentally in the difference between the cognitive level of experiencing, understanding, and judgment, on which even an atheistic historian could claim on the basis of historical evidence that Jesus existed, and the level of commitment and freedom, on which I decide to believe. This distinction grounds another one between the intellectual pattern of experience, one example of which is rigorous historical-critical inquiry, and the religious pattern of experience, which involves knowledge in sublated form, but which emphasizes and gives the highest priority to freedom, commitment, love, and falling in love with God.

Because religious belief is linked to the love of God here, there is an authentic sublating of cognition, a legitimate "overcoming" of metaphysics. In contrast to postmodern overcomings, however, the religious belief I am defending here builds on metaphysics while transcending it. The very desire to know and love that led me to metaphysics also leads me beyond it in religious faith and love.

Nonetheless, on this level of religion and love is a certain meditativeness and contemplation that recalls Heidegger's discussion of meditative thinking. Spiritual masters of Christianity such as St. John of the Cross talk about different spiritual disciplines such as periods of silence before God, spiritual reading of the Bible and other great religious texts, meditating or ruminating in a thoughtful, receptive, nonargumentative manner on such texts, prayer taking the form of a conversation with God, and silent, reverent awe-filled contemplation of the mystery. St. John of the Cross tells us, "Seek in reading and you will find in meditation; knock in prayer and it will be opened to you in contemplation."[25]

Philosophy relates to such religious disciplines in various ways. First of all, it leads up to and prepares for and gives way to faith-filled and love-filled contemplation as we have done in this book. Second, philosophy is nourished by such contemplation. Nourished and restored by the Christ event, philosophers return to their own proper work with greater faith, hope, and charity, greater depth and richness of experience, greater insight, and greater ability to deal with the mystery of evil as it arises in their own sphere of inquiry and influence. Philosophy now more fully and adequately and easily serves the mystery rather than giving in to attempts to master it that betray the philosophical impulse itself. In a way slightly different and yet similar to Martin Heidegger, the philosopher is the shepherd of mystery, serves it, and tries to understand and illumine it. Finally, philosophy as transcendental or dialectical-phenomenological method reflects on the Christ event; philosophy becomes theology. In this text, however, as I explained in the Preface, because the doing of theology in Part Two is seen as the completion and crown of philosophy, theology becomes a part of my philosophy of religion, whereas in other contexts it would not be. There is, therefore, partial identity and partial difference between philosophy and theology, but not in any way that would imply mastery of the mystery or any claim to exhaustively and totally understand the Christ event.[26]

Spiritual disciplines such as silence, spiritual reading, meditation, prayer, and contemplation allow us to receive the light and love and strength of God in a way that overflows into love for the other and into social action. Later in the last chapter I will show how such disciplines can help us in the North to distance ourselves from, detach ourselves from, and see through the pomp and trappings of the commodity form in late capitalism that has us, even those of us who try to be and claim to be critical of it, in its thrall. Indeed Sobrino reminds us that there is a spirituality of liberation that is crucial for the process of liberation itself. Without such spirituality the praxis of liberation too easily becomes or can become bitter, self-righteous, violent, and vengeful. The mystery of evil reasserts itself in the process of liberation itself.[27]

Here, however, we are focusing on the initial, contemplative, prayer-filled moment of liberation, in which I fall in love with God and Christ, who reveals himself to me as "the man for others," whose love expresses the love of God for human beings and of human beings for God, who is committed to and lives out an orthopraxis of love for the poor and oppressed and marginalized. The "preferential option for the poor" is not merely a Marx-inspired, philosophically grounded claim as I argued in CAL, but is God's viewpoint on human suffering. In such prayer filled contemplative openness to God, as I showed in Part One, I become disposable to God's love and truth (grace), as they are revealed to me. Here disposability and creative fidelity find their ultimate flowering. Here literally and figuratively I become a hearer of the word, and as a Christian that is my fundamental vocation, my fundamental life call.[28]

One episode from the Gospels expresses for me almost perfectly this stance of disposability and creative fidelity in hearing the word. When the angel appears to Mary in the Annunciation, the angel announces to Mary that she is to conceive Christ, the Son of God. Not understanding fully how such an event is to occur, Mary nonetheless abandons herself in loving trust to the mystery and prays, "Behold, I am the handmaid of the Lord; May it be done to me according to your word" (Luke 1:26–28). In Mary's stance before the angel and God, as Fra Angelico imagines her at prayer in his fresco of the Annunciation at San Marco in Florence, there is a "feminine" receptivity that responds to the inspiration and will of God.

We could say, therefore, that there is a relatively disinterested and a relatively interested aspect to religious experience in general and Christian religious experience in particular. In prayerful, contemplative abandonment to the mystery, I know and love God for God's own sake. In such abandonment and in the love for human beings, for the poor that is its offspring, there is that "useless self-transcendence" that is essential for all authentic religious belief and practice. God is no mere means to my projects, religious or otherwise, but is known and loved for God's own sake. "Useless self-transcendence," then, implies that such action is its own end and is not a mere means to something beyond it.[29]

Nonetheless, such actions are just part of genuine religious belief and practice. For, as I have articulated it in this book, belief in and commitment to a particular religious tradition emerges as a response to the mystery of evil, of bad will. Westphal in his own way makes the same point when he talks about all religions necessarily dealing with the guilt and death, which are the effects of sin and wrongdoing. All authentic religions—such as Hindu, Buddhist, Muslim, Jewish, and Christian—therefore, arise as responses to the human being's concern with sin, guilt, and death. In this sense, religion is "interested" as well as "disinterested." It arises not only as a response to the human being's desire to know, love, and serve God, but also from the need for individual and collective salvation. Liberation, properly so-called, includes both of these aspects, and they both function reciprocally in all authentic religion.[30]

These two concerns are to be distinguished from a third—namely, my own well-being in the world as that concerns such issues as physical pleasure and well-being, and functional, professional success. Up to a certain point, these are legitimate, but to the extent that the religious practice is deep and authentic, they are subordinated to the first two concerns. I pray for health or professional success, but say, "nonetheless not my will, but thine be done." Even my desire for liberation from sin begins to be permeated more by my disinterested love of God; I see sin more and more as a violation and betrayal of my personal relationship with God that is intrinsically valuable.

Through such a brief phenomenology of religion and of Christian religious practice, the reader is already prepared to see what I will discuss more fully in the next chapter—namely, the criticism of religious belief that Freud, Nietzsche, and Marx make when they see religion as serving merely worldly ends is one-sided.

From what we have already seen here, we can argue that such criticism describes either a total or nearly total subordinating of religion to merely worldly ends, an inauthentic use of religion, or a legitimate concern for worldly ends that is subordinated to liberation from sin and to disinterested knowledge and love of God. Such inauthentic practice may be quite prevalent and even dominant for the most part, but is at odds with the fundamental telos of religion as "useless self-transcendence" and as liberation from sin. There are therefore, four aspects to religious belief and practice and its Christian form that such critics do not keep distinct: inauthentic use of religion to achieve worldly ends, authentic concern for worldly ends that subordinates itself to higher ends, liberation from sin, and disinterested knowledge and love of God. In reducing religious belief and practice primarily to the first of these uses of religion, they do unphenomenological violence and injustice to religious experience.

Conclusion: The Christ Event

The Christ event, then, represents the culmination of the revelation of God's truth and love, and Christ expresses in a certain sense the ultimate fulfillment and term of dialectical phenomenological reason as it has unfolded in my three volumes. He is himself the union of universal and particular, transcendence and immanence, human and divine, transcendental and hermeneutical, unity and plurality, spirit and nature, knowledge and love, for which we have been striving and toward which we have been pointing throughout the three volumes. Christ in himself embodies the unity of opposites which is the touchstone and telos of dialectical phenomenology. Both Hegel and Kierkegaard make this point in different ways, but since the Christ event is first and foremost an object of faith-filled love, it is from Kierkegaard that I take my bearings more than Hegel. In committing itself to and believing in

Christ, dialectical phenomenology receives its religious salvation and liberation and enlightenment from without rather than generating it from within. At this highest, culminating stage there is "otherness," a difference in God that reason does not fully comprehend. Although this union of opposites is both partially mediated and paradoxical, paradox finally wins out. Paradox is the passion of thought, especially the thought that sees itself as completed and sublated in faith-filled love and commitment to Christ. To the extent that philosophy and a philosophical use of theology reflect and elaborate the Christ event in a way that leads to deeper understanding, a partial mediation occurs, but this always limps after and is subordinated to the Paradox and the Mystery.[31]

Because the Christ event occurs as the solution to a problem of evil, is based on a cognitional and transcendental structure that is universal, and implies the incarnation of God as an unrestricted act of understanding and love extending to everything and everyone, the Christ event is universal. Such a claim is true even though the event occurred in a particular place and time, and even though Christianity developed primarily, although not exclusively (remember Eastern Orthodox Christianity), in the West. Here the distinction I made and argued for in CAL between particular hermeneutical origin and universal validity is relevant. A philosophical, ethical, or religious discovery or manifestation can occur in one place, time, and region, but nonetheless be universal in scope and validity. Such is true of science, mathematics, ethical insights into human rights, and Christianity. A particular human being was born in Bethlehem, grew to maturity in Nazareth, and was crucified in Jerusalem, but the meaning and validity and appeal of the divine revelation and intervention that took place through this human being are universal in scope and validity. Thus religious revelation and experience do not deny but confirm my argument throughout the three volumes that it is possible to achieve objective, universal truth, and that it is possible to avoid the extremes of dogmatism and relativism. Indeed, Christianity and the Christ event are the final flowering and apotheosis of that orientation and that striving.[32]

All of which is not to imply that Christianity is the only legitimate form of religious revelation, only that, by the criteria of this essay, it is the most adequate. Christians can and should learn in dialogue and ecumenical exchange with other religions such as Judaism, Hinduism, and Buddhism, but they do find themselves legitimately preferring God as incarnate to the merely transcendent, abstract God of Judaism, and God as historical, personal, and incarnate to the more impersonal, ahistorical, and simply or mostly nontranscendent divinities of some forms of Hinduism and Buddhism. Such confidence in relative adequacy is based on a metaphysics affirming a God that is personal and processive, the heuristic structure of the solution to the problem of evil, and Christian revelation itself. Corresponding to the exigency of dialectical phenomenology itself for an adequate object of knowledge and love is the revelation of a God phenomenlogically present in a mediated way to our experience, knowledge, and love, and dialectically manifesting a unity of opposites such as human and divine, one and many, unchangeable and changeable, independent and dependent.[33]

EIGHT

༼ᗡᘏᗢ༽

Suspicion and Religious Belief

At the beginning of Part One, I questioned the possibility of meta-physics by reflecting on those masters of suspicion concerning that enterprise, Kant, Heidegger, and Derrida. At the beginning of Part Two, I confront the possibility of authentic religious belief and practice by considering three masters of suspicion concerning that enterprise, Freud, Nietzsche, and Marx. In doing so I will be presuming our results from Part One concerning the existence, compatibility, and relevance of God to human intelligence, freedom, and praxis.

The issue dealt with in this chapter is different—namely, the function of religious belief. Even if God exists, even if God is compatible and relevant to human freedom, how does religious belief function in the life of the believer? Does God function as consolation for ontological weakness (Freud), as sociological weakness seeking revenge (Nietzsche), or as sociological power seeking legitimation (Marx)? If any or all of these critiques make the case essentially and fundamentally against religious belief, then such belief is discredited.[1]

The questions posed by Freud, Nietzsche, and Marx, then, are not skeptical in an evidential sense—what is the evidence for God's existence—but speak to the existential-sociological function that religious belief plays in the life of the believer and society. All three thinkers are committed to the nonexistence of God in an evidential sense also, but that is not the primary focus of their critique. We will briefly consider their nonbelief on these grounds also but will concentrate on their main arguments concerning function.[2]

We are involved here, then, in a hermeneutics of suspicion, which is a "deliberate attempt to expose the self-deceptions involved in hiding our actual motives from ourselves, individually or collectively, in order not to notice how and how much our behavior and beliefs are shaped by values we profess to disown."[3] My strategy, first, will be to admit that the functional use of religion as a painkiller, as a form of resentment, and as legitimation for domination goes on a great deal of the time. We can note the self-deception involved in the Afrikaner attempt to portray apartheid as a divine mandate, "manifest destiny," and "anticommunist" theologies that have contributed to imperialist and neoimperialist domination and exploitation of indigenous populations in North, Central, and South America, as well as President Bush's call for religious celebration after the Gulf War (which I will show later was a manifestly unjust, imperialistic war), with which call most churches went along and complied.[4]

My further question, however, will be whether such a critique exhausts the possibility and actuality of religious belief. Are there in religious traditions resources for criticizing the invalid use of religious belief? Can the hermeneutics of suspicion itself function as a way of purifying religious belief?

My answer to the first question is a firm "no," and my answer to the last two questions is an equally firm "yes." When we consider the Old and New Testaments, my primary examples of religious texts, we note already a prophetic critique that anticipates what is going on in Freud, Nietzsche, and Marx. Such a biblical critique is complemented, filled out, and rendered more intellectually rigorous and contemporary by the masters of suspicion. On the other hand, religious belief helps such suspicion to keep from being overly cynical or despairing or hypercritical in itself, in the sense that I direct my suspicion toward others but leave myself off the hook. Rich complementarity, then, rather than mutual exclusion, seems to be the most adequate stance.[5]

Properly understood, then, religious belief requires suspicion, and suspicion requires religious belief. Suspicion can and must become a kind of spirituality that believers employ in order to move themselves and society from inauthentic to authentic religious belief and practice, from mere religion to faith. This is a faith that recognizes that the church crucified Christ.[6]

Freud

Freud puts his brief against religious belief in a nutshell when he says that the "whole thing is so patently infantile, so foreign to reality, that to one with a friendly attitude to humanity it is painful to think that the great majority of mortals will never be able to rise above this view of life." Religion is a system of doctrines and promises which on the one hand explains to him the riddles of this world with enviable completeness, and, on the other, assures him that a careful Providence will watch over his life and will compensate him in a future existence for any frustration he suffers here. The common man cannot imagine this providence other than in the figure of an enormously exalted father.[7]

Religion is a painkiller, analogous to chemical intoxicants and the illusions of art, that allows most human beings to deal with the pain, anxiety, and suffering of everyday life.

There are two claims linked to one another here: an evidential claim based on Freud's positivism and a suspicion based on his account of the role religion plays in the lives of human beings. The evidential claim can be rejected for reasons that I have already developed in this book and elsewhere: the self-contradictory character of positivism, the distinction between science as empirical method and philosophy as generalized empirical method, the reality of conscious interiority in human beings, the possibility and actuality of metaphysics, and the reality of God.[8]

Moreover, we can reject Freud's occasional, inconsistent use of ad hominem and genetic fallacies. In discussing illusion he asserts that it is not necessarily an error because of some defect in the believing soul or in the way I come to hold a belief. That a priest or teacher told me that something is true does not make it, by that very fact, false. A girl may believe that a prince will come to marry her, and in a few cases that has occurred. Delusion, however, in contrast to illusion, is utterly foreign to reality; it cannot possibly be true.[9]

Yet after making the above distinction, Freud simply identifies religious belief with delusion. Such an equation rests upon his linking his suspicion of belief as illusion with his skepticism, rooted in positivism, that religious belief is untrue in that it has no real referent. Moreover, Freud misses the point that no belief, religious or otherwise, can be refuted by showing the flaws in believing souls. I do not refute Kant's categorical imperative by showing that people sometimes or often do not act that way. For this reason the issue of religious truth remains an open question that psychoanalysis cannot answer. The answer to that question rests on the believer's own inquiring intelligence and reasonableness and freedom and commitment. The possibility remains open that psychoanalytically motivated suspicion can purify the believer's practice of faith.[10]

When he uses psychoanalysis to criticize the role religious belief plays in the life of a believer, Freud is on more solid ground. Here religion plays the role of a wish-fulfillment. To understand this we must briefly consider Freud's psychoanalytic theory. We have, according to him, an overwhelming desire for consolation, for protection against the overwhelming power of nature, and for rectification of the instinctual renunciation demanded by civilization. We want somebody strong enough to protect us from death and friendly enough to compensate us for the renunciations demanded by our culture; eternal life in paradise does both jobs quite well.[11]

Wish-fulfillment is rooted in the id, nature as instinct or drive. Ego and id are distinguished as reason and passion, and reason is in the service of amoral desire. Freud presents the ego as a weak rider on a powerful horse; the ego is guide, and the motive is powerful passion. The superego is culture internalized as conscience. As the voice of culture, which can be quite unreasonable, conscience is not the voice of reason or of God, but that of violence. As such, the superego can be cruel to the ego, and such cruelty is manifest in the intense feelings of guilt present in obsessional neurosis and melancholia.[12]

Freud identifies happiness with pleasure, and finds the purpose of life in the pleasure principle. The program of the pleasure principle is utterly in conflict with the course of the real world. Freud's stance here is one of resigned despair; happiness is not the purpose of the universe. The most that is possible is a mitigated unhappiness, which psychoanalysis can help us to negotiate. Religion is an attempt to compensate for this situation, to give us an illusory or delusional consolation that the human condition does not yield. His psychoanalytic critique of religion can be taken as an attempt to make us grow up. Just as we must sooner or later give up our belief in Santa Claus if we are to be mature adults, so also must we give up our belief in God.[13]

Freud comes to this account of wish-fulfillment by analyzing such phenomena as slips of the tongue, errors, misplacing objects, and, most importantly, dreams. A head of the board opens the meeting and says, "I declare the meeting closed." After having been though a painful experience in Stockholm, a woman forgets a word in her mind associated with that experience. A man forgets where he put a gift for his wife, from whom he feels alienated, and rediscovers the item later when he feels loving toward her. Another man, a scientist, who is about to marry the love of his life, forgets that it is his wedding day and goes to his laboratory instead.

Such phenomena enable Freud to offer the hypothesis of an unconscious. Because such an unconscious is repressed and forgotten, I have to recover it through an active remembering in psychoanalysis. And in such an unconscious, wish-fulfillment plays an important role. Because I secretly, at least in part, do not wish to be at the meeting, I declare it closed. Because I feel alienated from my wife, I misplace her gift. Because I really do not wish to marry, I go to my laboratory instead.[14]

It is in interpretation of dreams that Freud most fully develops his theory of the unconscious and of wish-fulfillment. Not only is interpretation of dreams a royal road to a knowledge of the unconscious activities of the mind in general, but it also provides a way of understanding Freud's critique of religion in particular. A dream is a disguised fulfillment of a suppressed or repressed wish.[15]

Freud analyses his dream of Irma's injection. Irma, a patient whom he is treating, was resisting his therapy and was consulting a medical colleague of Freud's, Otto. Freud's dream, as he interpreted it, was an act of self-justification. First, her not getting over hysteria is her fault. Freud reproaches her for resisting his therapy and gives her characteristics identifying her with two other patients who might be recalcitrant. Second, her problems are organic; since Freud is treating her for hysteria, he is not responsible if the illness has an organic basis. Third, Dr. M, who suggests an organic diagnosis, does not understand hysteria and is not as good a doctor as Freud. Fourth, the hysteria is Otto's fault. Irma's problems come from an unwise injection administered by Otto.[16]

Freud recognizes that it is not entirely consistent to take comfort from the organic diagnosis and then ridicule Dr. M for offering it. It is not only logic, however, but also decency that is sacrificed. Freud has revenge on Irma, Dr. M, and Otto for failing to agree with his, Freud's, diagnosis, or for reporting that his patient is not really well. While there may be a basis for reproaching Irma, the reproach of Otto is entirely fabricated. The dream is a fulfilled wish, in this case, the wish for revenge.[17]

Wishes, censorship, and disguise also operate in neuroses. Freud draws an explicit parallel between obsessional neurosis and religious ceremonies. The resemblance between the obsessive "ceremonial" aspects of such neuroses and religious ceremonials is not merely coincidental or accidental but grounded in a deep affinity. Obsessional neurosis is one of several ways that the self defends itself against threatening ideas of a sexual nature. The primary component of this complex idea is the person's memory of sexual trauma from infancy or childhood. Linked to this is an affective component, which includes anxiety over the somewhat unwelcome possibility of repetition of the experience, our guilt or shame, and our fear of punishment.

Because it proves impossible to forget the experience, symptoms arise through the mechanism of unconscious defense. The ego attempts to repress an idea that is incompatible with its own sense of moral or personal self-worth. In this way the ego frees itself from the contradiction, but only at the price of the regular recurrence of a symptom. The affect is separated from the idea and reattached to a symbolically suitable substitute sufficiently different to be bearable. In the hand washing compulsion of Lady Macbeth, for example, the unacceptable idea is the memory of murder. The painful affect, linked to the idea of an unclean soul, is transferred to the bearable idea of dirty hands, resulting in an abnormal concern for clean hands. "The washing is symbolic, designed to replace by physical purity the moral purity which she regretted having lost."

The analogy between obsessional neuroses and religious ceremonials has many different aspects. I note two differences and four similarities. The neurosis is private, whereas religion is public; the neurosis is rooted in repression of sexual instincts, whereas religion is rooted in repression of ambitious, aggressive instincts, which have their roots in the ego, and which Freud sometimes calls egoistic. The goal of the former is bodily pleasure and the goal of the latter is self-esteem, but both know how to "look out for number one."[18]

The four similarities are as follows. The first is the compulsiveness of both neurotic and religious acts, which expresses itself in the conscientiousness with which both are carried out and in the anxiety that accompanies any deviation, neglect, or interruption of the performance. If I miss Mass, even though it is not my fault, I feel terrible. Second is the isolation of both kinds of acts from other activities, making them relatively easy to conceal. The Sunday Christian, who is pious on that day of the week and exploits people as an industrial manager during the other six days, is an example. Third, both kinds of acts are symbolically meaningful, even in their details.

Fourth, religious acts are more meaningful than they seem, because they have hidden as well as overt meaning. Such a claim applies not only to the meaning of the ritual, which some participants may not fully understand or fully attend to, but also to deeper, unconscious meanings. Like obsessional neuroses, religious rituals are symbolic defenses against the temptation stemming from repressed evil impulses and symbolic protection against anticipated punishment. At the same time, because they are a compromise between warring forces of the mind, they reproduce something of the pleasure they are designed to prevent. They express the repressed instinct no less than the agencies that repress it.[19]

One example of such compromise is incest taboos of tribal societies. It is interesting that the very sexual acts normally forbidden by religion are expressed in riotous sexual orgies functioning as religious ceremonies. Another example is the excessive solicitude of the rites of sacred kingship, compensating for the deep hostility and envy of underlings. In one ceremony, for example, those electing the king reserve for themselves the right of beating him on the eve of the coronation. And finally, the Christian eucharist itself worships God by sacrificing God, Jesus Christ. Here is a rite in which, even though communion, resurrection, and hope are part of it and are linked to it, the one-sided focus of some religious communities is on suffering and sacrifice and death.[20]

Still another example of compromise formations is forms of religious magic in which, according to Freud, the community attempts to appropriate or control God. Rather than worshiping God and sacrificing ourselves to God for the sake of God's will, we appropriate God for our own ends and use God to legitimate and justify our interests. Thus, different nations can appropriate

God for their national ends, as Bush did in the Gulf War, and religion is used to legitimate and justify certain social practices of injustice, repression, and exclusion. The religious right in the United States promotes its attack on the poor administered by the welfare state as holy and just, and liberals present their policies of neocolonialism and neoimperialism toward Central and Latin America as being "on God's side." We bargain with God through our rites, sacrifices, and actions, and make God our own personal property. But what if the true God of the Old and New Testaments is not a God to be bargained with, is not a God of consolation, and refuses to be possessed?[21]

If so, then religious belief must be purified of such practices, and suspicion remains one of the useful strategies for doing that. It enables us to see that the mature believer does not seek the consolations of God but the God of consolations. Growth from religious childhood to adulthood implies the movement into a dark night of sense and spirit. Naked faith replaces consolation, and humility replaces pride and self-assertion.[22]

A further related point is that Christianity is a religion of the Cross; one does not get to the resurrection except by passing through Good Friday. Accordingly, Jesus in the Garden of Gethsemane prays that the cup of his suffering pass from him, but nonetheless says, "Not what I will but what you will" (Mark 14: 36). Again Jesus chastises his disciples when he tells them that he is going to suffer and die, and they resist. Christ rebukes Peter, saying, "Get behind me, Satan, you are thinking not as God does but as human beings do" (Mark 8: 31–33).

Christianity is not a religion either of consolation-pleasure or of functional success, but of joy won through a purified, disciplined heart and sacrificial, self donating love on the part of both Christ and the believer. Freud, in identifying happiness with pleasure, misses this possibility. Consequently, he is unable to see that great joy is possible even in the midst of great suffering and deprivation.

One example is Daniel Berrigan's reflection from the depths of a Washington, D.C., jail, after having been arrested with his brother Phil for civil disobedience.

> Anyway, here's my translation of that breakthrough. It's the gratitude that wells up in me, unforeseen, almost ecstatic, at being in jail. Now help me figure that one out! It's being here (even here) with Phil. I remember something Sam Melville wrote about Attica. Prison can be ecstacy. It's one's act of faith in choosing to be here—verified in the eyes, speech, conduct, style of another. Being here with Phil.

> This hole. They say even in a D.C. jail, you can't go lower than we've gone. We're in deadlock: 24–hour lockup, two in a cell hardly large

enough for one, sharing space with mice, rats, flies, and assorted uninvited fauna. Food shoved in the door, filth, degradation. And I wouldn't choose to be anywhere else on the planet. I think we've landed on the turf where the breakthrough occurs. I think it's occurred already.[23]

Berrigan and the Catholic left, which he helped spawn in the 1960s, are some of the main examples and inspirations of an authentic Christianity that regularly practices and lives, out of its own resources, its own kind of suspicion. As such, he is a counter-example not only to Freud's critique of religious belief, but to Nietzsche's and Marx's as well. Religious belief does not have to be (but often is) a search for consolation, does not have to be (but often is) born of resentment, does not have to be (but often is) uncritically supportive of an unjust capitalist status quo.

Pleasure and consolation, of course, are not to be despised, nor is functional success. But the main point of religious belief is not here. God does not exist to satisfy my need either for consolation or for success; rather we exist to fulfill God's projects, to do God's will. Not my will, but thine be done. Therein we find, if we are reasonably faithful, peace, joy, and happiness. But these are not the same as, nor can they be reduced to, mere pleasure or consolation, functional success or egoistic satisfaction.

True it is, nonetheless, that we as believers often turn religion into a means for consolation or success; we often try to domesticate God or to use liturgical sacrifice as a means of buying God off, as a substitute for the real sacrifice of doing God's will in the daily stress of ordinary living. Freud thus echoes the critique of prophets like Samuel.

> And Samuel said: Does the Lord desire holocausts and victims, and not rather that the voice of the Lord should be obeyed? For obedience is better than sacrifices: and to hearken rather than to offer the fat of rams.

> Because it is like the sin of witchcraft to rebel; and like the crime of idolatry, to refuse to obey. (1 Samuel 15:22–23)

Samuel here is practicing his own hermeneutics of suspicion, criticizing sacrifices that are motivated not by obedience toward and love for God and neighbor, but rebelliousness and idolatry.[24]

On this issue, the prophets may have a more complex reading of human nature than Freud. Rather than writing off religious belief as totally given over to such unacceptable strategies, a prophet-inspired reflection distinguishes among at least three kinds of believer. First, there are those who are totally or mostly given over to the use of religion as a source of consolation or functional success. Even here, however, are we to say that nothing authentic ever creeps through, that no hint of genuine love for God or other human beings ever manifests itself, that there is never even a tincture of genuine commitment to the will of God? I think not. Even on this level, it seems implausible to say that the practice of belief is totally corrupt. Human motivation is more complex than that.

A second group of people consists of those whose motivation is genuinely mixed, perhaps half-inauthentic and half-authentic, with some slightly more inauthentic than authentic or vice versa. A third group consists of those whose motivation is all or mostly pure, authentic, sincere, genuinely loving toward God and human beings, genuinely functioning as servants of the will of God. Here we are to think not only of Christ and the prophets, but of saints like St. John of the Cross and St. Teresa of Avila.

Now the point would be that growth in authentic religious belief means moving from focusing on the consolations of God to focusing on the God of consolations, for God's sake and because God's glory and will are worthwhile in themselves, whether or not our pleasure-seeking or functional selves are satisfied. Here I insist on the point made over and over again in the gospels on the necessity of dying to such selfhood if genuine religious belief and practice is going to occur and flourish. "For whoever wishes to save his life will lose it, but whoever loses his life for my sake and that of the gospel will save it" (Mark 8:36).

A hermeneutics of suspicion can contribute to such death of self. In this respect religious belief becomes less and less a flight from reality and more and more an encounter with it at its deepest and most comprehensive. Thomas Merton, a twentieth-century Catholic monk, expresses this orientation vividly.

> The monk who is truly a man of prayer and who seriously faces the challenge of his vocation in all of its depth is by that very fact exposed to existential dread. He experiences in himself the emptiness, the lack of authenticity, the quest for fidelity, the "lostness" of modern man, but he experiences all this in an altogether different and deeper way than does man in the modern world, to whom this disconcerting awareness of himself and of this world comes rather as an experience of boredom and of spiritual disorientation. The monk confronts his own humanity and that of his world at the deepest and most central point where the void seems to open out to black despair. The monk confronts this serious possibility, and rejects it, as Camusian man confronts "the absurd" and transcends it by his freedom. The option of absolute despair is turned into perfect hope by the pure and humble supplication of monastic prayer. The monk faces the worst, and discovers in it the hope of the best. From the darkness comes light. From death, life. From the abyss there comes, unaccountably,

the mysterious gift of the Spirit sent by God to make all things new, to transform the created and redeemed world, and to re-establish all things in Christ.[25]

Nietzsche

If Freud focuses on ontological weakness seeking consolation, Nietzsche dwells on sociological weakness seeking revenge. Unlike Freud, he focuses on what is historically specific. Unlike Marx, he focuses on the weakness rather than the strength of class power from whence domination and exploitation proceed. Because my approach in this book is so influenced by Marx, Western Marxism, and critical theory, therefore, Nietzsche will be an important, necessary complement. At what point does legitimate anger against social injustice turn into seething resentment? At what point does recognition of objective injustice and victimization turn into a certain willingness to be or play the victim? At what point does legitimate critique of power turn into anger against all legitimate self-assertion and excellence present in any society?[26]

Whereas Freud and Marx are committed modernists who buy into the modern project of enlightenment and critique, Nietzsche is perhaps the first postmodernist. He is committed to a counter-enlightenment or postenlightenment perspective; modern reason is inherently dominating and repressive and needs to be overcome. I have already criticized such postmodernism elsewhere and in this book, somewhat in Nietzsche but more in twentieth-century disciples. That will not be my main point here. Rather here I am interested in a more positive reading and use of Nietzsche, Nietzsche as master of suspicion whose insights can aid a modernist religious project.[27]

Nonetheless, a few brief comments are in order on Nietzsche's postmodernism and its basis. Nietzsche presents the will to power as a universal claim about the world as a whole. Such a claim is, first of all, in tension with Nietzsche's desire to overcome metaphysics. Second, the claim is inconsistent with a stated perspectivism. Each person tends to carve up the world interpretively according to his or her own will to power, her own drive to self-assertion and self-actualization. The feminist sees the world one way and the male chauvinist another. In contrast to the universality of the metaphysical claim, relativism has to be a consequence of Nietzsche's perspectivism.[28]

When we come to Nietzsche's account of the morality of mores, he is less metaphysical and more historical in his orientation. To be moral, correct, ethical means to obey an age old law or tradition. Custom and tradition arise out of a community's own will to power, its need to conserve and enhance itself. Superstition, fear, cruelty, and domination are some of the means by which morality is established and enforced. There is nothing universal about specific moralities; indeed moralities are inevitably plural. Also my enthusiasm for morality will be proportional to the extent that it constrains others, not myself.[29]

Nietzsche's form of suspicion he calls genealogy—that is, the inquiry into concealed historical, sociological origins of belief and practices. Here he asks what needs or interests rooted in an individual's or community's will to power motivate the adoption of moral values. We could say that there is a Freudian element to Nietzsche in that the motives for adopting a morality can be uncontaminated by moral restraint, repressed or unconscious. The reason for adopting a policy of morality is not moral; rather it is rooted in my will to power. Moreover, we note a Marxian component to Nietzsche's analysis insofar as such needs and drives are sociologically conditioned.[30]

Before I go on, we should note that, like Freud, Nietzsche has an epistemological skepticism. Religious belief functions as an opiate; God makes me happy, therefore God exists. Because I have dealt with such skepticism in a previous chapter, I will not consider it further here except to repeat that such an objection does not touch an argument for the existence of God based, as mine is, on the pure desire to know, which is the source of the suspicion concerning illegitimate wish-fulfillments. Here my main focus will be on the functional role religious belief plays in the lives of individuals or groups.[31]

Even though moralities are basically plural, there are two basic kinds running through the history of humankind, master and slave morality. Master morality arises in the soul of ruling tribes and castes. "The man who has the power to requite goodness with goodness, evil with evil, and really does practice requital by being grateful and vengeful—is called 'good'; the man who is unpowerful and cannot requite is taken as bad."[32]

Several points are worth noting here. First, the phrase "ruling tribes and castes" indicates that such morality arises from particular groups, not society as a whole. Here we find something very similar to Marx's class analysis, which, as we will soon see, argues that the ruling ideas in a society are those of the ruling class. Second, in master morality revenge is a virtue. We will see later why he condemns the vengefulness of slave morality. Third, the primary value is good/noble, not bad/base. Fourth, because spontaneous self-celebration of strength is the primary value and revenge is a primary virtue, the identification of altruism and morality is mistaken. The morality of love for neighbor is rooted in slave morality. Finally, the enemies of good are themselves good, not evil. The morality of the strong is shamelessly egoistic; others not as noble are subordinate by nature and should sacrifice themselves.[33]

The essence of slave morality is that those over whom the strong exercise their power see them as evil. The moral distinction is between good and evil rather than noble and base, and the two distinctions are significantly, really, importantly distinct. The most basic difference between master and slave morality is one of origin; master morality arises in the strong and slave morality arises in the weak. There is a further difference of content; justice is in the interest of the stronger in master morality, and slave morality speaks of equality, justice, and altruism. Consequently, in master morality noble is basic and base is derived, whereas in slave morality evil is basic and good is derived. Because they are evil, I am good. Westphal calls this "the Fonda fallacy." Journeying to Hanoi in the 1960s, Jane Fonda perceived U.S. policy as evil, and she uncritically affirmed Ho Chi Min as good.

Such evaluations express the revenge of the oppressed. Such revenge differs from that of the oppressor, the master class, in several ways. The origin of revenge in the oppressed is resentment rather than self-affirmation and self-celebration. Because such resentment cannot find expression in action or fears to express itself in action, it smolders and seethes within the breasts of the weak. Moreover, the weak deceive themselves about their morality in a way that the master class does not. Slave morality is contemptible because it is a big lie, giving itself high-sounding reasons to justify what is in fact ignoble, self-serving behavior and motivation. That here honesty and intellectual integrity are values for Nietzsche is true; that he has the right to uphold them as values is probably not the case, given his commitment to the will to power and perspectivism. Truth, therefore, is instrumental, whatever serves my will to power.[34]

Pastoral power, exercised by the minister or priest in society, is weak insofar as it is relatively powerless in a socio-economic sense, strong insofar as it has a social function. This strength is reinforced when it is linked to socio-economic power. The priest's weapon is the truth rooted in the ascetic ideal, the cluster of ascetic, altruistic, and moral values associated with religion East and West. Through the priest the resentment that originally had as its object a powerful group is turned against his subjects; "you are guilty, you are sinful." He alters the direction of resentment, and herein lies his power, which is often wielded despotically and tyrannically.

Such an account links up with Marx's account in several ways. Though Nietzsche speaks of castes and Marx of classes, the notion of hierarchy and domination is present in both. A second affinity lies in the way both argue that caste or class have a hermeneutical monopoly of means of interpretation. A third affinity occurs insofar as the state has a monopoly of means of violence and the church a monopoly of means of interpretation; the possibility of cooperation is very strong. Nietzsche gives us an analysis of the origins of priestly power, an account of the social origins of the Grand Inquisitor. Since Dostoevsky in *Brothers Karamazov* makes clear that Christ has no more cunning competitor, both philosophers and Christians would do well to look at his account. Dostoevsky presents Christ as a liberator interested in the freedom of his subjects, contrasted with the Grand Inquisitor who is interested in subjugating his subjects. Thus has priestly power, in fiction and in fact, in the past and present betrayed Christ while claiming to serve him.[35]

For all the above reasons, Christian morality is immoral, dishonest, weak, hypocritical. The virtues of the Christian are splendid vices—splendid because they represent a spiritual achievement, vicious because they mask a self-centered will to power that is immoral by its own criteria and because they engage in self-deception. Weakness, rather than being owned up to as a necessary fact of life, is treated as a virtuous achievement. The weakness can be physical or spiritual, and stems from and justifies different kinds of incapacity, lack of self-esteem, lack of intelligence, cowardice, and laziness. I am virtuous because I do not have Kissinger's intellectual brilliance, Mohammed Ali's boxing ability, or Donald Trump's wealth.[36]

Love of neighbor, preached by Christianity as a virtue, is often just a manifestation of low self-esteem, timidity, desire for peace at any price, inability to be alone, fear, laziness. Because I fear to be alone or fear conflict or fear rejection, I just go along and tell myself that I am being virtuous and loving. I am "nice," I am courteous, I am kind, I am gentle. One example of such false neighbor love occurred at a Catholic university where I was teaching. We as a faculty were confronting very unreasonable cuts in salary, faculty, and programs imposed by a fanatically cost-conscious, economist administration for whom academic quality had become unimportant. Only having warm professorial bodies in the classroom to meet tuition-paying undergraduates mattered. When I ran into a fellow male faculty member, a priest, in the recreation center, I discussed these cuts with him and proposed public faculty critique and opposition to the administration as a possibility. He nodded his head reluctantly, but then said that he did not wish to get into too much public critique and conflict "because he wanted to feel good about himself and the university."

When I made the same proposal to another faculty member, also a priest, he mentioned that such public critique and opposition would violate the love and togetherness and community to which we in a Catholic university are committed. "Christian neighbor love" in Nietzsche's sense has never been more virulent and for me this kind of interpretation reinforced and complemented my neo-Marxist critique of the university as one-sidedly mirroring and legitimating capitalist values. Such neighbor love, and here I register partial disagreement with Nietzsche, is a caricature of the tough love of real Christianity, exemplified when Christ forced the money changers out of the temple, and healed the blind and lame (Matthew 12:12–17) or when Christ says:

> Do not think that I have come to bring peace upon the earth. I have come to bring not peace but the sword. For I have come to set a man

against his father, a daughter against her mother, and a daughter-in-law against her mother-in-law; and one's enemies will be those of his household. (Matthew 10:34–36)

It struck me then during those years at the university that, as illuminating as Marx was to clarify the economic dimensions of university policies, Nietzsche was as necessary to articulate the pathological *sociology* operative in the university, one element of which was a timid, compliant, obedient faculty unwilling to take the bit in its teeth, unwilling, like Prufrock, "to raise the universe to an overwhelming question."[37] When such politics, values, and attitudes are generalized to become part of the whole society, it is easy to see how Christianity, or indeed any religion, can become a pacifying ideology and narcotic that props up a corrupt , unjust, exploitative status quo. The very victims of that status quo can refuse to criticize or rebel and call it virtue; they can remain stuck in their victimhood and call it obedience or humility or love. We are a long way from Merton or Berrigan or Martin Luther King or Christ here.

True it is that critique and suspicion can be overdone and one-sided at times, that a critique without love and compassion for what is criticized is suspect, that excessive anger can lead to excessive violence and terror and self-righteousness. What authentic Christianity points to, however, is a gentle and assertive tough love that avoids the extremes of either soft, one-sided love and one-sided, excessively angry critique. The civil disobedience of a King or a Berrigan, I would argue, is an example of such gentle and assertive religiously motivated love. It is nonviolent and loving toward the oppressor, but it raises hard questions about an unjust status quo, is willing to confront it publicly, is honest, and is willing to risk physical injury, prison, and even death in order to express its critique. Such love proceeds from and is modeled upon religion as liberation, Jesus Christ Liberator, which I will be discussing in a later chapter, and is as different from the neighbor love Nietzsche criticizes as day is from night.

Two other virtues that Nietzsche genealogically unmasks are justice and pity. Is there not, he asks, in the passion for distributive justice an expression of envy on the part of the have-nots? Is there not in the desire for retributive justice the passion for punishment and revenge? Those filled with resentment long for the hangman and the electric chair. "Mistrust all in whom the impulse to punish is powerful . . . the hangman and bloodhound look out of their faces. Mistrust all who talk much of their justice." The desire for justice can lead to a moral fanaticism that drowns everything in an orgy of class or race war. Extremists on the right and on the left fall under Nietzsche's critical, suspicious gaze. Is their call for justice genuine or only an expression of resentment? Nietzsche's tendency, of course, is to deny that such a call could be genuine.[38]

Rather than Hitler being a logical consequence and expression of Nietzsche's thought, a claim that some have made, it is more appropriate to see Hitler as a gifted, secular, ascetic priest skilled in the use of language to arouse the resentment of the masses and to lead them to support the final solution. In this respect, we can sympathize very much with Foucault, when he describes Deleuze's and Guattari's very Nietzschean (and Marxian) *Anti-Oedipus: Capitalism and Schizophrenia* as "the introduction to the nonfascist life." Along with them we can see how there is an unholy negativity that has nothing to do with critique, resistance, or liberation, and that blocks self-and-other-affirming revolutionary theory and practice. Unlike them, I think there is room for some negativity, that which is rooted in a legitimate critique and overcoming of injustice, but who can deny that this has often been accompanied by or even replaced by envy, resentment, revenge, and dishonesty? Who can deny that legitimate progressive leftist goals and projects have been corrupted in this way? In a Nietzschean spirit, we could say that leftist morality in practice is often immoral in its self-righteousness, violence, terror, domination, and resentment.[39]

The current rage for imprisonment, prison building, and capital punishment in the United States is another example of an unholy crusade for justice, masquerading under an assumed aura of religion and morality. Prison building has been on the increase; it has become one of the leading industries in the United States—the prison-industrial complex. Such an orientation, again, has socio-economic and sociological aspects upon which both Marx and Nietzsche can shed light. As city, state, and federal governments cut back on welfare and on funding for the cities, as the drug war increases, as the Latino and black ghettoes become more and more places of social despair and possible sources of social disruption, the prison-industrial complex becomes a source of investment for regions left bereft by capital flight, a way of employing otherwise unemployed white workers in these regions, and a way of containing unrest in the ghettoes. At the same time the rage and self-righteousness and obsessiveness with which we institutionalize and implement the death penalty makes us suspect on Nietzschean grounds. The United States is the only western country to have the death penalty now, and we have recently increased it to include over sixty crimes.

One example of these tendencies is Mumia Abu Jamal, a black journalist sentenced to death in 1982 on the trumped up charge of killing a white Philadelphia police officer. Mumia had been a thorn in the side of the Philadelphia political establishment, a strong critic of widespread police brutality, and a defender and advocate of MOVE, a radical black community whose homes were fire bombed and many of whom were killed in a police raid ordered by Philadelphia's mayor. Even while in jail, he continued to be a "voice for the voiceless," reflecting in tapes and writings on prison conditions nationwide as they affect incarcerated blacks and Latinos and as they reflect the institutionalized classism and racism in the United States. Consequently, I was not too surprised when Governor Thomas Ridge ordered Mumia's execution on August 17, 1995, thus morally and religiously keeping his promise to the electorate to revive the death penalty. I will be talking in other chapters about capitalism as an economy of death. Certainly one of the most visible aspects of that is the prison industrial complex.[40]

Pity for Nietzsche is also similarly motivated; in pity we see the structure of slave morality as such. It is rooted in resentment, can occur as a flight from self-esteem, and exacts a subtle revenge. By compelling in a superior way active gratitude from the recipient, it enacts benevolent revenge. Pity is paternalistic and exerts a moral superiority to the person receiving aid. It is pharisaic; the Pharisees "are all men of *resentment* . . . a whole tremulous realm of subterranean revenge."[41]

What is noteworthy here is that Jesus himself was strongly critical of the Pharisees and, consequently, was as strongly hated by them as is Nietzsche's Zarathustra by the "good and just." Organized religion can and does function as the antithesis to genuine religious belief and practice. Here again it is tempting to see Nietzsche as a plagiarist of the New Testament. He carries out a critique of religion similar to that already present in the Bible.[42]

In the Parable of the Pharisee and the Tax Collector (Luke 18:9–14), for example, we see a fundamental contrast between inauthentic religion and authentic religious belief. The Pharisee congratulates himself before God, thanking God that he is not like other men; the tax collector humbles himself and asks mercy for himself as a sinner. One point to notice here is the way in which the tax collector is marginalized by the Pharisee as outside the church; here is one indication of Jesus's identification with the oppressed. Another point to notice is that the tax collector calls himself a sinner. This action seems to escape Nietzsche's alternatives of master morality, in which we are good and they are bad; and slave morality, in which they are bad and we are good. The tax collector has some status in the larger, secular community, but does not use it to exalt himself and put down others.[43]

The story of the woman taken in adultery illustrates the same points (Luke 7:36–50). The Pharisees bring before Jesus a woman caught in adultery and ask him what he thinks. His response is to say, "let the one among you who is without sin be the first to throw a stone at her." In the story of the Prodigal Son (Luke 15:11–32), the father generously and compassionately forgives the repentant sinner and son returned home and has to confront the petulant older brother, who says, "Look all these many years I have served you, and not once did I disobey your orders." The father responds, "But now we must celebrate and rejoice, because your brother was dead and he has come to life again; he was lost and has been found."

The older brother represents and expresses the pharisaic attitude toward life, refusing to share in either the forgiveness or the meal celebrating it. In acting this way he reveals that the so-called righteous are more deeply alienated from God than are sinners. Compassion plays a key role both in this parable and that of the Good Samaritan. Both the Samaritan and the forgiving father are Jesus' critique and alternative to the dominant, self-righteous pharisaic culture. The ones who pass by the outcast and refuse to give are part of that culture. In a similar way we in the United States and in New York City (and most other major and minor American cities) sit numbed and indifferent as beggar after beggar comes through subway trains and walks our streets, telling ourselves in self-righteous, moral, religious fashion that they deserve their fates because they are lazy, welfare cheaters, and have not worked hard like us. Like the Prodigal Son despoiled of his substance or the man set upon by robbers, they deserve their fate.[44]

Further conflict arises in the debate with the Pharisees over the Sabbath. Jesus heals a man with a withered hand in the synagogue on the Sabbath, after which the Pharisees plot to kill him. He heals a man who had been unable to stand upright for eighteen years, and then heals a man with dropsy. In doing so, he notes that the Pharisees have no qualms about untying their livestock to lead them to water or about pulling an ox or ass that has fallen into a well to safety. How can they object to aiding a human being on the Sabbath (Mark 3:1–6; Luke 13:10–17; 14:1–6)?

Again Jesus questions the Pharisees concern for cleanliness. In their symbolic system, good vs. evil, righteous vs. sinner, and clean vs. dirty were more or less interchangeable. Consequently, when the Pharisees catch the disciples eating with unwashed hands on the Sabbath, they are critical. Jesus responds with:

> Well did Isaiah prophesy of you hypocrites, as it is written,
> > "This people honors me with their lips,
> > but their heart is far from me;
> > in vain do they worship me,
> > teaching as doctrines the precepts of men."
> You leave the commandment of God, and hold fast the tradition of men.
> (Mark 7:1–13)

Just as Nietzsche thinks that what is really important is not on the surface of our actions, so Jesus claims that what is most important is in the human heart. Also Jesus complains that the Pharisees do not take seriously the command to love their neighbor; they subordinate or sacrifice that commandment to religious rules or rites. Because they are indifferent to human need, theirs is a false piety. If one genuinely loves God with one's whole heart and whole soul, the First Commandment, then the test and expression of that is love for the neighbor, especially for the marginalized and poor and exploited.

Pharisaism is guilty, therefore, in Westphal's words, of "Third Commandment idolatry." The third commandment says that we should not take the name of God in vain. The Pharisees constantly speak of God, but in their actions and in their hearts they take the name of God in vain. The essence of such idolatry is human usurpation of the divine, the reduction of the commandments of God to merely human traditions and laws.[45]

I find Nietzsche enormously insightful and challenging here. As a leftist and believer, I think Nietzsche reminds us of the dangers of a self-righteousness on the left, of a simplistic identification with the poor, of the dangers of a hunger and thirst for justice that becomes vengeful and terroristic. How many good, progressive, movements, reforms, and revolutions in the twentieth century, I wonder, have been done in by such attitudes and values and practices.

There is a pharisaism on the secular and religious left that Nietzsche, and Jesus, properly warns us against. Such a stance might take the following form:

> Thank you, God, that I am not like other human beings. They have not run the political risks that I have run. They have not committed the civil disobedience that I have, they have not spent time in jail for conscience's sake and I have, they have not identified publicly with the oppressed and I have, they have not spoken out and I have. They are merely bourgeois, secure professionals and academics, and I am a heroic, radical academic. Thank you, God, that I am not like other human beings.

Nietzsche's point here, and it is one that I have been making throughout these three volumes, is the importance of self-affirmation. A chastity based on impotence or a love based on weak self-esteem or a meekness based on inability to become angry and assert myself are fraudulent in whole or in part. I have articulated different steps of self-affirmation throughout my three volumes and throughout this volume; cognitive self-affirmation of myself as knower, existential choice of myself as an experiencing, understanding, judging, and choosing subject in relationship to being, psychic conversion in which I rescue my sexuality, eros, and feelings from a punitive, repressive superego and integrate them into my conscious life, the ethical moment and its articulation into right, morality, and justice, radical political conversion as an implication of intellectual, moral, and, as we will see, religious conversion, and a radical praxis in which the oppressed become aware of themselves as not only oppressed but as worthwhile, valuable, responsible agents who organize, rise up, and resist.[46]

Freud, Nietzsche, and Marx also have a light to shed and a role to play in such self-affirmation and its implications. Freud helps us to become aware of our unconscious and sexuality and eros, but he needs Nietzsche in order to move from mere resignation to joyful affirmation of self, and they both need Marx in order to move adequately to social critique and transformation. Joyful critique arises out of such self-affirmation. "Laughing lions must come . . . I would only believe in a god who could dance."[47]

It is one thing to recognize that a group has been unjustly oppressed. Nietzsche tends not to do justice to this moment; here is where he needs Marx. But it is another thing to stay in that situation of oppression in a state of wretched contentment that takes easy revenge on the oppressor as a form of resentment. To do that, of course, is to play into the hands of the oppressor, who has ideologically tried to convince and to brainwash me that he is worthwhile and powerful, and I am not. I can do nothing and I am nothing.

Consequently, the beginnings of any reformist or radical praxis by oppressed women, laborers, African-Americans, the poor, and homosexuals should include a process of conscientization in which we become aware not only of our oppression but of our worthwhileness. "I am woman, and I am beautiful" or "black is beautiful" or "gay pride." Not only have we endured injustice from the oppressor but we have also introjected the ideological idea of us. "You are poor, therefore you are worthless and can do nothing." To stay in this stance merely plays into the hands of the oppressor, and a religious belief that does that just reinforces the rule of the oppressor. A liberator God and Christ who encourages me and empowers me to criticize oppression and to act against it are entirely different.[48]

There is, therefore, a bogus and authentic identification with the poor and oppressed. The bogus form is the one that stays stuck in resentment. The authentic form is that which is rooted in self-affirmation. As a radical, I affirm that there are people, maybe even I myself, who are illegitimately exploited, marginalized, and oppressed. But because such recognition is based on a legitimate self-affirmation and affirmation of the other, we can then proceed to act against and overcome such oppression, not just wallow in it.

The same distinction applies to religious belief. There is a religious belief based on flight from self and hatred of self. There is also a religious belief based on and proceeding from self-affirmation as I have argued for it in this book. Thus, the trajectory moves from self-affirmation to the intelligibility of being to God as the ground of such intelligibility to a liberator God and Christ working with us to overcome injustice to individual and group praxis necessary to achieve liberation. There is, therefore, an illegitimate and legitimate expression of weakness and dependence, that flowing from such self-hate and that which flows from self-affirmation as an aspect or part of liberation.

It is in this sense that the religious "without you I can do nothing" makes sense. It is analogous to and yet different from spouses who say something like that to their mates to whom they are linked for life. They are together not out of weakness, out of inability to stand on their own two feet as individuals. But this very need of the other paradoxically grows out of their strength: "because I affirm and love myself as an individual and social being, I need you." Similarly, because I affirm and love myself as a pure desire to know oriented to complete intelligibility and as openness to an actual and possible religious revelation, I love God and Christ. If I did not care enough about myself to undertake the process of self-affirmation leading to metaphysics, religious belief, and liberation, God and Christ would be empty words for me.

Marx

In moving to Marx at last, we are confronting somebody who launched what remains still the most searching and profound critique of capitalism. Twentieth-century Western Marxism, critical theory, and liberation philosophy and theology are enormously indebted to him. All decent social theory is a footnote to Marx, because the capitalism that Marx criticized has now become almost worldwide, with terrible, destructive impact on the world's poor, workers, and environment. I would argue that Marx's critique is more relevant than ever; in this respect, I agree with Michael Parenti, who says that Marx is more relevant than ever because the capitalism that he so trenchantly criticized is now worldwide. I have argued to some extent for such claims in PCM and CAL, and will in the penultimate chapter argue for them in the context of the current neoimperialism, which I am calling "The New World Order."[49]

Not only is Marx's critique still relevant, insightful, and valid, but so also is his solution to the contradictions of capitalism, full, economic, political, and social democracy. I agree with Gould, Harrington, Rader, Ollman, Peffer, and many others in thinking that Marx is most properly read as a democratic socialist. People such as Michael Novak, who read him as simply or primarily statist, reductionistic, and deterministic, factors certainty present in the subsequent, vulgar Marxist thought of people like Stalin and Lenin, simply miss the nuance and complexity in Marx's thought on these questions. They flatten him out into a one-dimensional thinker who is easily refuted. This ease of refutation, of course, is the point. If Marx were more complex, if his thought were less easily dismissed, then perhaps we would heed his critique of capitalism more seriously than we do.[50]

Related to this point is the issue of the demise of the Soviet Union, which is presented as the demise of "Marxism" and the triumph of capitalism.

There is an interpretive and a twofold logical problem here. The interpretive problem is related to what I said in the preceding paragraphs. If the equation of Marx with vulgar Marxism is wrong and if the Soviet Union is a version of that, as I think it was, then the demise of the Soviet Union does not mean a failure of Marxism in the genuine sense at all. Rather, now that this bogus example of Marxism has been thoroughly discredited historically, genuine Marxism can be taken seriously and given a chance.

Second, whatever we think of Marx's recommended cure to the ills of capitalism, we need to attend to his critique of capitalism. Just as a diagnosis of cancer does not depend for its validity on the success of any of the proposed cures of cancer, so also the validity of Marx's critique of capitalism does not depend on the success of any of the proposed cures. Third, it is hard not to see another version of the Fonda fallacy in all of this celebration of the fall of the Soviet Union and the triumph of liberal capitalism. Because the Soviet Union was evil, the liberal capitalism that opposed it was and is good. Another alternative, the one I am defending here, is that capitalism is equally or more pathological than Soviet Marxism. A plague on both their houses.[51]

Not only is Marx's general diagnosis of and cure for capitalism still valid, but so are many arguments and insights such as value theory, the essential connection between capitalism and poverty, and his account of ideology. It is that upon which I will be focusing on in this chapter.

Marx's critique of ideology and of religion as a form of ideology builds upon and completes Feuerbach's critique of religion as projection. There are several distinct layers to this account, a Hegelian, a Freudian, and a political-economic that Feuerbach does not and Marx does develop. When Feuerbach says that the idea of God is simply the idea of the human species as individual, he is saying that we project onto God perfections belonging to the human species. When he says that in religion consciousness and self-consciousness coincide, we are conscious of God as related to our consciousness but not as projected. The next step to be taken is to realize that we have simply created God in our own image and likeness. The Freudian element occurs when Feuerbach says that religion is a dream or dreamlike. Unlike Freud, he says that we project what is best of ourselves onto God. When he says that we project a god rich in human attributes because of our human material poverty, Feuerbach is stumbling onto a political-economic dimension that Marx will pick up and develop.[52]

What Marx does with this insight is to historicize it and contextualize it in a way that Feuerbach does not. For Feuerbach the projection of a god motivated by poverty is metaphysical, universal, eternal; for Marx the projection of such a god is rooted in specific conditions of poverty in our time caused by capitalism. In order for Feuerbach's humanism truly to become itself and to complete itself, therefore, it must become social theory and critique of political economy. Atheistic humanism is necessary for a fully human world.

This conclusion does not follow from anything Marx has said. As such, it is a dogmatic assertion. What does deserve more attention from religious believers is his claim that religion supports unjust social structures. The more effective refutation here would be practical: religion and religious believers would cease to support such structures and begin to work against them and resist them and overcome them.[53]

I take Marx as simply accepting and building on Feuerbach's critique of God as projection. In this respect I take my account of God in Part One as implicitly answering such a critique. Belief in God as uncritical projection or dream is distinct from an affirmation of God based upon the imperative of the desire to know, which is itself the source of the critique of invalid projection and illusion. If God is necessary to account for the existence and operation of the desire to know and for it not to fall into contradiction with itself, then belief in such a god cannot be a projection and an illusion. The very ontological and epistemic conditions of the possibility for criticizing projection and illusion cannot itself be a projection and illusion.

When Marx, then, in the *Introduction to the Critique of the Philosophy of Right* makes the claim that humanism equals atheistic humanism, that claim does not follow from anything he says; it remains dogmatic and arbitrary. Moreover, when he points to the role of religion as mirroring and justifying injustice *essentially*, his critique of religion is one-sided to the extent that religious belief and practice have also functioned as a critique and overcoming of injustice; consider Gandhi, Martin Luther King, Dorothy Day, and Gustavo Gutiérrez as examples. Moreover, Marx says that religious suffering is at the same time "true expression of real suffering and a protest against real suffering." Yet he does not develop that point about "protest" in a way that his text would seem to demand. Here again his account seems one-sided.[54]

Nonetheless, even if we deny that the most authentic humanism is necessarily atheistic, that God is necessarily a projection of human subjectivity, and that religion always functions as legitimating ideology for injustice, I would hold that Marx's concrete critique of religion as it functions has a good deal of truth. Religion often functions as an opiate, as a painkiller, as a consolation to the oppressed classes, and as a moral legitimation for the guilty conscience of the ruling class.

> Religious suffering is at the same time an expression of real suffering and a protest against real suffering. Religion is the sigh of the oppressed creature, the feeling of a heartless world, and the soul of soulless circumstance. It is the opium of the people.[55]

About this quotation, to which I have already adverted, we can make several points. First, religious suffering is an expression of real worldly suffering. Second, religion can and does function as a protest against such suffering. Third, rather than following up on this point, Marx claims that religion is an opium, a form of consolation or painkiller especially tempting when the will or opportunity for social action and protest are lacking. Fourth, not only is religion a painkiller and consolation, but for the masters it can function as moral legitimation. Earlier in the *Introduction* Marx has referred to the capitalist world's "moral sanction" and "justification." Finally, critique and action are necessary to remove the conditions of injustice making religious belief necessary. "The abolition of religion as the illusory happiness of the people is the demand for their real happiness."[56]

Also, and following on the above points, for Marx the relationship of religion to the secular state is very problematic indeed. Private religious belief echoes the separation within the human being between the private egoistic self and the public political self; in capitalist society the latter is subordinated to the former. The state is a means for private economic goals. Furthermore, the spirit of this private world, which Marx calls "civil society," is the spirit of egoism, the war of all against all.

Nor is the private sphere devoid of public influence. Although the state no longer requires prerequisites of class, birth, education, or property ownership for political participation, these function factually and "have an effect in their own manner . . . Far from abolishing these factual differences, its existence rests upon them as presupposition."[57] Religion is such a factual presupposition, which makes its presence felt even in the secular state. In North America, the land of religiosity par excellence, the legal separation of church from state has not prevented religion from functioning as a legitimation for imperialism, manifest destiny, slavery, racism, sexism, and heterosexism, prejudice against homosexuals. President McKinley's account of how he reached the decision to enter the Spanish-American war is illustrative:

> I walked the floor of the White House night after night until midnight; and I am not ashamed to tell you gentlemen that I went on my knees and prayed to almighty God for light and guidance more than one night. And one night it came to me this way—that there was nothing left for us to do but to take them all, and to educate the Filipinos, and uplift and civilize and Christianize them, and by God's grace do the very best we could by them, as our fellow man for whom Christ also died. And then I went to bed and went to sleep and slept soundly.[58]

The white man's burden takes a U.S. form; heavy lies the head that wears the imperial crown.

Marx's final point concerning the relationship between religion and the state is that religion also functions as an analogue of the state. Just as the political state has a spiritual, ideal, legal relationship to civil society, which nonetheless reinstates it, so also religion represents a "heavenly" overcoming of earthly life that nonetheless reinstates it and allows itself to be dominated by it. Just as politics is civil war carried on by other means, so also religion is bourgeois egoism carried on by other means. One example of this tendency is the focus in contemporary religious belief on the salvation of the individual soul to the exclusion of any concern for social justice. Another is the concern for private, sexual morality coexisting with indifference to real human life outside the womb oppressed or crushed by unjust social structures. If religion, we could say, in its practice and preaching encourages and emphasizes belief in individualistic, other-worldly salvation and morality, such belief in practice leaves the ordinary bourgeois professional and capitalist in the pew quite unchallenged, uncriticized, and indeed consoled. As long as he comes to church regularly on Sunday, supports the church financially, and does not commit abortion or adultery, he is upright. That he is an executive in a large corporation that exploits its workers, invests in imperial enterprises abroad, marginalizes the poor, and pollutes the environment is morally irrelevant. He is a "Sunday Christian or Jew," who is good to his children, wife, and God on weekends and exploits the rest of the world during the week.[59]

Marx's so called "materialism" is historical rather than metaphysical—that is, it is not an account determining whether the world is made up ultimately of spirit and matter, but an account of the relationship among economic, political, and cultural dimensions of modern society. What is the relationship between culture or philosophy or religion and fundamental economic structures and interests?

Marx's answer is to say "that the ideas of the ruling class are in every epoch the ruling ideas, i.e. the class which has the means of material production at its disposal has control over the means of mental production . . . The ruling ideas are nothing but the ideal expression of the dominant material relationships." To illustrate this point, that General Electric owns N.B.C. is a clue to deciphering why N.B.C. generally airs ideas and opinions favorable to or uncritical of G.E. and deemphasizes or ignores ideas and opinions critical of G.E. and capitalism.[60]

Such ideas become ideology when they reflect and legitimize the domination, exploitation, and hegemony exercised by this class over other people in the society. In capitalist society, Marx argues, such domination, exploitation, and hegemony are exercised primarily against and toward the working class, those who do not own and control the means of production but who produce the products that are the source of capitalist profit.

One characteristic of ideology for Marx is that it fails to notice the social conditioning of ideas. It also presents itself as neutral, independent, value-free, but in fact is not neutral, is dependent, and is value-laden. Thus, a liberal separating of the public and private spheres in capitalism, while claiming to be value-free and independent, in fact encourages and legitimizes that separation in capitalism and covers up the way political life serves economic exploitation and domination. Or the private, other-worldly orientation of some versions of Christianity leaves the real capitalist world unthematized and uncriticized. Or the apparently neutral, objective, value-free stance of the liberal, bourgeois academic, who in fact is committed to and supported by capitalism, writes off as "not real philosophy" or "not real social science" forms of thought such as Marxism, critical theory, or liberation theology that bring capitalism into question, and is not open to and gives short shrift to such methods of inquiry.[61]

Like all ideology, religious belief resorts to several techniques of neutralization. One of these is, in Westphal's words, "overt espousal." The behavior of dominant institutions is explicitly declared to be the will of God. Thus, the Nazis made unconditional obedience to the state a religious duty, the Dutch Reformed Church presented apartheid as a religious mandate, evangelical missionaries in Vietnam and Central and Latin America persuaded peasants under their tutelage to support repressive regimes kept in power by U.S. imperial support, and the war against communism became a holy war.[62]

Overt espousal, however, because it has few resources for persuading the victims of injustice that they should go along, is limited as a technique of neutralization. Consequently, other techniques become necessary. One of these is to encourage ignorance of the Bible among those at the bottom; such a strategy was employed in the U.S. in the nineteenth century with the slaves. They were prevented from reading politically explosive passages in the Bible such as Christ's distinguishing in the last judgment between those who were generous to the poor and suffering and marginalized, and those who were not as a criterion for entering the kingdom of heaven (Matthew 25:31–46); or Mary's Magnificat, which describes God as putting down the mighty from their thrones, filling the hungry with good things, and sending the rich away empty (Luke 1:46–55).[63]

Another technique is to edit selectively the Bible stressing the passages counseling obedience and leaving out others such as the Magnificat that are more critical and utopian. Or the ruling powers can allow reading of the Bible as a whole but interpret it in such a way as to render innocuous certain passages. One such technique is vague generality. We espouse the commandment to love our neighbor but do not apply it to the relationships between white and black, rich and poor, heterosexual and homosexual. Thus, the South African synod at one point openly decried racism as a sin, but could not identify apartheid as racist. Vague generality keeps us from the risks of siding concretely with the poor and oppressed, and from running the risks of being wrong in some of our political choices, policies, and strategies.

A final strategy for neutralizing the utopian content of the gospel is dualistic hermeneutics. We have already seen examples of this in the Sunday Christian and the privatistic, individualistic, other-worldly Christian not concerned with social injustice, focusing instead on the relationship with God and immediate, personal forms of interaction. Thus, in the United States the Pro-Life Movement, whatever one may think of its stance on abortion, is dominantly such an ideology because it focuses primarily on life within the womb and conspicuously ignores life outside the womb victimized by various forms of injustice such as racism, sexism, classism, and heterosexism. Another example is the current religious emphasis on "family values," oriented to the immediate family but ignoring or leaving unthematized the broader, less immediate forms of structural injustice or "social sin" characteristic of advanced capitalism and leading to poverty, unemployment, homelessness, and hunger. These seem to have nothing to do with family and, therefore, nothing to do with morality, except in the eyes of right wing Christians who see them as results of personal laziness, unwillingness to work hard, and so on. The widespread, conservative attack on the welfare state and on "welfare cheats" is another example of dualistic hermeneutics.

Dualistic hermeneutics is characterized by a series of interrelated dualities such as spiritual vs. material, future eternal life vs. present earthly life, personal and inward vs. social and public, vertical vs. horizontal, and so on. Using such dualities, the Christian message articulates itself in exclusively individualistic, privatistic, other-worldly terms; the social order is dealt with only to the extent that it is divinely ordained. One symptom of such dualism is the preference for Matthew's "blessed are the poor in spirit" (Matthew 5:3), over Luke's more materialistic "blessed are you who are poor" (Luke 6:20). Christianity can become the opiate of slaves or other oppressed because it builds its foundation on private ecstasy and spirituality; concrete injunctions to serve the poor and identify with them, as in Luke 11:29–37 (The Parable of the Good Samaritan), or claims such that it is harder for the rich man to enter the kingdom of heaven than for a camel to pass through the eye of a needle (Matthew 19:20) or that one must choose between God and mammon (money) (Matthew 6:24) are spiritualized and volatilized away. Masters can feel good because they are really poor in spirit; slaves can feel justified because they are conforming to God's will and will find their reward hereafter. There is then a Marxian as well as a Nietzschean-Freudian component to Christianity as a slave religion. It can function not only as false consolation and as a form of vengeance against strong rulers, but also to legitimize and cover up class or group injustice.[64]

What is the alternative? If such attitudes and practices are widespread in Christianity and other forms of religion, what would a more authentic form of religious belief and practice be? Obviously the way to "refute" Marx is not, as I have said before, primarily theoretical but practical. Religious people should begin to take seriously not only their relationship with God and immediate relationships of family and friendship, but those who are victimized by structures of injustice outside these immediate relationships to God and other people. These relationships are essential and important but not the whole story. Genuine Christianity is holistic; it does not divide people up into spiritual and material or private and public or individual and social, and then choose the former of these sets of opposites, but takes all of these into account and integrates them. Genuine religion and Christianity are holistic or, as Gustavo Gutiérrez tells us, liberatory. He distinguishes three, interlocking levels of meaning in liberation: socio-political liberation, full human, psychological liberation, and liberation from sin—in short, a full, integral liberation:

> There are three levels of meaning of a single, complex process, which finds its deepest sense and its full realization in the saving work of Christ. These levels of meaning, therefore, are interdependent. A comprehensive view of the matter presupposes that all three aspects can be considered together. In this way two pitfalls can be avoided: first, *idealist* or *spiritualist* approaches, which are nothing but ways of evading a harsh and demanding reality, and second, shallow analyses and programs of short-term effect initiated under the pretext of meeting immediate needs.[65]

One way that Christians can begin to be fully Christian in an authentic, liberatory sense is to take their own scriptures seriously. These are, I will be arguing in this and the next chapter, already liberatory, already holistic, already more comprehensive and nuanced than a dualistic conservative or liberal hermeneutics would suggest. In other words, dualistic hermeneutics translated into Christianity is *bad Christianity*, bad on its terms. God as liberator in both the Old and New Testaments wishes God's people to be both interior people of prayer and also people of justice. It is fine to say that "the kingdom of God is among you" (Luke 17:21) and "My kingdom does not belong to this world" (John 18:36). As we have already seen and have been emphasizing, there is a legitimate spiritual, contemplative dimension to Christianity.

But as well, God in the Old and the New Testaments is one who has a passion for justice. As Mary says in her magnificat:

> He has shown might with his arm,
> dispersed the arrogant of mind and heart.
> He has thrown down the rulers from their thrones,
> but has lifted the lowly.
> The hungry he has filled with good things;
> the rich he has sent away empty. (Luke 1:51–53)

Mary was undoubtedly deeply acquainted with the Old Testament. Perhaps Jesus himself learned from her, from Psalms 9–10, the link between pride, power, and wealth, and that God comes to the aid of those victimized by this unholy trinity. Did Jesus learn from her the contrast between the good king of Psalm 72, who gives justice to the poor and crushes the oppressor, and the kings in Psalm 82, who fail to do justice by delivering the weak from the wicked? When people like Archbishop Romero in El Salvador or Dom Hélder Câmara in Brazil or an Anglican archbishop in South Africa, Nobel Peace Prize winner Desmond Tutu, act in solidarity with the poor and oppressed, they are just practicing basic Christianity as articulated in the Old and New Testaments. That such solidarity displeases those in their parishes or dioceses who happen to benefit from or cause such oppression is a sign of the truth and authenticity of their religious preaching and practice. Authentic Christianity is radical and prophetic, or it is not at all.[66]

Christians have resources in the Bible for presenting a critique of contemporary capitalism and the religion that serves it that sound very Marxian: "One of the striking things about the Bible is its hostility to religion," and one of the striking things about this hostility is that it is directed not against other religions and worship of other gods, but against "our" Jewish or Christian religious practice. We note Jesus' critique of the worldliness of his disciples, as in Mark 9:30–41, in which Jesus criticizes his disciples for having a debate about which of them is the greatest and most prestigious in the kingdom. Jesus criticizes, as I have already noted, Jewish legalism focusing on the Sabbath, Paul criticizes Jewish legalism focusing on circumcision, and James criticizes cheap grace.[67]

Such critiques occur frequently in the Old Testament as well. For instance, in Samuel 15:22, we note the following:

> Does the Lord desire holocausts and victims in burnt offerings and sacrifices, and not rather that the voice of the Lord should be obeyed? For obedience is better than sacrifice and to hearken than to offer the fat of rams.

Over and over such themes occur in the Old Testament. Sometimes the call to obedience is generic; at other times it is very specific: "for it is love that I desire, love and not sacrifice, and knowledge of God rather than holocausts" (Hosea 6:6).

Sacrifice and other forms of worship are unacceptable to God when they coexist with or serve economic injustice; God in critique of such practices seems, outrageous as it sounds, "Marxist." Religion becomes "instrumental" religion, very similar to the instrumental reason criticized by Frankfurt school critical theory—that is, scientific, technological reason in the service of capitalist profit and power. With instrumental religion, we have again Third Commandment idolatry, the practical, effective taking of God's name in vain. Since God is on the side of the poor and oppressed, when we side with the oppressor, it is clear that we are not worshiping God. We have effectively substituted another god—money, power, or wealth.[68]

The protest against Third Commandment idolatry resounds throughout the Old and New Testaments. In Amos 5:21–24, we find the following, as he criticizes religious practice in Bethel and Gilgal:

> I hate, I spurn your feasts, I take no pleasure in your solemnities; your cereal offerings I will not accept, nor consider your stall-fed peace offerings. Away with your noisy songs! I will not listen to the melodies of your harps. But if you would offer to me holocausts, then let justice surge like water, and goodness like an unfailing stream.

Because organs and anthem music have drowned out the cries of the poor, the music has turned sour to God's ears.

Amos reflects on two other themes as well, the plight of the poor and the luxury of the rich. He focuses on the lavish eating and drinking habits of the rich and their luxurious homes. His complaint is not that the rich enjoy themselves, but that they do so at the expense of and in extreme indifference to the poor. He distinguishes between actively depriving the poor of what is rightfully theirs and consuming the fruits of such injustice without caring about their victims. These are two equally hideous forms of injustice, equally odious in the eyes of God. In active oppression, the courts are regularly the ally of the powerful rather than the defender of the weak. Moreover, the judges, legislators, and businessmen who are targets of this critique and "who trample upon the needy and destroy the poor" are not atheists but are in church every Sunday, "Sunday Jews," who ask when the Sabbath will be over "so that we may buy the lowly man for silver, and the poor man for a pair of sandals; even refuse of the wheat we will sell!" (Amos 8:4–6).[69]

Amos is not the only "radical" prophet. In the first chapter of Isaiah, we find an equally strong repudiation of false worship and an equally economic interpretation of why Yahweh sees it as an abomination (Isaiah 1:10–23). In this text we find Yahweh's first question about the ethical-religious quality of a society: How does it treat widows and orphans? Or we could turn to Jeremiah 7:1–15, in which he makes a critique of the temple of Jerusalem similar to Amos's critique of the shrines at Bethel and Gilgal. The text indicts not only oppression of foreigners, orphans, and widows, but also the worship of Baal and other false gods. Third Commandment idolatry, it seems, leads to first commandment idolatry, the worship of false gods.[70]

Or in Isaiah 58, we read the following:

Do you call this a fast, a day acceptable to the Lord? This rather, is the fasting that I wish: releasing those bound unjustly, untying the thongs of the yoke; setting free the oppressed, breaking every yoke; sharing your bread with the hungry, sheltering the oppressed and homeless; clothing the naked when you see them, and not turning your back on your own.

In its passionate identification with the poor and oppressed and its eloquent critique of injustice, this rivals anything in Marx.

As we will see more fully in the next chapter, the story of Exodus is paradigmatic for the biblical understanding of who the God of the Bible is. When God chooses a people, he chooses a rabble of slaves to whom he entrusts a new covenant. "I, the Lord, am your God, who brought you out of the land of Egypt, the place of slavery" (Exodus 20:2). God reveals the divine essence in the fact of "bringing out," freeing, "releasing," "saving" the oppressed people. "Say this to the Israelites, I am the Lord and I will free you from the forced labor of the Egyptians and will deliver you from their slavery" (Exod. 6:6–7).

This theme of liberation, of identification of God with the poor and oppressed, appears massively throughout the Old and New Testaments: in the Law, the Psalms, the Prophets, the Gospels, the Epistles, and even the Apocalypse. Liberation theologians properly see that this understanding comes to a climax in the Gospels. They invite us to see the Gospels as the story of the Son of God who liberated the slaves in Egypt. The Son of God is Jesus Christ, Liberator. For example, note Jesus' identification of his mission as "good news to the poor," both in the synagogue in Nazareth (Luke 4), and in his response to the delegation from John the Baptist (Luke 7), his teachings about wealth and power, his relation to women, lepers, tax collectors, Samaritans, and beggars; and the political character of his confrontation with the Jewish authorities, which includes the charge that the temple trade was thievery (Mark 11), his Parable of the Rich Man and Lazarus (Luke 16:19–31), and his healing and compassion for the sick (Luke 14:1–6, 15–24). The Son of God, then, is like the Father; throughout the Gospels we see a person who is incredibly and unfailingly loving and compassionate toward the poor and oppressed, and who becomes legitimately critical and angry toward their oppressors: no soft, weak neighbor love here.[71]

The biblical evidence, then, for the claims I am making is massive and overwhelming. Jesus Christ, Liberator, does not sink into clichés; we note throughout a *coincidentia oppositorum*, a unity of opposites in his person, preaching, and practice between love and anger, justice and mercy, the spiritual and the material, asceticism and pleasure, the inner and the outer, contemplation and action. He fasted for forty days and nights in the desert (Matthew 4:1–11), but then eats and drinks and performs miracles at the wedding feast in Cana (John 2:1–11). He praises Mary's contemplative absorption in him and is critical of Martha for "being anxious and worried about many things" (Luke 11:38–42), but praises those who not only hear the word of God, but act upon it (Luke 8:19–21). He insists upon the importance of spirit and of inner intention (Matthew 6:5–8), but insists also on the validity of the letter of the law (Luke 16:16–17). The dialectical unity of opposites for which I have been arguing all the way through the three volumes is here lived and expressed perfectly by Christ in his person, words, and actions. In relation to him, philosophical dialectic only imperfectly grasps and points to what he embodies perfectly but also mysteriously—incarnate mystery.

There is a sense, therefore, in which Marx already is biblical and the Bible is Marxist. Both the prophets and Marx have an account of justice that is economic, that suggests that no country with as much wealth and so much poverty as ours can be even close to adequacy on human rights, much as we regularly congratulate ourselves on human rights in the political sense. The biblical and Marxist criterion for justice is not our gross national product and our military power, but how we treat our poor, and here we need both the Bible and Marx. We need the Bible to manifest who the God is who calls us to liberation and to insist on the universal validity of this call: "liberate the poor" resounds in every historical epoch. We need Marx to update the critique, to interpret and develop and apply the norms of justice in today's capitalist world. What has emerged and what I will be arguing for more fully later suggests that any religion soft on capitalism, accommodating to it in various ways, as both liberal and conservative versions of Christianity do in the United States and in the world generally, is going to be inadequate as religious belief and practice. It will be tempted by and fall into, more or less, first commandment and third commandment idolatry.

What is necessary in churches both on the right and on the left is the willingness to preach, hear, and act upon the message of Christ and the Prophets; a hermeneutics of suspicion inspired by Marx can help us recover the ideology critique already present within the Bible. It may seem that liberal Christianity is less guilty of ignoring the prophetic critique of Christ and the Prophets than conservative Christianity. What happens, however, is that Christ's message is heard up to the point where reformist adaptation to capitalism should pass over to radical critique and transformation of capitalism. Moreover, the overt espousal and dualistic hermeneutics of conservative churches is replaced by the vague generality characteristic of more liberal churches.[72]

Conclusion

We have taken an important step toward elaborating a philosophy of religion that is not only cogent and true, but also authentic and ethically and politically liberating. First, we have seen that the skeptical critiques given by Freud, Nietzsche, and Marx are not the main nor the most valid aspect of their critiques. In my opinion, they are rather easily handled in terms of the framework and argument set up in Part One. Thus, Freud's positivism in the light of philosophy as generalized empirical method leading to metaphysics and the affirmation of God does not stand up. Nor does Nietzsche's overcoming of metaphysics leading to a metaphysics of the will to power, a self-contradictory perspectivism, and his characterization of religious argument as wish-fulfillment: God makes me happy, therefore God exists. An argument for the existence of God based on the desire to know and an overcoming and rejection of postmodernism undercuts these arguments.

Moreover, Marx's skeptical rejection of religion as projection misses the way the very critical thought and action to which he is committed presumes implicitly the intelligibility of being and, therefore, the reality of God. The account of religion as projection misses the distinctions in Part One between God as hypothesis and God as reality, between God as a projection of inadequate self-knowledge and God as an affirmation proceeding from authentic self-knowledge, and between God as a projection of irrational desire and God as an affirmation proceeding from rational desire, without whom I land in self-contradiction.

Second, we have seen a great deal more validity in Freud's, Nietzsche's, and Marx's critiques of religion as consolation, resentment, and ideology. Unfortunately, they are on the money too much of the time in their interpretation of the way religious belief and practice actually function. Third, however, the three masters of suspicion alert us to the degree an authentic suspicion already operates in the Bible. Jesus and the Prophets are critical, implicitly and explicitly, of the same kinds of religious belief and practice, what we might call the irreligious use of religion.

Fourth, consequently what emerges is a model of religious belief and practice that is relentlessly and continuously purified by suspicion. Religious belief and practice will be more authentic the less they are permeated by consolation, resentment, and social ideology. They will be more authentic the more they are permeated by an honest facing up to the dark night and the cross, genuine compassion, love, and humility, and a thirst for justice. The Gospels, like more recent documents, advocate a preferential option for the poor with radical implications. If capitalism is structurally, essentially unjust, as I have already argued in PCM and CAL and will argue further in this book, and if capitalism "intends" in a structural sense to produce poverty, then both conservative and liberal versions of Christianity, even though they possess some validity, do not go far enough. And Marx, critical theory, Western Marxism, and liberation philosophy and theology help us Christians to see that. If Marx is right and I am correct in my appropriation of him, then to say "radical, prophetic Christianity" is to be redundant.[73]

At the same time Christianity relativizes and transcends any particular philosophical, theological, or political solution. As we have seen somewhat already and will see more fully in later chapters, the Kingdom of God has a gratuitous, mysterious, spiritual dimension that does not allow us to confuse the Kingdom with any historical stage, any human achievement, or any revolution, even a democratic socialist one. No revolution or revolutionary result should be embraced idolatrously. Only God is God.[74]

NINE

The Liberating Christ

Dialectical Considerations

I have indicated in a preliminary way some of the main themes of this chapter. In previous chapters I have stressed that God is processive and loving, is a God of justice, is identified in a special way with the poor, and invites followers to commit themselves to a praxis of liberation.

Objections, however, are not lacking to this interpretation. One of them is that the model of liberation stresses too much the political dimensions of human life and Christianity, and neglects too much the interpersonal dimension and the dimensions of contemplation, grace, personal transformation, and salvation from sin. In the previous chapter, however, I indicated the basis for an answer to that objection when I suggested that liberation has at least three aspects to it: socio-political, human-psychological, and personal-redemptive.

Socio-political liberation, of course, is essential. It means transforming the institutionalized racism, sexism, heterosexism, and classism that oppress and exploit people. There is, however, another dimension to liberation that is more internal and psychological, and is not reducible to the social and political, even though it is linked to them. Liberation, we might say, following Nietzsche, Marcuse, and Deleuze-Guattari, is not only external but also internal, not only liberation from the external oppressor but also liberation from the internal oppressor or fascist who colonizes the mind and psyche, not only oriented to justice, but happiness, not only present and actual, but also futural and utopian. Liberation intends not only a new society but also a new human being. Justice needs to be linked to utopia. Liberation is the continuous self-creation by human beings of themselves as free and liberated.[1]

Finally, we note a spiritual dimension to liberation in the deepest sense: negatively liberation is liberation from individual and collective sin, and positively a turning to God, a falling in love with God. On this level is the prayerful, contemplative turning to God as the gratuitous source of faith and hope and charity, who will also help us to achieve liberation in the psychological and social senses. Religious contemplation is necessary and essential not only because it is valuable in itself as an expression of my love for God, but because it contributes to and leads to the praxis of justice. If I truly love God, if my contemplation is genuine, then I will love my neighbor in the practice of justice.

Theologically considered from the standpoint of faith, then, all these levels are essential and mediate one another. Merely political or socio-economic liberation without psychological-erotic liberation is incomplete and leads to a contradiction between just social structures and repressive psychological structures. Both political and psychological liberation without liberation from sin are, as we have seen in chapter 7, self-defeating and impotent; spiritual liberation not leading to psychological and social liberation is one-sidedly spiritualistic. A love of God that does not do justice to one's own vulnerable psyche and to the human other is false or a one-sided, incomplete love. Here, as the previous chapter indicates, we are just being seriously biblical.

The above distinction among social, psychological, and religious liberation overlaps with and cuts across another threefold: that of my relationship to social structures; to my immediate neighbor, my family, friends, wife, and children; and my relationship to God. Once again, the truth is mediation among these dimensions. Bourgeois Christianity, as we will see, deemphasizes or eliminates both the first and third dimensions. As regularly preached and practiced (witness many or most middle- or upper-class Christian churches on Sundays) such Christianity leaves out or minimizes both the political and mystical dimensions of Christianity and enshrines what we might call "bourgeois I-thou," a comfortable, superficial, easy, narcotizing relationship to my immediate neighbor, "Christian neighbor love" as Nietzsche characterizes it, that does not do justice even to that dimension. Both Daniel Berrigan and John of the Cross are out of place in such a religious preaching and practice. Norman Vincent Peale preaching the "power of positive thinking," on the other hand, is right at home.

A second kind of issue that critics bring up is the way liberation theology uses Marx and neo-Marxism. According to such critics, that use disqualifies the approach or at least leads to serious flaws. Because Marx is deterministic, reductionistic, undemocratic, and atheistic, so the story goes, the use of Marx has to be harmful or fatal to an account of human beings in the world that tries to be nondeterministic, multileveled, democratic, and theistic.

My response, and here I am basically articulating my own viewpoint while drawing on other sources in liberation philosophy and theology, is to say that I relate to Marx and neo-Marxism the way Aquinas related to Aristotle or Lonergan to Kant, learning from Marx but also rejecting invalid aspects and linking his insights to insights from other sources and traditions. In PCM and CAL I draw on Marx's criticism of capitalism as unjust, his labor theory of value, his account of class domination and exploitation, his account of praxis, and his notion of socialism in developing my own theory.[2]

While rejecting Marx's atheism on good phenomenological, epistemological, and metaphysical grounds, as I have already shown in the preceding chapters, I do think there is much to be learned from his critique of actual religion, "really existing religion." Marx teaches that religion often functions as a bulwark and justification for the ruling class. To that extent, I argue, absorbing but going beyond Marx's critique, religion dies, contradicting its own radical, prophetic substance. A religious belief not informed by ideology critique runs the risk of becoming merely bourgeois.

Moreover, there has been much work done on Marx that justifies denying the equation between Marx and Soviet Marxism or the claim that Marx is reductionistic, deterministic, and anti-democratic. I agree with this literature in rejecting these claims. Marx's version of communism, for example, is full economic, political, and social democracy, which Soviet Marxism and Marxism-Leninism contradicts and denies.[3]

Marx's "materialism," therefore, amounts to saying that human beings are in the world and are influenced by its economic, political, and social structures in a fundamental way. But such rootedness is not meant to deny the possibility of actively, critically distancing myself from such structures, criticizing them, and transcending them in aesthetic or philosophical manners.[4]

Whether one uses and draws on Marx's thought or not depends on how useful one finds his analysis for understanding social reality. Liberation philosophy and theology find that social reality as they experience it can be most fruitfully understood through a generous use of Marx's social analysis, but subsumed by and as a part of a broader philosophical, theological, and religious vision. This is a judgment with which I happen to agree and have argued for through three volumes; Marx's radical analysis and solution are more adequate to social reality than either a conservative or a liberal version.[5]

Moreover, I should not ignore that different theorists of liberation use Marx more or less extensively and some hardly at all. They go all the way from Dussel's quite extensive use, upon which I will draw in my last two chapters, to Gutiérrez who makes little reference to him in *A Theology of Lib-*

eration. Moreover, the critics miss the extent to which liberation theology becomes progressively more critical and nuanced in its appropriation of Marxism. None of them buy into the unacceptable Marxism mentioned above, Marxism-Leninism, and its aspects of determinism, reductionism, anti-democracy, and authoritarianism. Rather, they attend to Marx's ethical and systemic critique of capitalism, his class theory, his theory of value, his account of praxis and struggle, and his theory of socialism. All of these aspects, as I have argued in PCM, CAL, and in this book, are valid, legitimate aspects of Marxist theory.[6]

The conclusion that I would draw from the above reflections is that liberation philosophy and theology need not apologize for their positive use of Marx. I myself certainly do not. Indeed, what the critics see as a liability I see as an element to be praised. Good for them and me! To ignore Marx's insights is to risk condemning oneself to an ignorance about socio-economic reality akin to ignoring Einstein in physics, Darwin in biology, Kant in epistemology, and Whitehead in metaphysics. To understand national and international capitalism, one still must read and learn from its most profound and searching critic. Indeed, I agree heartily with Tony Smith when he says in one of his books that all twentieth-century economic theory is a footnote to Marx. Often, I would add, a very bad footnote.[7]

What needs to be said also is that such criticism of liberation often just manifests a beam in the eye of its critics. They are often just people who have bought into the capitalist system so wholeheartedly and so uncritically that they are unable to be open to or even moderately sympathetic to a form of theology that is critical of capitalism, and that, therefore, draws on Marx and brings into fundamental question the bourgeois Christianity of the critics. Such critics—Michael Novak, for example, about whom I will have more to say in my penultimate chapter—often resort to facile equations of Marx with Marxism-Leninism or with the caricature of Marx as one committed deterministically to iron laws of history, and so on. What needs to be evaluated and criticized therefore is not so much Marx or liberation theology's use of Marx as the narrow, dogmatic stance of the critic.[8]

The question remains, however, concerning the radical stance of liberation theology toward the capitalist system. How legitimate is that stance? If, with Dussel, we argue that in the Old and New Testaments there are general injunctions to liberate the poor and also to criticize prophetically institutionalized forms of injustice, the question arises concerning how to apply those injunctions to contemporary social reality. Is a conservative, liberal, or radical social analysis the most adequate, comprehensive, and nuanced version?

In CAL I criticized Nozick's conservative defense of the minimal and Rawls's defense of the liberal welfare state as inadequate, and argued for democratic socialism as the most adequate form of justice. It alone can satisfy my four principles of justice: 1) everyone's security and subsistence rights should be respected; 2) there is to be a maximum system of equal basic liberties, including freedom of speech and assembly, liberty of conscience and freedom of thought, freedom of the press and the right to hold personal property, and freedom from arbitrary arrest and seizure as defined by the rule of law; 3) there is to be, first, an equal opportunity to attain social position and office; second, an equal right to participate in all social decision-making processes within institutions of which one is a part; third, equal opportunity for meaningful work; 4) social and political inequalities are justified if, and only if, they benefit the least advantaged and are consistent with the just savings principle, but are not to exceed what will seriously undermine equal worth of liberty and self-respect. Because capitalism violates all four principles, it is intrinsically unjust. This claim is true of national capitalism in the North, and, as I will argue in the last two chapters, of international capitalism as it links North to South in a system of unjust dependence. Democratic socialism, on the other hand, satisfies these principles.[9]

The radical interpretation and application of "liberate the poor" is, therefore, the most adequate interpretation. What is called for is a critique of and liberation from national and international capitalism as the dominant and most fundamental and far-reaching form of contemporary injustice. Central and Latin America went through their own partial verification of this point as they experimented with "development" as proposed and implemented by Presidents John Kennedy and Lyndon Johnson. What development meant and led to, however, was greater economic slavery, impoverishment, hunger, unemployment, terrorism, and repression for the South. The Alliance for Progress was used to bring into existence the national security state, which has as its main enemy not an external force but its own people, those within the country with the will and energy to challenge the reign of capital. Development or developmentalism merely reformed or made smooth the running of an international capitalism, which is the problem, not the solution.[10]

"Development" as a theme, of course, in the 1980s and 90s has given way to the "free market" as a solution to the economic woes of the Third World. However, as I will argue more fully in the last two chapters, the free market is less a solution to those woes than an intensification of them, and for the same reasons. An international capitalism that is the main source of these woes is reigning ever more supreme, and is achieving its ends of exploitation, domination, control of markets, and access to cheap labor and raw materials through the mechanisms of the so-called free market.[11]

All of the above is true in spite of the proclamation of free market miracles in countries like Brazil, Chile, and Guatemala. Even when there has been a statistical increase in gross national product, such miracles have meant increased misery for most of the population. There was during the 1980s, for example, an increase of 44 million poor in Latin America as a result of free market policies. All this is not surprising, of course, when we remind ourselves that a virulent capitalism is using "development" and "free market" to achieve its exploitive ends, which generally do not benefit but make worse the lot of most of the people in a country or region. Capital's approach: "if free market doctrines and politics achieve my ends better than development, then so be it."[12]

The radical interpretation of liberation, therefore, is the only one that does not involve a compromising of Christianity's radical, prophetic substance, that does not turn it, at least to some extent, into a comfortable illusion and consolation for the upper and middle classes. The radical social analysis of PCM and CAL is, therefore, subsumed in a broader, deeper, and more comprehensive metaphysical, religious, and theological vision. Liberation, I would argue, is the most comprehensive account available. It includes not only the three aspects mentioned above—social, psychological, and spiritual—but it also includes the spiritual dimension of theology dominant in the first centuries of Christianity and the speculative, theoretical dimension that began to develop in the thirteenth and fourteenth centuries and continues up to the present day. The spiritual and theoretical, however, need to be linked to ethical, political praxis more adequately than they have in the past.[13]

In this sense the spiritual as articulated in the ninth chapter; "falling in love with God," expressed in disciplines such as silence, spiritual reading, meditation, and contemplation; and a transcendental, methodologically grounded account of human beings in the world, experiencing, understanding, judging, and deciding in relation to a processive being, God, and Christ, must be completed in and expressed in a radical, liberating praxis—which itself is the most adequate response in love to a God and Christ who first loved us by being incarnated here on earth and being put to death by unjust political and religious authorities. Christ was himself a victim of political and ecclesial injustice, mainly because he opposed it and called it into question. Thus, his life outlines for us the path of discipleship; like master, like disciple.[14]

The Content of Liberation

The basic biblical text for the theme of liberation is articulated in the story of Exodus, of the liberation of the Jewish people from Egypt. This story follows upon the account of creation, which is part of salvation history. The story of creation is not developed to satisfy some merely philosophical concern but rather as a part of salvation history. One of the best indications of this fact is Isaiah, who says, "But now, thus says the Lord, who created you, O

Jacob, and formed you, O Israel: fear not, for I have redeemed you; I have called you by name; you are mine" (Isaiah 43:1; see 42:5–6). Yahweh is at one and the same time both creator and redeemer: "For he who has become your husband is your maker; his name is the Lord of hosts; your redeemer is the Holy One of Israel, called God of all the earth" (Isaiah 54:5).

The liberation from Egypt follows upon this theme in the Old Testament. Liberation is a political act delivering the people from the oppression described in the initial chapters of Exodus: "that place of slavery" (13:3; 20:2; Deuteronomy 5:7); repression (1:10–11); alienated work (5:6–14); humiliations (1:13–14); enforced birth control policy (1:15–22). To overcome such oppression, Yahweh awakens a liberator, Moses:

> I have witnessed the affliction of my people in Egypt and have heard their cry of complaint against their slave drivers, so I know well what they are suffering. Therefore I have come down to rescue them from the hands of the Egyptians and lead them out of that land into a good and spacious land, a land flowing with milk and honey . . . So indeed the cry of the Israelites has reached me, and I have truly noted that the Egyptians are oppressing them. Come now, I will send you to Pharaoh to lead my people, the Israelites, out of Egypt. (3:7–10)

Moses began a long, hard struggle for the liberation of his people. At first the Israelites did not listen to him, were tempted to retreat and give in when threatened by Pharaoh's armies, and told Moses that they preferred a life of slavery to the insecurity of life in the wilderness (6:9; 14:11–13; 16:3). A gradual pedagogy of the oppressed was necessary in order that the Jewish people become aware of the roots and causes of their oppression, struggle against it, and understand the profundity of the liberation to which they were called. The creator of the world is the creator and liberator of Israel, to whom God entrusts the mission of establishing justice:

> Thus says God, the Lord, who created the heavens and stretched them out, who spreads out the earth with its crops, who gives breath to its people and spirit to those who walk on it: I, the Lord, have called you for the victory of justice, I have grasped you by the hand; I formed you, and set you as a covenant of the people, a light for the nations, to open the eyes of the blind, to bring out prisoners from confinement, and from the dungeon, those who live in darkness. (Isaiah 42:5–8)

The creator God who is an unrestricted act of understanding and love is a God of justice and liberation. Yahweh summons Israel to a promised land free from misery and alienation.

You have seen for yourselves how I have treated the Egyptians . . .
Therefore, if you hearken to my voice and keep my covenant, you shall
be my special possession, dearer to me than all other people, though all
the earth is mine. You shall be to me a kingdom of priests, a holy nation.
(19:4–6)

The covenant and liberation from Egypt are two aspects of the same historical process. Insofar as this is a march toward a new city, a promised land,
the Book of Exodus is shot through and through with eschatology. God as a
historical, processive God is the creator of nature, but is the Lord of history
more than of nature. God is a God of promises who keeps promises. Exodus
is shot through with hope.[15]

With Exodus a new age has begun, marked by cooperation between
human beings and God. The work of Christ is part of this process and brings
it to fulfillment. The redemptive action of Christ is conceived as re-creation
and presented in a context of creation (Colossians 1:15–20; 1 Corinthians
8:6). Not only is the work of Christ a new creation, but it is liberation from
sin in all its consequences: injustice, hatred, poverty, exploitation, and so on.
Creation and salvation therefore have a christological sense: all things have
been created in Christ, all things have been saved in him. Even after Christ's
death and resurrection, the work of salvation is not complete. Rather, his life,
death, and resurrection point toward and invite us to participate in a future liberation of nature and human beings, the liberation of the Kingdom. Even the
triumph of Christ's resurrection is shot through with futurity, with promise,
and with hope (Colossians 1:15–20).[16]

The human being is the heart of this work of creation and re-creation,
and is called to continue it through human labor and praxis (Genesis 1:28).
The liberation from Egypt is initiated by God but entreats and requires the
active participation and cooperation of human beings. Faith desacralizes creation by making it the proper domain for human praxis. In working, transforming the world, breaking out of servitude, and taking responsibility for
their destiny in history, human beings create and fulfill themselves. Because
work is alienated and exploitative in Egypt and contributes to widening the
gap between rich and poor, human beings must leave Egypt and thus overcome alienation and the gap between rich and poor. To engage in such praxis
on the earth means nothing if it does not lead to human self-creation and serve
the good of human beings. When work ceases to serve this end, then it
becomes alienated, contributes to building idols and fetishes, the fetishism of
commodities. Commodity fetishism today, of course, leads to and is part of
the money fetish and capital fetish, on whose altars over twenty million people are sacrificed every year in forms of war, imprisonment, torture, terror,
starvation, and poverty. National and international capitalism is the main,

most fundamental, most dominant form of injustice and fetishism to which a praxis of liberation and a liberator God and Christ is opposed.[17]

The history of the Exodus and the covenant is a story of the Promise, the Promise made by God to human beings, which is the revelation of God's love and reveals human beings to themselves. We discover who we are fully by believing in, committing our lives lovingly to, and hoping in the Promise. The Promise is a gift accepted in faith; it begins in God's promise to Abraham and is fulfilled, partially, in those who have faith in Jesus Christ (Galatians 3:22).

The Promise unfolds in the particular promises made by God throughout history. The first expression of the Promise is the covenant; the kingdom of Israel is another concrete manifestation. When the infidelities of the Jewish people rendered the old covenant invalid, the Promise was incarnated both in the proclamation of a new covenant, awaited and sustained by a saving remnant and in the promises that prepared for and accompanied its advent. The Promise enters on its last days with the proclamation in the New Testament of the gift of the kingdom of God in Christ.

The Promise is not exhausted by these promises nor by their fulfillment; it goes beyond them, explains them, and gives them their ultimate meaning. A dialectical relationship exists between the Promise and its fulfillment. The resurrection is the fulfillment of something promised and is the anticipation of a future. The resurrected Christ is still future to himself, not identical with himself, permeated with difference. The Promise is gradually but not fully revealed in its universality. It is already partially fulfilled in historical projects but not completely. With the incarnation, life, death, resurrection, and sending of the Holy Spirit, the Promise has entered into a decisive stage, but even so it illumines the future of humanity and anticipates a future fullness. Past, present, and future aspects are essential to the Promise and the history of its fulfillments. As retained from the past, it is fulfilled and received in faith; as present, I am able to respond to it with contemplative gratitude and love; as future, I work toward it in a praxis of justice rooted in hope.[18]

Jesus in his life and death did not generally preach himself, but the Kingdom of God. We can initially describe the Kingdom of God, salvation, as the content of the Promise: political, psychological, and spiritual liberation. Spiritual liberation is defined here negatively as liberation from sin and positively as loving union with God. The Kingdom of God as the reign of God implies two things: human beings are to orient themselves vertically to God in faith, hope, and charity, and horizontally to human beings in praxis, service, and justice. Filiation with God, being a son of God, implies brotherhood with other human beings. No love of God without brotherhood, no brotherhood without love of God.[19]

Love is proved more in deeds than in words. The deeds of Jesus are signs of the coming of the Kingdom: "the blind regain their sight, the lame walk, lepers are cleansed, the deaf hear, the dead are raised, and the poor have the good news proclaimed to them" (Matthew 11:5–6). Miracles and forgiveness of sins are most properly interpreted as signs of the Kingdom, instances of a praxis of justice and mercy.[20]

The content of the kingdom is liberation in its different senses, and this content is the will of God. "I come down from heaven not to do my own will but the will of the one who sent me" (John 6:38). Doing the will of God means conversion from individual and collective sin. The sinner is one who uses created power both to secure himself against God and to lord it over others.

Sinners are frequently described as hypocrites by Jesus, and their hypocrisy is verified in their sin against the Kingdom. Jesus hurls anathemas against the Pharisees because they pay no attention to justice, at theological experts because they unilaterally impose burdens on people and have appropriated knowledge for themselves, at the rich because they refuse to share their wealth with the poor, at priests because they impose unreasonable restrictions on people's freedom, and at political rulers because they govern despotically and arbitrarily. Jesus in his solidarity with the poor thus manifests kinship with the God of the Old Testament, who is a God of justice. Like Father, like Son.

These anathemas are always collective, directed against institutionalized group egotism. Jesus is critical of the abuse of power, religious, intellectual, economic, or political. He notes and criticizes a relationship between such power and oppression. Religious oppression exists because the Pharisees impose unjust burdens. Ignorance exists because the priests have appropriated the keys to knowledge. Poverty exists because the rich do not share their wealth. Existence of oppression is not some necessary law but the historical consequence of collective sin.[21]

Only one kind of power is proper to the realization of the kingdom: love, sacrifice, service, truth. "So the Son of Man did not come to be served but to serve and give his life as a ransom for many" (Mark 10:45). Jesus' life is a being-for-others.[22] To live life as a gift and to spend it on behalf of others:

> If death is not merely the final moment of life, but part and parcel of the structure of life, inasmuch as moral life ebbs away, moment by moment, slowly emptying, dying, from the moment it is conceived—and if death as this gradual emptying is more than just biological fatality, but an opportunity for persons to accept, in liberty, the finitude and mortality of life, and thus open themselves to something greater than death—if to die, then, is to make room for something larger, if to die is to empty oneself in order to receive the fullness of the advent of the one who is greater than life—then we can say that the life of Christ, from its first

moment, was an acceptance of death, with all the courage and mettle of which anyone is capable. Jesus was completely empty of himself, so that he could be full of others and God. He accepted mortal life, accepted the death that hung like a dark cloud over his commitment to the life of itinerant prophet and the messiah who rescues human beings.[23]

Jesus is not only oriented to the Kingdom, but it itself is already present in him. "The Kingdom of God is at hand" (Mark 1:15). "But if it is by the finger of God that I drive out demons, then the Kingdom of God has come upon you" (Luke 11:20). This advent of the Kingdom implies solidarity with the oppressed. He takes sides with all of those criticized on the basis of established canons of respectability and righteousness: the prostitute, the Samaratan heretic, the tax collector, the Roman centurion, the person born blind from birth, the paralytic, the hunchback, the pagan Syno-Phoenician, the apostles when they are criticized for not fasting after the manner of the disciples of John. Because of such solidarity, consequences follow; Jesus is vilified, insulted, accused of keeping bad company, labeled subversive, heretical, possessed, insane, and more. But such a life and such consequences flowing from such a life are what a life lived for God and human beings means and implies.

If Jesus expresses and is oriented to the will of the Father, then one who is a disciple, a genuine follower or son of God or Jesus, does the will of the Father by following in Jesus' footsteps. Like him, our call is to be human beings for God and others, poor in spirit, dying to ourselves daily, doing justice, and oriented to and filled with something greater than ourselves. Like him, we have to be willing to accept and live with the consequences of such discipleship even unto death.[24]

The disciple or follower of Jesus is thus called to a new life, to be a new man or woman, able and willing to forgive enemies, to live generously and magnanimously, to live in faith and hope for the kingdom, to live a life of ecstatic, committed, outgoing love. We have already noted in previous chapters Jesus' sanity, his unity of opposites such as anger and gentleness, goodness and toughness, friendship and critique, joy and sorrow, masculine and feminine, obedience to the will of God and creativity and lack of conventionality.

He walks among forbidden people and accepts doubtful persons in his company such as Simon the Canaanite or Judas Iscariot. He completely overturns and reverses the social framework, saying that the last shall be first (Mark 10:31), the humble shall be masters (Matthew 5:15), and tax officials and prostitutes will find it easier to enter the kingdom of heaven than the scribes and Pharisees. He does not discriminate against anyone, neither heretics nor schismatic Samaritans (Luke 10:29–37; John 4:4–42), nor people of ill repute like the prostitute (Luke 7:36–40), nor the marginalized, sick, leprous, poor; nor the rich whose houses he frequents even while saying to them, "Alas for you rich, you are having your consolation now" (Luke 6:24). Nor does he refuse the company of his opposition, the Pharisees, even though he says to them many times, "Alas for you, scribes and Pharisees, you hypocrites and blind guides," (Matthew 23:13–39).[25]

The Christian as disciple is called to share in this new life of love and generosity and freedom and solidarity with the poor. To live in this way, however, requires conversion of heart. "Repent, and believe in the gospel" (Mark 1:15). Such conversion is both personal and political; it requires both a contemplative falling in love with God and a lived solidarity with the poor, a preferential option for the poor. Discipleship is both contemplative and active, personal and political, God-centered and human-centered. In being this way and acting this way, the Christian is simply following in the footsteps of Jesus, who himself brings new life and affirms the possibility, in his life and ours, of becoming new human beings.

For this reason the life and message of Jesus are revolutionary, not in any narrow sense having merely to do with the acquisition of political power, but in a more fundamental, universal, nonnationalistic sense. In his attack on personal sin, psychological alienation, and unjust social structures, Jesus offers us the possibility of transcending and going beyond these. In so doing, he and those who follow him lay the groundwork for revolution in the more narrowly political or socio-economic sense. This also, at times, is necessary and legitimate.[26]

Fundamental Christian morality, then, is not the fulfillment of this or that moral norm, but the following of Jesus to realize the Kingdom as Promise. Because there is a nonidentity between the Promise and any particular embodiment of it, there can be no simple adherence to the status quo if one is Christian. Such a claim is doubly true if the status quo, like our contemporary capitalist status quo, is unjust. To say "bourgeois Christian" or "capitalist Christian" is to utter a contradiction in terms.

The following of Jesus means, then, following him in a situation of conflict, a class-divided, race-divided, sex-divided society. Such a stance implies participation in class struggle, in solidarity with other struggles centered around issues of sexual, racial, and heterosexist injustice, and a taking of sides in that struggle, for the poor and against the rich. Solidarity with the poor means that I am on their side because they understand the meaning of the Kingdom best, because they have been exploited, and because they realize most fully their need of liberation or salvation. Moreover, because the poor are the victims of injustice, on the receiving end of the slings and arrows of the outrageous misfortune handed out by an unjust society, they have a privileged epistemic standpoint for perceiving injustice and accepting the Kingdom as an alternative. To the extent that I side with the poor epistemically, morally, politically, and religiously, I am more likely to be "in the truth" and to act according to it. To the extent that I do not side with the poor, on the other hand, I am more likely to miss the truth and to live falsely and unjustly.

Because the Christian is necessarily for justice and against injustice, then he must side with the poor against the rich as perpetrators of injustice. There is a fundamental "either-or" here that a stance of neutrality most often just sidesteps or ignores to cover over an unjust status quo. Neutrality most often leads to or implies defense of an unjust status quo. Finally, such solidarity is not in contradiction with the imperative to love universally and extend the kingdom universally. I side with the poor against the rich for the sake of the rich as human beings. I hate their injustice, but I love them truly insofar as I attempt to free them from injustice through identification with the poor. I best love the rich by liberating them from their injustice. The poor here are not just the exploited in Marx's sense of the proletariat, but all of those who have been rendered marginalized, destitute, and outcast by an unjust system. Moreover, the Bible locates the primary cause of poverty in this sense in material oppression by the rich.[27]

Moreover, not only the end but also the means must be Christian. Such a stance implies, I think, a basic preference for nonviolence personal and political. As I argued in CAL, such a stance does not exclude some minimal, reluctant use of violence in particular cases, but it does imply a general attitude and spirit of gentleness and nonviolence as the most effective way of loving the oppressor and oppressed. Such a stance was expressed many times by Jesus, as when he admonished Peter in the Garden, when Peter cut off the ear of one of the captors. Jesus said, "put your sword into its scabbard. Shall I not drink the cup that my father has given me?" (John 18:11); or "take my yoke upon you and learn from me, for I am meek and humble of heart; and you will find rest for yourselves" (Matthew 11:29); or on the cross when Christ forgives his tormentors, "Father, forgive them for they know not what they do" (Luke 29:34); or his forgiveness of one of the criminals crucified with him, "Amen, I say to you, this day you will be with me in paradise" (Luke 23:43).[28]

The path of discipleship, then, is the path of nonviolent, gentle, suffering love, the path that Christ trod in his life up through his passion. This is "the law of the cross," returning good for evil, as I argued in chapter 7, the most fundamental and fruitful way of confronting evil. That this path took the form of suffering and death is to be explained by the fact of what he is and stands for in an unjust, conflictual society. Christ's suffering and death were simply the consequence of his life and message, and willingness to follow him as the way is part of the essence of discipleship. "Whoever wishes to follow me must deny himself, take up his cross, and follow me. For whoever wishes to save his life will lose it, and whoever loses his life for my sake and that of the gospel will find it" (Mark 8:34–35).[29]

In case we are still committed to a false notion of God, totally immutable, impassive, unable to feel pain, God on a power trip, Jesus on the cross reveals God to us. For it appears here that God can and does suffer. God is not all-conquering but humiliated and weak; God is not all-powerful but impotent in the way of suffering love. Through his suffering and death, Jesus reveals God as love that conquers evil through suffering, not power from on high. He reveals himself as the man and God for others. From Jesus we learn that the only kind of love worth talking about is that gentle, suffering love and service. As we see a little later in discussing the church, a Christianity that is lordly and triumphalistic is in contradiction with itself and its own origins.

Jesus on the cross brings into question the God of religion, in whose name one subdues human beings, and expresses the God of good news, who brings liberation. The representatives of Jewish religion put him to death because he called into question religion as they represented it: legalistic, literal, superficial, dominating, and unjust. When the Pharisees criticize the disciples for picking grain on the Sabbath, for example, Jesus says, "The Sabbath was made for man, not man for the Sabbath" (Mark 2:27).[30]

What is the significance of the Resurrection for liberation? It has at least three: historical (what really happened), theological (what is the significance of the Resurrection event), and hermeneutical (how is it possible to comprehend the event and its meaning). We have already considered the historical aspect, and to some extent the theological and hermeneutical aspects, in chapter 7. Here I will go more fully into the theological and hermeneutical aspects. As theological, the resurrection says something about God as the one who brings Jesus back from the dead, who acts as a liberative power that has become a historical love after the life and death of Jesus, and who has handed Jesus over out of love for human beings.

The Resurrection, theologically interpreted, also manifests something about humanity and history. God has pardoned and revitalized human beings rather than exercising retribution toward us and condemning us. We have been offered a new kind of life based on faith, hope, and love. Jesus Christ, in triumphing over sin, suffering, and death, has become a place, a *topos*, a domain in which utopia is realized and which legitimates hope against hope. As human beings, we now live a new life here and now in history. Utopia becomes real in Jesus and a real possibility for us.

Finally, the Resurrection theologically considered confirms the life and message of Jesus. If God did resurrect Jesus, then he stands in a special relationship to God. If God did raise Jesus from the dead, then he confirmed Jesus' concrete way of living, his preaching, his deeds, and his death on the cross.[31]

Hermeneutically the Resurrection can be understood as legitimizing a hope against hope for a total transformation of the person and history. This is a hope that overcomes all the negative aspects of the world. It is a hope against death, suffering, and injustice while going through these and struggling against them, not a hope above them.

We as disciples grasp history as promise, and we are conscious of a mission to be performed. We have a mission not only to witness to Jesus but to transform the world in the light of his promise; we must establish a new creation. Understanding the Resurrection of Jesus thus implies a radical hope in the future, a commitment to history as promise, mission, and radical discipleship that concretizes Christian hope and carries out a love-inspired praxis. Such love opens history up. The Resurrection is not simply an event that happened just once in the past but has to be kept alive and enacted by a love-inspired praxis operating in the present and oriented hopefully, hoping against hope, to a liberated future. Dialectical phenomenology as oriented to a hermeneutical retrieval of the past, eidetic reflection on the present, and critical orientation to the future finds its completion and fulfillment and transcendence in such a praxis.[32]

Such discipleship never eliminates, however, the dialectical tension between Cross and Resurrection. It does not cut off in a triumphalistic way, as Christianity at times has tended to do in the past and present, the Resurrection from the Cross to affirm an all-powerful God operating in history, God on a power trip. Rather, the Jesus who arose from the dead is a Jesus who trod the path of ordinary living, suffering, and death, subjected himself to the slings and arrows of misunderstanding, persecution, humiliation, and calumny, and remained faithful to God's will in humility and love unto death. In this respect, the disciple is no better than the master. The path of discipleship is his path.

It is a fundamental dictum of Christianity that the risen Lord is a Lord of power, but how we conceive this power is crucial. If the risen Lord is the crucified one and the slain lamb, then power is manifested through the praxis of discipleship, and Christians will produce a political theology. On the negative side this will entail prophetic denunciation of injustice and will maintain a certain eschatological reserve: the parousia is yet to come fully. On the positive side it will entail efforts to organize society along the lines demanded by justice and preached by Jesus. Such a Christianity is not triumphalistic; rather, it will realize that the only kind of power worth talking about is that which is embodied like that of Jesus in humility, self-surrender, and service. When Christians forget this point, they form a political religion that is contrary to the spirit of the gospels and most often allied with the powers that be. Christianity, instead of being the praxis of suffering love, becomes ideology serving and legitimating the status quo.[33]

I began these three volumes with a search for the truth expressing the eros of the desire to know. Through the three volumes and especially in this volume, I have discovered that such a search for truth leads to commitment and love, affirmation of God as an unrestricted act of understanding and love, and Jesus Christ as both truth and love, identification with the poor and oppressed as victims of national and international capitalism, and engagement in a praxis of justice. Such praxis leads me back to intensified reflection on and loving, prayerful contemplation of truth and love, out of which flows an increased and deeper engagement with justice and the poor. I thus inscribe a circle in which reflection and contemplation lead to justice, identification with the poor, and praxis. And praxis drives me back to intensified reflection and contemplation and love of incarnate truth and love.[34]

Conclusion

Jesus Christ, Liberator, presents us with a call to discipleship, and such a call is the basis for a praxis oriented to justice. I would be less than honest, however, if I did not own up to the fact that in its concrete embodiment in the church, Christianity is a part of the problem as well as the solution to sin and injustice. Concrete Christianity is a lived tension or contradiction between Jesus Christ, Liberator, and God on a power trip, a postbourgeois message and a bourgeois church, a practice of discipleship in love and a religion administered from on high by a hierarchy treating people as objects, not as subjects working together in a community of servant love.[35]

I hasten to add that this is not simply a tension or contradiction between Christ and church but within the church itself. The church itself contains within itself both liberating and nonliberating elements, both postbourgeois and bourgeois aspects, both truth and ideology. The normal access to Jesus Christ for the believer is through a tradition mediated by and present in a church, but this tradition and that church need to be interpreted not only receptively and faithfully, but also suspiciously and critically. If I am a believer, I operate in the church out of love for the church, but my love is both receptive and critical, both childlike and adult, loving and suspicious. In this way we are being faithful to dialectical phenomenology as involving both openness to tradition and critique of tradition. My love for the church is prophetic as well as faithful.[36]

The tradition itself and the church in which it is embodied and carried is not only something to be criticized but also something that nourishes me, which is the source of a "dangerous memory" that can be drawn on in the process of liberation. In meditating on Christ on the Cross or his identification with the poor or his love for others or his denunciation of the Pharisees, I use these dimensions of the gospels to call into question our hedonistic, consumeristic, hypocritical capitalist present. In drawing on the Old Testament prophetic critique of empire, I bring our own United States involvement in the current New World Order into question. As I will show in a later chapter, the contemporary New World Order in its worldwide domination, exploitiveness, and destructiveness makes the Old Testament empires look positively benevolent by contrast. We have turned empire into an art form.[37]

Nonetheless, Christianity, we must face it and be honest about it, is significantly bourgeois in both its Protestant and Catholic versions; so also, by the way, is Judaism. Such a characteristic is manifested in the way it practices and preaches an apolitical, nonpartisan love that does not take sides, in its tendency to privatize its message into a comfortable form of "bourgeois I-Thou" leaving out or minimizing both the political and mystical dimensions of Christianity, in its tendency to reduce the messianic future to an endorsement of the present for those who already have wealth and power and status, in its tendency to substitute a faith in praxis for the actual praxis of discipleship, in its theology and preaching that smooth over contradictions and tensions, and leave believers consoled rather than challenged, feeling good about themselves rather than anguished about the poor, in a rigorism of rules about issues such as celibacy, birth control, and divorce, and slackness about the demands of radical discipleship, and in a hope that tries to conceal from itself its own messianic uneasiness—namely, that it is still awaiting something. Hope becomes a power without expectation, and such hope is a hope without joy. Bourgeois Christianity is too often a religion without joy, because it is narcotizing, loveless orthodoxy without radical, prophetic orthopraxis and loving community. Individualistic, bourgeois religion reigns supreme in those joyless, gray, lifeless supermarts of the spirit, the normal or all too prevalent parish or community churches.[38]

Bourgeois Christianity is a paternalistic church that takes care of people rather than being a mature church of the people. The form of love that is preached is often a weak form of Christian "neighbor love," which we have already seen is suspect from the perspectives of both Marx and Nietzsche, as well as the Old Testament prophets and Jesus Christ. Its support for the capitalist status quo occurs and is expressed not only in a theology, preaching, and practice that refuse to bring the status quo into question and legitimize it and support it, but in a monopoly by a clerical, hierarchical, mostly masculine, white, and straight elite of theological production, teaching, and preaching that echoes the white, racist, heterosexist capitalist monopoly of means of production and propagation of ideology. Such a bourgeois church has its historical origin in the way the hierarchical structures of ancient Rome were taken over, imitated, and institutionalized in the early church by the fifth century and have continued up to the present day with little change. Such a bourgeois

Christianity, need it be said, while it retains some of the truth of the Christian message, does so in a way that distorts it and betrays it.

The betrayal is manifest in the many ways in which human rights already institutionalized in secular society are regularly violated in the church, freedom of conscience is violated, diversity of opinion discouraged and repressed, and the legitimate rights of women and homosexuals to participate fully and be ordained are ignored. Hans Küng and Leonardo Boff being called on the carpet in Rome are outstanding examples of such tendencies, as is the disciplining of Charles Curran in the United States. Roman Catholicism is much worse than Protestantism in many respects; some Protestant churches are at least ordaining women. Roman Catholicism is noteworthy in trailing behind Protestantism in the refusal to learn lessons about human rights, freedom, and democracy. In contrast to Protestantism, Roman Catholicism can perhaps be more adequately characterized as a church that is becoming increasingly more bourgeois, as Protestantism already is, but retains pre-bourgeois, paternalistic, feudal elements.[39]

I agree with Boff and Metz when they say that a preferable model for the emerging church in the twenty-first century, a postbourgeois church that would help bring about and reflect a structurally more just society, is the base communities in Latin and Central America, which are beginning to be instantiated in North America and Europe as well. The people of such communities are no longer taken care of paternalistically, but participate fully in the practice, preaching, and organizing of the church. The movement, then, is not so much from the top down, as in the paternalistic church, in a way that discourages participation, freedom, and diversity, but from the bottom up. Such base communities offer the rest of the world models of solidarity with the poor in a way that contrasts with the individualism of the bourgeois church, concrete ways of linking salvation with liberation that would actualize and instantiate what we have established in this book philosophically and theologically, and an ideal of real community as opposed to an alienated church administered from on high but not really in touch with its people, who remain isolated and lonely in a deadly way.

Such base communities are decentralized, not centralized as is the bourgeois church, horizontal primarily rather than hierarchical, emphasize orthopraxis rather than simply orthodoxy, are identified with the poor and oppressed rather than simply the rich and powerful, are interested in freedom more than in order, and emphasize more than does the bourgeois church the particularity of the church present in a particular region and nation. Again I do not mean to give the impression of disjunction between such opposites as centralization and decentralization, hierarchical and horizontal, universal and particular, but rather a mediation. The bourgeois church tends to emphasize one opposite to the minimizing and excluding of the other, universality imposed on a particular region or country in a way that does violence to its particularity rather than universality that is properly integrated with and giving full play to such particularity, as in base communities. Such base communities, I might say, represent a more adequately dialectical model of the church in which opposites are mediated and integrated.[40]

I am suggesting here that the First World church needs to learn from the Third World base communities, which provide a more mature, more Christian model of church. Indeed, as I have already suggested, such learning is already going on. In so arguing, I am not claiming that we need to create a new church, but that Christianity needs to be transformed from within itself through the interplay between North and South. In so doing First World Christianity takes a significant step toward overcoming its own Eurocentrism and ethnocentrism and becoming a truly universal, world church, and such interplay between First World and Third World church becomes part of the international praxis of liberation on a cultural-religious level. I have more to say about the significant political role of such base communities in my final chapter on liberation in the center.[41]

❦

TEN

Intellectual, Moral, and Religious Conversion as Radical Political Conversion

In my three volumes the notion of conversion has been operative all along. In PCM I argued that adequate self-knowledge, adequate self-appropriation, implies intellectual conversion. The real is not something that I look at according to an empiricist model of knowing, but is intended through a process of experiencing, understanding, and judgment. Furthermore, objectivity is not arrived at through taking a good look, but is the fruit of authentic subjectivity. Finally, the self is not known through some kind of inward look or mere experience or intuition, but is experienced, understood, and affirmed.[1]

Similarly in CAL the necessity and importance of moral conversion was affirmed. After intellectual conversion an exigency emerges that doing conform to knowing. For if I am committed to intelligence and reasonableness, then I cannot coherently and nonarbitrarily commit myself to living irrationally. For if I am committed to inquiring intelligence and reasonableness in my knowing, then I cannot consistently commit myself to irrational living, contrary to the dictates of inquiring intelligence and reasonableness, without falling into contradiction with myself. The question, "Should I live according to inquiring intelligence and reasonableness?" admits of only one intelligent and reasonable answer, "yes." A "no" answer is incoherent; I intelligently and reasonably argue that an unreasonable life is preferable to a reasonable life.[2]

In arguing that doing conform to knowing, then, I am led to take seriously the moral level of consciousness as opposed to the merely cognitive. The moral level arises on the fourth level of freedom, decision, commitment, and action. As articulated in CAL, this moral level has three stages, aspects, or levels to it—right, moral in the narrow sense, and ethical.

The level of right calls to me to obey the exigencies of communicative action as spelled out in a principle of universality, U, which leads to and grounds the basic principle of discourse ethics, D. The principle of universality states that any legitimate norm requires that all concerned can accept the consequences and side effects its universal acceptance can be anticipated to have for the satisfaction of everyone's interests (and that these are preferable to any other alternative). D states that only those norms can claim to be valid that meet (or could meet) with the approval of all concerned in their capacity as participants in a rational discourse. U and D cannot be denied without self-contradiction or arbitrariness. If, for example, I try to deny U, then either that denial is rational or it is not. If it is rational, then it does in fact meet with universal acceptance on the basis of the better argument; I implicitly contradict the content of what I affirm explicitly. If the claim is not rational, then what is arbitrarily asserted can be rationally questioned or denied.[3]

The level of right, however, proves to be insufficient, for the issue arises concerning the requisite material and social conditions such that people can participate freely and equally in communicatively active, moral, political discourse. Equal opportunity to participate that is more than merely formal and verbal demands approximately equal material and social conditions. Accordingly, the Principle of Generic Consistency, PGC, is affirmed: act in accordance with the generic rights of others as well as yourself. Negatively this implies that I ought to refrain from coercing or harming recipients of my actions. Positively the PGC implies that I ought to assist others to have freedom and well-being whenever they cannot otherwise have them, and I can help them at no great risk or cost to myself. Accordingly, if I see a person drowning in a lake as I am walking by and I am a good swimmer, I have an obligation to attempt to save the person.[4]

On the moral level, moreover, the PGC implies Freedom as Self-Development, or FSD. Because freedom and well-being are both dispositional and occurrent, habitual and present in individual actions, any choice must imply the willing of the basic conditions and dispositions that are necessary for the essential unfolding and realization of the project of being a self. Self-development is the freedom to develop myself through my actions. It is a process of realizing my projects through activity in the course of which I develop my character and other capacities. I develop myself when I engage in political activity over a period of time or learn to be a pianist or go to graduate school in philosophy.

Because, however, freedom in the full sense is positive and not merely negative, because it implies the capacity to realize one's choices, and because control by one group over the enabling conditions of self-development implies a domination incompatible with freedom, self-development implies equal positive freedom. Such a freedom implies and includes the right of each individual to the enabling conditions, material and social, without which individual purposes cannot be realized. Among material conditions are means of subsistence, labor, and leisure activity. Among the social conditions are cooperative forms of social interaction, reciprocal recognition of each one's free agency, and access to training, education, and other social institutions.[5]

Both the level of right and the level of morality lead into and imply four principles of justice in light of which we can evaluate social institutions:

1. Everyone's security and subsistence rights are to be respected.
2. There is to be a maximum system of equal basic liberties, including freedom of speech and assembly, liberty of conscience and freedom of thought, freedom of the person along with the right to hold property, and freedom from arbitrary arrest and seizure as defined by the rule of law.
3. There is to be (A) a right to an equal opportunity to attain social position and offices, and (B) an equal right to participate in all social decision-making processes within institutions of which one is a part, as well as (C) an equal opportunity for meaningful work.
4. Social and political inequalities are justified if, and only if, they benefit the least advantaged and are consistent with just savings but are not to exceed levels that will seriously undermine equal worth of liberty or the good of self-respect.[6]

One implication of my principles of right, morality, and justice is the injustice of both capitalism and state socialism. The orientation to full communication present in U and D is violated by both capitalism and state socialism. State socialism openly represses any kind of dissent, and late capitalism covertly represses it through such mechanisms as campaign financing largely supplied by the rich and corporations, media subservient to capitalism, and different kinds of selection mechanisms operative in government such as limiting the range of available options considered, and forming committees in Congress largely sympathetic to the corporations they are overseeing.

Both state socialism and capitalism are also incompatible with equal positive freedom on the moral level. If such freedom is to be realized, it requires equal access to the means of power, production, and culture. Both capitalism and state socialism, because they allow some to own, control, and derive the primary benefit from the means of production, power, and culture, essentially violate the imperative of equal positive freedom.

Both state socialism and capitalism also violate one or more of the principles of justice. Both systems violate the principle of equal opportunity to make decisions in the economic arena, and both systems violate the fourth principle inasmuch as the levels of income and wealth exceed the limits necessary for equal worth of freedom and self-respect. Democratic socialism, however, involving ownership and control of firms by workers, full economic, political, and social democracy, a minimal welfare state, a market forbidding exchanges between capital and labor, and local, regional, and national planning associations to coordinate and plan investment and disburse funds to needy, deserving firms and individuals, does satisfy the principles of right, morality, and justice.[7]

Moreover, another consequence of moral conversion as leading into right, morality, and justice is solidarity with the poor and oppressed. For insofar as people are exploited, dominated, and marginalized by an unjust racist, sexist, heterosexist, classist capitalism, then I have to hear and respond to their cry and side with them against the oppressor. There is a preferential option for the poor that can be argued for philosophically as well as religiously.[8]

Radical political conversion, therefore, is an implication of intellectual and moral conversion. Such conversion has and implies the following aspects and levels: the shift on the level of freedom to moral value as requiring a transcendence of egoistic self-centeredness, expansion of moral conversion into the principles of right, morality, and justice, a critique of state socialism and capitalism as unjust, an option for democratic socialism, a solidarity with the exploited, marginalized, and oppressed, and a praxis directed against individual and institutional injustice and oriented to establishing through reformist and radical measures a more just social system.

Finally, I come to religious conversion. The necessity and legitimacy of this has already been argued for in previous chapters. Such religious conversion, falling in love with God and Jesus Christ, is required positively as the natural completion of our desire to know and love, and negatively as the overcoming of individual and social sin. Moreover, because religious conversion sublates intellectual and moral conversion, it also sublates their consequences. Radical political conversion is, therefore, a consequence of religious as well as intellectual and moral conversion.

Moreover, I have discovered specifically religious grounds discussed in previous chapters, for radical political conversion. For I have affirmed liberation theology as the most adequate, comprehensive interpretation of Christian revelation and its relation to contemporary economic, social, and political reality. Such a stance requires and counsels a radical, transformative, revolutionary, not merely a reformist approach toward contemporary capitalism and, to the extent that it still survives, state socialism. Conservative and liberal Christianity, both forms of bourgeois Christianity, are inadequate *as Christianity* for reasons that we have already seen and for other reasons that we will see in this chapter and further chapters.

Description of Radical Political Conversion

Intellectual Conversion

I have established, therefore, the necessity of radical political conversion. What I propose to do in this part of this chapter is to reflect upon the content of such conversion, first on intellectual, then on moral, and finally on religious conversion. My procedure in each subsection will be to describe each conversion and then to interpret the consequences for radical political conversion. Conversion in general results from a vertical exercise of freedom whereby I shift from one horizon to another. Such a vertical exercise of freedom contrasts with a horizontal exercise, where my choices all take place within a certain context of assumptions, meanings, and values. Conversion may involve either a progressive deepening or broadening, in which my world gradually expands by building on previous knowledge and commitments. Or it may involve a wrenching in which previous judgments and commitments are overturned. What was real now seems illusory; what was important is unimportant; what was central is now peripheral. The scales have dropped away. Now my life makes sense where before it was absurd, now I see where before I was blind, now I am alive where before I was dead.[9]

Conversion is, then, a function of the whole person, but most fundamentally of the so-called fourth level of freedom, building on, retaining, and going beyond the first three cognitional levels of experience, understanding, and judgment. Conversion in the full sense leads to my choice of a different life and a different world, where I cease to drift and take responsibility for my life. Intellectual conversion, therefore, even though its focus is on cognition, is chosen. I freely choose to live up to and obey the four transcendental precepts corresponding to experience, understanding, judgment, and choice: be attentive, be intelligent, be reasonable, be responsible. Because these precepts themselves are values chosen by freedom, I reject the myth of neutral, value-free intelligence.[10]

In my three volumes I have treated intellectual conversion first, then moral conversion, then religious conversion. Really and existentially, however, religious conversion often flows over into moral conversion, which then leads to intellectual conversion. The falling in love with God proper to religious conversion attunes me to the values of justice and right essential to moral conversion, which then alerts me to the meaning and reality proper to intellectual conversion. Conversion as self-transcendence gradually expands from the religious through the moral to the intellectual, until the whole person is brought under its sway.[11]

Intellectual conversion, as we have seen throughout Part One, is the shift from a very erroneous myth concerning reality, objectivity, and human knowledge. This myth is that "knowing is like looking, that objectivity is seeing what is there to be seen and not seeing what is not there, and that the real is what is out there now to be looked at."[12] This myth overlooks the distinction between the world of immediacy and the world mediated by meaning. The world of immediacy is the sum of what can be sensibly seen, touched, tasted, and so on, and conforms to a degree to the myth's concept of knowing, objectivity, and reality. This world of immediacy, however, is but a part, the experiential part, of the world mediated by meaning. The most obvious level of knowing, experience, is not what knowing obviously is. The world mediated by meaning is what is known through individual and social experience, understanding, judgment, and belief.

A consequence of accepting transcendental method—fully experiencing, understanding, judging, and deciding to live according to my structure of experiencing, understanding, judging, and deciding—is that variants or offshoots of empiricism, such as objectivism, positivism, and scientism, must be rejected. Such methods ignore the distinction between data of sense and data of consciousness. For empiricists all data are data of sense. Empiricist methods also miss the distinction between empirical method and philosophy as generalized empirical method. Moreover, these stances miss the reality and importance of philosophy as reflection on interiority, because they have no cognitive access to interiority.[13]

The question that now faces us is this: What are the implications of transcendental method for my life as a self-appropriated, intellectually converted subject in late capitalist society? The answer is that intellectual conversion and capitalism are flatly contradictory. Capitalism, because it is essentially, structurally objectivistic, fetishistic, reifying, and scientistic, is at odds with critical realism. Capitalism, if you like, is in certain essential respects a lived counter-position that a fully reflective, fully appropriated person should reject. I should stress here that because capitalism is essentially contradictory, its counter-positions are in tension with its valid breakthroughs, positions, on an intellectual, moral, and aesthetic level. "Capitalism" I am here defining as a socio-economic system in which the primary goal governing the whole system is economic profit, in which workers are separated from the means of production privately owned by capital, and in which workers are free to sell their own labor power to the highest bidder.[14]

To begin at the beginning, in chapter 1 of *Capital*, Marx utters a commonplace: that the capitalist social world is characterized by buying and selling of commodities. Right away, however, he introduces a crucial distinction between use value, the capacity of a commodity to satisfy real human needs, and exchange value, the amount of abstract or socially necessary labor time measured in money that is contained in a product. Labor time is the source of value for Marx here because it alone can serve as a basis for measurement among objects that are diverse in use values: a car, an airplane, and a house have quite distinct use values, but become commensurable because of the labor time contained in each of them.[15]

Because, however, products in a market economy are separated from their producers and because they are measured by a thing, money, and because their value is quantified, commodity fetishism is a necessary result of capitalism. Human beings as subjects produce things as products with value; the human subjectivity, however, that is the source of the value is forgotten. We forget that money is a commodity produced by workers, and money seems to be itself a source of value. "It is nothing but the definite social relations between men themselves which assumes here, for them, the fantastic form of a relation between things."[16]

As capitalism develops, this fetishism extends more and more from production into private consumption. Because of the intrinsic possibility of overproduction, capitalism must develop mechanisms that persuade the populace to consume up to the level required by the system. One mechanism developed for this purpose is advertising, which appeals to us by equating being with having. If I wish to catch the woman or the man, wear Calvin Kleins. If I want to get the job, wear expensive Florsheims. If I desire to play good golf, buy this expensive set of Arnold Palmer golf clubs. I am what I make or wear or own—and the more I have, the more I am.[17]

Corresponding to the supremacy of exchange value over use value in the product—profit after all is measured in exchange value—is the supremacy of abstract over concrete labor in the activity of laboring itself. Labor, in order to get a job, must sell itself on the open market; labor power becomes a commodity. Contradicting this emphasis on labor as commodity is capital's reliance on labor as use value, as subject, to produce more than the value of its wages. Labor must produce the surplus value that is the source of capitalist profit. Surplus value, then, the amount of labor time over and above necessary labor time, the time necessary to reproduce the value of one's own labor power, arises from labor as subject. Capital simultaneously denies and affirms labor as subject, as use value for capital is its capacity to produce surplus value. The result, then, of the supremacy of abstract labor over concrete labor is a commodification of labor power. Labor becomes a thing whose distinctiveness from other things, its capacity as subjectivity to produce surplus value, capital must simultaneously affirm and deny.[18]

As capitalism develops, it is an easy step from commodification to reification—that is, the extension from the corporation throughout society of a form of rationality that Horkheimer calls instrumental rationality, scientific, quantitative rationality ordered toward the good of profit. In relationship to this goal, everything becomes a means, everything, as Marx puts its, becomes subject to universal prostitution. Nothing is sacred.[19]

Because it becomes increasingly important for capital, in order to insure its well-being and survival, to extend its sway over everyone and everything, a formal, bureaucratic kind of rationality emerges, a version of instrumental reason that Habermas describes as purposive rational action. Because this rationality is oriented to quantity rather than quality, the abstract rather than the individual, administration rather than participation, any concern for subjectivity or self-appropriation dwindles or dies. The world so aptly described and depicted by Kafka develops—the organization man, the man in the gray flannel suit, the other-directed person. Like Prufrock, my self-confidence drains out of me—"Shall I part my hair behind? Do I dare to eat a peach?"[20]

The final flowering of this process of objectification, commodification, and reification is scientism as the form of reason most appropriate to late capitalism. Capitalism, we can say, has moved through four stages historically. First, capital posits the supremacy of exchange value over use value; I must invest money to make money. If the miser is an irrational capitalist, piling up his money in order to make money, the capitalist is a rational miser, investing his money in order to make money, losing his life in order to find it.[21]

Second, there is the supremacy of absolute surplus value in the early stages of capitalism, the acquisition of surplus value by lengthening the working day. Third, there is the supremacy of relative surplus value, in which capital acquires surplus value by decreasing the amount of necessary labor time going to the worker in the form of wages. Capital achieves this end by an increased productivity, based on developing technology and machinery, which allows products necessary to feed, clothe, and house labor to be produced more cheaply and more quickly. Accompanying the reign of relative surplus value is greater investment in technology compared to labor, greater division of labor, cheapening of labor. Labor, already a commodity, becomes a degraded commodity, a mere appendage to the machine.[22]

Finally, in the twentieth century science becomes not only productive force but ideology. Corresponding to a one-dimensional society ruled by a calculus of profit is the reign of one-dimensional thought governed by a logic of quantity. All other forms of rationality—aesthetic, moral, metaphysical, religious—are shunted to the side as capitalism finds the form of reason most appropriate to itself. If science is essentially descriptive of facts and capitalism is *the* fact, then any kind of critical transcendence of capitalism is by definition impossible. Science becomes a peculiar kind of legitimating ideology, an ideology that denies itself as ideology, an ideology that claims to be value-free. If science equals rationality, then such a claim legitimatizes the jettisoning of democracy and the rule of experts like Kissinger or Brezinski.[23]

Intellectual conversion can be compared to Plato's Parable of the Cave.[24] Movement from knowing as looking to knowing as experience, understanding, and judgment is a movement of the whole person from illusion to truth, analogous to the person staring at images on the wall moving out of the cave into the sunlight of reality. If my claims here are true, capitalism provides a way of understanding the Parable of the Cave in twentieth-century North America and western Europe. It systematically and structurally produces illusion, mystification, obfuscation, distortion. As late capitalism matures, it moves from "being" to "having" to "appearance"—the society of the spectacle. The spectacle is *capital* to such an extent that it becomes an image. Knowing as looking becomes a way of life.[25] If so, then full liberation from the cave implies a critique and liberation from capitalism. Short of such a critique, we have not asked all the relevant questions, come to all the relevant insights, or made all the necessary judgments.

Because capitalism is systematically and structurally productive of illusion and mystification, it covers up the ultimate reality of subjectivity, being, and God. The subject becomes a reified object, being becomes a quantified thing, and God becomes mere projection of feeling. To change Plato's Parable of the Cave a bit, we can imagine a family of four staring at images on their television forty to fifty hours a week, deliberately and systematically produced to convince them that being is having, uncritical patriotism is virtuous, certain persons are inherently evil, and certain others inherently good. The loss of being so bemoaned by thinkers such as Heidegger has its roots here. Capitalism is institutionalized group bias reinforcing and legitimizing the general, empiricist bias, and thus blocks the unfolding of the desire to know. Capitalism is an institutionalized refusal of insight.[26]

Moral Conversion

Moral conversion occurs when I cease to live a hedonistic, self-indulgent, narcissistic life and begin to commit myself to the genuinely valuable. I move from satisfaction to value as the controlling norm of my life. Satisfaction is the empirically pleasurable or unpleasurable; value is experienced, understood, affirmed, chosen. When satisfaction and value conflict, the morally unconverted person goes for satisfaction, the morally converted for value.[27]

Moral conversion implies a shift to action or praxis as essential in my life. To know is one thing, to do is another; to know what is right is one thing, to do what is right is another. From the perspective of moral conversion, merely knowing the true and the good is not enough. The question arises about the conformity of my doing to my knowing. If they do not fit, then my life is a lie. If they do fit, then I am integral, authentic, together.[28]

When moral conversion and intellectual conversion take place in the same consciousness, then moral conversion sublates intellectual conversion. What sublates goes beyond what is sublated, introduces something new, and at the same time retains and builds upon what is sublated. I go beyond the particular value, truth, to values generally as I explicitly become a conscious, practical agent in the world. Such moral transcendence, however, in no way interferes with my devotion to truth. Indeed, I need the truth if I am to know and realize the genuinely good. Now, however, my devotion to truth is on a firmer basis because I am armed against egoistic, group, dramatic, and general bias, and because the search for truth is in the far richer context of the pursuit of values.[29]

Moral conversion is lived out and expressed in an adult universe of meaning. There is a cognitive dimension to meaning when I move out of the infant's world of immediacy and into the adult's world mediated by science, psychotherapy, philosophy, and theology. In addition to cognitional meaning there is efficient meaning in which human beings work and bring forth products, constitutive meaning in which human beings produce social institutions and cultures, and communicative meaning in which a history of common, shared meanings is built up, transmitted, and enriched within a community. We communicate intersubjectively, artistically, symbolically, incarnately.

Meaning, in other words, is not only discovered cognitively but created practically. For this reason a conjunction of the constitutive and communicative functions of meaning yields the three key notions of community, existence, and history. A community is not just a number of people living within a certain geographical place, but an achievement of common meaning. Such meaning is potential when there is a common field of experience, formal when there is common understanding, actual when there are common judgments, realized when there are common shared commitments and aversions, values and disvalues, ends and means. Community coheres or divides to the extent that this commonality of meaning holds together or breaks up, survives or perishes, increases or decreases.

The individual develops as an authentic or inauthentic individual in relation to the common meaning of the community. There is minor authenticity or inauthenticity of the subject in relation to the tradition itself. "The chair was still the chair of Moses, but it was occupied by the Scribes and Pharisees. The theology was still scholastic, but the scolasticism was decadent. The religious order still read out the rules, but one wonders whether the home fires were still burning."[30]

History, because it is a human product, differs radically from nature, which unfolds in accordance with law. Logical meaning has invariant structures and elements, but the content of history is the structures subject to cumulative development and decline. Human beings do not simply conform to traditions and institutions the way they would to systematic law, but are free to shape and transform these traditions and institutions. Meaning in the social-political sphere is not simply discovered but created.[31]

For Marx, the person is eminently and primarily a practical, creative being, able to create and overturn human institutions. Such an affirmation underlies Marx's critique of capitalism and his projection of different social arrangements beyond it. What had a human beginning can have a human end; what human beings choose to create they can choose to reform or destroy. There is in human practical rationality a necessary going beyond, rooted in the ability to ask the further question, conceive a higher viewpoint, overturn mistaken judgments, reject distorted values.[32]

Because human rationality is essentially utopian in these senses, a rationality unwilling and unable to do this is a mutilated, incomplete, half-hearted rationality. It is the contention of critical theory that bourgeois, ethical-political rationality is such a half-baked rationality, inconsistent, obscurantist, exploitative, absurd. Bourgeois ethical and political rationality is at odds with itself. Counter-positions, however, whether in the intellectual or political realm, invite reversal.[33]

Capitalism, one could say first, is wrong not because it violates moral and political ideals brought in from outside, but because it systematically and structurally violates its own ideals. One example of such a violation is the conflict between such ideals as they are present in the marketplace and in the work place. In the marketplace, freedom, equality, property, and Bentham's "the greatest happiness of the greatest number" seem to prevail. I am free to sell what I own, whether it be my car or my own labor power, to someone else and to receive the equivalent in money. In the work place, however, such values are betrayed and turn into their opposites. Freedom turns into rigid subjection to the capitalist manager or machine, equality turns into domination and appropriation of surplus value, property turns into the appropriation by the capitalist of the product produced by labor, and Bentham turns into the unhappiness of deskilled work within the work place and poor living conditions, squalor, poverty, and homelessness outside the work place.[34]

Another example of the same kind of contradictoriness resides in the justification for property. From Locke on, the standard bourgeois justification for private property has been that I put my own labor into what I own: whatever I have worked on, I can legitimately appropriate. What happens, however, in capitalism is that the right to own what I have produced turns into the capitalist's right to own what others have produced.[35]

To take still a third example, we can consider the Kantian commonplace of bourgeois morality that human beings should be treated as ends and not merely as means. Such a claim has the implication that in the production process, human beings should be the ends of that process and not mere means to it. This claim is one of the main points made in the U.S. Catholic Bishops' pastoral letter on the economy:

The dignity of the human person, realized in community with others, is the criterion against which all aspects of economic life must be measured. All human beings, therefore, are ends to be served by the institutions that make up the economy, not means to be exploited for more narrowly defined goals.[36]

Yet what happens is that capitalism necessarily, essentially, structurally violates this imperative in practice. Being treated as an end means work that is meaningful and satisfying; capitalism, however, subdivides and mechanizes work in the name of efficiency oriented toward profit and maintenance of political control, so that the worker becomes a mere appendage of the capitalist manager or machine. That which should be the means of self-expression instead becomes the source of alienation. Also, treating someone as an end means full participation in the decisions that shape the work process. Workers, however, are essentially victims of decisions they have not made and of processes over which they have no control. Finally, being treated as an end means that my work serves and benefits me as a worker. Capitalism, however, subordinates the worker's gain to capitalist surplus value and profit. As a result, workers remain at least relatively poor compared to capitalists, and there is enormous poverty, unemployment, and homelessness.[37]

Still a fourth example of capitalism violating its own moral ideals is the incompatibility between the moral, political imperative of democracy and the domination essential to capitalism. Democracy in the full sense means participation in decisions affecting me, not just a formal exercise every two to four years to choose among candidates chosen by elites. Democracy implies equal claims by all to influence decisions, run for office, voice their opinions, air their grievances. Democracy implies that no arbitrary limit be placed on questions asked, alternatives considered, criticisms offered, proposals made.[38]

Capitalism reveals itself as structurally incompatible with such democracy for several reasons. First, it is difficult or impossible for someone to get elected without money or the support of those with money. This fact means that those with questions, criticisms, or policies offensive to capital will not be supported by capital. Moreover, just as capitalism economically rests on unequal access to the means of production, so also politically it rests on unequal access to political power. Corporations and the wealthy have much greater access to and influence on decision-making through membership on or influence on key committees, and the lobbying of political action committees. Because the "business of America is business," government looks after the well-being of the business community more than that of workers and the poor. Because the government depends for its own survival and well-being on the good fortune and support of business, it goes out of its way to please business.

Because of the preceding point, there is a tendency for Congress and committees in government to favor those alternatives approved by business and not to consider alternatives that displease business. Cutting military spending, for example, is anathema; cutting welfare is not. Also there is a positive correlation between one's wealth and participation in the political process. One reason for the decreasing participation of workers and the poor is the strong perception that what they do and say makes little or no difference to the outcome, and that their concerns are not being addressed. Media, which are primarily financed by business, overwhelmingly express opinions, attitudes, and values that are favorable to business and have the largest audience. Contrast both the opinions and readers of *Time* with those of *Nation*. Finally, politics, because it functions in a government basically ordered to the good of business, increasingly becomes a politics of public relations and image, insuring that substantive issues are not raised and relevant questions are not asked. In place of honest, full discussion of issues in an election, the emphasis is on selling a presidential candidate.[39]

Capitalist democracies, therefore, rather than being "of, by, and for the people," are "of, by, and for the capital and the rich." Democracy, rather than fulfilling Mill's ideal of full, unlimited, equal participation and discussion for all, is reduced to a mere formal exercise. This is not to say that state socialist experiments in Russia and China are any better. Indeed, because of the lack of a democratic tradition, respect for individual rights, and a public sphere of criticism and opinion, they fall behind, at least in some respects, the achievements of bourgeois democracy. Rather than an economic domination peculiar to capitalist societies, state socialist states practice a bureaucratic, political domination that is equally or more reprehensible. From the point of view of moral conversion, both late capitalism and state socialism are inadequate.[40]

Building on such arguments as these, we can argue that, if we are committed to full political democracy, then we require economic democracy—decentralized, worker ownership and control. Not only is economic oligarchy contradictory to political democracy, but, following Walzer, we can see that arguments validating or invalidating the one validate or invalidate the other. If, using *modus ponens*, we are committed to political democracy, then the same reasons oblige us to endorse economic democracy. If A, then B; A, therefore B. If, on the other hand, using *modus tollens*, we wish to endorse capitalist, economic plutocracy, private ownership and control of the means of production, then the same reasons oblige us to reject political democracy. If A, then B; not B, therefore not A.

Walzer argues this point through using a real historical example: Pullman, Illinois, in the nineteenth century set up by George Pullman both as a town and a business. Pullman thought this investment of money in the town gave him the right to run it like a benevolent dictator. However, Walzer argues, we do not recognize such a claim as valid in the political arena. Essentially people entering the town would be giving up rights of self-government they already had as American citizens. Nor does the idea that the citizens did not have to live there justify Pullman; that they chose to live in Pullman does not justify denying them rights as citizens.

Now Walzer's point here is that if these arguments are not justified for denying political democracy, then they are not valid for denying economic democracy either. Pullman's entrepreneurial energy and investment went equally into his town and his business; by his standards and his arguments, both were his private property. He had as much right to choose his worker's wives as he did their wages; he could as legitimately control their privacy as their productivity. Since, however, his arguments are clearly not valid for the town, then they are not valid for the plant either. Economic and political democracy are parts of a seamless web; denying or affirming the one implies denying or affirming the other.[41]

Up to this point, we have been performing what critical theory calls immanent critique, measuring capitalism against its own norms and values, and finding it wanting. This is an elementary, straightforward form of critique very much in accordance with our spirit and method. If the doing does not conform to the knowing, then the doing is ethically and politically suspect. Rationality in the cognitive and ethical arena implies performative and logical consistency. If a system is essentially self-contradictory, as capitalism is, then that system is essentially flawed morally and politically.

The argument of this section, then, entitles us to say that capitalism is structurally unjust and, therefore, at odds with moral conversion. In CAL I concluded that a society, in order to be just, must allow individuals maximum freedom to participate in the life of that society and fundamental equality in wealth and income, with some allowances for individual preference, initiative, talent, and need. Capitalism fails on both counts. Freedom is not adequately present because of the conflict between political democracy and capitalist oligarchy, and because of the regimentation of the capitalist work place. Equality is also not present, because of unequal access to means of production and power.[42]

As my earlier discussion of right, morality, and justice shows, freedom and equality go together or not at all. Loss of freedom implies inequality because of the domination of one group over another. Fundamental inequality leads to loss of freedom because some have greater resources to realize their aims than others and can impose their preferences on others. In twentieth-century capitalist society, then, there are basically three alternatives: Nozick's minimalist state, Rawls's welfare state, or a decentralized democratic socialism. Nozick's minimalist state is basically inadequate, because it intentionally leaves capitalist unfreedom and inequality intact, legitimizes that intactness, and discourages any form of welfare whatsoever. Rawls's welfare state, while it is an improvement over Nozick, is also deficient, because its difference principle, that inequality in income and wealth is legitimate if the well-being of the worst off in society is increased, legitimates enormous gaps in income and wealth, endorses a contradiction between political democracy and economic oligarchy, and legitimates such economic oligarchy. Since neither the minimalist state nor the welfare state measure up to the standards of justice, only democratic socialism will do.[43]

Full moral conversion, then, implies critique of and transformation of capitalism and movement toward a democratic socialism. The principles of right, morality, and justice are the middle terms between moral conversion and democratic socialism. If I am committed to full moral conversion, I must be committed to right, morality, and justice. If I am committed to right, morality, and justice, then I am committed to maximum freedom and equality. If I am committed to maximum freedom and equality, then I must reject capitalism as unjust. If I am fully morally converted, then I must reject capitalism as unjust. Conversely, if I do not reject capitalism as unjust, then I am not fully morally converted. I am either insincere, inconsistent, misguided, misinformed, confused, or all or some of these in combination. A merely bourgeois moral conversion is an incomplete, truncated moral conversion. Justice in the moral sphere is fundamental and essential; capitalism as injustice contradicts such meaning. As negation of such meaning, capitalism is not only intellectually but morally absurd.

I have been discussing here only the issue of justice in one country. However, I wish at least to note that there is also an international problem of justice arising when capitalism exports its system abroad in various forms of direct or indirect imperialism, which problem I will take up in the last two chapters. Expropriation of surplus value at home expands to become expropriation of surplus value abroad. The limits of this chapter, in which the ground covered is already fairly extensive, do not allow me to go into the issue at length. Here it is only appropriate to note that radical political conversion has international as well as national implications. Condemnation of U.S. capitalism as unjust at home will then, very probably, lead me to condemn it abroad as well. This issue, as U.S. involvement in Central America and in the Middle East indicate, is not a trivial one.[44]

Religious Conversion

Religious conversion is the peak of self-transcendence. Intellectual conversion promotes self-transcendence by orientation to the totality of being and moral conversion by its commitment to justice in community, but religious conversion is other-worldly falling in love with God without restriction. As such, it occurs primarily on the fourth level of responsibility, choice, and commitment. The openness or disposability to the other that has its roots in intellectual and moral conversion flowers in religious conversion as disposability toward God, emptiness for God as absolute mystery.[45]

When religious conversion occurs, my life is put on a new basis. Whereas before the initiative came from me, my own efforts toward intellectual and moral self-transcendence; now the initiative comes from God as I receive God's love. The results are increased peace and joy, attentiveness to God in prayer and to God's loved ones in action, relinquishment of self and love of the other. Religious conversion sublates intellectual and moral conversion in that it retains all that is valid and legitimate in them but puts them on a new basis. I live now no longer, but Christ lives in me. "It is the first principle. From it flows one's desires and fears, one's joys and sorrows, one's decisions and deeds."[46]

It is in this notion of sublation that we find the first connection with radical political conversion. For if the results of my first two sections are true, then we can say that religious conversion sublates radical intellectual and moral conversion. If such sublation occurs, then religious conversion also possesses as part of its meaning and one of its fruits radical political conversion. Otherwise there would be a contradiction between the sublated radical intellectual and moral conversion and the conservative bourgeois religious conversion. A Christianity that merely legitimates and reproduces the bourgeois, middle-class subject is incomplete and self-denying.

Second, religious conversion also has its own proper content to contribute to radical political conversion. Part of this content is the orientation to community that is at odds with the individualistic, bourgeois subject, regarding others either as obstacles or means on the way to affluent living. If we are, as Christianity says, all members of one mystical body, then we are not essentially rugged individuals, would-be entrepreneurs or consumers, "Rambos" or "Ronbos" deriving our meaning from our private property and profit, but social individuals oriented to finding meaning in community. Even when I am most alone, in reflection, writing, or prayer, I am still communal in the language that I use, the traditions that nourish me, the persons about whom and for whom I think, write, or pray.

Third, since love of God is fruitful, it overflows into love of all those that God loves or might love. Essential to Christianity is the preferential option for the poor, the oppressed, the persecuted, the homeless. Essential to the ultimate reality of God and Christ is that God is on the side of the poor. We side with the oppressed against the oppressors, the elite, the powerful. Here Christianity proclaims an either-or: either we are on the side of the poor or the rich, oppressed or the oppressors, the powerless or the powerful. There is no middle ground. If I am committed to justice, then I have to be against injustice.[47]

Empirical research bears out that capitalism intends to produce its poor. In 1984 in the United States the bottom 20 percent of the population received only 4.7 percent of the total income in the nation and the bottom 40 percent only 15.7 percent, the lowest share on record in U.S. history. In contrast, the top 20 percent received 42.9 percent of total income, the highest share since 1948. The top 10 percent of families own almost 57 percent of the net wealth of the nation and the top 2 percent own 28 percent of this wealth. When we subtract homes and other real estate, these figures go up dramatically from 57 percent to 86 percent and from 28 percent to 54 percent. The U.S. Catholic bishops, from whom I got these figures, judge that the distribution of wealth and income in this country is so unequal that it violates minimum standards of distributive justice. Unemployment in the United States, when one calculates not only those out of work but those who have given up looking and those only working part-time, amounts to one-eighth of the work force, between 13 and 15 million people. In the United States at the end of 1983, there were 33 million poor by the government's official standard and another 20 to 30 million by any reasonable standard.

During the Reagan-Bush "revolution" in the 1980s and 90s, the average after-tax income of the top fifth of the population rose by 35 percent while the bottom fifth's share fell by 10 percent. The richest 1 percent of all Americans, about 2.5 million people, now receive nearly as much income after taxes as the bottom 40 percent, about 100 million people, whereas in 1980 the top 1 percent received about half as much after-tax income as the bottom 40 percent. The 75 percent growth in the incomes of the richest 1 percent of the population from 1980 to 1990 equals the total after-tax income of the poorest 20 percent received in 1990.

The gap between the wealthy and the middle class has widened to such an extent that, while in 1980 the after-tax income going to the middle 60 percent of the population was 12 percent greater than the income of the richest fifth, in 1990 the income of the middle three-fifths was 7 percent less than that of the top 20 percent. Increasingly the so-called middle class is being afflicted by the injustice of capitalism. With respect to ownership of wealth, the disparities are even greater.

Contributing to these disparities is a much greater tax burden on lower income groups and a much lighter one on upper income groups. The federal tax burdens increased during the 1980s, from 6.7 percent to 27.7 percent on the poorest tenth of the population and from 8.4 percent to 16.1 percent on the poorest fifth. Such burdens decreased for upper income groups: 9.5 percent on the richest 5 percent and 14.4 percent on the richest 1 percent of the population. From such figures, it is hard not to conclude with Piven and Cloward that Reagan-Bush, in their attacks on the welfare state, assault on labor unions, and redesigning of tax policies conducted a new class war on the poor, labor, and even the middle 60 percent of the population, meanwhile convincing large portions of that 60 percent that they had never been better off.[48]

Not only the empirical facts but a Marxian conceptual reflection on capital logic give scarce comfort to those who wish to defend the possibility of a fully humane, welfare state capitalism. Indeed, there are significant indications that poverty, unemployment, and gaps between rich and poor are increasing. The general law of capitalist accumulation, then, Marx states as follows: "The greater the social wealth, the functioning capital, the extent and energy of its growth, and therefore also the greater mass of the proletariat and productivity of its labor, the greater is the industrial reserve army."

Capitalism structurally produces unemployment, poverty, homelessness, hunger, and so on. These are the effects of the original relationship of domination in the work place, in which the worker is hired not for his own self-satisfaction and profit, but the capitalist's. From this relationship all bad things follow. Flowing from and based on this relationship is the critical worsening of the lot of labor over the years as capitalism moves from absolute to relative surplus value, increased division of labor, relatively and often absolutely more investment in means of production rather than labor, and the industrial reserve army as a direct consequence and outgrowth of these tendencies. Capital is a Moloch on whose altar the poor and oppressed are sacrificed.[49]

Religiously converted Christians, then, in their preferential option for the poor, necessarily are in conflict with the imperatives of capital. Such imperatives require poverty not only as structural effect but as a way of lowering wages and making labor less rebellious. In the context of the twentieth-century welfare state, governments can and do consciously intend to manipulate such unemployment and poverty in order to reduce the political resistance of the working class and to lower inflation.[50]

Finally, I may note the opposition between religious conversion and capitalist instrumental reason oriented to the useful. If the desire to know is a natural desire to see God, then we can note the natural completion of that in the falling in love with God in which I become contemplatively, prayerfully attentive to God. From the perspective of instrumental reason, however, nothing could be more impractical and nonfunctional than such prayerful, contemplative attentiveness. From the perspective of such prayerful openness to God, the dominance of instrumental reason serving only the capital fetish is an offense, and such contemplation constitutes a breach with and form of resistance to the reign of such rationality.

From the perspective of religious conversion, the most valuable things in human life—thought, art, friendship, love, contemplation—are "useless" in this sense. This perversion and absurdity lies in its subordinating the essential to the accidental, the "useless" to the useful, the intrinsically valuable to the instrumentally valuable. That which should be highest becomes lowest and the lowest highest; that which should be the means becomes the end and the end becomes the means.[51]

In summarizing this section, I argue that a radical interpretation is more faithful to the Gospel and Christian tradition than either a conservative or liberal interpretation. I have supported this claim, first, by insisting that religious conversion sublates radical intellectual and moral conversion. Also, as the U.S. Catholic Bishops' economic pastoral indicates, a merely individualistic reading of the scriptures, experience, and the Christian tradition is less comprehensive than one doing justice both to the individual's relationship to God and the social expression of that relationship. A strictly individualistic reading of the gospels has trouble with such passages as that dealing with The Last Judgment, Matthew 25:31–45, in which personal salvation is linked to the doing of justice.

The preferential option for the poor, moreover, is necessary if personal conversion is to be authentic. Intellectual, moral, and religious conversion leads to a commitment to justice; commitment to justice leads to a preferential option for the poor. A radical political conversion is a more consistent expression of the preferential option for the poor. The true God is not a God who protects and legitimizes the bourgeois status quo but a God who liberates us from such a status quo—Jesus Christ-Liberator. The true God is not the God who exploits the poor, but the God, Jesus Christ, who is identified with the poor.[52]

A merely individualistic, conservative or neoconservative Christianity produces and reproduces the privatistic, bourgeois subject. Such a Christianity does not do justice to the social dimension of the gospel. The real debate is between those who wish to seriously reform capitalism in the light of the imperative for social justice and those who wish to transcend capitalism altogether. As we have seen in previous chapters and in this chapter, the radical alternative is preferable.

Conclusion

It might be helpful, at this point, to sum up the usefulness of intellectual, moral, and religious conversion in bringing about social change. Intellectual conversion is useful to the extent that it arms one against positivism, scientism, reductionism, and technocracy. Moral conversion is useful in order to prevent a "cynicism about means," a playing fast and loose with democracy, freedom, equality, and individual rights. Religious conversion is useful in that it prevents a fetishizing or divinizing of the political party or state in a way that short-circuits meaningful reform or revolution.

Now if intellectual, moral, and religious conversion imply radical conversion, then the opposite is also true. Radical political conversion is incomplete, truncated, and self-contradictory without intellectual, moral, and religious conversion. A positivistic, technocratic, reductionistic politics, a moral cynicism about means, and authoritarian, terroristic, totalitarian left movements and government are the results of radical political change severed from the requisite intellectual, moral, and religious conversion. I will develop this point more fully in the next chapter.[53]

ELEVEN

༻∽∾༺

Religious Belief and Critical Theory

At this point, after reflecting on the bases and implications of radical political conversion, I am ready to consider a new but related question, that of the relationship between religious belief and critical theory. This issue has already arisen or been anticipated in certain parts of this work. In Part One, we saw how speculative metaphysics has an ideological-critical aspect to it. Correspondingly, throughout Part One I have argued that ideology critique has a speculative-critical dimension. Being as the object of the pure desire to know allows us to critically evaluate from a metaphysical perspective empiricism, scientism, individualism, consumerism, and reification as various ideologies supportive of, manifesting, and legitimating late capitalism. Such ideologies are not only illegitimately objectivistic in a way that suppresses subjectivity and selfhood in a phenomenological sense and do not only legitimate injustice in an ethical sense, but are also false in a metaphysical sense. They contribute to a degradation of being and the life-world. As a result the depths of being and God conceal themselves and withdraw to the technocratic wasteland of late capitalism. Being conceals itself or is concealed by such ideologies and the social practices that they legitimate.

Similarly here in Part Two, as I have already indicated briefly in certain places of the text, ideology critique and religious belief dig into one another. In the chapter on faith and suspicion I indicated what a religious belief informed by suspicion would look like. In this chapter in the dialectical sec-

230

tion I will demonstrate that point further by reflecting on the interplay between Kierkegaard and critical theory. Then in the descriptive section I will lay out a positive description of a religiously informed ideology critique and critical theory.

Thoughts of complementarity, therefore, suggest themselves. Can a form of ideology critique be argued for that integrates both perspectives, that brings the social and individual, outer and inner, economic and religious together? This question will be the theme of this chapter. The full purview of social critique, I will argue, includes economic, political, social, and religious levels. Critical theory in its fullest manifestation embraces both secular and religious ideology critique. The secular critique fleshes out and renders incarnate the ideals and aspirations of religious critique, and guards against and criticizes the ideological abuses of religious belief. Religion can be and often is an opiate, but does not have to be such. In its own fundamental core it is prophetic and critical.

The religious dimension of critical theory, on the other hand, prevents a merely secular critique from absolutizing itself epistemologically and ethically—there is more in heaven and earth, Marx and Habermas, than is dreamt of in your philosophies. Religiously inspired persons ask whether there is not a form of pathology more fundamental than class or group domination, a pathological, demonical flight from intelligence and freedom into the aesthetic, a flight that class or group domination encourages and twists and uses for its own purposes. Finally, we ask whether existential and religious self-appropriation is not necessary for an adequate social critique. If individuals are not living in reflexive integrity before God and others, how can they carry out an adequate social critique and praxis? If such critique and praxis express and incarnate authentic individuals, are not they necessarily at the same time the ground of such critique and praxis?[1]

This chapter, therefore, in its dialectical section will be divided into four parts: economic, political, social-cultural, and religious. As we move through these parts, Marxism-critical theory will play less of a role and Kierkegaard more; both, however, play a role in all stages. By "Marxism-critical theory" I understand a tradition of Western Marxism extending from Marx through Hegelian Marxists in the 1920s such as Bloch, Gramsci, Korsch, and Lukacs, to the Frankfurt School theory of such thinkers as Marcuse, Adorno, Horkheimer, Benjamin, and Habermas. Such theory is distinguished from "vulgar Marxism" or "Soviet Marxism" in its emphasis on dialectic as opposed to merely positive science, the necessity of normative social critique, the importance of the political and social-cultural domains, and the significance of the free, reflective subject. Already obvious, therefore, should be the affinity between such social theory and Kierkegaard's thought, which in its own way, as I will show later on, is dialectical, normative, culturally aware, and emphasizing the subject—truth is subjectivity.[2] As I will use the terms in this paper, "Marx," "Marxism," and "critical theory" are roughly synonymous.

Dialectics of Religious Belief and Ideology Critique

The Economy

In Marx's theory the basic root of alienation in modern society is capitalist social relations. Because of capitalist ownership and control of the means of production, labor is alienated from the object produced, the process of work, its consciousness of itself as labor, and other people. Because labor in capitalist society is initially divorced both from means of subsistence and means of production, labor has to work on capital's terms, and capital has a right to appropriate the product produced and profit for itself. Labor, because it is in an unequal relationship of power with capital, has to be content with wages that remain at a subsistence level.[3]

Because capitalists are animated by a "vampire thirst" for profit, they try to make work as efficient as possible by divorcing the worker from organization and control of the process of work, and transferring the mind of the work to the capitalist manager and machine. Division of labor is progressively introduced as the laborer becomes an automaton, more and more just an appendage of the machine.[4]

Because profit measured by money is the goal of capitalist investment, labor becomes a mere means to such profit. The enjoyment of workers and the workers' consciousness of themselves, their species life, is sacrificed on the altar of profit, and they become alienated from themselves. Such alienation from oneself is accompanied by alienation from other people, the capitalist and other people with whom they are competing for a job. In an individualistic society with little or no community, money becomes the real mind and community of all things, and others become either obstacles or means on my way to Wall Street or Greenwich. Capitalist society becomes a "pursuit of loneliness" in which wealth is the goal and general human misery is the result.[5]

Capitalism as Marx defines and articulates it has a certain logic: expansionary, quantitative, exploitative, and inverted. If making some money is good, then making more money is better, and making the most money is best. Capital as a process of self-expanding value (abstract labor time measured in money) tends to extend its sway over more and more areas of human life. If consumer demand is a problem, then advertising emerges as a way of solving this problem. If market instability is a difficulty creating the possibility of depressions and recessions, then state investment in the economy becomes legitimate and necessary. If inadequate national demand or shortage of raw materials or excessively expensive labor is a problem, then capital expands into areas with more consumers, more raw materials, and cheaper labor. Imperialism is rooted in and is a natural consequence of capital logic. Imperialism as I will show more fully in chapter 13, is simply unjust capitalist social relations transplanted abroad.[6]

Because the goal of expansion is surplus value or profit, surplus, unpaid labor time measured in money, quantity reigns over quality in capitalism. Commodities have to have a real or imagined use value in order to be salable to the consumer, but this use value ultimately serves profitability. The subordination of real human need to profit is itself a perversion manifested in such phenomena as planned obsolescence, creation of artificial or unnecessary needs, and spending for relatively useless but very profitable items such as weapons rather than education or health care or housing for the poor.[7]

Capitalism is exploitative because, as our account of alienation already shows, people are used as mere means for the sake of profit. Surplus labor time is stolen from the laborer in a way that contradicts the bourgeois justification for private property that people should have the right to appropriate the objects containing their own labor. Capitalism turns this right into the legal right to appropriate the fruits of other people's labor.[8]

Because capital logic is expansionary, quantitative, and exploitative, it is also inverted, means are turned into ends and ends into means, the lowest into the highest and the highest into the lowest, the intrinsically valuable into the instrumental and vice versa. Because of the thirst for surplus value, capital extends its sway into more and more areas of human life; nothing is sacred, everything becomes salable, everyone becomes a commodity.

> Money is the hangman of all things, the moloch to which everything must be sacrificed, the despot of commodities. . . . Universal prostitution appears as a necessary phase in the development of the social character of personal talents, capacities, abilities, activities. More politely expressed, the universal relation of utility and use.[9]

What happens as a result of all the above is the minimizing or denying of real individuality. Capitalism creates the conditions for full individuality, but because of the lopsided distribution of wealth and income, these are not shared with most of the population. Because of the division of labor and the dehumanizing conditions of work, the laborer becomes a mutilated monstrosity and a deformed human being. Because of the domination of exchange value over use value, a quantitative sameness is forced on the population. Individualism is substituted for individuality, a deep, qualitative awareness of myself and other. I think that I am being an individual when I purchase the same perfume, watch the same program, or read the same magazine as everyone else. "The really with-it, fashion-conscious man reads *Playboy*."[10]

Capitalism creates the conditions for a rich, many-sided individuality, but is unable to realize it because of the alienated, class-based exploitative nature of capitalist social relations. One of the little known aspects of Marx and critical theory is their passion for genuine individuality, which passion they share with Kierkegaard. Unlike Kierkegaard, they stress the socio-economic conditions for the emergence of such individuality, which is full economic, social, and political democracy. This is the so-called "communism" of Marx, which has little to do with the Soviet version. Communism as Marx envisions it is simply the creation of the socio-economic framework for the emergence of the rich, many-sided, social individual. How this solution relates to Kierkegaard's religious faith, the primary focus for him of the emergence of the genuine individual, is one of the central issues of the chapter. What I will be arguing is that both are necessary. Full individuality requires both the transformation of capitalism into full democracy and religious belief. Neither critical theory nor Kierkegaard are adequately dialectical in that they have not synthesized adequately the opposites of radical social practice and religious belief.[11]

In this way communism is a dialectical solution to the alienation of capitalism, bringing the conditions for the fulfillment of individuality into relationship with those individuals themselves. Human history will have moved from a stage of one-sided immediacy of workers to land and to each other in precapitalist societies, through a stage of one-sided capitalist mediation, dualistic, alienated, individualistic, to a stage of mediated immediacy. Community is restored but now in a context where expression of individuality is given full play.[12]

Kierkegaard does not place the same emphasis on the economy as Marx; the economy for him is an instance of and manifestation of the public, which I will discuss later. Since both Marx and Kierkegaard, however, refuse to reduce the economic to the social or vice versa, we can note an approximation of their positions to each other. One of the ways in which the economy expresses the public is the dominance of money in our lives. "What is a woman's loveliness if it is for sale for money? And what is a bit of talent when it is in service of vile profit?"[13]

In Kierkegaard's encounter with *The Corsair*, which he criticized for being a form of journalism that was extremely commercial, meretricious, and degrading, he also encountered the universal, leveling, quantifying, expansionary power of money.

> But, alas, when passion and commercial interest determine the issue, when there is no ear for the harmony of spheres of category relations but

only for the rattle of money in the cash box, and when passion is propelled to the extreme by the consciousness that every subscriber buys along with the paper the right contemptibly to dispatch what is being written—this is another matter.[14]

Kierkegaard indicates here the way money corrupts and degrades authorship by way of turning it into a kind of prostitution, and the way money plays a role by covering up or obliterating differences between categories. Publications such as *The Corsair* arouse a superficial, commodified passion that allows people to think that they can dismiss significant, profound authors who resist any reduction to a least common denominator. For this reason there is no middle ground between publishing significant material and being condemned for earning money by writing for and editing *The Corsair*. For this reason Kierkegaard does not wish to waste the time of businessmen.[15]

Because the capital-public possesses a quantifying, expansionary, exploitative logic, it is also inverted. Both critical theory and Kierkegaard develop this point in different ways. Enterprises such as *The Corsair*, Kierkegaard argues, turn relationships upside-down. Because of such inversion, the nonessential, Kierkegaard's trousers, is substituted for the essential, inwardness. Cowardice in *The Corsair* appears as inwardness, false comedy as true comedy, irresponsibility as responsibility. People reading *The Corsair* find his critique of it dull and pedestrian, its critique of him funny and satirical.[16]

In the face of such an expansionary, quantifying, homogenizing power, genuine individuality is more and more eclipsed. Because all human beings are simply numerical units of a quantitative mass, quantity has driven out quality, mediocrity has eclipsed excellence, and fashion has triumphed over originality. No person makes his own decisions. Like Marx's worker, Kierkegaard's citizen is passive, "distracted from distraction by distraction," easily manipulated by the media, willingly seduced by the latest entertainment fad. The public becomes a fetish supplying the community, thought, security, and authority that human beings are unable to supply for themselves. Public opinion invades interiority more and more. If I am unable or unwilling to come up with my own opinions, convictions, and commitments, I can always have recourse to Tom Brokaw or Dan Rather or David Letterman.[17]

Like paper money, ideas, opinions, and witticisms circulate at second hand, divorced from passion, thought, and responsibility. Abstract, inauthentic reflection buys everything at secondhand prices. Because thought has become a commodity, a dog the public keeps for its own amusement, and a technique that anyone can learn, the only way thought can be redeemed is through the leap of religious faith.[18]

In the leap of faith individuals themselves are able to establish links with other human beings:

But through the leap out into the depths one learns to help himself, learns to love all others as much as himself even though he is accused of arrogance and pride—or of selfishness—for being unwilling to deceive others by helping them, that is, by helping them miss what is highest of all.[19]

Kierkegaard's approach here is dialectical insofar as contemporary mass society, which is alienated and one-sidedly mediated, points back to antiquity, in which there was an immediate relation of human beings to one another; and points forward to faith, in which alienation is overcome and there is true reconciliation between such opposites as silence and speech, inwardness and revelation, individual and community. In contrast to the present age's false reconciliation of opposites, creating the public and crushing the individual, the religious individual is no longer isolated and reaches out to other human beings.[20]

The Ethico-Political

In the history of Marxism there is a developing awareness of the importance of the ethico-political level. Underemphasized and undeveloped in Marx himself, the political in thinkers such as Gramsci and Habermas comes more into prominence in itself as a reality and category distinct and yet related to the economic. In this part of the essay I will focus on Habermas himself as the most fully developed account of the ethico-political within Western Marxism. His is the most thoroughgoing rethinking within this tradition of the relationship between the economic and the political.[21]

This rethinking occurs on a number of distinct, but related, categorical levels, moving from abstract to concrete. 1) On the level of a theory of historical materialism, Habermas argues that moral learning is a pace-setter for historical change, and the institutionalizing of such learning allows a society to respond to crises arising on an economic level. 2) On a descriptive-phenomenological level, Habermas distinguishes between a communicative praxis governed by qualitative norms and a purposive rational action oriented to quantitative prediction and control, and among moral, scientific, and aesthetic forms of communication, each with its own telos, norms, and logic. 3) On the level of a theory of modernity, Habermas argues that moral, scientific, and aesthetic forms of rationality have been differentiated, and that these forms of cultural rationalization are distinct from social rationalization, that is, the institutionalization of purposive rational action in the economy and state.

4) On the level of a synchronic account of modern capitalist society, Habermas argues that there are not only economic and rationality crises (eco-

nomic crises mediated by the state) but also legitimation and motivational crises. The latter two have their roots in capitalist society's inability to meet the legitimate ethical and political expectations of its participants. Can modern capitalist society be adequately democratic if the state and economy must serve the preservation of capitalist profit over against the interests of the polity as a whole? Habermas questions whether there is not an inevitable contradiction between democratic legitimation and capitalist accumulation, universal and particular, capitalism and democracy. Is not American capitalism, for example, ostensibly "of, by, and for the people," ultimately of, by, and for capital? Are not such tendencies manifest in the way we prefer military spending, very profitable for corporations, to spending for other human needs such as housing or food or rapid transit, the way money influences disproportionately the formation of state policy, and the way other voices, such as those of the poor, the unemployed, and the homeless, are shunted to the side? Communicative action is oriented to the universal claims of truth, sincerity, and rightness, and to the universal good of the whole society, but is ultimately contradicted by and, too often, overridden by particular capitalist class interest.[22]

For Habermas the critique of society has a moral-political component as well as an economic component. The moral-political component manifests itself in early Habermas's critique of science-technology as ideology shoving to the side the claims of ethical reason and making politics merely the art of selling the president according to an economic model of rationality, and in late Habermas's account of the different kinds of crisis and his critique of a capitalist colonization of the life-world, in which domains normally governed by communicative action are subject to economic imperatives. Universities become primarily launching pads for Wall Street, television programs become primarily ways of making money for the sponsor, and politics becomes the art of "manufacturing consent," in which a manipulative strategic action (purposive rational action used against people) prevails over communicative action.[23]

In its growing awareness of the importance of the ethico-political, critical theory approximates Kierkegaard. Fundamental to his whole project is the notion of ethical self-choice leading to and implying commitment to the human or divine other. The movement from the aesthetic to the ethical level of existence is a move from a life of rootless floating and experimenting to a life of existential commitment, from sensuous particular to ethical universal, from selfishness to selfhood. The highest religious level, in which the ethical is brought out of its conflict with the aesthetic, completes this process of self-becoming. I will discuss this level more in the last main sub-section of this dialectical reflection, Religious Belief.[24]

Suffice it to say that Kierkegaard speaks to the necessity of a series of conversions or leaps, from the aesthetic to the ethical and from the ethical to the religious, in which the inwardness or interiority of the self manifests itself. I find fruitful complementarity here with Western Marxism's emphasis on individuality, but which, compared to Kierkegaard, remains undeveloped. Crucial to individuality according to Kierkegaard is inwardness, the reflective, free consciousness of the individual as a self choosing itself in relation to a human and divine other. Even Habermas, whose own interpretations of Mead and Durkheim point to such interiority, finally does not take the full turn into it, for reasons that I will develop in my next chapter. As I will show, this refusal has atheistic consequences.[25]

I find complementarity and not contradiction for two reasons. First, such interior, existential conversion to selfhood can strengthen and enhance communicative praxis, whereas this formalizes, expresses, and externalizes inwardness. I commit myself firmly and habitually to an ethical form of life, from which communicative praxis springs and without which it remains fitful, inconstant, and vacillating. The existential and the political, inwardness and communicative praxis, self-awareness and ideology critique complement one another; no adequate communicative praxis without full choice of myself as existentially and historically ethical, no adequate selfhood without communicative praxis.

Kierkegaard thinks and lives this reciprocity in his participation in the *Corsair* affair in which he allows himself to be pilloried by the *Corsair* as a way of revealing its cultural bankruptcy, and in his later critique of Christendom. Even the social expression of his critique has more of the private, inward, and individual in it than the forms of public, political action and protest favored by Marxism. Against the corrupt *Corsair* and corrupt Christendom, he manifests the full resources of an authentic inwardness, reminding Marxism and critical theory that within the heaven of critique, there are many mansions.[26]

Adorno, who perhaps has a more developed idea of inwardness than Habermas, recognizes the above claims in a way that approximates Kierkegaard:

> In the face of the totalitarian unison with which the eradication of difference is proclaimed as a principle in itself, even part of the social force of liberation may have temporarily withdrawn to the individual sphere. If critical theory lingers there, it is not only with a bad conscience.[27]

In the face of a commodified, exploitative, one-dimensional society, the struggle for individual enlightenment and authenticity can be the beginning of political resistance and have at least an indirect political resonance.

Culture

It is perhaps on the level of culture, a public domain where exchange of information, ideas, and values occurs, that critical theory and Kierkegaard are closest. For Marxism, culture produces ideology that expresses, legitimates, and covers up class and group domination: racist, sexist, heterosexist, classist. For this reason the leading ideas of an epoch are those of its ruling class. The individualism, for example, so rampant during the Reagan era expresses and legitimizes the private ownership of the means of production, the orientation to private profit, and the reluctance to use the state for public spending that helps the poor, the unemployed, and the homeless.[28]

As capitalism develops and economic and legitimation crises emerge more frequently, ideology becomes more of an issue. If depression is to be avoided, people need to be persuaded to buy goods that they might otherwise not buy. If revolution is to be avoided, a population whose interests the economy and the state generally do not adequately serve needs to be convinced that its interests are served. As a result, in the twentieth century a "consciousness industry" emerged that is in most respects the same as and a development of Kierkegaard's "public." The economy and consciousness industry require one another and lock into one another. Indeed, media such as radio, television, newspapers, and movies not only sell money-making as a way of life, but are themselves committed to making a profit. General Electric buying NBC during the 1980s and newscasts praising its military weapons used during the Gulf War are typical examples. The very Patriot missiles you see being deployed are produced by GE; "GE brings good things to life."[29]

Within the consciousness industry there are at least two main functions: reporting and interpreting the news in a propagandistic manner and the creation of "phantasmagoria." Both of these functions have as their ultimate goal the subjugation of the viewing, consuming public to the imperatives of capital. Reporting of the news occurs in a way that is selective, biased, one-sided, and false. For example, the press understates the number of protesters going to Washington to protest the Gulf War, or fails to mention crimes of client regimes supported by the United States, or mentions such crimes on the back page, or describes as "democratic" what are actually repressive, undemocratic client regimes in Brazil, Argentina, and Guatemala. An "economic miracle" of free trade is proclaimed in Central and Latin America, which actually leaves most people in those countries worse off, more hungry, more illiterate, and more repressed than they were ten or fifteen years ago.[30]

Another function of the media, however, is to create "phantasmagoria," images functioning as commodities and commodities functioning as images. Phantasmagoria are a cultural expression of the fetishization of commodities described by Marx, in which relations between people take the fantastic form of relations between things. The commodity becomes fantastic, seeming to have properties it does not have and having properties that are not apparent. In the consciousness industry images become commodities as sports figures are used to sell basketball shoes, sexy models to sell clothes, and movie stars to sell deodorant. Michael Jordan, Cindy Crawford, and Clint Eastwood become reified, fetishized gods and goddesses, expressing the reign of the gods capital and money. At the same time commodities like basketball shoes become images, seeming to possess magical qualities. If you buy Nike, then you too can "be like Mike."[31]

Like postmodernists such as Baudrillard, Marx and critical theory recognize the fantastic, fictional, "simulative" character of the commodity. Unlike Baudrillard, however, they relate this simulation to the real capitalist world of production and consumption. In this way they do more justice than does postmodernism both to the fiction and reality of the late capitalist consciousness industry. Benjamin's account is that these phantasmagoria "express," not simply reflect, this real economic world, the way a dream expresses the interplay between id and superego. Ideology critique consists in showing the relationship between such expression and economic-political processes and in criticizing both as false and unjust. Late capitalism promises what it really cannot deliver, happiness, and claims to practice what it really violates and frustrates—namely, justice. Because of the gap between promise and reality, the consciousness industry has to intervene in order to prevent people from seeing what would be otherwise obvious, that the American dream is a nightmare. Indeed, the function of the consciousness industry is to create a mass, collective dream, from which critical theory tries to awaken us.[32]

Kierkegaard's notion of the "public" also recognizes the unreal, fantastic dimension of the consciousness industry. He describes the public as "an evasion, a dissipation, and an illusion. . . . The public may take a year and day to assemble and when it is assembled it does not exist." Further, the public is "an abstract void and vacuum that is all and nothing" and "reflection's mirage . . . the fairy tale of an age of prudence." Like Marx and critical theory, Kierkegaard relates the public to its basis in real social life, criticizes it normatively in the light of criteria proceeding from ethical selfhood, evaluates it dialectically in the light of an ontology of the self, synthesizing such opposites as necessity and possibility, finitude and infinitude, and points toward its overcoming in a more just society. Like Marx and critical theory, Kierkegaard's conception of self, normativity, rationality, and critique is fundamentally modernist, or at least has significant modernist strains, not simply postmodernist as some are wont to argue.[33]

What is the public? It is a collection of inauthentic individuals living amorally as a mass or crowd and expressing itself anonymously, abstractly, passionlessly, and irresponsibly. The public is the expression of a conformist society in which individuality has lost all depth and social life all ethically defensible mediation. Nothing is sacred, everything is for sale, and no one is willing to take seriously anything besides her or his own pleasure or profit.[34]

As we have already shown in the first section of this chapter, the press for Kierkegaard is an instance of the public, consuming everything in its path, turning everything into grist for its mill, making everyone a celebrity for fifteen minutes. The genius of Kierkegaard lies in his understanding so early the quantitative, homogenizing, infinitizing, inverted, exploitative logic of the public or capital-public; twentieth-century capitalism has turned emergent tendencies in Kierkegaard's Denmark into an art form. The later critical theory of Adorno, Benjamin, and others develops these insights of Marx and Kierkegaard and shows how their claims are even truer today. Merely emerging tendencies have turned into a system of "totalitarian" or "quasi-totalitarian" control.[35]

Such claims may strike the reader as overstated and one-sided. Do not we in the United States have a real set of freedoms and rights unlike those of the formerly brainwashed Russians and the currently brainwashed Chinese? Critical theory's response is to admit that such freedoms and rights are institutionalized and even operative in a minimal sense, but are significantly compromised and violated in practice. Indeed, that we are legally and formally free makes ours a more efficient system of brainwashing. When people in Russia, prior to 1989, sat down for the evening news, they knew they were just receiving propaganda, the party line. When we hear Dan Rather or Tom Brokaw, we think we are getting the unvarnished truth. Because propaganda comes bearing gifts, ideology under the guise of truth or fantasy in the guise of fact, the brainwashing is even more effective. For this reason as well as others, an ideology critique inviting us to rediscover the socio-economic roots of such ideology and our own authentic individuality is necessary.

Religious Belief

Here on this level is affinity and difference, agreement and disagreement between Kierkegaard and critical theory. For critical theory, religion is something to be criticized and transcended, because it represents an alienation of human beings from their own essential powers and because it often functions as an ideological prop for a corrupt, unjust social status quo. Critique of religious belief as such a prop, therefore, functions as an element of ideology critique.[36]

Kierkegaard argues against Marx and critical theory that authentic religious belief helps the human being overcome alienation and that such belief can function as ideology critique. Inauthentic religious belief, such as operated in Kierkegaard's Christendom, can and does function in the way that Marxists describe it. Coming down to the present, we can see that this process continues. We have only to note the way organized religion celebrated and supported the Gulf War, ringing its church bells all over the country on a day designated by Bush to celebrate the great triumph, or the way an individual-istic interpretation of religious belief mirrors individualistic capitalist society, the individualism Reagan and Bush raised to an art form. For religious believ-ers, therefore, such critique can purify their notion of God. God is not, and should not be conceived as, simply the God of the ruling classes. If this is all God is, then God is dead and deserves to be dead. Rather God is identified with the poor and exploited and suffering; we can find in Kierkegaard begin-nings of a "preferential option for the poor":

> In order to invite them to come to one in this way, one must live in the very same manner, poor as the poorest, poorly regarded as the lowly man among people, experienced in life's sorrow as anguish, sharing the very same condition as those one invites to come to one, those who labor and are burdened.[37]

The only kind of God worth talking about is God as liberator, as partner and companion in the project of overcoming racist, sexist, classist, heterosex-ist injustice. Such a conception of God, I would argue, is necessary if critical theory is to achieve its full range and effectiveness. Critical theory can and should include a religious component. The first strand in this critique is the negative critique of religious belief undertaken both by Marxism and Kierkegaard.

A second strand is that religious belief has positive resources upon which one can and must draw in order to make one's critique. If, as I have already argued in this chapter, interiority and critique dig into one another and if interiority in its full aspiration and range implies religious belief, then cri-tique and liberation in their full range imply religious belief. Kierkegaard argues that human subjectivity is a passion for the infinite, for that in which I can believe and entrust myself unreservedly as an unrestricted source of intel-ligibility and love. Short of such an adequate "object" for my belief, I am in danger of committing myself unreservedly to a finite object, of divinizing it. If a contradiction emerges between the infinite passion and finite object, this contradiction can be adequately resolved only by making the full-fledged commitment to God and to Jesus Christ as the most adequate historical reve-lation of God.[38]

Marx and critical theory, because they fail to take the full turn into inte-riority, miss the positive reality and importance of religious belief and thus shortchange themselves. Interiority, as I have already shown and will develop in the next chapter, becomes a crucial middle term mediating political critique and religious belief.

The argument up to this point may seem abstract. This is not necessar-ily a bad thing, since any good philosophical argument will have an element of abstractness about it. A third step, however, that is more concrete is to show hermeneutically how Kierkegaard's Christianity has positive resources for making such a critique. Here it is important to note how he insists, in the *Corsair* affair and in the critique of Christendom, that Christianity most comprehensively and deeply interpreted not only resists being incorporated into an unjust status quo, but can function as a critique of that status quo. In identifying reason with a corrupt public sphere mediated by the Danish state and economy, one makes reason irrational by uncritically deifying it and by ignoring the authenticity of the individual.

In making Christianity merely an affair of the educated middle and upper classes, a person does violence to the universality of Christianity as it extends to the poor and oppressed. If Christianity is genuinely universal and it extends to the poor, oppressed, and suffering, then like Christ and any Christian who follows him seriously, one must wish not merely to aid these people from on high but to be with them, suffer with them, identify with them. Here is a religiously motivated identification with the oppressed similar to Marxism's identification with labor and other victims of capital. Identification with the poor and oppressed becomes the epistemic and ethico-religious vantage point from which I make my critique and engage in praxis. Short of such identification my critique is not fully true nor my praxis fully ethical. Also, in making religion state-supported and financed, one does violence both to the secular character of the state and to the transcendent character of religious belief. One divinizes the state and renders immanent religious belief. In doing so one also misses the legitimate modern differentiation between secular and religious. Once again Kierkegaard's modernist roots are apparent. Like Habermas, he insists on legitimate differentiation occurring in modern society.[39]

Kierkegaard, then, undertakes from the perspective of a vantage point outside reason itself, the level of freedom and commitment oriented to a transcendent God, a critique of reason. Such a critique, however, benefits reason by allowing it to become fully self-critical and not to divinize itself; in so doing it becomes uncritical and therefore irrational. Similarly, a right wing Hegelian reason, or in the twentieth century a liberal, scientific reason that divinizes the status quo, sacrifices its ethical, critical substance and becomes irrational. To the extent that such a reason invites individuals to identify with the social whole and ignore their own individuality, such a reason becomes inauthentic, and, therefore, irrational. Reason in order to realize itself fully must become fully self-critical by transcending itself. Short of such self-transcendence reason remains partial, limited, truncated, and in danger of divinizing itself. The benefits of such an approach for a Marxism always in danger of divinizing itself in the dialectic, the party, and the state should be obvious. Only God is God.

Finally, the life of Kierkegaard himself most concretely expresses and conforms to his thought. Fact proves the genuine possibility of a religious belief that is genuinely, prophetically resistant to and critical of a corrupt, unjust society in his time and our time. In the presence of God the "single one" recovers his sense of self, uniqueness, and integrity. In the face of the conformity encouraged by mass culture, the single one becomes an original creative self. In the face of the leveling tendencies of consumer culture, the single one develops capacities for self-transcendence toward God and other human beings. In the face of the mindless togetherness of such a society, the single one learns to choose and cherish a life-giving solitude. Through such solitude persons develop a critical distance enabling them to see through the myths of such a society: consumerism, militarism, rugged individualism, imperialism, "the new world order," technocracy, sexism, and hedonism. Kierkegaard's life and thought manifest the possibility of a prophetic philo-sophical and religious critique that can be wedded fruitfully to critical theory. Such possibilities continue to be expressed in our own time by such people as Martin Luther King, Malcolm X, and Daniel Berrigan. Each in his own way testifies to the falsity of a religious belief that identifies with and refuses to question an unjust status quo, the necessity to join faith with justice, the importance of linking peace with justice, the identification with the poor and oppressed, and the truth of a prophetic religious critique and transcendence.

Description

I have noted here many affinities between critical theory and Kierkegaard: the importance of the individual, the significance of ideology critique, the relationship between capital and the public, the necessity of praxis, a pathological logic in capital and the public that is inverted, quantita-tive, exploitive, and expansionary, the importance of the ethical-political, a use of dialectic moving from one-sided immediacy to one-sided, contradic-tory mediation to integrative individualism and social transformation, and the critique of fetishism.

At the same time, at each stage in my inquiry I have noted differences and disagreements: the relative weight each gives to capital and the public, the different importance each gives to interiority, the different weights given to public, collective action versus a resistance and critique that is more on the individual level, and the differing evaluations each gives to religious belief. I think that most of the differences are complementary rather than contradic-tory. If one realizes, for example, that for both Marxism and Kierkegaard the relationship between economy and the public is reciprocal, dialectical, and nonreductionistic, then the only question remaining concerns priority, importance, and dominance. I have indicated elsewhere why I think the Marxist answer is preferable. Again, as I have already shown, existential inwardness complements the public and communicative, and vice versa. Individual, religious, and ethically motivated resistance can complement a Marxist emphasis on public mass action.[40]

Critical theory enables religious faith to be sufficiently suspicious of itself, to be critical of and transcend practices and ideologies of racism, sexism, heterosexism, and classism. Religious belief building on but going beyond metaphysics allows critical theory to be sufficiently open to God as the ground even of its orientation to a critique and praxis of radical liberation, to be aware of the dialectic of sin discussed in chapter 7, to have a firm basis and infinite, personal, divine referent such that all socio-economic solutions can be criticized and relativized as finite and not divinized or fetishized. Critical theory helps religious belief to be more adequately and fully religious; religious belief helps critical theory to be more adequately critical and radical.

Where the differences are less easily resolved is on the religious question itself. Is religious belief merely ideology or is it also a positive component essential to ideology critique? I have briefly argued in this chapter and more extensively in prior chapters why I think the latter is true. An approach integrating both the negative and positive evaluations of religious belief is, therefore, more comprehensive hermeneutically than one that emphasizes simply the negative or the positive.

The formal result of my essay is, then, a conception of critical theory as having at least four different levels, economic, political, cultural, and religious, which interrelate in different ways. If I add the metaphysical level discussed in Part One as distinct but related to the religious, then we have five levels. One way in which the levels interrelate is that we can affirm the necessity of radical political conversion as a basis for doing critical theory. Such a conversion establishes a habitually lived horizon within which I as theorist and human agent operate rationally, ethically, politically, and religiously. The movement from aesthetic to ethical to religious, which Kierkegaard describes as a series of leaps, has a social, political component to it, an identification with the oppressed, a preferential option for the poor, and a commitment to work for justice.

Such radical political conversion has at least four components. The first is a commitment to rational, communicative praxis, in which I habitually am oriented to affirming and living out the implications of the better argument.[41] A second level is ethical, in which I move from mere self-centered aesthetic enjoyment to ethical commitment to the other as an end in itself. A third level is social, in which I act and live and theorize from the perspective of a preferential option for the poor, marginalized, and oppressed. A fourth level is religious, in which I commit myself to a God inviting me to share in the work of liberating the oppressed. Radical political conversion, therefore, wedding an existential, reflective component and a critical, political component, is the final fruit, and, at the same time, the basis of the marriage between critical theory and religious belief that I present here.

Conclusion

At this point I have completed my demonstration of the mutual interpenetration of ideology critique and religious belief. As we saw in the discussion of faith and suspicion, adequate religious belief has a moment of suspicion and critique. As we have seen in this chapter, ideology critique has a religious as well as a metaphysical dimension to it. Now in the next few chapters we need to extend these insights into the parameters of modern and contemporary capitalism on national and international levels. What implications does our account have for the interpretation of modernity, neoimperialism, and liberation in the imperial center, acting in tandem with liberation in the periphery of the Third World?

The Religious Significance
of Modernity

At this point in the book my discussion needs to become still more historically concrete and comprehensive. I have affirmed the reality and importance of Jesus Christ and Jesus Christ liberator, and faith illumined by suspicion and radical political conversion as a consequence of intellectual, moral, and religious conversion. Now I need to confront in this chapter the role of religious belief in modern history. Has modern history rendered religious belief obsolete or irrelevant?

Here I propose to reflect on Habermas as the strongest, most developed, and most sophisticated version of a "yes" answer to the above question. According to him, part of the progress of modernity has been the gradual withering away and growing obsolescence of religious belief as modernity discovers its fundamental, ethical, rational core. According to him, religious belief during the progress of modernity has been subject to a "linguistification of the sacred" in which its ethical core is cognitively redeemed in ethical praxis. Modernity represents an *Aufhebung* of religious belief in which its properly religious aspect is rejected and its ethical core retained and sublated into the higher viewpoint of communicative praxis.[1]

Nonetheless, as I hope to show in the course of this chapter, such skepticism about religious belief is premature. Not only is it important for believers to ascertain the validity of his arguments for overcoming religion, but there is a relevance of Habermas's theory for religious belief itself, a form of religious ideology critique that can enhance Habermas's own project, and there are positive openings in Habermas's thought that allow for a positive relationship to certain kinds of religious belief. There are, then, multiple lines of significance between Habermas and religious belief that need to be thematized and evaluated.

Habermas's social theory as a progressive, synthetic movement from abstract to concrete has four moments: eidetic-descriptive, hermeneutical, structural, and political. What are the different kinds of rationality as we experience, describe, and understand them essentially? What is the best interpretation of rationality as it develops, differentiates itself, and is twisted to serve class and group domination in modernity? What is the economic and political structure of late capitalism and to what contradictions does it give rise? What social movements have emerged in late capitalist modernity that are or can be efficacious? Correspondingly, this chapter will have four parts in which I first positively and negatively evaluate his position in relation to religious belief, and then lay out my positive account. In contrast to other chapters, dialectic and description operate in each of the four sections.

The Structure of Communicative Action

The most abstract level of Habermas's work is his eidetic-descriptive account of communicative action—that is, his attempt to articulate the invariant universals in communicative action that we spontaneously employ and that are continuously present to us in an intuitive manner. Such a descriptive move becomes necessary in order to become clear about how we experience rationality in its various forms. This serves to evaluate various one-sided accounts of rationality. If Husserl's own descriptive turn to "the things themselves" became necessary to order to avoid a "philosophizing from on high" proceeding from such questionable premises as the atomistic character of perception or the dichotomy of mind and body, then Habermas's descriptive turn in a postmodern climate of thought becomes necessary to avoid an "anti-philosophizing from on high" proceeding from such premises as "all judgments are expressions of power" or "all rationality is instrumental." Further theorizing is necessary and Habermas does plenty of that, but we "get our feet on the ground" philosophically through an initial description of how we employ different forms and kinds of rationality. In this way he avoids a facile reductionism.[2]

What first becomes apparent in communicative action is that it is governed by three validity claims—truth, sincerity, and rightness. When I converse with somebody, we presuppose that what we are saying is true, is sincere, and right or appropriate, in the sense that we are not trying to impose on each other arbitrarily or assume authority arbitrarily.[3]

Although in his later work at times Habermas seems to back off from using "transcendental" to describe such validity claims, they retain some of the functions of the transcendental in that they are necessary, putatively universal conditions of the possibility for communicative praxis. They make possible an "ideal speech situation," the projection of a regulative ideal of communication in which no objection, expression, or opinion is excluded from consideration, full symmetry, reciprocity, and equality reign among participants, and the only force is that of the better argument. Such an ideal speech situation is neither empirically real in the sense of being totally realized nor is it purely fictional, since it functions as an implicit norm and measure in the light of which we can spontaneously evaluate some conversations as closed and repressive and others as open and liberated.[4]

Related to the three main validity claims are three main possible kinds of sentences: constative, regulative, and expressive. The constative sentence—for example, "John is five feet tall"—makes truth claims about the objective world. The regulative speech act, for example "Bush's intervention in the Middle East is unjust," articulates what is morally wrong. The expressive speech act, for example "I am happy that you won the award," expresses my subjective response to something. Each kind of sentence specializes in or emphasizes one validity claim, but the others are present as implicit presuppositions. For example, my expression of joy at your success presupposes my recognition that you have succeeded.[5]

Communicative action includes the above speech acts and their validity, and is distinguished from an instrumental action oriented to success. Such action can only achieve its perlocutionary aims by keeping them secret, and always involves a kind of manipulation, coercion, or violence. Contrast parents trying to convince their child to go into medicine in order to fulfill the secret needs of the parents for status or prestige with parents who are honestly open with their son about his career choice, their own desires and expectations for their son, and their own commitment that the son do what best suits him and fulfills him. There is a nonviolence and noncoerciveness about communicative action that instrumental action implicitly trades on and presupposes, even in arguing that "all communication is violent." For the claim to have any validity at all, it tacitly presupposes a nonviolent process of persuasion in which the better argument wins. Otherwise the claim has no more validity than that of a Chilean prisoner tortured into making the admission that Pinochet is a just ruler.[6]

There are many positive merits to Habermas's conception of communicative action. Such a conception allows him to do justice to the different forms and kinds of rationality in a way that avoids modern and postmodern reductionism. Nonetheless, some reservations do arise. We may note the exclusion in Habermas of metaphysical-religious constative sentences such as

"God exists," expressive sentences such as "I love God," and regulative sentences such as "God's will is that I do this." On a strictly descriptive level there seems to be no reason to exclude these sentences as legitimate examples of communicative praxis. Yet Habermas excludes them as legitimate because of presuppositions informing his descriptive account. Such presuppositions most likely include (and here I am interpreting and extrapolating) Kant's critique of metaphysics, Feuerbach's critique of religion, and Marx's critique of religion as ideology. More precisely Habermas's Marxism, albeit reconstructed, informs his descriptive account in a way that may prejudice it illegitimately.[7]

I hasten to add that there is nothing methodologically illegitimate in having such presuppositions, because I do not think that a totally presuppositionless account is possible. What is possible, however, in Habermas's own spirit in the context of the ideal speech situation, is a questioning of such presuppositions. Do they withstand the force of the better argument? It shall be the burden of the rest of this chapter to show that they do not.

Taking a hint from Parsons, I am raising at this point the hypothesis of a fourth domain, perhaps most adequately conceived not as running alongside normal constative, expressive, and regulative sentences indicating three different worlds—objective, subjective, and social—but as grounding, surrounding, and rendering completely intelligible these three worlds.

Adding to the plausibility of such a hypothesis is Arendt's criticism of Marxism in general and, by implication, of Habermas in particular of being insufficiently attentive to and appreciative of the contemplative, and too one-sidedly focused on praxis in the triple forms of art, political action, and labor informed by science. I question Habermas here for being too uncritically Marxist in focusing on objective spirit and excluding absolute spirit too much, especially its domains of religion and metaphysics. Is Habermas too uncritically interested in reason as a form of world *transformation* and not enough as a form of world *disclosure*? I am reminded here of Adorno's self-critique, insofar as he asks whether the Marxist utopia is just capitalist busyness and bustle democratized and more equally distributed? Perhaps true utopia is just closer to "rien faire comme une bete, lying on water and looking at the sky, being nothing else, without any further definition and fulfillment."[8]

I have to be careful here to be fair to Habermas. He does admit to an aesthetic, contemplative component to rationality; also to a form of discourse or conversation in the constative domain in which there is an aiming at the truth for its own sake, and, of course, science has a theoretical component. Nonetheless the questions persist. Is significant justice done to a kind of metaphysical-religious questioning of the whole? Do even the purely theoretical moments in Habermas arising in discourse about the moral, scientific, and aesthetic domains take their bearings too much from world-transforming praxis? Is there a danger on the descriptive level of excluding too much world-disclosing forms of rationality (Arendt in her critique undoubtedly has in mind as an alternative a receptive, meditative Heideggerian *Denken* about being) and emphasizing too much world-transforming forms of rationality? Again on a strictly descriptive level there seems to be no reason for such exclusion and emphasis. Such contemplative, receptive, meditative questioning of being does go on and needs to be described. Arendt does exactly this in her posthumously published work on thought and willing, in which such contemplation and thought serve as necessary complements to praxis in its different forms, political, aesthetic, economic.[9]

A related issue is whether Habermas's conception of individuality is too thin and impoverished. Using Mead's conception of socialization, Habermas distinguishes between a socialized "me" and a creative, free "I" not reducible to the content of such socialization and able to resist it. Such a distinction suggests an opening into an existential phenomenological reflection on interiority, which Habermas does not take and which we have taken throughout this book. Such a path of reflection articulates a domain of human experience that itself can plausibly be said to open up to being completed in a metaphysical-religious affirmation and commitment.

Kierkegaard's account of the three states of existence—aesthetic, ethical, and religious—and Lonergan's account of conversion—intellectual, moral, and religious—are probably the best recent examples. We move from a finite individuality to existential-phenomenological explication of such interiority leading to metaphysical-religious affirmation and commitment as the fullest actualization and completion of such interiority. As I have shown, not to make such an affirmation and commitment is to short-circuit and arbitrarily limit the fundamental human drive to intelligibility and value, or, in Habermas's terms, to introduce an arbitrary block and limit into the ideal speech situation, which requires that no a priori limits be put on questioning.[10]

Habermas, of course, has his own reasons for not using such an existential phenomenological account of subjectivity: the fascism of Heidegger, the validity of a shift from a philosophy of consciousness to one of language, and the link of phenomenology to constative or instrumental reason. These reasons do not seem cogent to me. The validity of phenomenology, even of Heidegger's, does not have to be rejected because of his fascism; there is a certain transcendence of the philosophy to the real person that, for good hermeneutical reasons, we need to affirm. It seems to me that Habermas overstates the significance of the linguistic turn insofar as he either denies or at least fails to thematize that there are mental acts such as understanding, judging, and choosing that are causative of and completed by external gestural or linguistic expression but are not reducible to such expression. The true reality, therefore, is "consciousness-expression."

It also seems to me that phenomenology is neither inevitably monological nor confined to instrumental reason. Schutz and others have developed a phenomenology of the social world, Husserl has criticized scientism and positivism for claiming to monopolize the definition of rationality, and Sokolowski has recently worked out a phenomenology of moral action. Properly understood, existentialism and phenomenology practice a descriptive, eidetic sensitivity to the multiple kinds of human rationality and action similar to Habermas's. They are allies, not adversaries.[11]

To return to the main thread of my argument, I have developed earlier in this book the idea of a domain of interiority that is structured by relationships of experience, understanding, judgment, and decision. For example, I see the apple fall, I formulate hypotheses to explain its falling, I verify these in experiments, and I decide to publish the results. I have argued, second, that such a transcendental structure is present in the various patterns of experience, aesthetic, scientific, moral, in a way that Habermas does not articulate. For example, I hear the poem read, I begin to grasp its meaning, I judge that my interpretation is true or that the poem is a good one, and I decide to read more of this poet. There is thus a principle of unity between and among the various patterns of experience that Habermas misses.

Third, questions concerning ultimate reality and meaning inevitably arise. In Lonergan's terms, "Is being ultimately intelligible?" or "Does an act of unrestricted understanding exist?" In Kierkegaard's terms, we might ask whether there is a being whom I can completely trust and believe in and love, who can satisfy completely my infinite passion, who can deliver the aesthetic from its conflict with the ethical in me. Here I would insist that commitment to the unlimited questioning of the ideal speech situation cannot exclude such questions as illegitimate. They are not meaningless because we can understand them, they are not absurd because they are not self-contradictory, and they are not illegitimate on positivistic grounds because Habermas has already rejected positivism. There is not just one form of rationality, scientific, but three. I would ask, "Why not a fourth?"[12]

Peukert has further argued that Habermas's own project requires a "yes" to the above questions. Operating as a presupposition of Habermas's communicative ethic is unconditional solidarity with all other human beings, past, present, and future. Such solidarity is rooted in the temporal aspects of the ideal speech situation, as well as the recognition of the other as an equal partner in speech, inviolable and free. Imagine, Peukert argues, a situation in which the ethical demands of communicative action were realized in full economic, social, and political democracy. In this situation, how is solidarity possible with the dead, oppressed, and innocent victims of past generations? Short of some kind of present solidarity with them as currently existing, do they not become mere means to our happy socialist present in a way that contradicts the unconditionality and universality of communicative praxis? If we try to forget them in order to remain in such a present, do we not contradict again such unconditionality and universality? How can a happiness based on evasion be true happiness?

Only the affirmation of past victims of oppression as currently existing and God as the guarantor of such existence delivers communicative praxis from its own contradictions. "The reality disclosed in communicative action, asserted as the saving reality for others and at the same time as the reality that through this salvation of the other makes possible one's own temporal existence unto death, must be called God." Such an analysis of human action, Peukert goes on to argue, is barely conceivable without the Old Testament and New Testament as hermeneutic revelations of such a God.[13]

Thomas McCarthy intelligently presents the strongest argument against this move of Peukert's. Are there not, McCarthy asks, any number of possible outcomes of such reflection on the conditions and implications of communicative action ranging from Horkheimer's pessimism about reconciliation with past victims and futural redemption to stoic resignation or existential commitment to Benjamin's empathic solidarity with past victims stopping short, however, of affirming God as a guarantor of solidarity to Habermas's compassionate solidarity modeled after Benjamin? Maybe one or the other of these stances is just the best we can do, McCarthy surmises, and thus inference from demand for perfect justice to God as guarantor is not valid.[14]

If, however, we recall what has already been affirmed about the intelligibility of being, then Peukert's argument is defensible. If being is intelligible, then it is completely intelligible. If it is completely intelligible, then God exists. Peukert's argument is just a variant of this general argument. If communicative action is intelligible, then it is completely intelligible. If it is completely intelligible, then it demands and requires real, effective solidarity with past victims of injustice. If such solidarity is to be present, then God must exist.

McCarthy's stance, then, rests upon a stance of "partial intelligibility," which I rejected in chapter 6 as incoherent. If communicative action occurs, therefore, it is either totally absurd or intelligible. It is not totally absurd; therefore, it is intelligible. If it is intelligible, then it is completely intelligible. If it is completely intelligible, then God exists. This metaphysically grounds and strengthens Peukert's argument and allows us to affirm some validity to it prior to recourse to Jewish and Christian sources. In the broadened and deepened content of Part Two of this work, recourse to these sources is certainly legitimate also.

If this all too brief sketch of an argument with and against Habermas is correct, then the following seems to be true: 1) At the eidetic-descriptive level there exists a fourth realm, the metaphysical-religious, that serves to ground the objective, subjective, and social realms. 2) On the same descriptive level, there is a contemplative dimension to which Habermas does not do justice. 3) There is an existential depth to individuality that must be affirmed and that opens, in its questioning and choosing, onto the transcendent. 4) Communicative ethics finds its ultimate completion and fulfillment in the affirmation of and commitment to such transcendence.

Hermeneutics

Because of problematic decisions, presuppositions, and exclusions on the descriptive, eidetic level, Habermas is already predisposed to interpret modernity in a certain way as a "linguistification of the sacred" that separates out and cognitively redeems ethical content and leaves behind specifically religious reference, belief, and commitment. Those belong to a superseded premodern stage of history governed by metaphysical-religious worldviews. If one rejects Habermas's problematic assumptions, then a different hermeneutical reading of modernity becomes possible. His interpretation of modernity as a contradictory tension between forward moves in learning and a pathological colonization of life-world by system requires and implies a metaphysical-religious dimension.[15]

The key word in Habermas's account of modernity is "differentiation" 1) among the spheres of aesthetic, scientific, and moral knowledge-cultural rationalization; 2) between cultural rationalization and social rationalization, in which purposive rational action, action utilizing technically chosen means ordered to technically achievable ends, is institutionalized in the economy and state; 3) between life-world and system, understood here as a functional connection among unintended effects of human choices (an economic crash or depression is a good example); 4) between a beneficial mediating of life-world by system and colonizing of life-world by system, in which the imperatives of capitalist or state socialist modernization impinge on, disturb, and corrupt spheres of the life-world. By "life-world" I here mean the social whole to which actors have access in a first-person, intuitive manner. As I speak to you in this room, this room opens onto a corridor in a building, which itself is in a university in a city. You and I share a common language and traditions, cultural, political, philosophical, religious, upon which we draw when we communicate. "Life-world" is to "communicative action" as implicit to explicit, prethematic to thematic, taken-for-granted to questionable, context to figure, indeterminate to determinate.[16]

Modernity is a contradictory blending of progress and decline, enlightenment and pathology, rationality and irrationality. In Habermas's view, his account is more comprehensive and nuanced than either an optimistic, harmonizing Parsonian account or a negative, postmodern account. Modernity is progressive in that forward moves in aesthetic, moral, and scientific learning have occurred and have been institutionalized. Modernity is pathological in that these very forward moves have been twisted in the interests of class or group domination. Habermas's Marxism comes in here to save modernist rationality. It is not modernist rationality *as such* that is the problem but its misuse and narrowing in the service of class and group domination.[17]

We have, then, four possible ways of relating to the modern: conservative regression, liberal commitment to a contradictory status quo, postmodern transcendence, and a dialectical, Habermasian "critical modernism." If the first three are inadequate, then Habermas's is the most preferable. Modernity and the Enlightenment are projects that need to be completed and redeemed, not rejected and scorned. Although Habermas is somewhat vague and indeterminate about his political program, it, in keeping with his Marxism, points toward significant economic, social, and political democratization. Because of the complex nature of modernity, such democratization will inevitably be accompanied by representation and expertise, and elements of bureaucracy and market. Because differentiation of system from life-world is a positive, forward move in modernity, and market and bureaucracy are elements of system, they would survive in any future democratization of society. There is a "Hegelian" realism that Habermas brings in here to qualify any naive Marxist hopes about total participatory democracy.[18]

As far as it goes, therefore, Habermas's account of modernity is illuminating and valid, a light shining in a darkness characterized by facile, contradictory attempts to transcend and reject the modern. But his account, in my opinion, does not go far enough and stands as inadequate by Habermas's own hermeneutical standards of comprehensiveness and respect for nuance. Taking a cue from Taylor in his recent, magisterial *Sources of the Self*, we may ask whether there is not a fourth strand of the modern that has been differentiated, the ontological-religious, in addition to the aesthetic, moral, and scientific. Once again quaternian rather than trinitarian thinking.[19]

Here I would have in mind the following phenomena, though I am not claiming an exhaustive description: the separation of church from state and economy in a way that allows for the greater autonomy of the former, the emergence of distinctively modern metaphysico-religious forms of thought such as Kierkegaard, Marcel, Lonergan, Barthes, Gutiérrez, and Tillich; the interaction between these forms of thought and the wider religious community; the mutual questioning of world by church and church by world such that the modern principles of freedom, reflexivity, and critique enter into the life of the churches and religious belief acts as a leavening influence on the world, allowing it to be more critical of the fetishes of money, sex, and power; and the emergence of distinctively modern political-religious movements led by such people as Berrigan, King, Day, and Camaro.[20]

Habermas's reply to this claim, of course, would be further insistence on and development of his thesis of the "linguistification of the sacred." There is an ethical core to religious belief that settles out in the course of modernity's development, leaving the proper religious reference and meaning of such belief in the dustbin of an outmoded premodern age.[21]

But has such a discarding occurred? To read the writings of a Kierkegaard or Berrigan or Gutiérrez or Moltmann is to witness an ethics essentially linked to and profoundly involved with religious belief. Such belief has not dropped out, but is the central motivating core. Maybe Habermas, because of the predilections mentioned in the first part of this essay, thinks that it should have dropped out or that it will drop out, but so far it has not. Without such predilections, does not a more comprehensive hermeneutic of modernity point to quaternity, not trinity? Is not the metaphysical-religious, if not alive and well, at least alive and kicking?[22]

Here I would not reject the phrase "linguistification of the sacred" but would qualify and differentiate it: 1) As indicating a complete or mostly complete jettisoning of religious reference and meaning, the phrase is false. 2) As indicating a certain process of secularization, this phrase is legitimate. Such secularization, however, is the differentiation of the religious-metaphysical from other spheres of human endeavor and does not imply the denial of the metaphysical-religious. 3) As indicating a widespread theoretical and practical atheistic, reductionistic interpretation of such secularization, the phrase is true, but this interpretation is just one strand of the process of secularization. Another is metaphysical-religious. 4) As indicating that certain forms of metaphysics and religious belief deserve to die, those that are ideological, escapist, and do not relate sympathetically to and learn from legitimate modern discoveries about freedom, subjectivity, rationality, and critique, the phrase is true. For example, the true God is not the bourgeois God of the ruling classes or a God that despises women, racial minorities, or the poor. Rather, in keeping with legitimate feminist, postmodern, and Marxist discoveries and critiques of modernity, the true God is on the side of the oppressed. There is a "preferential option for the poor" that is essential to any properly modern form of religious belief.[23]

5) The legitimate forms of religious belief that deserve to survive have learned from the modern and vice versa. Here I think of Lonergan's use of Kant, Kierkegaard's of Hegel, Metz's of Benjamin, Dussel's of Marx. In this sense of a mutual testing in which religious belief has passed through the crucible of modern questioning and critique, there is a "linguistification of the sacred." In my opinion, the best formulation of such religious belief is Tracy's "revisionism" in which there is total questioning of church by world and world by church. Religious belief allows itself to use and to be brought into

question by modern questions, insights, and methodologies. At the same time religious belief functions as a transcendent reference point allowing us to be critical of simplistic forms of progress trampling underfoot the poor, the homeless, the oppressed.[24]

The latter point is quite important and needs to be emphasized. Employed in the context of a critical modernist religious belief, even pre-modern religious texts do not have to be exercises in a conservative nostalgia trip, but are themselves sources of a dangerous memory bringing into question certain structures of modern domination. Thus, Christ's description of the Last Judgment and those who will sit at the right hand and left hand of his Father brings into question modern tendencies to valorize too much the rich, the victorious, and the powerful and to ignore the poor, the defeated, the weak. Mary's contemplative, receptive "be it done unto me according to thy word" brings into question our modern fetishizing of productivity, business, "busy-ness," efficiency, usefulness. Christ's warning that it is harder for a rich person to get to heaven than for a camel to pass through the eye of a needle warns us about the dangers of reducing Christianity to the measure of the bourgeois, middle-class subject.[25]

Hermeneutic receptivity to religious sources, then, is essential, but so also are suspicion and critique both of world and church: critique of the world insofar as it deifies or fetishizes such finite realities as money, sex, and power; and critique of the church insofar as its ideas, institutions, and practices con-flict with the genuine prophetic content of Old and New Testaments. If Tracy is correct in asserting that there is an ideology critique internal to religious belief and texts, then such modern insights and methodologies of suspicion and critique can enhance, explicate, and serve such critique. For example, using the insights of feminism, can we not ask whether there is a solid theo-logical basis for ordaining women, or is the justification for not doing so just a fancy, disguised form of male domination? Using the results of a liberation theology informed by positive appropriation of Marx and Western Marxism, can we not, as Boff has done, criticize many practices of the Catholic Church as undemocratic, dominating, and unjust?[26]

Crisis Theory

Here we consider the economic and political structure of late capitalism and the contradictions to which it gives rise. There is a certain parallelism and connection as we move from abstract to concrete in Habermas's thought. In relation to traditional Marxism, his description of communicative action reduces science-technology, in itself and in its use by labor as a form of pur-posive rational action, to simply a part within a more comprehensive theory including the aesthetic-expressive and the moral-political. There is similarly a de-absolutizing but not a complete rejection of science and labor carried out in his reconstruction of historical materialism, in which moral-political learning becomes the pacesetter for historical development. Similarly, on the level of a hermeneutic of modernity science is distinguished from morality and art as one form of rationality but not the only form, and purposive rationality in social rationalization as that occurs in the economy and state is distinct from cultural rationalization. Labor and science, which in traditional Marxism too often tend to become the whole story, are subject to a general *Aufhebung* in Habermas, retention, negation, and transcendence.[27]

This fundamental rethinking of Marxism that remains in some sense still Marxist continues on the more concrete, political level of crisis theory, in which Habermas develops an interpretation and critique of late capitalism. His theory of communicative action, theory of historical materialism, and hermeneutics of modernity give him the tools to reconceptualize the notion of crisis in a way that is fruitful. Here again there is a relativizing but not denial of the economic; other kinds of possible crises in late capitalism are rationality, legitimation, and motivational crises. Indeed late capitalism, because of its orientation toward total administration, creates the possibility for other kinds of crisis not envisioned by a more traditional Marxist analysis.

The pessimism in Marcuse's *One-Dimensional Man*, for example, about the possibility of meaningful social change may be seen from a Habermasian point of view as manifesting the deficiencies of traditional Marxism, even though Marcuse in many ways is not a traditional Marxist. Nonetheless, he is wedded to a traditional account to the extent that if late capitalism seems to close off the possibility of economic crisis and to incorporate labor into its bosom, pessimism about the possibility of meaningful social change seems to be a logical conclusion. Habermas, on the other hand, is committed to a more dialectically hopeful account of late capitalism. His positive endorsement of communicative action, history and modernity prepares him to see positive elements in late capitalism not accessible to a more traditional Marxist account.[28]

A rationality crisis, for example, is like an economic crisis in being a crisis primarily in systems identity, a breakdown in late capitalism conceived as a well-running, functional, objective structure. Unlike economic crisis, however, rationality crisis is mediated by the state. Carter's inability simultaneously to control both unemployment and inflation is a rationality crisis.[29]

Legitimation and motivation crises are crises in social identity based upon the willingness or unwillingness of people to support and actively participate in the social and political life of society. A legitimation crisis arises in the modern state because of the contradiction between the imperative to secure capitalist accumulation and the imperative to secure legitimation through recourse to a communicative ethic institutionalized to some extent in the democratic institutions and practices of the modern state. A contradiction arises between particular capitalist imperatives and universal criteria of a communicative ethic stressing the good of all. If, for example, some kinds of military spending very profitable for capitalist firms cannot be justified through rational discussion, then problems of legitimation arise for such spending.[30]

For Habermas legitimation deficits finally are based on motivation crises that are endemic to late capitalism. Such crises occur through a negative erosion of attitudes favorable to capitalism such as a work ethic and individualism and asceticism, and the positive emergence of values and practices in tension with late capitalism such as science, communicative ethics, and modern art. Their commitment to rational verification, normative universality, and disinterested aesthetic enjoyment are in fundamental tension with the limited arbitrariness, particularism, and utilitarianism of bourgeois rationality.[31]

Once again effectively operative in producing crisis tendencies are the same three elements of modern Western rationality: science, morality, and art. Once again, rather than triplicity, why not quaternity? Could we not argue for enlightened religious belief and practice as other powerful sources of motivation that are in tension with the maintenance of the capitalist system? Consider the service of a Dorothy Day, the resistance of a Berrigan, and the protest of a King. Do we not have in the fidelity to the desire to know culminating in religious belief, in the religious preferential option for the poor, and in disinterested contemplative prayer powerful motives for resisting capitalism that complement, enhance, and complete Habermas's communicative ethic? If some have found this ethic too formalistic, too lacking in content to be effectively motivating, is not such a metaphysical-religious motivation a marvelous, strong, additional and deepening form of motivation?[32]

We have to be careful here. There clearly are certain forms of religious belief that act as ideological supports of capitalism reflecting and legitimizing its privatism, individualism, and conformism. Such forms of belief, however, are not only inadequate by the standards of the ideology critique, communitarianism, and the solidarity present within religious belief itself, but also are inadequate by the standards of a critical modernity interacting creatively in mutual critique and enlightenment with such belief. As we have seen, certain forms of religious belief deserve to die because they have been untrue to their own radical prophetic substance. A Judaism or Christianity that has become merely ideological is untrue to itself as Jewish or Christian.[33]

It makes sense here on this level to talk, first, about the way secular ideology critique can benefit religion not only by reminding it of its own radical, social, prophetic substance, and giving it tools to articulate and deepen such substance, but also by purifying its notion of God. God is no longer a cozy father in the sky, an escape for neurotics, and a prop for the ruling classes, but rather a loving freedom inviting me, you, us to become free in a process of individual and social transformation. Jesus Christ Liberator![34]

It makes sense also to discuss the way religious belief drawing on its ideological critical resources can itself contribute to and be ideology critique. If there is, as we have seen, a domain of freedom, love, and faith beyond rationality and cognition, then such faith oriented to its religious "object" enables us to criticize tendencies on the part of rationality itself toward self-aggrandizement, domination, and fetishization. Here I am thinking not only of obvious deformations of rationality such as technocracy, positivism, and scientism but even the temptation of a secular communicative ethic to set itself up as the sole guide and norm, to deify itself, to be insufficiently receptive to alien, irrational, aesthetic, revelatory aspects of self and world. One can with Habermas perform a rational interpretation and critique of capitalism. But what if reason itself becomes the problem? Reason criticizes the capital fetish or state socialist fetish, but then sets itself up as a fetish or god.[35]

To illustrate the role religious belief can play in a critique of society, we may compare Kierkegaard and Berrigan. Kierkegaard played a prophetic religious role in relationship to the nineteenth-century Danish church and society similar to that of Berrigan in relationship to the Catholic Church and American society in the twentieth century.

Kierkegaard's critique of the homogeneous mass society and public of the "present age" parallels Berrigan's critique of and resistance to the American-military industrial behemoth. Both were forms of religious ideology critique forcing believers to ask themselves what happens when religion simply becomes a flatterer of the age, a servant of the status quo, a slave to current economic-political fashion. In their hands religious belief becomes a powerful source of critique and resistance to a corrupt economic-political status quo.[36]

Habermas would reply, of course, that he can already affirm fallibilism and the aesthetic and nature from within the structure of his own theory. And there is all the difference as well between a "Protestant," Kierkegaardian tendency to find secular, natural reason to be limited and sinful, and a "Catholic," Thomistic tendency to validate such a reason and to go as far as it will take one. Yet even a Catholic can ask whether there is not a natural pridefulness, if not in reason itself, then in the human being who tries to live rationally without faith? And is not this pridefulness a worm that can eat away at even the most righteous of social reform and revolutions? And even if Habermas can rightfully say that he builds fallibilism into his theory, is there not a difference between the conceptual recognition and the existential living out of that fallibilism? Does not communicative ethics itself, therefore, need to be subjected to a religious ideology critique and to incorporate that into itself or, more adequately, allow itself to be incorporated into that critique?[37]

Social Movements

What social movements emerge from the contradictory structure of late capitalism that have a chance to bring about meaningful social change? I note here that just as there is a relativizing of the claims of labor and science on descriptive, historical, and structural levels, so also is there on the level of concrete, political action. Like Marx, Habermas takes it to be a responsibility of critical theory to indicate systematically what groups or movements present the best possibilities for social change. For Marx, the answer was the working class; for Habermas, it is social movements such as feminism, civil rights, ecology, antiwar, and antinuclear that burst into bloom in the 1960s and early 1970s.[38]

Just as Habermas removes an economist, productivist bias from Marxism on the first three levels discussed above, so also on this level. Indeed, this articulation of these first three levels prepares him to look for potentially liberating groups outside of and distinct from the economic sector. There is more than a suggestion, following Offe, that crisis is more likely the further away one is from the economic sector, especially the big monopoly portion of that sector. Capitalism has done so well in containing economic crisis that one could expect, on the assumption that capitalism is a unified, contradictory social system, contradictions to break out elsewhere. The events of the 1960s and early 70s bear Habermas out. Universities, not corporations, were the more likely sources of conflict; students, not workers, were more likely agents of resistance to late capitalism and all its pomps; feminist groups, not labor unions, are the leading progressive movement today; damage to the environment, not happiness in the work place, is the more potent issue.[39]

Habermas, and along with him Offe, has better than anyone else provided the revised conceptual, Marxist framework for understanding such events and movements. If communicative action is aesthetic and practical as well as scientific and technical, if moral-political learning is even more of a pacesetter in historical evolution than scientific-economic learning, if modernity has institutionalized the differences among scientific, moral, and aesthetic learning, if crises can be legitimational and motivational as well as economic and rational, then it makes sense to expect that social movements are the most likely agents of liberating social change.

Capitalism has engaged in a colonization of the life-world, imposing its logic and commodification on spheres intrinsically alien to it such as education, art, culture, and politics. Thus, the person most likely to make it to Harvard and Yale is not the best and the brightest but the richest and best-born. The program that is shown on television is not the most aesthetically stimulating and socially provocative, but that which is the least threatening and most profitable to the sponsor. Universities more and more are not places to pursue the examined life but rather launching pads for Greenwich and Wall Street. Politics more and more centers not on discussion of real issues but on "selling the president" or congressman or senator.[40]

Thus, Habermas argues, if our life-world is colonized in this way, we would expect protest potentials to emerge not in an old politics concerned with economic distribution but in a new politics concerned with quality of life, or as he puts it, "the grammar of forms of life." If one thinks, as I do, that the potential for economic and rationality crisis has increased since the early 1970s with such events as OPEC's raising of oil prices, recession, unemployment, and inflation, which all reflect a cessation in the expansion of late capitalism taking place from 1955 to 1970 and a contraction from 1970 to the present, then workers as workers might have more of a role to play. But, because of the changed structure of late capitalism, they are no longer privileged or even the most likely agents of social change.[41]

Habermas distinguishes here between more conservative movements such as proposition 13 in California based on defense of property and more progressive social movements such as the peace movement or feminism. Here we need only to add and emphasize, in a way that he does not, the contribution of religion to both these tendencies. The Pro-Life movement, because of its unenlightened stance on life outside the womb such as the poor, unemployed, African-Americans, women, and the victims of imperialism, would count as conservative. The religious contribution to the civil rights movement, peace movement, and ecology movement would count as progressive. Again the names of Dorothy Day, Martin Luther King, and Daniel Berrigan in the U.S. and the movements they have spawned come to mind, including the recent Plowshares movement which Martin Sheen has joined. Properly conceived, interpreted, and articulated, religious belief has been, is, and can be a progressive force for social change. When we shift our gaze to the third world in such areas as Latin America, then progressive movements for liberation become other obvious instances. As the film *Romero* showed, Archbishop Romero went through a radical political conversion in which he realized that the Christianity most worthy of the name is that which stands explicitly on the side of the poor and oppressed against the rich and the oppressors.[42]

Conclusion

We have discovered multiple lines of significance between Habermas and religious belief. First of all, we have criticized his negative judgment concerning religious belief. Neither on descriptive nor hermeneutical nor structural nor political levels does his argument work.

Indeed we have discovered, second, that religious belief can contribute to Habermas's project, making it more consistent and comprehensive, supplying another resource for critique, providing a strong resistance to late capitalist exploitation, and acting as an ingredient in liberating social movements. Third, Habermasian modernity and rationality can act as critical leavening agents on religious belief, enabling it to discover and enhance its own ideology critique, reflectivity, social consciousness, notion of God, and option for the poor.

Finally, what the above points suggest is a reciprocity between Habermas and religious belief; communicative action flowers and completes itself in a religious commitment to God, "a being in love with God." Religious belief comes more into its own through encounter with the legitimate chastening, vivifying, purifying aspects of communicative action.[43]

THIRTEEN

༄ঌ

Beyond the New World Order: A Critique of Neoimperialism

At this point we are ready to take another step in our inquiry. I have affirmed thus far in this part the reality of Jesus Christ as Liberator, intellectual, moral, and political conversion as radical conversion, the link between ideology critique and religious belief, and the religious significance of modernity. I have been progressively broadening and deepening my critical theoretical and theological reflection in space and time, synchronically and diachronically. Now in this chapter the task is to inquire more fully into what, in North and South American philosophy and theology of liberation, we need to be liberated from. International capitalism in all its pomp and viciousness, a worldwide Auschwitz, comes into full view. This investigation completes and fills out the inquiries in PCM and CAL focused on a merely national, Northern capitalism and thus makes good on the promise of dialectical phenomenology to be free of any lingering Eurocentrism or ethnocentrism. Only an interpretation, critique, and overcoming of neoimperialism fully accomplishes this task. Finally, in the last chapter I will reflect, using secular and religious sources, on what liberation in the center of the empire requires.

Right now in the 1990s, we are in the midst of a national and international celebration. The Soviet Union has fallen, the Berlin Wall has come tumbling down, threats to "free world democracy" in places like Nicaragua, El Salvador, and Haiti have been beaten back, and the free market and democracy have now been extended all over Europe and, indeed, the world. Capitalism, private ownership, and control by one class of the means of production for the sake of profit, has now come closer than ever to realizing its concept, worldwide, limitless expansion, consolidation, and domination. Only a few stubborn holdouts, like China, North Korea, Vietnam, and Cuba, remain. Thus, thinkers like Fukayama celebrate the "end of history" and the arrival of the capitalist parousia, and thinkers like Michael Novak proclaim the glories of democratic capitalism.[1]

I think that such celebration is not only naive and premature, but severely misguided and unenlightened. All the way through my three volumes I have been developing a critique of capitalism, first in its national, Northern version in PCM and CAL, and now in its international, Northern-Southern version in this book. In my critique I have been arguing that capitalism in its national, Northern version is reifying, commodifying, exploitative, and unjust. International capitalism is simply the same inhumane system externalized and internationalized. The New World Order (NWO) is simply capitalism externalized and internationalized as neoimperialism, and as such the same reification, commodification, exploitation, and injustice are now worldwide in an even more virulent way.[2]

If one had any doubt about the injustice of capitalism in the North, countries like the United States or Great Britain or Germany, then one should have no doubts when we consider how it operates in places like Honduras, Guatemala, and Brazil. If capitalism in the North is or seems relatively benign, capitalism in the South is stark in its visible amount of repression, war, cruelty, disease, hunger, starvation, poverty, and mass death. One thinker estimates that well over twenty million people die per year as direct or indirect victims of the NWO; thus a multiple holocaust occurs every year. The NWO, rather than something to be praised and celebrated, is something to be mourned and resisted.[3]

One challenge to the current celebration comes from an unlikely source (because of the apolitical interpretations and uses to which his thought is put, especially in the U.S.), Jacques Derrida, in his book *Specters of Marx*. Not only does he argue that the announced death of Marx is premature and construct a critique of Fukayama, but he claims that the NWO is deeply problematic and pathological. He lists several different aspects of that pathology: massive unemployment, marginalization of the homeless, ruthless economic war among Europe, the United States, and Japan; contradictions and inconsistencies in the so-called free market, which often means free market for the South and protectionism and state intervention in the North; a foreign debt that is contributing to the starvation and despair of a large portion of humanity, an arms trade that shows no signs of abating, the spread of nuclear weapons, interethnic wars in places like Bosnia, Rwanda, and Somalia, drug cartels and mafia that function as capitalist states, and an international law that functions in an excessively formalistic way and at the behest of the rich,

powerful states in the North and which is set aside or used and abused ideologically when the ends of profit and power demand such moves.[4]

In the face of enthusiastic celebrants of the NWO like Fukayama and
Novak, Derrida says the following:

> Never have violence, inequality, exclusion, famine, and thus economic
> oppression affected as many human beings in the history of the earth
> and humanity. Instead of singing the advent of the ideal of liberal
> democracy and the capitalist market in the euphoria of the end of his-
> tory, instead of celebrating the "end of ideologies" and the end of the
> great emancipatory discourses, let us never neglect this obvious macro-
> scopic fact made up of innumerable singular isles of suffering: no
> degree of progress allows one to ignore that never before, in absolute
> figures, never have so many men, women, and children been subju-
> gated, starved, or exterminated on the earth.[5]

Derrida here is functioning the way an authentic intellectual should in a
deeply unjust society, as a critic of power rather than its sycophantic cele-
brant. In this same spirit, Derrida proclaims that Marx is not dead; deconstruction is rooted in a certain, radical questioning spirit of Marx. Marx is part
of the heritage of the West which we must appropriate, and he is part of any
decent humane future. I agree. In this same spirit and with deep sympathy and
gratitude toward Derrida, I propose to undertake first a dialectical and then a
positive construction, interpretation, and critique of the NWO.[6]

Dialectical Considerations

Initially there was some hope that capitalist led modernization and
development would contribute to the political and economic well-being of the
Third World (TW). Such was, for example, the stated intent, in contrast to its
hidden imperial motivations, of John F. Kennedy's Alliance for Progress for
Central and Latin America. Unfortunately, three decades later the life
prospects for people in these regions are worse as poverty, unemployment,
homelessness, illiteracy, terror, and repression have grown apace. One little
known aspect of the Alliance for Progress was the creation of national security states throughout the region that took as their major task defense undertaken by the governmental and military apparatuses of these states and the top
economic ruling elite against their own people.[7]

In the 1980s and 90s free market doctrines took over in Central America (CA) and Latin America (LA) and the rest of the so-called TW—that is,
the parts of the world that function in a relationship of dependence, subordi-

nation, and servitude to dominant capitalist states like the U.S. or Great Britain. Northern states no longer, with the same hype and to the same degree, give money and advisors for "development" as in the Alliance for Progress. Rather, TW countries are told to open themselves up to the beneficent influence of U.S., European, and Japanese multinational corporations and banks. During the 1980s U.S. investments in LA were heavy; the result was $230 billion transferred to the U.S. through debt service, dividends, and profits. The result for most Latin Americans has been disastrous. Over half the population, 222 million in 1994, were living in poverty, 70 million more than in 1980.[8]

Responding to the perceived failure of the models of modernization and development, thinkers and activists in CA and LA developed the model of liberation. Development and modernization failed, they argue, and necessarily must fail, because they preserve and enhance a *dependence* of TW economies and polities on the First World (FW), which works to the benefit of the FW. TW economic and political well-being, they argue, was never the main intent of development. Rather, the intent was to keep the TW in thrall to the FW and subordinate to it as a source of profit, raw materials, and cheap labor. Because such dependence is the main cause of the problems of the TW, these countries must liberate themselves from such dependence. They must overcome capitalism in its national and international aspects, and move toward socialism, full economic, social, and political democracy. Rather than the TW functioning as a servant or means to FW well-being and profit, TW countries should become autonomous, and their own labor, natural resources, and economic productivity should serve primarily their own well-being, not the well-being of the North.[9]

So far, so good! The liberation model simply takes seriously, as one of its main influences, concepts developed in the West and North by such thinkers as Kant and Marx. It is wrong, Kant says, for one person or group of people to function simply or primarily as means for someone else's well-being. Capitalism is unjust, Marx argues in politicizing Kant, because most of the population is exploited as a means for capitalist profit. The liberation model simply takes seriously and renders consistent and comprehensive concepts and theories developed in the North, as well as traditions and theories more indigenous to the South. Who could reasonably object to this procedure?[10]

Yet Michael Novak and other thinkers find liberation philosophy and theology very objectionable. They have no problems with the morality of capitalism; rather than seeing "democratic capitalism" as a contradiction in terms, as I think it is and as I argued at length in CAL, they see it as providing for the flowering of full economic, political, and social freedom. Empirically it is not that, not even in the North, but it is even more obviously not that in the

South. Indeed Chomsky and Herman draw an empirical correlation between increasing terror and repression and increasing U.S. aid.

The reason for such a correlation, Chomsky and Herman point out, is a safer investment climate for U.S. and European and Japanese multinational corporations. Repressive, terroristic regimes keep down and discourage popular, democratic challenges to the reign of capitalist business in those regions. Rather than Roosevelt's Four Freedoms—freedom of speech and worship, freedom from want and fear—being operative, it is really the fifth freedom that is dominant and normative, "the freedom to rob and exploit." Rather than democracy being the real goal of American foreign policy, it is really, as coups and interventions against democratic governments in Guatemala, Iran, Brazil, the Dominican Republic, Chile, Nicaragua, and Haiti since 1954 indicate, the deterring of democracy that is the goal. Real, effective democracy threatens capitalism, unsettles it, undermines it.[11]

Capitalism and democracy, then, are absolutely, essentially incompatible with one another, not only within the capitalist firm in which the basic investment decisions are made by the capitalist owner and manager and the profit flows back to them, but in the larger society as well, because capitalism in different ways distorts and manipulates and subjugates the political and cultural life of the country to its own ends. I have argued this point in CAL, for national northern capitalism, but the same is even truer for international capitalism. Because it is the same capitalist beast in southern dress, we can expect the same exploitiveness, the same trampling on human freedom, the same poverty, unemployment, and homelessness. Indeed, as I have already indicated and will develop more throughout this chapter, these evils are even more virulently present in the South.

Novak and others point to the so-called free market miracles that have occurred in these countries during the 1970s and 80s and 90s. In response I ask, "Miracle for whom?" Certainly the top two or five or in some cases ten percent of economic and political elites in those countries benefit and the gross national product may even increase, but I have already shown how in CA and LA such apparently good things go along with a worsening of life prospects for the majority of the population: increased poverty, unemployment, hunger, illiteracy, ill health, pollution, and repression. And indeed this pattern is standard and is repeated throughout the TW with very little variation. A privileged elite at the top, a poor majority, a government that serves that elite and exercises greater or lesser terror and repression toward the majority, and the increasing presence of northern multinationals glad to move in because of the improved investment climate. Economic miracle indeed!

Incredibly enough, however, there are some like Novak who argue that the major cause of underdevelopment in CA and LA is CA and LA. Inadequate cultural development has prevented people in those countries from being sufficiently entrepreneurial like their enterprising brothers and sisters in the North, if only they would imitate us. For centuries CA and LA have been hostile to commerce. In contrast North America delights in free enterprise. Many thinkers criticize dependency theorists like André Gunder Frank for overemphasizing the role of external factors and ignoring factors internal to the countries themselves. CA and LA, Novak argues, have chosen to depend on the more developed countries. Moreover, the option for socialism in those countries is too simplistic, ignoring the undemocratic nature of socialist governments and providing little specific information about socialist institutions.[12]

This is a classic international case of what goes on domestically and nationally all the time, "blaming the victim." One initial way of responding to Novak is to note that other theorists such as Cardozo have dissociated themselves from Frank's strong version of dependency theory putting the blame totally or mostly on external factors. This move is as one-sided as a strong version of the modernization thesis such as Novak's putting the blame mostly on internal factors. "Latin America is responsible for its own condition."[13]

Cardozo argues that a combination of internal and external factors has caused LA and CA to deviate from the pattern of normal development. This deviation involved a structure of property ownership that concentrated land in the hands of a few and left the majority propertyless, a Spanish culture imposed on an indigenous Indian people creating a rigid class stratification, a political system that kept power in the hands of the land-owning oligarchy or military, and an economy geared for external markets to meet domestic needs, a consequent dependence on foreign markets and foreign investors, and frequent U.S. military interventions when countries threatened to step out of line.[14]

What the proponents of modernization fail to see or do justice to is, first, the colonial heritage of Spain and Portugal from the fifteenth through the eighteenth century. Because of this heritage, Latin Americans did not begin with the relatively egalitarian agriculture and production for home consumption that is deemed essential if countries are to develop normally. Rather, development from the fifteenth through the eighteenth centuries was skewed and became underdevelopment as LA geared its mining and plantations—the sources of its most important goods—first and foremost to foreign markets.[15]

From the fifteenth century onwards, therefore, there were no strictly internal factors in CA and LA. Rather, Spain and Portugal introduced a foreign cultural, political, economic, and military domination that subordinated the well-being of these countries to that of Spain and Portugal. They plundered these countries for minerals and left a legacy of disdain for work and a failure to encourage entrepreneurial skills and productivity. Novak is certainly right about this point, and it is admitted also by Enrique Dussel, a Latin American liberation philosopher and theologian. Spain chose to take the easy out of exploiting mines with Indian labor rather than taking the hard way that England chose—the hard work of an industrial people. What Novak misses and Dussel sees is that in English development there is serious exploitation of labor by capital and enormous suffering caused by capital. The choice, therefore, was between two different forms of exploitation, and Spain chose and imposed on CA and LA the less economically fruitful form.[16]

Such lopsided ownership of land and wealth continued after independence from Spain and Portugal was achieved in the nineteenth century. At this time a neocolonial dependency was developed in relationship to the U.S. and Great Britain. As more and more foreign investment in these countries occurred and production for export was encouraged, countries became dangerously dependent on one or two commodities for export such as coffee in El Salvador or bananas in Honduras or cotton in Brazil. As discussions took place among ruling elites divided between a "European" party favoring foreign investment from without and production for export and an "American" party favoring protectionist policies to safeguard and encourage small businesses and an autonomous industrial development, the European party, except for Paraguay, won out.[17]

Internal and external factors thus operated and continue to operate together in the history of the region, but the point is that they are aspects of a world capitalism developing and functioning internationally from the fifteenth through the twentieth centuries. Separation of internal and external aspects is undialectical; they are distinct but related. Ruling elites in the South thus "chose" to be dependent but in the context of bribe and threat and coercion and terror from the North. Thus, when Guatemala chose in 1954 to nationalize United Fruit and Chile in 1972–73 to nationalize Anaconda Copper, coups led and encouraged and financed by the U.S. occurred to reverse and prevent such events. Since 1850 the U.S. has been involved in literally hundreds of political-military interventions to ensure that these countries stay on the right "European" path. For example, it intervened unilaterally and militarily in Haiti in 1891, in Chile in 1891, and Brazil in 1894 to "protect American interests, lives, and property," in other words, to secure the fifth freedom.[18]

Part of the Spanish-Portugese legacy was political as well as economic and cultural. And therefore, after independence was achieved, a tradition of authoritarian, absolutist rule remained. This perdured through the nineteenth and early twentieth centuries. The point is here again that, as these countries tried to democratize themselves in liberal and radical ways in the twentieth century, the U.S. stepped in. Thus, Arbenz's government in Guatemala in 1954 and Bosch's in the Dominican Republic in 1966 were moderately liberal and democratic; Arbenz even sided more often with the U.S. in the U.N. than with the Soviet Union. Yet the U.S. stepped in and successfully deterred democracy, because these governments threatened to do something for their people. Dangerous talk of land reform and increased welfare and rights of labor offended their "friend" to the North. Nicaragua in the 1980s and Haiti in the 1990s are other examples of such successful deterrence of democracy.[19]

No one today can deny the fact of economic interdependence between and among nations. What has been and is operative, however, are two kinds of interdependence. One is that among relative equals such as the United States, Great Britain, and Germany. The other is an interdependence of subordination between the U.S., on the one hand, and Guatemala and Colombia, on the other. The economy, politics, and culture of one country are dependent on the other country in such a way that the former functions as means to the well-being of the latter. And such a relationship of dependence did not just "happen" historically nor does it "happen" to obtain today. Rather, structures, policies, and different kinds of power, the most obvious and extreme of which is military, are exerted to maintain and enhance this relationship of dependence.

One example of such unequal dependence is the flow of revenue from one country to another. Prior to Allende in Chile, only 11 percent of the revenue gained from foreign-owned copper enterprises remained in that country. Only 10 percent of oil profits ($600 million out of $5 billion) remained in Venezuela during the 1950s. In the heyday of British imperialism (1870–1913), the flow of income to Great Britain exceeded the flow of capital from Britain by 70 percent. Foreign investments by U.S. corporations (1950–63) were similar: flow of capital from the U.S., $17.4 billion; flow of income to the United States, $29.4 billion.[20]

Another indication of the same unequal, one-way dependence is debt service. As countries in LA lost money through the unequal exchange between their lower priced commodities and the higher priced commodities of the First World (in 1960 three tons of bananas could buy one tractor; in 1970 the same tractor cost the equivalent of ten tons), the economic condition of these countries worsened. As a result they were forced to borrow more and more, and now a good deal of earnings from exports goes to debt service paid to international banks, corporations, and organizations such as the World Bank and International Monetary Fund. By 1982, Mexico was using 59 percent, Brazil 69 percent, and Argentina 78 percent of their export earnings to service debt.[21]

Diachronically the tendency has been that dependence and exploitation increase as LA and CA move from colonialism through the era of political independence to neocolonialism to the current, sophisticated neoimperialism of the NWO. Today transnational corporations are present more than ever on the international scene, and foreign companies have gained majority ownership of many leading industries in LA and CA. In Brazil around 1970 foreign interests controlled 50 percent of all manufacturing, including 81 percent of the rubber industry, 83 percent of electrical machinery, and 88 percent of transportation equipment. In Peru and Columbia foreign companies controlled 43–44 percent of all manufacturing. In many instances, 42 percent of the time according to one study in the 1960s, the foreign control came from buying out local companies.[22]

The result is that synchronically a tight system of neoimperial control prevails that works to the advantage of the North and to the disadvantage of the South. I will go into this synchronic structure more in the second part of this chapter. What seems clear, however, is that this neoimperial network includes and implies strong economic power linked to political and military power as enforcers of last resort.

Underlying the critique of Novak and others is a dependence on Niebuhrian realism that wishes to reject the approaches of liberation philosophy and theology, as well as those of Marxism, critical theory, and political theology as one-sidedly utopian and soft-headed, not recognizing in a hard-nosed way the realities of power. Better a realistic working within the parameters of the welfare state or the neoliberal state or the neoliberal NWO than some wild scheme of revolution and socialism.[23]

I have dealt with this issue of realism and utopianism in CAL. There I argued, first, that reason and freedom in their orientation to questioning, to community, to justice, and to social transformation are essentially utopian. Niebuhr and Novak truncate and mutilate human reason and freedom by confining them too much to the reality of a false, one-dimensional status quo. Next, I argue more explicitly than Marx does that different kinds of evil exist, one of which can be fully overcome by socio-economic reform or revolution. One kind of evil, historical evil as I define it, can at least in principle be eliminated; the abolition of slavery and the gradual emancipation of women are instances. But other kinds of evil, the existential evil that inclines me to go against the light of conscience or the ontological evil making it inevitable that any particular, historical incarnation of a political or moral ideal will be imperfect or the institutional evil making inevitable a certain gap between insitutionalized values and the emerging, new values and ideals of creative individuals and groups, will not be eliminated but only at best mitigated by historical reform or revolution.[24]

The overcoming of capitalism as a form of historical evil will not, therefore, bring total salvation in a secular or religious sense. The above kinds of evil will remain as actualities and possibilities, as well as different kinds of bias, egoistic, dramatic, group, and general. What would happen, and has happened in the past, is a step forward in the process of the human race achieving liberation. Historical liberation as democratic socialism, full economic, social, and political democracy, will be a step forward toward full liberation.

It will provide a context whereby human beings individually and collectively can more adequately and fully achieve and receive salvation.

Moreover, as Marx himself did, I reject the antithesis between utopia and realism. Marx distinguishes between his own position and that of utopian socialists who posit some kind of dreamed-of future without relating it in a tough-minded way to the hard capitalist present. What are the contradictions in this present that can give rise to movements for liberation? What concrete agents and groups can be appealed to as potential or actual agents of liberation? What is the concrete content of the liberation and socialism to which I aspire and which I desire? I have dealt with these questions in detail in CAL and will do so further in the rest of this chapter and the following chapter. Realism without utopia becomes merely cynical adjustment to an unjust status quo. Utopia without realism becomes mere abstract dreaming. Novak is no more adequate for conceptualizing this unity than Neibuhr; indeed Novak is simply an updated version of Neibuhr's own separation of utopia and realism and opting for realism.[25]

Finally, Novak and other defenders of a realism counseling adjustment to and acceptance of the NWO are in a religious and moral dilemma. If the welfare state in its earlier Fordist phase was unjust (I will define this more fully later on), then it is even more obviously unjust now in its post-Fordist phase, what I will later define and analyze as "flexible accumulation." The welfare state in the North from 1940 to 1970 managed to contain and manage the contradictions of capitalism and to provide a minimally decent standard of living for most of its population. Now, however, as more of the suffering comes home, as the "Third Worldization" of the U.S., Great Britain, and Eastern Europe proceeds relentlessly, the pathology of national and international capitalism becomes more apparent, even in the North. I will argue in the next chapter that this pathology presents both a danger and an opportunity. For these reasons I would argue against Novak that my radical version of Lonerganian self-appropriation leading to intellectual, moral, and religious conversion and grounding radical political conversion is more adequate. His neoliberal use of Lonergan leads to an acquiescence to an unjust status quo and, therefore, to a flat contradiction between the realist stance and the implications of self-appropriation. If racism, sexism, classism, and heterosexism are unjust manifestations of group bias in late capitalism, then pragmatic, realistic accommodation to their embodiment in our current, institutional framework is unjust. Lonergan's philosophy, which can function as an occasion for critical transcendence, in Novak's hands becomes part of an abject capitulation to a corrupt, unjust status quo. Lonerganian realism becomes pragmatic accommodation.[26]

Novak is a beautiful example of what I described in another book as "triumphalistic modernism," in distinction from my "critical modernism."

Such a triumphalistic modernism has much to learn from its postmodern critics who describe it as Eurocentric, imperialistic, closed to and dominating over its "other," blind to the damage the North has wrought on its brothers and sisters in the South. Novak's modernism, we might say, is "North Americacentric" or "United Statescentric." If only CA and LA had the wit to learn from us and follow our entrepreneurial example, they would be in better shape. The blindness and arrogance here in somebody so well-educated, intelligent, and, at times, insightful, is astounding, expecially in the face of the obvious damage that has been and is being wrought on the South by the North. But in that respect Novak is all too typical of most North American neoliberal or conservative intellectuals, who have become apologists for the established order. The more things change. . . .

All of this is not to deny that we in the North may be and, indeed, probably are in a prerevolutionary situation. Consequently, a legitimate realism counsels at this point not revolutionary activism, but "radical reformism." Women's rights groups, peace groups, antinuclear groups, and environmental groups work for reforms, and even more importantly now in the face of the right wing onslaught on the welfare state, defend already institutionalized but now threatened reforms, but as steps on the way to a possible revolutionary future. Again Marx, critical theory, Western Marxism, and liberation philosophy and theology thematize more adequately this distinction between revolutionary and prerevolutionary situations and their corresponding forms of practice than do Niebuhr and his disciples. Such utopian realism is the only kind of realism that is not a cop out.[27]

An Articulation of the New World Order

At this point I have demonstrated the fact of an international dependence that exploits and disenfranchizes and marginalizes and impoverishes a significant portion of the world's population. A nuanced account of such dependence, doing justice to both internal and external components, can be defended. Now the task is to positively describe, articulate, and verify the lineaments of this international system of domination, which I am describing as the New World Order (NWO).

Here I am going to lay out a preliminary model of the NWO and then go more deeply into its structure, goal, parts, means of implementation and defense, and implications. I see the NWO as a worldwide imperial or neoimperial system with at least the following interlocking parts or aspects: national and transnational corporations whose primary goal is profit; armed forces dedicated to securing the conditions for the realization of profit; international organizations like the World Bank and International Monetary Fund ostensibly formed to benefit countries in the TW but actually functioning to keep them in thrall to FW capital, and to a lesser extent TW capital in the hands of a minority; corrupt local monarchies, oligarchies, and governments that are democratic on paper; capitalists and professional elites in TW countries supported by the North and working with it; national and local military groups and police in these countries that repress dissent from below and are trained by the U.S. in places like the School of Americas (described by its victims in the South as "the School of Assassins"); agencies such as the Central Intelligence Agency (CIA) functioning as sources of information and subversion and money and armed coups against governments that threaten to step out of line and do something for their people; and finally, the poor majorities in TW countries and, increasingly, in FW countries that emerge as the main victims of the whole neoimperial system. By "neoimperial" here, I mean a form of domination that is indirect, not direct, that does not involve the direct, colonial administration of one country by another.

What is the goal of the NWO? I would argue that the goal is The Fifth Freedom as defined earlier, the freedom to rob and exploit. Fundamentally, the Fifth Freedom is the freedom of corporations in the FW and TW to rob, kill, and exploit domestic and native peoples with impunity. Other cultural and political freedoms, while not being reducible to this freedom, ultimately serve it, are subordinated to it, and, if necessary, are sacrificed to it.

Putting this same point in more explicitly Marxist terms, we can say that the goal of the NWO as imperialistic is the national and international extraction and transfer of surplus value from poor to rich, labor to capital, South to North. The FW enriches itself at the expense of the TW; the TW functions as a servant of the FW. When it tries to step out of that servile role, then military and political force is used to put down such insubordination. People who step out of line—like Bosch in the Dominican Republic in 1965, Allende in Chile in 1972, Ortega in Nicaragua in 1979, and Aristide in Haiti in 1990–91—are demonized as enemies of freedom, "totalitarian," "terrorist," and "communist."[28]

Value, as I defined it in PCM and CAL and earlier in this book, is the abstract, socially necessary amount of labor time required to produce a commodity. Surplus value is the time of labor over and above necessary labor for which labor is not paid. "Capital" has three meanings. First, it is the class who owns, controls, and derives the primary benefit from means of production and their employment. Second, it is an exploitative social relationship between this class and labor. Third, it is a process of self-expanding value. Capital in the economy functions like Hegel's absolute spirit, in that it is continually trying to expand, to subject more domains to its sway, to incorporate more and more, to produce more and more. If making some money is good, then making more money is better, and making the most money is best.[29]

Furthermore, we can describe different relationships within capitalism as a socio-economic system. First, we note a vertical relationship of exploitation between labor and capital in both North and South. In this relationship surplus value, unpaid labor time, is extracted from labor. Second is a horizontal transfer of surplus value, indirect exploitation as I am defining it in departure somewhat from normal Marxist usage, based upon a relationship between or among supplies of capital. Within countries this relationship can occur among branches of capital such as the steel industry and automobile industry; or between sector one, producing means of production, and sector two, producing means of consumption; or among industrial capital devoted to production of commodities, commercial capital devoted to the selling of commodities, and financial capital devoted to the management of money as the privileged commodity, measure of value in other commodities, means of circulation, and means of payment to pay off debts and to finance new projects.[30]

Capitals can also relate across borders. Advanced capital in the North can compete with and ultimately triumph over capital in the South. Transfer of surplus value occurs here in various ways. Capital appropriated by one subject, the bourgeois class in the FW country, appropriates capital and surplus value produced in the TW. One way such appropriation occurs is that capital in FW countries with advanced, sophisticated technology can produce items for less cost, put them on the market in the TW at a cost above their value but still lower than the price of commodities produced by a less technologically advanced TW capital, and reap enormous profits. When the wealth is drained out of less developed countries, the bourgeois classes in those countries must superexploit their laborers in order to make money at all and to stay wealthy. Consequently, the need grows for a repressive state, armed forces, and police to discourage and put down revolt from the "unreasonable" masses.

At this point we may require a more comprehensive and precise distinguishing and relating of terms. "Value" is the average socially necessary amount of labor time necessary to produce a commodity. "Surplus value" is unpaid labor time. "Profit" and "rate of profit" is this surplus value seen in relation to the total investment of the capitalist in means of production and labor. "The rate of surplus value" is the relation of surplus to necessary labor time. The "cost price" is the value of the commodity that includes what is invested in necessary labor and means of production, but excludes surplus value. The prices arising when the average of different rates of profit is drawn from different spheres of production and is added to the cost prices of these different spheres of production are prices of production. Market price is what a product actually sells for, and average market price is the average price a commodity sells for over a period of time.

Obviously all of these terms are distinct but related; surplus value is not profit, even though profit ultimately depends on and is constituted by surplus value. Price is not the same as value, and as averaged out in an average rate of profit and average market price can diverge significantly from value. Consequently, if a FW capitalist selling cars in a TW country with an average price of $3000 can, because of superior technology, decrease his cost price of $2000 by 50 percent, then he stands to make an enormous profit. And if he underprices his car by $400 or $500, he can still make more than average profit. It is competition between and among capitalists that tends to produce an average rate of profit and an average market price. Such competition occurs not merely in the TW but in the FW. As we will see more fully later, transnationals selling in the FW at average rate of profit and market price products produced in the TW can make an enormous profit because of cheaper raw materials and labor in the TW. And consequently, they can also sell below the average market price and make an enormous profit.[31]

The transfer of surplus value from South to North, then, is the transfer of surplus labor or life. "Dependence" is the name of the international system by which the peripheral peoples are sacrificed to the fetish of world capital. We can talk, then, about unjust exploitation of a people in the peripheral country, not only labor but the poor, peasants, and Indians whose life is sucked out of them by national and international capital, vertically through the exploitation of labor by capital and horizontally as value passes from one national capital to another, one people to another. Dominators in the TW are themselves dominated, but often there is little explicit consciousness of the domination and sin, because they are rooted in seemingly objective and objectively justified structures.[32]

Transnational corporations are relative newcomers on the scene. They represent, if you like, the fourth major stage in the development of dependence. The first two, mercantalism and free trade, pertained to colonialism. The third, imperialism in the strict economic sense, implies that capital sells in the periphery industrial products produced in factories located in the central country in the North and imports raw materials from the peripheral country. In the fourth, transnational stage, capital locates factories within the peripheral countries.[33]

In this last stage the relationship between the corporation and the support nation (General Motors in the U.S.) diminishes but does not cease. The corporation originates in the support nation. This nation supplies security in the form of military intervention when the reign of capital is threatened in the TW, and most of the profit flows to the support nation. On the other hand, transnational capital reinforces its relationship with the host peripheral country. Not only do such nations provide a market, but they are the source of cheap labor, raw materials, and underdeveloped banking—and are the point of departure for sales to the home market (in the host country) and the export market (from the host country).[34]

In the stage of transnational capital, horizontal dependence increases. Not only can transnational capital produce products in the host country at lower cost because of advanced technology and at lower prices than competing national capitals, but still above the value of the product in that country, but it can ship products home to the support country, undersell or underprice competitors at home, but still make enormous profits because of the cheap labor and raw materials in the host country. Thus, a car produced at a cost of $3000 in the host country and sold at $7000 in the support country, $1000 below the going average price for an automobile of that size and make, will have a profit of $4000, twice as much as automobiles made in the support country at a cost price of $6000; labor and raw materials cost more to produce in the support country.

We can talk, then, about a triple injustice of transnational capital: that between transnational capital and underdeveloped peripheral capital in the form of excessive profit, transfer of surplus value from periphery to center, and relationship between transnational capital and developed central capital in the support country. This triple injustice comes on top of and presumes the vertical injustice of exploitation in both countries. Quadruple injustice.[35]

Concerning the first form of injustice, transnational capital competes with peripheral capital on an unequal basis. Because transnational capital wields a better technology and produces products at lower cost, transnational capital produces commodities at a lower price and often of a better quality. Furthermore, because it is more capital-intensive, investing relatively more in means of production than in labor, transnational capital wipes out traditional sources of production. The twenty vendors of the 7–Up company throw thousands, such as fruit vendors, employees of small soft-drink companies, and sales persons in small stores, out of work. Unequal competition reigns in the market of a peripheral country, and is proclaimed by its defenders as manifesting the parousia of the "free market."

The second form of injustice is the transfer of surplus value or surplus life, which, let us recall, is human labor time. The normal relationship that occurs is that between a parent company such as Ford and its subsidiaries in places like Buenos Aires. A high percentage, as high as 40 percent in U.S. firms, of international trade occurs in such intrafirm transfers, thus giving the lie to current celebrations of the "free market." Money from the subsidiary flows to the parent company in various ways. One is "fictitious payments" by subsidiary to parent such as the sale of production plans or payment on loans given by the parent company or buying of parts by the subsidiary company.

Another way of transferring surplus value is by "exporting" products manufactured in the peripheral subsidiary. The parts of a Ford motor will be sent from Brazil to the U.S. to be assembled and sold in the U.S. The product is underbilled, sold at less than its actual value, by billing it either at less than cost but thereby at a price below its "product value"—which will include gratuitous surplus value. Also the market price in the central country will be a great deal higher than it could have been in the peripheral country by reason of the low wages paid to the peripheral workers. Thus, we have direct transfer of surplus value from the periphery to the center.

Finally, in the third form of injustice, transnational capital has at least two advantages over merely national capital in the support country. First, the transnational corporation acquires money from the subsidiaries that it is able to use in research, advertising, and so on. Coursing through its body is the blood of workers not only from the support but from the peripheral country. Second, because the product has been produced at lower cost due to a lower average wage in the periphery (and the resulting hunger, poverty, and death of the overexploited peripheral worker), the product can be offered for sale at a more favorable market price, lower than that in the support country but higher than that in the peripheral country, that provides extraordinary profit.

To summarize, we can talk about three ways in which the blood of the poor circulates in the capitalist system. First is the vertical relationship of exploitation between capital and labor in which the blood of living labor is transferred to capital. This is the first and the most abstract injustice or sin of modernity, first in Europe and then in the rest of the world.

Second, building on this relationship, albeit in a more concrete way, developed central capital extracts surplus life or surplus value from the underdeveloped peripheral capital. This international social relationship is less visible and more complex than the first social relationship of sin. Third, a part of developed central capital establishes a direct relationship with the workers of the host country. While still competing with central and peripheral capitals, it effects an overdetermination of the law of dependence not merely through unequal exchange but through a wage difference as well. Consequently, there is an increase in the rate of surplus value, the relationship between surplus labor and necessary labor for which labor is compensated, functioning as the basis for an increase in the rate of profit. The rate of profit, again, is the relationship between surplus value and the total investment of the capitalist in means of production and labor.[36]

The multinational corporation, rather than being a great civilizer and source of benefits to the majority of humankind, is a Moloch on whose altar most of humanity is sacrificed:

> Far from being instruments of "civilization," the transnational becomes the universal vampire, extracting blood, "surplus" human life, from the periphery of the capitalist economy. "Thou shalt not steal. Thou shalt not kill." And yet theft and murder only penetrate more deeply and spread their tentacles even further as they become technologized and

universalized. To boot, they now do this in the name of democracy, liberty, and civilization. Humanity's mighty potential benefactor has become its pitiless predator.[37]

National and international capitalism in the age of the NWO is a horror story, the multinational is the main character and villain in that story.

Filling out the economic picture are two other aspects that reinforce these kinds of economic injustice and really constitute two other forms of it. The first is international loans made by organizations such as the IMF and World Bank. These, in contrast to industrial capital producing goods and commercial capital selling goods, are agents of financial capital lending or selling money to make money. Such money lent out at the cost of interest paid flows from surplus value as the source both of the money lent and the interest paid back. And, as we have already seen, such debt payments constitute an enormous drain on the peripheral country. Mexico, Brazil, Venezuela, and Argentina were over $300 billion in debt in 1983. Mexico paid $12 million in annual interest beginning in 1984 (and this is a country whose dominant class kept some $70 billion in North American banks; a Mexican worker earned about a dollar an hour that year).[38]

Military spending and investment is another kind of mechanism for acquiring surplus value and for protecting the international system geared to producing it. It reinforces other kinds, helping to keep in line countries who unreasonably depart from their service role. And it functions as an enormous source of surplus value in its own right, in the center and in the periphery. In the central country this surplus value and profit, at least three or four times higher than normal rates of profit, occurs as a result of enormous state subsidies to corporations like Boeing or McDonnell-Douglas. In the periphery such surplus value takes the form of purchase of arms produced by the central country. The government of the central country comes bearing gifts—"look what I have for you"—and ruling capitalist and military elites in those countries buy the gifts at enormous cost. And this money for arms in center and periphery is, of course, not spent on real human needs such as housing or rapid transit or education or poverty or hunger. Sin is piled on sin, injustice on injustice.[39]

At this point we can see how capitalism is an economy of death. Military spending, war as an immensely profitable business, renders explicit this aspect, but it is more or less present at least implicitly in all parts of the capitalist system and manifests itself in different ways: through the unjust exploitation of labor by capital, through environmental devastation, through the international transfer of surplus value leading to poverty and death in the periphery, through marginalization of the poor, homeless, and unemployed, and through policies of torture, repression, and terror which increase and enhance such marginalization. The underlying logic of these various forms of death is a socio-economic system in which human beings are means to be exploited for the sake of profit, and the poor periphery is simply a means for the well-being of the center.

The environmental devastation is perhaps worth emphasizing because I, perhaps, have not emphasized it enough in previous works. Such devastation is a direct outgrowth of the logic of capital, which sees nature functionally as just a means for profit, a storehouse of raw materials. Nature as a manifestation of the mystery of being to be appreciated contemplatively is simply shunted to the side. The result is that every North and Latin American city has its Newark, and nature is more and more despoiled and polluted. Capital following its own logic cannot but regard human beings and nature as mere means to profit or surplus value.

Drawing on the discoveries of my speculative-political metaphysics, which emphasizes the importance of nature as a part of being, and on my hermeneutics of Christianity, especially my feminist reading of Christianity, we have resources to criticize such devastation of nature. Rosemary Reuther, for example, in her feminist interpretation of Christianity, emphasizes how a resulting valorization of nature, woman, and the earth must and should occur. What is required is a "conversion to the earth" such that we relate to nature receptively and appreciatively as a "quasi-thou," as an intrinsically valuable partner in the project of liberation rather than a mere means. Important also in this respect is that a liberating hope for transcendence also be seen as recuperative return to nature as matrix and God/dess as source and ground of our being. God/dess is both God whom we seek as transcendent goal and to whom we return as ground and creator. Nature similarly is not to be left behind as hindrance to freedom, but recovered and redeemed as essential to freedom.[40]

Up to this point in my descriptive articulation of neoimperialism, I have been dwelling mostly on its economic dimensions. Nonetheless, while these are important and while capitalism as a world system subordinates everything else to this economic injustice, there are irreducible social and political dimensions. To the extent that they are subordinated to the Fifth Freedom, they become distinct forms of injustice. To the extent that they incarnate progressive, forward moves in learning, they can be used to contest capitalism. Democracy, free speech, and human rights, for example, to the extent that they are institutionalized in the North and South, can function as the basis for counter-hegemonic movements and revolutions. Such is the case in the Sandinista movement in Nicaragua and Aristide's election in Haiti; such is the case with the Zapatista revolt in Mexico and Allende's election as a socialist in Chile.

Social-cultural hegemony in North and South is exercised in various ways. One is racism, in which dark-skinned people are taught to think of themselves as inferior to their light-skinned counterparts to the North, and which is used by the North to sell its interventions to its own populations. Racism was a crucial feature of the Gulf War in 1990–91, in which not only Saddam Hussein but Arabs in general were demonized. Another form of hegemony is to teach native peoples through education, media, and indoctrination of elites at universities in the North and South that their culture, language, and religion are inferior to those of the North. Still another are conservative religious viewpoints that counsel obedience rather than revolt against an unjust status quo. These can be and have been contested with some success by liberation movements rooted in a progressive Christianity. A final way of exerting hegemony is through advertising and fashion imported from the North or forced on the South by the North, in which people are taught that "things go better with Coke" or Calvin Klein jeans are better than their own native products. And we should remember here that media are themselves big businesses out to make a profit, and that their business is to sell or market capitalism as a way of life by deliberately and structurally creating false consciousness.[41]

Political hegemony is still another form of injustice, and this functions in various ways. One is through educating political, police, and military elites in places like Harvard or the School of Americas. Another is through cooperation in making and carrying out of policy with the dominant class and its professional and military flunkies in peripheral countries. And a third, when all else fails, is political or military intervention. Send in the ambassador or the marines. And such intervention serves the implementation of The Fifth Freedom. As I have already indicated, such interventions have occurred hundreds of times in the last century and a half.

Such is the state of things in the world as we approach the twenty-first century. Changing the terms and expanding them somewhat from the way I used them in CAL, I would argue that late capitalism as it operates internationally is subject to a triple form of injustice: exploitation in the economic sphere (either direct in the vertical sense or indirect in the horizontal sense), tyranny in the socio-cultural sphere, and domination in the political sphere. These refer to the three forms of hegemony already discussed and include within them or underneath them sub-forms of injustice, especially in the economic sphere. Tyranny and domination are subordinated to and serve the economic sphere as dominant. "Marginalization" as I defined it in CAL occurs in all three domains—economic, cultural, and political—and "colonization," the structural imposition of values of the economic and political spheres on other spheres, occurs in the economic and political spheres.

We are in a position now to see how nonsensical the talk about the "free market" and "free market miracles" in the South is. Even though in some cases the overall national gross national product rises, the standard of living for the poor majority stays in its same wretched state or decreases. Although I have already stressed this point, I wish to emphasize here another point, the degree of control built into the three forms of injustice. Multinational corporations, for example, do a great deal of trading between parent and subsidiary, are aided in their project of making profits by state subsidies through the Pentagon, and are helped through policies enforced by the World Bank and IMF requiring reductions in welfare, production of crops for export rather than home consumption, and tax breaks going to foreign corporations.

Socio-cultural hegemony is a form of control and containment, brainwashing people into believing that they are not beautiful without their Calvins and that they are racially inferior. Political hegemony, with its use of militarism and political power, is most obviously controlling in a way that works systematically to the benefit of capital, but political hegemony rests upon and is reflected by less obvious forms of economic and cultural power. Free market ideology, then, coexists uneasily in a contradictory way with these massive forms of control. This fact is nothing new about capitalism, which even in its national, Northern versions is already contradictory. What neoimperialism does, of course, is to externalize and internationalize these contradictions.

I do not wish to overstate the above point. Free markets have some reality; referring to them is not purely, only significantly or mostly, ideological. What I am insisting on here is that, whether as reality or ideology, they coexist uneasily with forms of control. A further point is the way this coexistence works to the benefit of the North and to the detriment of the South. Chomsky puts the point dramatically when he argues that the policy is essentially "free markets for them (the TW), control, protectionism, and state subsidy for us."[42]

Even in NAFTA and GATT, the insistence is on the TW opening itself up to the invasion of powerful Northern multinational corporations and banks, their investments, and products. We in the North, on the other hand, tacitly exempt ourselves from free market discipline in all sorts of ways, retaining intellectual property rights to biomedical discoveries and inventions, encouraging through tax breaks, loans, and subsidies other countries to buy and sell our products rather than those of some other country, protecting our own products with tariffs, strong-arming countries such as China and Japan to go along with our policies or else, and, of course, using massive state subsidies not only for military spending but also biomedical research, the next major area of investment and already the source of huge profits for U.S. corporations.

Not only is this claim true synchronically about the world capitalist system as it functions now, but it is true diachronically as this system has developed over the centuries. Both the U.S. and Great Britain in the nineteenth century, for example, required a good deal of protectionism for industries such as cotton, steel, and wool. Protectionism, state subsidies, state intervention prevailed more and more in the North because these were essential for capitalism to develop. The South, meanwhile, was bribed and threatened, forced and coerced to cut down on its protectionism and state subsidies to domestic industry and investment in education and welfare for the poor. It was forced, ironically, to adopt a free market system that has never been in effect in the North, and that is a recipe for disaster. Indeed such "forcing" has been one basic cause for underdevelopment in the South. India and Egypt, for example, in the late eighteenth and nineteenth century, were relatively equal to Great Britain and the U.S. or even ahead in such industries as textiles and cotton, but were coerced in various ways into allowing their countries to be free markets, while Great Britain and the U.S. used protectionism to develop their fledgling textile and cotton industries.[43]

At this point I have fully laid out my model of the NWO, capitalism in its latest stage of international exploitation, tyranny, and domination. Such international injustice corresponds on an international level with what in CAL I defined as "flexible accumulation" on a domestic level in the North. Flexible accumulation as I defined it in CAL is manifested in attack on wages leading to destabilizing and lowering of wages, a deregulation of environmental standards, rules governing work and control of the financial industry, a greater reliance on small businesses, smaller inventories, and subcontracting, weakening of labor unions, attack on welfare for the poor while increasing welfare for the rich, a greater strength of financial capital relative to productive capital, small producers in which "everyone is a celebrity for fifteen minutes," and a volatile postmodern aesthetic.[44]

Fordism preceded flexible accumulation and was characterized by increasing management of consumption based on higher wages, positive state intervention in the economy, big corporations, big labor unions, increase of wages, increase in welfare both for the poor and the rich, significant economy of scale, and a relatively stable modernist aesthetic. Fordism domestically roughly corresponds to imperialism as I have defined it here, capital selling its products in the TW and buying raw materials from the TW. Capitalist industrial investment in the TW, although it begins during the era of Fordist imperialism, does not take off and incarnate itself fully until flexible accumulation and transnationalization, roughly the last forty years.[45]

Is the model that I articulated, however, true? What I have done so far, for the most part, is to lay out a hypothesis on the level of understanding. Throughout the second part of this essay, I have indicated or referred to various kinds of evidence on various levels, but my main intent has been to articulate the model. Now our main intent has to be to evaluate it. Is it true? How does it stack up against liberal or conservative models that more or less endorse the NWO? Some of these thinkers admit some of the empirical evidence that I have adduced, but would deny that this evidence indicates anything systematic that undermines the legitimacy of the NWO. Most instances of poverty or terror or repression indicate exceptions or failure in execution or miscalculation in an otherwise well-functioning, well-intended system

I obviously disagree. I think that the evidence for the pathology of the NWO is massive and overwhelming, but my argument itself is not without presuppositions that I have articulated elsewhere or in this book. First of all, I have phenomenological-hermeneutical presuppositions argued for in PCM for the reality of conscious, embodied, communal subjects in the world and the legitimacy of hermeneutical interpretation and critique. Second, I have presuppositions rooted in an account of right, morality, and justice in CAL and articulated in this book in previous chapters. One ethical claim here is that capitalism is unjust in that it violates the tenets of right, morality, and justice. Capitalism is essentially at odds with intellectual, moral, and religious conversion. Radical political conversion is the appropriate, consistent response to an unjust capitalism. The ethical argument argued for and stressed in this chapter is that capitalism is unjust because it systematically extracts surplus value from living labor. In this respect, capitalism is exploitative.

A third level of presupposition argued for in this book is the metaphysical-religious. I have subjected capitalism to a metaphysical-religious ideology critique in which I argue that capitalism violates the inherent multidimensionality of being and human beings, commodifies and reifies human beings, obliterates the mysterious and sacred, and illegitimately deifies itself. Jesus Christ is a liberator God identified with the poor and oppressed. Since capitalism necessarily and inherently produces poverty, the preferential option for the poor, which I have argued for both ethically and religiously, obligates us to oppose capitalism.[46]

Phenomenological-hermeneutical, critical theoretical-ethical, and metaphysical-religious presuppositions operate in the explanatory-hermeneutical argument I am developing and stressing in this chapter. Why is my interpretation of late capitalism as transnational, flexible accumulation preferable to other more benign modes and interpretations? The criteria that I employ in verifying my hypothesis are the canons for a critical hermeneutic developed both in PCM and CAL: parsimony, comprehensiveness, consistency, coherence, successive approximations, and residues.

Parsimony is observed when claims are verified in the empirical data present in any mode of inquiry. Comprehensiveness is a norm in the light of which we can say that one explanation is better than another if it explains more of the data, retains more of previously valid insights from the past, does more justice to the differences and nuances in data, and gives rise to more fruitful future investigations. An interpretation is consistent if it does not contradict itself and other true propositions, and coherent if it hangs together.

Coherence combines consistency and comprehensiveness. The canon of successive approximations is observed when we in successive readings achieve a more adequate interpretation than before. No exhaustive or totally certain interpretation is possible; further questions will always arise. But interpretations can more and more approximate a fully adequate reading. Finally, the canon of residues counsels me to look for and be open to inconsistencies and anomalies and contradictions in the text or reality, and to try to account for them. The more adequate observing of this norm is one indication of the superiority of my account, in contrast to other accounts that overlook or explain away or do not explain contradictions in the NWO.[47]

Why is my interpretation true or truer than other competing versions? First of all, in the dialectical section I have considered what I deem to be the chief objections to my interpretation and chief alternatives, that of modernization and that of the so-called free market. Frank's initial account of dependence was seen to be a one-sided emphasis on external factors, and Novak's an equally one-sided emphasis on internal factors. What I have argued for was a model of dependence that integrates external and internal factors into a dialectical account of capitalism as it develops over the centuries from mercantilism through colonialism to neocolonialism to flexible accumulation.

Next, I note a dialectical interplay between our general model of empire and particular empirical data, and between these two extremes, less general phenomena such as particular capitalist states or corporations, institutions such as the IMF or World Bank, and policies of these states, corporations, or institutions. Hermeneutical verifications can move from the general or universal, the upper blade, to the particular, the lower blade, or from particular to general and universal.[48]

For example, moving from the general to the particular, we can expect increasing poverty and misery in the TW for most of the people in those countries, and such is the case as we have already seen. Or again, if my model is correct, then we would expect it to explain what is otherwise anomalous from the point of view of liberal and conservative bourgeois theory, curious exceptions to the general rule. Hundreds of interventions and subversions of democracy by the U.S., Great Britain, Europe, and Japan in the TW over the last century and a half become immediately intelligible using my model. It explains more, not only capitalist democracy and human rights, but capitalist pathology and exploitation. My model employs the canon of residues much more adequately than liberal or conservative bourgeois theory. What such theory cannot explain and my theory can, is, if the Western capitalist democracies in the North are committed to democracy, human rights, and the well-being of peoples, why have policies emerged and hundreds of interventions occurred to negate democracy, human rights, and the well-being of peoples?[49]

Now someone influenced by liberal or conservative models might object that I overstate or overdo the negative and pathological. Are there not good things about capitalism that my model does not articulate adequately? I would argue that there are such good things but that they function in tension with and in contradiction with the bad things I have described. In CAL I argued that capitalism is in tension with democracy, accumulation with legitimation, manipulation with communicative action. Similarly, on an international level democracy and human rights as they are institutionalized in the U.N., World Court, and democratic capitalist states represent forward moves in learning that can be used in the struggle against racism, sexism, heterosexism, and classism. When the World Court by norms of international law condemns the U.S. for mining one of Nicaragua's harbors, that condemnation can be and was used by TW liberation movements in their struggle against the U.S. and its client states.[50]

Liberal supporters of the U.N. are right to note and applaud its forward-looking commitment to human rights. What such supporters miss, however, and what my model comprehends more adequately, is the way the U.N. functions as an instrument used by the neoimperialist powers to carry out their unjust designs. In the Gulf War of 1990–91, the U.S. bribed and threatened most of the members of the security council to go along with its designs. I will discuss the Gulf War as a neoimperialist war more fully later on in this chapter. Habermas's mistake as a liberal, at least in this instance and in this respect, is to note the forward-looking commitment to human rights in the U.N. charter but to miss or not do justice to the way the U.N. was used by the U.S. and Great Britain to achieve their imperial ends. I think that my position is more comprehensive and more adequately suspicious in using the canon of residues.[51]

There are models of the NWO that in a one-sided illegitimate way stress the negative and deemphasize the positive in modernity and in modern capitalism. In CAL I exhaustively criticized postmodernism for such an undertaking. A one-sided postmodern view of the world capitalist system would do the same thing. It sees imperialism as Eurocentric and perceives little or nothing good about that European tradition.

Even someone like Derrida in his late work, however, in a more critical modernist fashion, argues that the European tradition in philosophy and politics and culture has something to offer the world. European universalism can be used in two ways. It can be used ideologically to justify imperialism and it can be used critically to criticize and overcome imperialism, as I have been doing in this essay. To take a European universalism seriously is to overcome Eurocentrism and to become genuinely open and listen to its TW other. Indeed the main thrust of my argument is that European universalism, if it wishes to avoid being logically and self-referentially contradictory, remaining incomplete and partial, not fully universal, must and should lead to a critique and overcoming of neoimperialism. The problem with Novak's and Habermas's liberalism, which has much substance, is that it does not do that. It is a contradictory substance and, therefore, remains Eurocentric.[52]

Moving back to the main thread of my argument, I can also move from the particular to the general. A shocking disclosure in the spring of 1995 is that journalist Jennifer Harbury's husband was shot by a Guatemalan officer in the employ of and trained by the CIA. The further revelations showed that this incident was just the tip of a murderous, neoimperial iceberg. Hundreds of officers similarly employed and trained in places like Fort Benning's "School of Assassins" have been operating for decades not only in Guatemala but throughout LA and CA. All of this has been occurring with the knowledge and support and conscious direction of the White House, State Department, and Pentagon. The murder of Harbury's husband was not the result of an atypical rogue operation of the CIA, the way it was interpreted by the mainstream press, but was quite typical and systematic. My radical interpretation satisfies the canons of parsimony and comprehensiveness much more than the bourgeois interpretation. It is not hard to see how such an incident and such politics maintain a climate of terror favorable to the Fifth Freedom, because they discourage dissent and revolt from below and maintain in power regimes supportive of U.S. corporate interests.[53]

Or again, we can look at the Structural Adjustments Programs (SAPS) promoted by the World Bank and IMF. On the books and officially, these organizations are supposed to help TW economies. Bourgeois theory, because it sees U.S. policy as basically well-intentioned toward the world and benign and not fundamentally flawed, cannot explain such matters. In fact, and as part of a pattern, the World Bank and IMF function to keep TW economies in thrall to FW capital. "Death through international finance" is the result. This subordination occurs in at least seven ways. First, emphasis on production for export, a standard feature of SAPS, further weakens the subsistence sector devoted to domestic consumption. A second negative consequence is that emphasis on exports can result in overproduction and a further deterioration in terms of trade between TW and FW. If twenty or thirty countries are exporting the same basic products, then prices go down. Next, higher interest rates mandated by SAPS often encourage speculation, fuel inflation, and further aggravate class divisions by limiting lending to the most affluent and powerful economic sectors. Further, removal of trade and export controls fosters dependence on foreign imports, increases the domination of foreign firms over TW economies, and encourages capital flight. Elites from CA and LA have more than $200 billion of assets in the U.S. These elites exploit the poor and then transfer their wealth to U.S. and other Western banks.

Next, privatization encouraged by SAPS results in greater concentration of wealth and loss of economic sovereignty. Local elites and foreign investors purchase publicly developed enterprises at sharply reduced prices. Also, mandated currency devaluations erode the purchasing power of workers while benefiting the foreign corporations operating in export zones. As a result of devaluing the peso, for example, the U.S. dollar cost of employing young women in Mexico's export processing zones fell by two-thirds. Finally, in order to satisfy foreign creditors, TW governments drastically reduce government spending. The result is a reduction of funds for development of the economic and social infrastructure and aggravation of poverty and hunger. Painful adjustments occur on the backs of the poor. According to the United Nations Children's Organization (UNICEF), the world's thirty-seven poorest countries cut health care budgets by 50 percent in the 1980s. UNICEF estimates that more than a million African children died in the 1980s as a result of SAPS imposed on the poor. In 1988 alone, 500,000 children died in underdeveloped countries as a direct result of SAPS induced austerity measures.

"Death by international finance" flows from capitalism as an economy of death. SAPS developed by the World Bank and IMF play their role in empire, to serve the Fifth Freedom and to keep the TW in thrall to the FW. In 1989 alone TW peoples spent $52 billion more in debt payments to the North than their nations received in new credits. Between 1978 and 1983, LA's total interest payments increased by 300 percent, and by 1984 every 1 percent rise in interest rates added $700 million in annual payments of Brazil alone. By 1990 LA's debts were four times as large as its latest earnings from exports, which meant that every 1 percent rise in interest rates necessitated a 4 percent increase in exports if the continent was to pay. Death through international finance is one crucial way the empire runs.[54]

My final verifying instance is the Gulf War of 1990–91. This war illustrates and instantiates many of the basic lineaments of empire. It reveals the pathology of the NWO on an international level the way the Los Angeles riots in the spring of 1992 reveal it domestically. Such a war was devastating to Iraq; a minimum of 100,000 people were killed, and the environment was devastated. Burning oil wells, oil spills, and damage to the fragile desert ecology threatened environmental catastrophe. In May of 1991 a Harvard medical team estimated that at least 170,000 more Iraqi children would die throughout the year as a result of typhoid, cholera, malnutrition, and other problems caused by the massive devastation as Americans bombed not only military targets, but power plants, water plants, fuel supplies, and hospitals. All of this is obvious war crime material, as Ramsay Clark leading an international commission so demonstrated; according to this commission, nineteen war crimes were committed in the Gulf War. One of those war crimes was the bombing and strafing of thousands of Iraqi soldiers retreating from Kuwait after the cease fire. Capitalism is an economy of death and a death culture; militarism is its explicit, extreme expression.[55]

Why was the war fought? The standard reasons given by our leaders for public consumption do not stand up to even momentary scrutiny. "Deterring naked aggression" does not work as a reason, because the U.S. as standard policy supports naked aggression when that serves its interests—for example, the war in Vietnam, our support for the Contras against Nicaragua, our support of Israel's attacks on Lebanon in the late 1970s and early 80s, our support of Indonesia's invasion of East Timor in the 1970s, and our invasion of Granada in 1983. That the U.N. approved and went along with the intervention scarcely carries weight, because the U.S. bribed and threatened members of the Security Council to go along. For example, we forgave a multimillion dollar debt to Egypt, approved a $140 million loan to China, and promised $7 billion in economic aid to Russia. "Restoring democracy" will not stand up to any scrutiny because Kuwait does not even come close to being a democracy and because the U.S., as we have seen, regularly subverts democracies such as Nicaragua in the 1980s and regularly supports tyrannical, undemocratic regimes such as Colombia in the 1990s.[56]

Most of the evidence indicates now that Bush did not seriously negotiate but that the Iraqis were open to negotiation at least by the end of August 1990, barely a month after their invasion of Kuwait. The evidence suggests that Bush wanted a confrontation that would enhance U.S. economic, political, and military power in the Gulf. Such a confrontation could take the form of the Iraqis' servile backing down and withdrawing without negotiation and with no saving of face, or war. The latter is what obviously occurred, and it was quite welcome to Bush.[57]

The stated official reasons, then, for intervening in the Gulf do not hold up, and from what we have seen already, it is understandable that they do not. "Restoring democracy" does not serve the end of empire, the Fifth Freedom; "deterring democracy" does, and this has been the policy of the U.S., at least since 1850. Democracy has to be deterred, because a democratic polity poses a threat to domestic and international capitalist hegemony. Thus, interventions or CIA engineered coups have occurred over and over again as in Guatemala (1954), the Dominican Republic (1965), Chile (1973), Nicaragua (1980s), and Haiti (1992).

The standard state justifications then, are ideological ploys to mask the real reasons. These are, in the instance of the Gulf War, at least six; our account is multicausal. First, U.S. and British corporations secured and strengthened their hold over Middle East oil; two-thirds of the world's oil reserves lie in the Middle East. A second reason is U.S. dependence on surplus oil revenue from the Middle East. Most of the profits made from the sale of oil by the Kuwaitis and Saudis are reinvested in the U. S. and in Europe in the stock market, purchase of real estate, and government treasury bonds. Saudi Arabia has $400 billion invested in Western Europe, and North America and Kuwait has between $100 and $200 billion invested. Such investment obviously helps to mitigate U.S. balance of payment problems and to enrich Northern corporations and banks.

A third reason for our involvement in the Gulf was that it distracted the population from domestic problems. Here is standard Machiavellian state-craft, and Bush employed it to the hilt as he confronted a short-term recession and an even deeper long-range economic crisis rooted in unemployment, excessive debt, and relatively little industrial investment. A fourth reason was intimidation. "What we say goes," whether we are dealing with Ortega in Nicaragua, Noriega in Panama, or Aristide in Haiti. We have no problem with tyrants as long as they do our bidding. We supported Saddam Hussein with money and arms all through the 1980s in his war with Iran. But when he stepped out of line by moving into Kuwait, he had to be put down and taught a lesson. The empire does not tolerate disobedience. Again this is standard operating procedure: witness Noriega in Panama in 1989 and the generals in Haiti in 1994; they were formerly supported by us but stepped out of line.

A fifth reason was to forestall the peace dividend. Once the Soviet Union fell apart, the chief stated reason for our high military budget disappeared, and a real danger emerged that money would be diverted from the Pentagon and devoted to real, authentic human needs such as education, housing, job training, remedying poverty, and the infrastructure of the cities. As Chomsky argues convincingly, however, and as has been somewhat explicit in my account up to now, the dominant reasons for military spending are huge profits, much above the average rate of profit, and the North-South conflict. The empire needs an enforcer of last resort, and Saddam Hussein was a pre-text to keep Pentagon spending at roughly the same levels. The search for a plausible, strong, permanent enemy, however, continues. Will it be Arab ter-rorism, druglords, unreasonable despots like Saddam Hussein "threatening democracy," or a combination of the above? As long as a plausible, suffi-ciently menacing enemy is not found, the military budget remains more open to democratic challenge than it was during the Cold War.

A sixth and final reason for the Gulf War was the U.S. desire to more firmly establish and assert a military presence in the Gulf, which at the same time is linked to and enhances an economic and political presence. For reasons already stated, the empire needs a global policeman, and the U.S. is now the only military superpower. This military presence allows the U.S. to assert enor-mous leverage in the Middle East and elsewhere, especially as European and Japanese corporations compete more successfully with us on a purely economic level. Because Japan and Europe are more strongly dependent than the U.S. on Middle East oil for its own consumption, such economic-political-military power gives us leverage in the interimperialist rivalry among states on such issues as trade, agriculture, and the conflict between Israel and the Palestinians.

One result of our self assertion in the Gulf is that the U.S. and Israel basically got their way in the recent Middle East accords (1993), the Palestinians received relatively little, and Europe and Japan just went along. Fundamentally, except for a few minor concessions, such as recognition of the Palestinians, Israel continues to control Jerusalem and key resources on the West Bank and Gaza. A feared Palestinian state, once again a potential threat to imperial, corporate hegemony in the Middle East, is avoided. Israel's role as our major imperial enforcer has never been stronger, and the credibility of the Palestinians has never been weaker.[58]

One final point to make about the Gulf War is that it was a television war. This point is in keeping with the emphasis on media spectacle in capitalism as flexible accumulation, the commodity as image and image as commodity. The war, even though it had its own reality, in spite of somebody like Baudrillard who minimizes the distinction between the war as reality and the war as spectacle, was made for the media and mediated by and for them in a way that others were not. The initial bombing of Iraq, for example, was coordinated with prime time evening news. Reporters' access to sources and events was very severely restricted. Viewers in the U.S. were continually subjected to an onslaught of prepared press releases, conferences, and briefings to put the war in the best light. Patriot missiles were celebrated for their accuracy, and generals like Schwarskopf for their ruthless efficiency in this "techno-war." What emerged later is that the missiles were not all that accurate and that the efficiency was overstated and excessively destructive.

In many ways the war as "techno-war" was a manifestation and celebration of capitalist technology and technical expertise. One interesting manifestation of this phenomenon was that General Electric, owner of NBC, was involved in the building of missiles like the Patriot missile. As a result, the very organization that contributed to building the missile was that which was singing its praises at night on television. "G.E. brings good things to life."

Further manifestation of the Gulf War as techno-war was the way it was managed and organized and orchestrated; I have already pointed out the way Bush's initial bombing was scheduled for prime time. The war was integrated and planned under a single commander, and integrated science, technology, and comprehensive planning functioned to control the battlefield and destroy the enemy. In a way that was impossible in the jungle terrain of Vietnam and designed to overcome and reverse the "Vietnam syndrome," reluctance to engage in imperial adventures because of our failure in Vietnam, the Gulf War was a "demonstration war" to showcase U.S. weapons, to display American political-military power, and to illustrate what happens when anyone steps out of line. "What we say goes." Saddam Hussein was a tyrant, it is true, but we realized that when we supported him with money and arms during the 1980s in his war with Iran. The problem was that, when he moved into Kuwait against our orders, he ceased to be "our tyrant."[59]

Conclusion

What, then, is to be done? What is the solution? To paraphrase Reagan, there is an evil empire, but it is us. I think the solution to the problem of empire is contained in my interpretation and critique. If neoimperialism is simply a racist, sexist, heterosexist capitalism externalized and transnationalized, and if capitalism involves control and domination and exploitation of one class by another and full command by this class of the resources of the world, economic, political, and cultural, then what has to emerge is the negation of capitalism, full economic, political, and cultural democracy. If neoimperialism is simply capitalism internationalized, then the solution is simply democracy internationalized—democratic socialism.

In CAL I argued for democratic socialism as a solution to the injustice of national capitalism in the North. This socialism I defined as full economic and political democracy, which employs some representation, a market forbidding exchange between capital and labor, three distinct but related domains—economic, political, and cultural—some technological expertise subject to democratic control within the firm, worker owned and managed firms, a state allowing for maximal decentralization and supplying welfare when necessary, and local, regional, and national planning councils. Here in this chapter I have stressed that national and international capitalism is unjust because it is exploitative in extracting and transferring surplus value. In CAL I presented at least three other arguments for the injustice of capitalism. It violates the imperatives of right insofar as it compromises and violates communicative action and its four validity claims of truth, rightness, sincerity, and comprehensibility; it violates morality insofar as it violates The Principle of Generic Consistency and Principle of Equal Positive Freedom, and it violates the four precepts of justice (here I am using justice in a more narrow sense).

Because neoimperialism is capitalism internationalized, the same beast in international dress, these ethical arguments also apply on the international scene. The structure of empire insures that the conditions for communication are not equal, adequate material conditions for communication and participation are not present for the vast majority of humanity, most human beings do not have anything like relatively fair access to means of economic, cultural, and political participation, minimal subsistence and security needs are less adequately satisfied in the TW than in the FW and becoming worse, freedom to participate is hampered and threatened by systematic repression and terror, inequities in income, wealth, education, food, housing, and effective economic, political, and social power make anything like equal opportunity seem like an unreal dream; and investment by multinationals and banks is systematically increasing, not decreasing the gap in income and wealth between rich and poor, and are not designed in any significant way to benefit the poor.

From the ethical point of view I am developing here, national and international capitalism is an ongoing, developing horror show.

If capitalism is unjust in the FW for all of the above reasons, then it is even more obviously unjust in the TW. Capitalism in the TW is more exploitative, more undemocratic, more productive of poverty, more marginalizing, more death-dealing. Consequently, if democratic socialism is ethically and systemically necessary in the FW, it is even more necessary in the TW.

There are obstacles to realizing this vision, of course, and I will get to these in the next chapter, but here one might object that because the TW is so underdeveloped industrially, it needs capitalism to foster productivity. Here is Novak's argument in a nutshell. Socialism is a luxury that we cannot afford because it is based on and presumes a productivity that is not yet present in the TW. The first problem with this argument is that it misses the ethical argument against capitalism. Developing productivity is turned into a fetish that justifies injustice toward the poor majority.[60]

A second problem is that all or most of the TW is already capitalized, is already structurally in the capitalist orbit, even though some elements of a peasant, feudal economy have been insufficiently capitalized and there are hold-out socialist or communist countries like Cuba, communist China, and North Korea. Given the high degree of unemployment, illiteracy, poverty, and starvation already documented in this book, one is tempted to ask how a socialist economy that is in principle democratic and participative and, therefore, does not use terror and repression against its people and that more fairly and equitably distributes the wealth and income already produced in the country would be any worse than capitalism already is in that country. Indeed a genuine democratic economy could not but be better both ethically and in terms of insuring a minimal level of material well-being to its people.

An example that supports the point is Cuba, which even with the massive terror and sanctions directed against its people since 1959 by the U.S. was still able to provide its people, at least by 1993, with an acceptable level of material well-being, education, and health, much higher than the so-called "free world democracies" supported by the U.S. Even beyond 1993, when the U.S. use of sanctions began to affect the economy in a much more negative and drastic way than before when the Soviet Union was in the picture, my choice would probably be to live in Cuba rather than in Guatemala or Brazil if those were the only choices. At least I would not be subject to systematic terror and repression, and I would be better off materially because of the government's commitment in principle to care for its people's material welfare.[61]

Capitalist productivity is already present throughout the TW, but unevenly distributed so that the majority of people not only do not benefit but have steadily become worse off in the last forty to fifty years. Responding to Novak and others, we could say that the Alliance for Progress and free market economics in CA and LA are both versions of their recommended alternative, and they have failed miserably. Capitalist productivity as capitalist does not and cannot benefit the majority of people in those countries. But such productivity appropriated and democratized and used for socialist ends will benefit the people, and this is what the philosophy and theology of liberation is all about.

The objection about preconditions for socialism and productivity, then, rests upon the same discredited capitalist developmental model and premises that gave rise to the philosophy and theology of liberation. Moreover, because capitalist productivity has already taken hold to a significant extent in the TW, the concern about preconditions for productivity has already been, at least partially, satisfied. The next step is to democratize and socialize such productivity for the people. What would happen, we are tempted to ask, if the wealth, income, and technology of the so-called economic miracles of the last twenty years in Brazil or Chile or Colombia, in which at least in some cases the gross national product did increase while the fortunes of the poor majorities declined, were actually appropriated for socialist and democratic ends? The question answers itself.

My criterion argued for in CAL of a situation where democratic socialism would work is "moderate scarcity," in which I mean some minimal access of everyone to two levels of goods necessary for self-development. The first is those conditions necessary for any self-development whatsoever: means of subsistence such as housing, clothes, food, health care, education, civil and political liberties, job opportunities, and equal participation in decision-making in domains of common economic, social, and political activity. Such minimal provision is and would be possible in situations even of relative scarcity, on the lower end of a spectrum of moderate scarcity, of all or most of CA, LA, Africa, and Asia.

A second level of access is a right to equivalent conditions of self-development rather than exactly the same conditions: an artist does not need the same education as an engineer. Both artist and engineer, however, have a right to some minimal access to some of the specialized training required for self-development. What this minimum is depends on the resources in the society, but some are present even in relatively poor countries such as El Salvador and Nicaragua. Even here there are universities and colleges providing some specialized education.

Beyond the first two levels, a third type of provision is possible and necessary that depends upon considerations of merit, individual need, and community need. A person's past achievement and ability as well as the community's need for trained, educated professors, doctors, and lawyers may entitle her to a fuller, more advanced education than is available on the first two levels. Indeed some of this education is necessary to meet needs of the first two levels.[62]

Now my point here is that within the domain of moderate scarcity, some countries will be more rich in resources than in others. Countries in the North are generally on the higher end of the spectrum than countries in the South, but even here there is variability. Brazil in the early twentieth century, for example, was a country rich in natural resources; now, however, it has been reduced to a shadow of its former self, polluted, poor in most of its population, and depleted of resources. Contra Novak, the capitalist North, working with elites and politicians and military in Brazil, did this to the country.

Nicaragua, again, after the Sandanista revolution against Somoza illustrates the same point, as it moved toward a more fully socialist, democratic society. It won an award from the World Health Organization for the best health achievement in a TW nation, agrarian reforms were carried out, GNP expanded by 5 percent in 1983 in contrast to other countries in the region, and production and consumption of beans, corn, and rice rose dramatically, Nicaragua came closer to economic self-sufficiency than any other CA nation, and Nicaragua made the most impressive gain of any CA or LA nation in quality of life index as measured by the Overseas Development Council, which index is based on literacy, infant mortality, and life expectancy. According to one commentator, "Nicaragua should, in many ways, stand as an example for Central America, not its outcast. The grim social statistics from Hondouras, a country in which the population is literally starving to death, stand in sharp contrast to the recent achievements of Nicaragua." Hondouras, as one would expect, is supported by and virtually run by the U.S.

Chile's democratic socialism under Allende was making similar strides: it raised production and real wages, conducted effective agrarian reform, and implemented policies such as milk distribution for children. These measures increased consumer demand and permitted industry to take advantage of underutelized plant capacity and idle labor while at the same time increasing real, parliamentary democracy. For these reasons, both Nicaragua and Chile stood as real counter-instances to the capitalist hegemony in the region and had to be undermined and destroyed. Like Cuba since 1959 and Haiti since 1991, the examples of these countries threatened to spread throughout the TW. They were possible "rotten apples" that could spoil the imperial barrel.[63]

Contrary, then, to the arguments of Novak and others, capitalism, not socialism, is a luxury that we can no longer afford. Almost without exception, capitalism has made things worse for the majority of the people in TW countries, not better. Because of policies encouraged by international capital, many TW countries formerly able to feed themselves but now forced to grow crops for export, no longer can feed themselves and have to import food from the North, which activity increases TW dependence on the FW, enriches the North, and further impoverishes and plunges into debt the countries in the South.

A final point is that many TW countries, at least in their rural domains, do not need high industrial development and high consumption as much as they need redistribution of land and a form of industry appropriate to that context. A peasant, who, under a socialist regime, is finally able to farm his own plot of land and thus support himself and his family, does not need the heavy industry employed by agribusiness. Such opportunities are lacking to him under the current capitalist regime in CA in which the vast majority of the land is owned by two to five percent of the population.[64]

In the state of Kerala, India, for example, an organized population has achieved major economic and social gains despite a per capita income that is two-thirds the average throughout India. In a survey of a half-million Indian villages, Kerala ranked first in fifteen of twenty categories measuring economic and social well-being. Economic reforms such as extensive land reform and availability of basic goods at fair price shops are linked to policies and programs that benefit the poor. The people of Kerala have easy access to health care, education, libraries, clean water, immunization, and family planning services. Kerala's adult literacy rate is nearly twice the national average, its people live approximately eleven years longer, its infant mortality rate is two-thirds lower, the birthrate is one-third lower, and inequality between sexes and castes are less severe than in other states of India.

High capitalist or socialist productivity, therefore, and heavy extravagant, sophisticated technology are not necessary in many parts of the TW. Indeed they would distort and destroy it. Rather, for Kerala, and for many states or many parts of states in the TW, we require a technology appropriate to the needs and lifestyle and ecology of the people, a "small technology," "small is beautiful." Needless to say, the example of Kerala is another potential "rotten apple" utterly at odds with the priorities of the NWO, which regularly brings inequality, poverty, disease, environmental devastation, hunger, terror, and repression in its wake. Consequently, we may wonder when this "threat to freedom" as currently defined will have to be removed.[65]

❦

FOURTEEN

Liberation in the Center

In the liberation philosophy of Enrique Dussel we have a significant new philosophical vision. His work is important in its own right as a unique philosophical synthesis incorporating insights and methods from Marxism, critical theory, phenomenology, existentialism, and Thomism. This chapter is less a commentary on Dussel's work, necessary and important as that is, than an attempt to use his basic insights and methodology and my own prior work in phenomenology, hermeneutics, and critical theory in reflecting on liberation in a North American context. What is the meaning of liberation in the center?

Dussel's philosophy is one developed from the periphery, Latin America, in relation to the center, North America. If he is right, and I think he is, the relation of center to periphery is one of exploitation and domination. If the center is rich, the periphery is poor; if the center is powerful, the periphery is weak; if the center is master, the periphery is slave. "Liberation," then, initially means liberation of the periphery from the center's economic, political, and social domination. As the chapter develops, the meaning of liberation will gradually expand, deepen, and become more nuanced.

The question that arises, then, for readers in a North American context is that concerning liberation at the center. Such a question is philosophically, ethically, and politically important. It is philosophically important because the center's domination of the periphery occurs with the help of obfuscating ideologies that more or less distort the truth. If we as philosophers are interested in the truth, we must liberate ourselves from the ideologies of the center: militarism, scientism, individualism, racism, sexism. The question is ethically important because the relation of domination is one of injustice; liberation from the domination of the center means actively working against the injustice perpetrated by the center.

The question of liberation is politically significant because liberation at the center contributes to liberation at the periphery and vice versa. In reflecting on, criticizing, and trying to overcome our own powerlessness and exploitation in the center, we work against domination at the periphery because, to a significant extent, the cause of both kinds of domination, internal and external, is the same, a racist, sexist, heterosexist capitalism. Reflecting on domination at the periphery gives me clues about the domination directed against me at the center; resisting domination at the center helps me more to understand and sympathize with those exploited at the periphery. Thus, exploited, powerless groups at both the center and periphery can begin to work together against the common system of domination that is alienating and exploiting us both. The CIA, for example, as one part of that system, does neither of us any good and is the enemy of us both.

Such reflections carried on by a North American philosopher are both paradoxical and difficult. They are paradoxical because we at the center in different ways benefit from and live off the exploitation of the periphery. Our standard of living, for example, depends significantly on the cheap labor we exploit in the periphery, the raw materials we extract, the markets we create. Such reflection is difficult because we in the center *seem* more content, happy, and at peace with ourselves than those in the periphery. Putting it another way, we can say that alienation and exploitation at the center come bearing gifts, whereas exploitation at the periphery stalks its victims with a gun. Listening to Bill Clinton charm us politically, Calvin Klein jeans seduce us erotically, and TWA tempt us exotically, we might be lulled into the illusion that capitalism and capitalist America are the best of all possible worlds. "Every day in every way we are getting better and better."

Yet one of the main propositions of this chapter is that such an illusion is simply that, an illusion, a mere "seeming." Injustice and unhappiness at the periphery make real, full justice and happiness at the center impossible. As one indicator of the truth of such a claim, we can note the widespread narcissism, poverty, unemployment, homelessness, anomie, drug addiction, alcoholism, nuclear paranoia, and high divorce rate at the center. For all our wealth and power in North America, a casual, disinterested observer who dropped in from Mars might wonder not only whether it has made us happier but whether it has not made us more unhappy.[1]

Another indicator of the truth of such claims is the Western philosophical tradition itself. Plato's *Republic*, for example, and many of Plato's other works as well, insists on the essential connection between justice and happiness. The main burden of the *Republic*, I take it, is that someone with a magic ring, who could undetected work his will on any woman or steal from any bank or commit any murder, although he might have the illusion of happiness, could not be truly happy.[2]

Again Hegel's *Phenomenology* develops the dilemma of the master-slave relationship, in which the master, because the recognition that he receives comes from the slave, someone not truly free or worthy, is not satisfied with such recognition. What the master really wants is recognition from an equal, which, as master in a master-slave relationship, he cannot have. Hegel argues here that the happiness of the dominator as dominator, even though the slave supplies him with an adequate material standard of living, is an inadequate, unsatisfactory form of happiness. The happiness of the dominator, in which we North Americans participate, is an unreal, illusory, inadequate form of happiness.[3]

My chapter, then, will have two parts: first, consideration of Dussel's concept of liberation in the context of the periphery, and then a reflection on liberation in the United States as the center. The movement of the chapter is from far to near, more global to less global, more universal to more specific, more theoretical to more practical. Theoretical reflection on liberation moves to reflection on liberating praxis within a North American context.

Liberation in the Periphery

The relationship between the center and periphery in Dussel's thought is a relationship between countries such as the United States, Europe, Japan, and Soviet Russia, and other countries dependant on them: Latin America, the Arab world, black Africa, India, and Southeast Asia. Two things are to be noted: first, the relationship between center and periphery is not that between capitalist and socialist or countries calling themselves capitalist and socialist. Soviet Russia as a socialist country, for example, was in the center, and Argentina and Brazil as capitalist countries are in the periphery.[4]

Second, the relationship between the center and periphery is systemic, which idea we begin to get at when we discuss relationships of dependence, exploitation, colonialism, and the like. As Dussel describes such colonialism, there are three stages through which world history has passed in the last five centuries. In the first, the English colonize North America and Spain South America. This stage comes to an end when New England colonists put an end to the English presence in North America, and countries such as Argentina, Peru, and Mexico emancipate themselves from Spain in the nineteenth century.

Around 1850 the imperialist center begins a second colonial age in which the Arab world, black Africa, India, Southeast Asia and China undergo the onslaught of a monopolistic economic imperialism using the colonies as markets, sources of raw materials, and cheap labor. By the end of World War II, the United States has replaced England as the leading imperial power in the world. The new imperialism is a neocolonialism, structured primarily by the transnationals and not requiring direct political administration of the colony by the United States.

The transnationals own the key industries in these countries and also pursue a new policy of cultivating needs and desires through mass media advertising. "Things go better with Coke" not only in New York but also in Managua. Such ideological imperialism enables the center to dominate peripheral peoples and their own national oligarchies. If Gandhi and Sandino are heroes of resistance against the second colonial phase, Allende and Ortega are heroes of resistance in the third phase. The recent war in Nicaragua should be seen in this context. The United States has shifted from a stance of liberation in the first colonial phase to a stance of domination in the third. This is the sobering fact from which philosophers of liberation in the center take their bearing. Also, we should note, in a way that Dussel does not emphasize, the emergence of the Soviet Union and its satellites as a component of the third phase of colonialism.[5]

Modern European philosophy, even before the *ego cogito* but certainly from then on, often relates to all human beings outside its boundaries as manipulable tools, instruments. The *ego cogito* constituted the periphery and asked itself, along with Fernandez de Oviedo, "Are the American Indians human beings, that is, are they Europeans and rational animals?" The practical answer was that Indians were suited to forced labor and were, if not irrational, at least brutish, wild, undeveloped, uncultured—because they did not have the culture of the center.

The ontology implicit in the *ego cogito* did not come from nowhere, but rather from a previous experience of domination of other cultures and other worlds. "Ego conquiero," "I conquer," is the lived, practical basis of the *ego cogito*; and homo homini lupus its real political expression. Philosophy in the bourgeois center, first Spain, then France and England, and now the United States becomes the ideological expression and legitimation of the bourgeois class.[6]

Ontology as a philosophy of the center becomes ontology that denies and annihilates distinction. Because being is defined by the system, the exterior other is nonbeing. As such, human beings must either be incorporated into the system or annihilated. If they resist being incorporated into a one-dimensional system, then they are subject to military attack by the SS or CIA. Militarism is essential to maintaining and enhancing the system. To resist the system, "being," is to risk literal nonbeing, death. The heroes of resistance on the periphery, such as Lumumba, Ben Barka, or Oscar Romero, often die in their resistance. "The conquests of Latin America, the enslavement of Africa and its colonization, as well as that of Asia, are the dominating dialectical expression of 'the same' that assassinates 'the other' and totalizes 'the other' in 'the same.'"[7]

War is the ultimate fulfillment of the praxis of domination, domination in its pure state, annihilation of others. In order to make war, I have to turn the human face of the other into an abstract mask, "the enemy," "the communists." To kill in Vietnam or El Salvador or Nicaragua I have to reduce the other to an abstraction. When this is done, then anything is possible, from making soap with the fat of tortured bodies in Nazi Germany to training dogs to violate women through torture in Chile.[8]

Domination in the oppressor corresponds to alienation in the oppressed. When I use the other, I appropriate the fruits of the other's labor as my own. When I do not recover the fruit of my work, my work is alienated. When such alienation is systematic, institutional, and habitual, then alienation is the fruit of unjust production. Ownership, the right to the other's product, is the counterpart in the dominator to alienation in the dominated. In a consumer society like the United States, it is ownership of capital that is decisive; in a bureaucratic society like the Soviet Union, it was control of political functions. In the United States domination takes a predominantly economic form; in the Soviet Union a predominantly political form.[9]

Domination of the periphery by the center is political and economic: political in the sense of the power of the United States government working through international agencies such as the IMF, the CIA, corrupt local oligarchies and monarchies; economic in the sense of the wealth produced going to the center to benefit the center primarily. Consequently, liberation is a negation of the negation, denial of a denial. In liberation oppressed peoples democratically and popularly shake off their oppressors and take control of their own destinies. The base religious communities all over Latin America are one example of such democratic, grassroots political movements, the Sandinista revolution is another. If domination is economic and political, then liberation is also. Nationalism leads to nationalization.[10]

There is an ethics of liberation in which we hear the other; the abstract mask of the other changes to a face. In such listening I cultivate an "atheism" toward the system and respect the other as outside the system, about whom I know nothing or relatively nothing. Someone who runs the risk of listening to the other runs the risk of being persecuted by the system as an outsider, corrupter of the young, a fifth columnist. In taking creative and courageous responsibility for the other outside the system, I come to be persecuted by the system or denied tenure or promotion. Such creative, courageous responsibility is the essence of a revolutionary ethic, not to be confused with "do-goodism":

In this way, the liberating act (act of gratuitous goodness), inasmuch as it is beyond intrasystemic interest, is and can be only illegal, contrary to present laws, which, because they are those of an old just order that is now oppressive, are unjust. It is the inevitable position of liberation: subversive illegality.[11]

Liberation in the Center

I have given a brief sketch of the liberation of the periphery from a system of domination emanating from the center. We, however, who are writing, reading, or listening to this chapter, are for the most part in the center. The question that emerges, then, is how we in the center can become liberated. Somehow we in the center have to be liberated from the center. We in the center in our own way have to become imprudently prudent, illegally subversive toward the center. Such liberation is, from the point of view of the center, evil, disobedient, lawless, irresponsible. We in the center who wish to become liberated have to move beyond good and evil as defined by the center. If, as I will show, the center equates human goodness and well-being with having, possessing, control, domination, then evil toward the center identical with liberating goodness will challenge that equation theoretically and practically. To be good in a liberating fashion means and implies that I am more or less at odds with the system, not at home in it, critical of it. Because living within the system is a living death, I risk disapproval, loss of tenure, promotion, persecution by taking a stand against the system.

Liberation in the center from the center implies that there is a periphery in the center, economic, political, and social, that is distant from and alien to the center. The periphery of the center and the center of the center relate to one another as rich to poor, capital to labor, possessed to dispossessed, male to female, exploiter to exploited, powerful to weak, employed to unemployed, manipulator to manipulated. Within the system constituted by the relation of the center to the periphery, we can say that there are overlapping subgroups that are relatively powerless, dispossessed, exploited, disenfranchised. Indeed, if I am correct in my analysis, most Americans are in the periphery to a greater or lesser extent. One of the systematic tricks of the center, carried out through government propaganda, mass culture, and education, is to convince most of us that we do indeed benefit from the center, need it, identify with it. To the extent that the Freudian-Marxist analysis is relevant here, we can say, following Marcuse and Deleuze-Guttari, that internalizing the rule of the center means internalizing the rule of the father. Liberation from the center, on the other hand, is anti-Oedipal, antihierarchical, antiauthoritarian—liberation from the center implies a world without the oppressive father.[12]

There is, then, in the United States enormous inequality between the center and the periphery. Economic considerations alone show that most of us are on the periphery. Now it is one of the main assumptions of this chapter that such inequality is unjust. Here I am building on prior arguments in this book that demonstrate, roughly, two criteria for a fully just society: full individual and political freedom and economic equality. Economic equality is necessary first, because without it there is no full individual or political freedom. Second, there is an incompatibility between democracy and such economic inequality; inevitably the dominant economic class will have the resources to limit options, control debate, and influence decisions in such a way that full public discussion and participation is impossible. Because capitalism is essentially a system that operates to keep the wealthy happy, too much democracy is dangerous for the system. Political action committees that predominantly represent corporate, upper-class wealth lobbying in congress are one example of such disproportionate power; the interlocking, reciprocal interactions between corporations and the government, in which persons move back and forth between the two, is another.

Third, because of this dominance of economic power, most work in the United States is still alienated, mindless, unhappy. As Braverman and others have shown, even white collar work is increasingly subject to the same kind of division of labor and subordination to the machine that characterized blue collar labor. Consequently, most computer workers are key punch operators whose work is as mindless and dissatisfying as that on most assembly lines.[13]

All of these tendencies toward economic marginalization have increased under flexible accumulation, described in the last chapter. Attacks on labor unions, migration of capital from one region to another or out of the country, attacks on parts of the welfare state, tax breaks and policies that favor the rich have worked to dramatically increase the wealth and income going to the top 10 percent in the society, and to drastically decrease in absolute and relative terms the wealth and income going to the bottom 40–50 percent of the population. In addition poverty, unemployment, homelessness, hunger have dramatically increased in the countries of the North, and show no signs of abating.[14]

In the United States the center for political domination is the welfare state. Because of the tendency toward economic crisis and problems with legitimacy that emerged in early capitalism prior to 1900 in the United States, a new relation of the state to the economy emerged that was more interventionist, positive, and committed to planning. In answer to the question about economic crisis, "How do we avoid depressions?," the solution that emerged was more government intervention in the economy, taking the form of taxation policies to increase investment in the private sector, unemployment insurance, minimum wage, and military spending. In answer to the question about legitimacy, "How do we keep workers and other groups in the society from revolting?," the answer that emerged was welfare embodied in such mechanisms as social security, unemployment insurance, and the minimum wage. The formula that various thinkers have used to capture the state's dual role of securing both accumulation and legitimation is the "warfare-welfare state."[15]

In relation to the political center defined as the welfare state are those who are administered by it, kept under it, or excluded by it, but whose interests are finally and ultimately subordinated to those of capital. The poor, women, blacks, students, unemployed are some of the groups who have a legitimate claim on the welfare state, but whose interests are not adequately or fully represented by it. Because such interests, however, express legitimate claims on the welfare state, a tension between accumulation and legitimation arises. This tension comes out in the following sets of alternatives. Which do we need more, military spending or spending for education, more money for super highways or more money for rapid transit, more spending for high and middle income housing or low income housing, private health insurance or national health insurance? The unjust accumulation emphasis is present in the first member in each set, the just legitimation emphasis in the second. Because of this contradictory tension, the groups who have a just, legitimate claim on the government do not have their claims fully recognized or implemented.[16]

Related to the first political center-periphery contrast between administration and the administered, is a second, that between the powerful and the powerless: between those who have easy access to the organs of government and those who do not. As Lindbloom argues this point, capital or its representatives have much more access to government than do labor, consumer groups, and others. He describes, first of all, the way in which government spontaneously adapts its policies to the needs of business. One small example of this tendency is a judge refusing to award punitive damages against Richardson-Merrill for producing a product MER/29 that resulted in a variety of bad symptoms, including cataracts. The judge refused, even though it was established to the judge's satisfaction that over a ten-year period the company had repeatedly suppressed evidence of the drug's dangers and had filed falsified reports to the Food and Drug Administration. Yet the judge refused to award damages because "a sufficient egregious error as to one product can end the business life of a concern that has wrought much good in the past."[17]

A second form of disproportionate business influence on government is represented by the actual grants of government authority to businessmen. Grants of eminent domain to private utility companies, veto power over appointments to regulatory agencies such as the Army Corps of Engineers, the thousands of business councils that consult regularly with government agencies on common policies, the business council composed of leading corporate executives that meets regularly with the president and cabinet, governmental inducements such as tax breaks to business, the much greater relative contribution of business than labor to electoral campaigns, the delegation of decisions affecting the common welfare, such as the level of steel or automobile prices, to private business. We can affirm, Lindbloom argues, not only much greater access of business to government, but also a much easier access.[18]

A third related political center-periphery relationship is that between purposive rational action, essentially science and technology, ordered to controlling and manipulating things and people, and symbolic interaction, popular, participatory democratic action. Such a gap develops because government more and more is a matter of technical, bureaucratic administration from on high, and less and less a matter of ethical, political democracy. If the welfare state is to be administered according to the needs of capital, then too much democracy is dangerous to the system's efficient survival and well-being. People should not take to the streets but rather should leave government to the experts. Kissinger and Brezinski, not King and Hayden, are the norm.[19]

As a result there is, Habermas argues, the phenomenon that ethics in government and politics is becoming increasingly anachronistic. Rather than rational discussion of issues in election campaigns, there is "selling the president." There emerges a distance between technocracy and genuine popular democracy that is contrary not only to Marx but to Mill. The most explicit conflict in late capitalist societies, in relation to which class conflict is real but latent, is that between purposive rational action and symbolic interaction, technocracy and politics, and the practitioners of symbolic interaction are relatively powerless. In science and technology late capitalism has found the form of reason most appropriate for itself. They have become not only productive forces, increasing through the use of science and technology the productivity of capital, but also ideology.[20]

The third major kind of center-periphery in American society is the socio-cultural level. Here I am referring to two different phenomena, the alienation in social relationships that occurs outside the work place and the production and reproduction of ideology. First of all, we can note the social relationships present in the different living situations of capitalist and laborer, white and black, man and woman, heterosexual and homosexual. To a significant extent, the spatial indicator of the first two sets of relationships is that between the suburb and city, the white upper middle class and the poor, the respectable neighborhood and the black ghetto, the clean outer city and the polluted inner city. To be in a ghetto, whether it be one of economic class, race, or sex, is clearly to be on the periphery. "White, male, wealthy, heterosexual" is in; "black, female, poor, gay" is out.

The social realm is also that sector of society concerned with the production and reproduction of ideology. By ideology here I mean a social rationalization simultaneously expressing, legitimizing, and covering up class or group domination. At this point in the chapter, the necessity for ideology in late capitalism should be clear enough. First, there is the fact of structural injustice or inequality already mentioned. Second, there is the possibility of legitimation crises, because of the state's contradictory role of securing both accumulation and legitimation. Finally, there is the structural possibility and increasing probability of motivation crises because the system is increasingly doing away with the motivation necessary to secure adherence to it and increasingly producing motivation that makes support of the system less likely. An example of the former is the erosion of the traditional work ethic through welfare programs; an example of the second is the production through education of people oriented to quality rather than quantity, use value rather than exchange value, enjoyment *in* work rather than money *from* work, service industries rather than productive industries.[21]

Clearly then, if late capitalism is going to keep people enthusiastically producing and consuming up to the levels required by the system, it needs ideology mills or ideology factories. One of these is the mass media and advertising, another is organized religion, still a third is the fine arts, and a fourth is education. The production of false consciousness is an essential part of the capitalistic system itself.

Perhaps the chief objection that might be made to these reflections is that my discussion of the periphery-center relation misses the reality of the middle class and that the existence of such a middle class makes the U.S. different from Argentina, Nicaragua, and Brazil. There is some legitimacy to the claim, I think, in that we clearly have more people in the so-called middle income brackets, $30–70,000 a year, than those in other countries. Even on this matter of income and wealth, however, as the statistics quoted earlier indicate, after the top 10 percent, income and wealth drop significantly. Even in this realm, the so-called middle class is peripheral, although not as peripheral as the sixty billion poor or near poor. Moreover, when we move into the question of actual power over decision-making in the work place, the "middle class" is even more peripheral. Decision-making for the most part is in the hands of a controlling group of stockholders and managers employed by them who are often part of the stockholding class. One of the moves late capitalism has made is to grant more income while reducing power.

Furthermore, if my analysis of the political sector is correct, political powerlessness is even more pronounced among the middle class. The influence of business over political decision-making, the rule of the expert, and the substitution of bureaucracy for democracy all mean that most of us are relatively powerless in a political sense.

Also, one of the elements underlying the belief in the middle class is the claim that we are moving from a blue collar to a white collar society. However, evidence indicates that, when we take into account the kinds of work not normally classified as blue collar work, such as picking up the garbage and delivering the mail, America will be a blue collar society through the 1990s and beyond. Moreover, even white collar professional work is in many instances underpaid, mechanized, and increasingly subject to the division of labor. Even when these problems are not present, the goals that the work serves make it absolutely or relatively meaningless. The doctor continually on the phone to his stock broker, the lawyer greedily searching out wealthy clients, and the academic breathlessly pursuing grants are classic, stock examples.[22]

Finally, the consciousness industry, the popular media such as television, newspapers, magazines, and the advertising present in all of these present an illusion of middle-class well-being that causes us to ignore our real condition, that of being in thrall to capital. The notion of a happy, well-off middle class, I would suggest, is to a significant extent a myth. The perpetuation and maintenance of false consciousness is itself part of the capitalistic system insuring that those on the periphery do not know the extent to which they are peripheral, buy into the naive, uncritical equation of being with having, possessing, consuming, and controlling, and, therefore, think that they are better off than they really are. Undermining and seeing through such false consciousness becomes an important, radical act, one of the chief roles of the radical, activist, artist, and academic.[23]

We have, then, in this section been discussing the center-periphery relationship in the United States. What we have seen is that, contrary to appearances, more Americans are in one way or another on the periphery, powerless, alienated, poor, unemployed. We might symbolize the center-periphery relationship in the United States by thinking of three places, Washington, D.C., Wall Street, and Madison Avenue, that are the centers of political, economic, and social domination respectively. In relation to these three places most of us are on the periphery.

Toward a Praxis of Liberation

I have already noted that there is a contrast between center in the North and periphery in the South, or third world as a whole: the North is rich, the South is poor; the North is powerful politically, the South is impotent; the North is literate, the South is illiterate or at least educationally disadvantaged in much of its population, through no fault of its own. The North is subject to propaganda and ideology as a way of containing democracy; the South is much more subject to violence and terror. The North has institutionalized democracy and human rights to some extent; the South is much more undemocratic and denying of human rights. The North is consumeristic; the South is hungry and poor in its majorities.

As a general pattern, of course, this characterization admits of qualifications and exceptions. Cuba, for example, under Castro did much better in feeding its people, clothing them, educating them, and caring for their medical needs than most of the so-called democracies in Central and Latin America supported by the United States. And even now, when Cuba is weaker than ever because of international pressure led by the U.S., it is not clear that one faced with a choice between living there and living in Guatemala or Brazil would not and should not choose Cuba. Chile under Allende's brief reign was more democratic than before or since. Guatemala under the reign of Arbenz was more democratic and more economically egalitarian and redistributive than before or since. Unfortunately, both regimes were brought to premature ends by U.S. led and financed coups, in which the CIA was heavily involved. These are two more instances of a general practice and pattern of deterring democracy when it conflicts with or does not adequately serve the Fifth Freedom.[24]

Nor do I mean, in presenting this picture and set of contrasts, to say and imply that Third World peoples are primarily or mostly responsible for their plight. Indeed the opposite is the case. Because of the nature of neoimperialism discussed in the last chapter, the main, leading cause for the plight of the Third World rests upon the imperialistic North now tripolar in including the United States, Western Europe, and Japan. Wealthy and powerful Third World minorities have participated in this process, as have repressive military and police, and educated elites who are easily bought off to serve the internal and external oppressor.[25]

Nor is it the case that poor majorities in these countries have mostly been passive, compliant, cowed victims. Rather the history of the North's subjugation of the South is one in which dozens, even hundreds, of uprisings, revolutions, and different forms of protest and resistance occurred, only to be put down and repressed. To realize the truth of this claim, we only have to consider Arbenz in Guatemala, Bosch in the Dominican Republic, Allende in Chile, the Sandinistas in Nicaragua, and Aristide in Haiti, at the moment restored but on U.S. terms and significantly weakened politically. Instance after instance of democracy is successfully deterred; after each one the leaders in the North breathed a sigh of relief. So far, in the whole of Central and Latin America, Castro's revolution has been one of the few not totally vanquished, and now, with the decline of the Soviet Union and unrelenting U.S. pressure, Cuba has become more problematic.[26]

Working out a philosophy and theology of liberation in the North has its own set of advantages and difficulties. Although they have insights that can illuminate our situation, one cannot simply transfer the analysis of thinkers like Dussel, Freire, Guttiérrez, Segundo, Sobrino, Miranda, and Boff to the North. The main difficulty is that I am not an abstract but a situated thinker, and my theorizing should reflect that. My theory intends universality, phenomenological, ethical, and metaphysical, but it also intends and incorporates hermeneutical specificity, psychological, social, and religious; an aspect of that specificity is my own personal, familial, and national situation.

As situated in the North, therefore, I think and speak and act out of a situation of relative privilege that has advantages and disadvantages for the project of liberation. Advantages are that I can use my education to criticize privilege and exploit a context in which human rights and democracy are much more securely institutionalized than in the South. Disadvantages are that my economic well-being can blind me to the poverty of others even in my own country, and consumerism can take me captive as I become addicted to the pleasures and seductions of the media, the society of the spectacle.[27]

The praxis of liberation, therefore, in the North has to use and respond both to positive, enabling and negative, disabling conditions in our situation. In general, the positive would imply a theoretical and practical praxis that is democratic, communicative, and non-violent; I theoretically grounded such praxis in CAL.[28] The response to the negative conditions has to include a theoretical and practical praxis that is "downwardly mobile," that tries in theory and praxis to identify with the oppressed and to own up to one's own oppression to the extent that it obtains, and that attempts a theory and practice that is disillusioning and "dislocating" in relation to the illusions and privileged location of the center. In the rest of this chapter I will attempt to spell out the praxis of liberation in relation to these positive and negative factors.

But my point here is that in many of its positive and negative conditions, this praxis is different from that of our brothers and sisters of the South. It does not have as many of our positive, enabling conditions, and it does not have as many of our negative blocks to liberation. We do share some, of course, and to an increasing extent. In the North, since flexible accumulation has taken over in the last thirty years, we experience growing poverty, unemployment, homelessness, hunger, powerlessness, repression, and marginalization. Indeed, some have commented on this phenomenon as the growing "third worldization" of the North. And this phenomenon is not only economic but political, as the lineaments of a police state emerge. Cities are more and more becoming armed camps, police repression grows, the attack by the right wing on the Bill of Rights continues, and the building of prisons has become a major growth industry.[29]

An effective theoretical and practical praxis of liberation, therefore, will involve and imply blending and relating both aspects common to the situations of North and South and those that are specific to either North or South. For radical theorists and activists in the North and South, the basic, shared negative, against which we both unite, is a national and international capitalism that is exploitative, oppressive, and dominating. The basic positive values are commitment to self-appropriation and to the liberation flowing from it as a process of creating individual and social justice and happiness, the transcendental precepts, the validity claims, the principles of right, morality, and justice, and democratic socialism as the goal of liberation.

I propose to begin such reflection by internationalizing the concept of crisis that I worked out in CAL for national, Northern capitalism. In that book I argued, drawing on Habermas and later Frankfurt School theory, that capitalism is prone not only to economic crisis rooted in overproduction and the resulting recessions and depressions, but also rationality crisis, the inability of the capitalist state to manage successfully and administer economic evils such as unemployment and inflation to the satisfaction of most of its citizens. Two other crises are legitimation crisis, in which a tension between capitalistic needs for accumulation and the polity's need for rational, democratic legitimation conflict in society and the state; and motivation crisis in which in the welfare state some motivations essential for consent to the status quo such as willingness to work hard erode and others such as a communicative ethic or post-auratic art emerge that are at least dysfunctional for capitalism as a socio-economic system.[30]

Because it is capitalism that externalizes itself and internationalizes itself abroad in the form of imperialism, there is no reason that these same crisis tendencies cannot arise in that context as well. Thus poor performance by the state in negotiating economic and rationality crisis gives rise to the Chiapas rebellion in Mexico and a crisis of the peso and the dollar. The resulting economic instability made U.S. investors nervous, leading them to encourage a military move against the peasants in Chiapas. Such a policy, however, led to widespread protest and demonstrations in Mexico and the U.S., questioning its legitimacy and undermining the motivation of people to participate and go along.[31]

When we consider flexible accumulation as the latest phase of national and international capitalism, some chinks begin to appear in the capitalist armor and opportunities for resistance emerge. In CAL I developed the account of the structures of flexible accumulation for national capitalism but not for imperialism. When we reflect on imperialism, we note the phenomena of capital flight from the country, the reduction of portions of the welfare state, or better yet, reduction of welfare for the poor and increase of welfare for the rich, attacks on labor unions, and the growing dominance of money capital over industrial capital on the national and international scene.[32]

One effect of flexible accumulation on the national and international scene is the growing possibility of economic crisis, in a way different from the reign of Fordism, which preceded flexible accumulation. As the movement of money capital internationalizes and increases, there is no guarantee that crashes, recessions, and depressions can be avoided. Indeed, because of the internationalization of capital now nearly achieved and certainly achieved in principle in flexible accumulation, the power of the national state to deal with and administer economic and rationality crisis, as it could more easily under Fordism, decreases. Capital can always vote with its feet if the state does not give it sufficient concessions and incentives, and if it tries too much to maintain or increase its budget to the poor. NAFTA and GATT put the finishing touches on this internationalization of capital and give capital enormous bargaining power against the state, labor, and labor unions. Reduce your taxes and lower your wage demands or I vote with my feet.[33]

As capital moves from the North to the South, within this country and out of this country, pressure is put on unions and workers to go along and allow reduction of wages and fringe benefits to remain competitive with third world labor. Therefore, the possibility and necessity of working class discontent, organization, and resistance grows in a way that was more unlikely under the reign of Fordism.

The welfare state arose as a way of dealing with both accumulation and legitimation crises. In order to make sure that people have enough money to generate sufficient demand for goods and to contain massive discontent flowing from unemployment and poverty, welfare programs like unemployment insurance, aid for dependent children, social security, medicaid, and medicare were generated. If flexible accumulation means, among other things, decline of such programs and provisions for the poor and working people, accumulation and legitimation pressures can be expected to increase.[34]

Different thinkers have stressed the way the decline of Fordism was hastened by an "accumulation crisis": the poor, workers, and educated professionals were receiving too much wealth and income from capital to make an adequate profit. As a result of a falling rate of profit, capital had too little incentive to invest. The results, which emerged fully with Reagan and Bush in the U.S. and Thacher in England, were attacks on labor unions, reductions in welfare for the poor, and bureaucratic and economic deregulation. These moves had the intended effect of decreasing the social wage, direct and indirect, and therefore, increasing the amount going to capital. Consequently, in the North we note a growing poverty, unemployment, homelessness, and hunger similar to the conditions that gave rise to Fordism in the first place and allowing increased possibilities of resistance and revolt. These emerge as a response to economic and rationality crisis.[35]

During the reign of Fordism, part of what allowed most of the population to support the system was a rising standard of living for many, the possibility of a good life after high school and college, and the hope to participate in the American dream—a house in the suburbs, two children, a beautiful wife or handsome husband, and a clean, healthy environment. As capital migrates out of the country, however, as unions are weakened, as labor in the North is forced more and more to compete with Third World workers for scarce jobs, as attacks on the welfare system continue, these aims become more problematic, and the possibility of a motivation crisis grows. Why should I work hard, why should I support this socio-economic system, why should I vote for or work for political candidates, when the consumeristic dream that kept me hooked into the system and that was a part of a tradeoff for decreased political power and minimal power in the work place is increasingly out of reach for more and more people?[36]

Even though capital's new class war is justified as an attack on the poor, homeless, marginalized, it is not simply or even dominantly that. Rather, cuts in education, medical care, public transportation, student loans, welfare, and job training affect all of us or most of us. Many people on the streets are formerly middle-class and white collar people who were thrown out of work in the 1980s and 90s as firms downsized, became more capital intensive, and moved out of the country in search of cheaper labor and less rigorous environmental regulations. The picture of a Ph.D. driving a cab because he cannot get an academic job is almost a cliché of current social life.[37]

With all of the above, the conditions for a legitimation crisis grow. What made capitalism in its Fordist stage apparently and, to some extent, really more legitimate and beneficent was the welfare state. As that is rolled back, the subordination of government to capital's priorities becomes more manifest and obvious. When mayors such as Giuliani in New York City and governors such as Pataki in New York state announce $300 million in cuts for welfare, education, and hospitals, while, almost in the same breath, announcing the same amount in subsidies and tax breaks for Wall Street, the contrast between accumulation and legitimation is stark and brutal. In the era of flexible accumulation, the gloves are off in the class war, which is also a war against women, blacks, Latinos, and homosexuals.[38]

The challenge for us as progressive, radical theorists, professionals, and secular-religious activists is to get ourselves together to organize and resist and overcome in the face of and because of these contradictions, in which a national and international capitalism has rarely been more virulent. But, in spite of the fact that things do not look good for the progressive cause, there is reason to hope. We must not forget that capitalism is contradictory ethically and systemically. It exploits most of us, and it is internally antagonistic, undermining the conditions of its own survival and well-being. One indication of such antagonism, in addition to those mentioned above, is the inability of the environment to sustain capitalist growth. Worldwide pollution and worldwide depletion of raw materials manifest the fundamental way, in addition to its exploitiveness, tendency to marginalize the poor and unemployed, and its militarism, in which capitalism is an economy of death in its undermining and destroying the conditions of survival and well-being upon which even it depends. Capitalism is a luxury that we can no longer afford.[39]

For these reasons, I think that world process is ultimately on the side of the oppressed, ethically certainly but also historically insofar as the more rational solution becomes more probable. Such a solution is not inevitable, certainly, because we have no guarantees. But socialism becomes the more obvious, sensible solution, as capitalism takes over and despoils Eastern Europe, as it destroys the environment, as its militarism spreads even in a post-Soviet age, as it brings into being more and more repressive regimes to deal with its own economic, rationality, legitimation, and motivation crises. "Socialism or barbarism"—this phrase is truer now than when it was first uttered.

As the current growth of a repressive apparatus in the U.S., the current list of sixty capital crimes, the building and staffing of prisons as a major growth industry in the U.S., an incarceration rate for all people and for blacks that is several times more than South Africa before Mandela took over, and the attempt to remove the exclusionary rule banning search and seizure without a warrant indicate, neofascism arises as one way to resolve the accumulation and legitimation crises in late capitalism. One alternative way to do that would be to move in the direction of legitimation by abolishing capitalism. The other is to reduce legitimation pressures through different forms of repression, policing, and containment. The police state, neofascism, or fascism arise as possible solutions to the motivation and legitimation crises of late capitalism in its phase of flexible accumulation.[40]

As all of this begins to happen, however, as the gloves come off in the class war, the structural possibility of motivation and legitimation crises grows. The apparent benevolence of the Fordist welfare state toward much of its population drops away and the obvious antagonism of the "flexible accumulation" state toward these same people increases. More and more of us are becoming either superfluous, redundant, or threatening to the accumulation of profit. As the possibilities for economic, rationality, motivation, and legitimation crises grow in this changed post-Fordist context, therefore, we note a basis of hope. When we add to these the role of a processive God as the ground and telos and exemplar of a world process oriented to liberation and the role of Jesus Christ, liberator, we have additional motives for hope. All is not lost, but the capitalist wasteland grows, and there is no time to lose in organizing resistance.

What, then, is to be done and how? In general, as I have already argued in CAL, because late capitalism is an identity in difference, racist, sexist, heterosexist, and classist, so also we need a movement that is also an identity in difference. Different groups and classes and parts of classes need to come together in a national and international coalition that avoids the extremes either of a monolithic labor organization centered primarily or exclusively on economic issues, and liberal and postmodern fragmentation and identity politics. Because the economic drive toward surplus value subordinates other forms of injustice such as racism, sexism, and heterosexism to itself, that remains hermeneutically the most fundamental form and telos of capitalism as a social system. But the other forms of injustice are not reducible to this economic orientation in origin, structure, or goal. Consequently, an adequate form of progressive resistance and organization has to take account not only the unity in late capitalism but pluralism and differences, and different social movements as they are affected and brought into being in different ways by our current social pathology. Such social movements in the last thirty years in the United States and western Europe include antiwar, antinuclear, feminist, environmental, and gay rights movements; and include thirty to forty million people in the United States.[41]

As I argued in CAL, when we link social movements with those emerging or already working on behalf of unions, labor, the unemployed, homeless, the poor, and hungry, movements that are related more directly to economic exploitation, then we have a significant basis for resistance. As economic and rationality crisis grows under flexible accumulation, then we can expect these economically based movements to grow, as they are already doing in New York City as we confronted the unholy trinity of Gingrich, Pataki, and Giuliani in the spring of 1995 advocating billions of dollars worth of cuts in programs affecting the poor, unemployed, homeless, children, welfare mothers, and medically needy and providing an equal or greater amount in various kinds of tax incentives, tax breaks, and subsidies to the rich and corporations.[42]

The point is that these two groups, labor, economy-based groups and social movements, need one another. Neither is sufficient by itself, and both have a common but multifaceted enemy, a racist, sexist, heterosexist capitalism. Direct and indirect victims of economic exploitation need to see how that affects and impinges on other apparently noneconomic sectors and movements such as the environment and military spending and use of racial and sexual division to foster disunity in resisting groups. Social movements need to realize the way that their own concerns link up to capitalism. Military spending, for example, is enormously profitable, and it is required to sustain our empire around the world. Destruction of the environment is linked to capital's "werewolflike hunger for surplus value," need for raw materials, and unwillingness to regard the environment as anything other than a source of raw materials. Spending on the environment or environmental regulation is resisted because it cuts into profits and acts as a brake on investment.[43]

Following Dussel and Gramsci, I wish, therefore, to articulate the notions not only of class but of oppressed peoples. Dussel, in discussing Latin and Central America, argues that the different poor majorities composed of women, peasants, labor, and progressive activists and intellectuals are oppressed by dominant elites and classes in those countries and in the North. "People" is broader and more inclusive and more concrete than class, including not only labor, but peasants, Indians, women, students, and progressive professionals. Each of these has its direct form of injustice that feeds into and is affected by economic, class exploitation. Peasants, for example, are affected by capital as they are forced off the land and go hungry when the World Bank and IMF force structural adjustment policies encouraging crops for export and discouraging crops for local consumption, especially by the poor.[44]

A people, then, will be a distinct national group with its own identity-in-difference, subject to class domination and exploitation that affects everyone, but plural and multiple in that women, blacks, homosexuals will be affected differently and will respond differently to such domination and additionally have their own form of domination with which to deal and which is related to economic oppression and feeds into it in different ways. A "people" is this identity in difference of a nation's exploited and oppressed, potentially and in different ways and at different times partially or totally united in its opposition to a common enemy, a racist, sexist, heterosexist capitalism, and united by a common ethical criteria of right, morality, and justice, and by a common goal, full economic, political, and social democracy.[45]

Emerging from and articulating and relating to the people or to specific classes or groups within it are "organic intellectuals" in Gramsci's sense, thinkers, artists, reflective leaders, organizers, and activists who lead their specific group and others as well not by imposing solutions from on high but through public dialogue, communication, and persuasion. Such persuasion occurs in the "public sphere" in the North, which is much more prevalent and operative and institutionalized than in the South, although even in the North it is heavily compromised by capitalist manipulation, control, propaganda, and advertising. Nonetheless, the public sphere is a real source of resistance in the North in the institutionalized domain of public, free, political discussion occurring in media, public forums, universities, political campaigns, demonstrations, and so on.[46]

Examples of such organic intellectuals in the United States are Daniel Berrigan for the Catholic left, Noam Chomsky for the academic, secular-Jewish community, Edward Said for the educated politically active Arab, Muslim community, bell hooks for black men and women, Mike Davis for a working class and academic constituency, Mumia Abu Jamal and Cornell West for the black progressive community. These relate to and emerge from but are not confined in their influence to one or more groups that may be called base communities, people organized in such a way that they live out and try to embody in their lives the just, liberated society that they are trying to create. Such communities exist by the thousands in the United States, Latin and Central America, and Western Europe.

Organic intellectuals and base communities are beginning to reach across national borders and to connect with one another. Examples are North American priests, ministers, religious, and lay Christians who interact with and learn from their brothers and sisters in Central and Latin America, supporting them, giving them money, visiting with them, learning from them, being inspired by them, and agitating politically on their behalf. Witness for Peace is one example of such cooperation; the sanctuary movement, the response to the slaughter of Jesuits in El Salvador, and the International Society for the Philosophy of Liberation are others. Enrique Dussel, an organic intellectual from Argentina and Mexico, has made contact with significant numbers of us in North America and Europe.

We need, therefore, to think about a "new internationale" in Derrida's sense, a loose alliance of activists, workers, the poor, intellectuals, white, black, brown, and red people of conscience that extends across borders and that would, and here I am going beyond Derrida, institutionalize forms of resistance and solidarity. I am as skeptical as Derrida of rigidly organized, hierarchized, elitist, dogmatic workers' parties and state apparatuses, but finally resistance to the NWO, if it is to be effective, needs to be institutionalized. To capitalist globalization we need to oppose socialist internationalism.[47]

A "new internationale" is still largely to be created, but it is an ethical and political necessity if effective national-international resistance to the NWO is to be mounted. Such a new internationale would be and could be an international linking and cooperation of different national peoples and groups and intellectuals representing peoples, democratic, institutionalized, decentralized as much as possible, involving, like effective democratic organizations within nations, some representation, operating at different levels, economic, political, and social. It plugs into and integrates different national groups and organizations already operative such as unions, political parties like the New Party embodying my identity-in-difference model of resistance and organization, philosophical and scientific and artistic organizations and groups, and so on.[48]

One effective way, therefore, to counter the ideology and propaganda that try to keep people hooked into the status quo is through an effective use of the public sphere by organic intellectuals and their communities through writing, speaking, organizing, petitioning, demonstrating, protesting, and civilly disobeying. Another is a spirituality and praxis of resistance. Religious traditions, properly understood, interpreted, and lived out, are terrific resources for mounting such resistance and indeed already have been in the United States. One has only to mention Martin Luther King's civil rights crusade based in Protestant Christianity, Malcolm X's Muslim resistance, Dorothy Day's Catholic Worker, and Berrigan's Plowshares and Kairos movements.

Not only Catholics, Protestants, Jews, but also people of other religions are sources of resistance and a basis of hope. Examples are the Voodoo religion of the indigenous peoples of Haiti, the Mayan religion of Chiapas, the religion of John Africa and Move espoused by Mumia Abu Jamal, and various other Indian religions in the United States, Canada, Central America, and Latin America. Indigenous peoples in the western hemisphere, whose lives and land have been scorched, raped, exploited, and terrorized by the imperial West and North serve, then, as powerful bases of resistance and hope. A Christianity of *liberatory incarnation* can be related to such movements sympathetically, drawing on its own tradition but also allowing itself to be enriched by and learn from these other traditions, especially about the renewing power of the land and positive resources in racially different traditions, religions, and movements. The land can be contemplated for its beauty and its sublimity but also, when we see the way that it has been despoiled in the service of profit, can be a source of prophetic anger. Racially distinct movements of liberation, such as those centered around Aristide, the Zapatistas, and Mumia Abu Jamal, originating in the distinct, naturally beautiful and sacred but also exploited, plundered, and polluted places of Haiti, Chiapas, Mexico, and Philadelphia, can be powerful sources of resistance and liberation. Here we find "earth power" linked together with "people power" in a collective resistance rooted in a collective, narrative memory oriented to a liberated future.

Drawing on disciplines of prayer, contemplation, literacy, and reading to supplement more secular forms of analysis and motivation, religious people can begin to free themselves from the narcotizing addiction of consumerism, advertising, and the TV culture. Motivated by a "preferential option for the poor," people have begun a "downward mobility," identified with Christ in his downward mobility, opting out of the reckless pursuit of money, power, pleasure, and success, and opting for justice, happiness, community, and genuine social liberation. Rooted in base communities, people can in their way of living, their simple lifestyles, their economic sharing, their decisions to live in poor neighborhoods and to serve and to work with people in those neighborhoods, and in their regular practice and support of nonviolent civil disobedience begin to foreshadow and anticipate and create a more just, liberated society, as well as to work for institutional, structural, social change. The nonviolent love of God and Christ translates into a non-violent love of the neighbor and praxis of liberation.[49]

Because we in the North are "rich" and well taken care of in relationship to our brothers and sisters in the South, the spiritual disciplines of prayer and contemplation and meditation and spiritual reading can be used to disillusion ourselves about the role capitalism plays in our own culture. Also to the extent that these spiritual disciplines are "useless forms of self-transcendence," valuable in themselves, they act as implicit or explicit critique of an instrumental culture subordinating everything to the dollar and to profit.

Liturgy can function as a way of remembering the suffering and oppressed; for example, Christian leftist groups in New York City sponsor on Good Friday a stations of the cross that ends with civil disobedience at places like Riverside Research Institute, which does research on Star Wars, and the Intrepid Museum, which celebrates events like the Gulf War. Bible study undertaken by religious groups, in which the Bible is linked to themes of economic justice and injustice, becomes a way of thinking about what the capitalist economy is doing to us. Such disciplines allow us to distance ourselves intellectually, spiritually, and politically from the dominant culture, to see through it, to see that the capitalist economy is really an economy of death.

Working for institutional change and living out in community the values motivating such work, thus, are complementary. Indeed thinkers and activists such as Daniel Berrigan describe this blending as basic sanity in our situation, not extraordinary, as the basic living out of a commitment and resistance that alone makes full sense in human and religious terms. Anything less is a compromise, a half-life, an invitation to inauthenticity. As Berrigan argues it, such sanity contrasts with the insanity of a late capitalist society that presents itself as normal and sane, but which is deeply irrational and pathological.[50]

Late capitalism in its latest national-international phase of flexible accumulation is becoming increasingly dominant at home and abroad. In this way, it can seem irresistible and overpowering. Important, therefore, are not only organic intellectuals and groups who unceasingly, in season and out of season, point out the deep contradictions and weaknesses and loopholes of this system; as well, we need continual efforts to organize disparate groups into an organized whole and to thematize and theorize a unity that up to this point has remained merely implicit, a unity in multiplicity that would begin to mount an effective resistance to the ongoing insanity of the NWO. And finally, we need groups and communities that in their way of living anticipate the liberated society that is trying to be born. Let a thousand, let ten thousand, let a million base communities bloom.

Conclusion

Ideology and social critique, massive organization and action, and individual and communal radical lifestyle, then, constitute a kind of blessed trinity of resistance, each leading into the other and mediating the other. Critique that does not lead to public organization and action is ineffective and incomplete; organization and resistance not rooted in and flowing from roots in personal and communal lifestyles is ungrounded, inconsistent, and inconstant; individual and communal lifestyle not nourished both by critique and organization will become too privatistic, isolated, and simplistic.

Secular and religious sources can nourish this trinity. Ideology critique, as I have already argued, has a religious as well as a secular component. Communal praxis and resistance can take secular forms, as in parts of the antiwar movement and feminist movement, or religious forms, as in the Plowshares movement; or both can work together, as in the antinuclear movement. Individual and communal living can be dominantly secular, as in the South End Collective that produces *Z Magazine* and publishes many radical books; or dominantly religious, as in the Catholic Worker Movement or forms of Quaker resistance.

On the lived level of praxis, therefore, opposites such as contemplation and action, universal and particular, tradition and innovation, secular and religious, private and public can be, as I have argued throughout this book, linked and reconciled. A fully effective praxis of resistance needs to embody such mediation theoretically and practically. There is no fully effective action without contemplation, no effective praxis without theorizing, no adequate universality without respect for and immersion in particularity, no effective public resistance without roots in personal and communal living, no effective social and communal living without leadership of organic intellectuals that relate to this community dialogally and democratically.

∽᷍᷍᷍ᢒ

Notes

Preface

1. I derive this distinction between foundational and systematic theology from David Tracy, *The Analogical Imagination* (New York: Crossroads, 1981), 47–82.

2. CAL, 291–92. I will fill out the imperialistic aspects of flexible accumulation in chapters 15 and 16 of this work.

3. The emphasis in this sentence should be on "conceptually systematic" and "philosophy." Others such as Stringfellow and Berrigan and Meyers have worked out powerful hermeneutical, biblically based theologies of liberation in a North American context.

Chapter One

1. I am choosing these three critiques of metaphysics because they are linked in a genealogical way in the tradition of Western, continental philosophy. Because Heidegger consciously links up with Kant while going beyond him, and similarly Derrida with Heidegger while trying to deepen his critique and complete it, the three comprise a developing unity. It seems to me, also, that these are the three most fundamental and most influential critiques of metaphysics; other critiques flow from them and depend on them.

2. Immanuel Kant, *Critique of Pure Reason*, trans. Norman Kemp Smith (New York: St. Martin's Press, 1965), 65–175.

3. Ibid., 257–75.

4. Ibid., 21–23.

5. Ibid., 65–67. PCM, 47.

6. Kant, *Critique*, 220–22.

7. See PCM, 47–54, for further, more detailed development of this point.

8. Kant, *Critique*, 257–75, 195–244.

9. Edmund Husserl, *Formal and Transcendental Logic*, trans. Dorion Cairns (The Hague: Martinus Nijhoff, 1969), 278.

10. Kant, *Critique*, 327–67. Bernard Lonergan, *Insight: A Study of Human Understanding* (New York: Longman's Green and Co., 1957), 341.

11. PCM, 106–14.

12. Ibid.

13. Ibid. Lonergan, *Insight*, 339–42.

14. PCM, 183–238. CAL, 17–45, 64–70.

15. Lonergan, *Insight*, 672–77.

16. Jürgen Habermas, *Theory of Communicative Action*, vol. I, *Reason and the Rationalization of Society*, trans. Thomas McCarthy (Boston: Beacon Press, 1984), 1–39. It might be that Habermas could be said to be advocating an ontology insofar as the three major speech acts refer to domains of the world: constative acts to the physical world, regulative speech acts to the moral, human world, and expressive speech acts to subjective, inner human nature.

17. Edmund Husserl, *The Crisis of European Sciences and Transcendental Phenomenology*, trans. David Carr (Evanston: Northwestern University Press, 1970), 389. It is important to note that this is not Husserl's claim, but rather he is attributing this view to others.

18. Martin Heidegger, "What is Metaphysics?" trans. F.F.C. Hull and Alan Crick, in *Existence and Being* (Chicago: Henry Regnery Company, 1949), 349–61. *What is Called Thinking*, trans. J. Glenn Gray and Fred Wieck (New York: Harper & Row, 1968), 143.

19. *What is Called Thinking*, 6.

20. Martin Heidegger, *The Question Concerning Technology and Other Essays*, trans. William Lovitt (New York: Harper & Row, 1977), 131.

21. Ibid., 168.

22. Ibid., 118–28.

23. Ibid., 16.

24. Heidegger, *What is Called Thinking*, 212. *The Piety of Thinking*, trans. James C. Hart and John C. Maraldo (Bloomington: Indiana University Press, 1976), 22–31. *On the Way to Language*, trans. Peter D. Hertz (New York: Harper & Row, 1971), 74, quotation from 108.

25. *The Piety of Thinking*, 26–27.

26. Paul Ricoeur, *The Rule of Metaphor*, trans. Robert Czerny, with Kathleen McLaughlin and John Costello (Toronto: University Press, 1977), 312.

27. PCM, 75–89.

28. Ibid., 45–54, 81–82.

29. Ibid., 82.

30. Ibid., 83.

31. Ibid., 82–83.

32. Ibid., 85.

33. Ibid., 83.

34. Ibid., 84.

35. Ibid., 84–85. Jean-Paul Sartre, *Being and Nothingness*, trans. Hazel Barnes (New York: Citadel Press, 1964), 3–45.

36. PCM, 86–89.

37. Ricoeur, *The Rule of Metaphor*, 311–12.

38. Bernard Lonergan, *Method in Theology* (New York: Herder & Herder, 1972), 3–25. Husserl, *Formal and Transcendental Logic*, 56–62. PCM, 112.

39. Hans-Georg Gadamer, *Truth and Method*, trans. Garrett Barden and John Cumming (New York: Seabury Press, 1978), xi–xii. PCM, 111–12.

40. Paul Ricoeur, *The Philosophy of Paul Ricoeur*, ed. Charles Reagan and David Stewart (Boston: Beacon Press, 1978), 165–68. *Hermeneutics and the Human Sciences*, ed. John B. Thompson (Cambridge: Cambridge University Press, 1981), 131–44. PCM, 176–77.

41. Husserl, *Crisis*, 16–18.

42. Ricoeur, *Hermeneutics and the Human Sciences*, 87–100. Hans-Georg Gadamer, *Philosophical Hermeneutics*, trans. David Linge (Berkeley: University of California Press, 1976), 26–42.

43. Jacques Derrida, *Of Grammatology*, trans. Gayatri Chakravorty Spivak (Baltimore: The Johns Hopkins University Press, 1976), 20.

44. Jacques Derrida, *Margins of Philosophy*, trans. Alan Bass (Chicago: University of Chicago Press, 1982), 3–27.

45. Derrida, *Of Grammatology*, 3–14. Rodolphe Gasché, *The Tain of the Mirror: Derrida and the Philosophy of Reflection* (Cambridge: Harvard University Press, 1986), 271–83.

46. Derrida, *Margins of Philosophy*, quotation from 22. Gasché, *The Tain of the Mirror*, 163–76. *Of Grammatology*, 157–65. *Positions*, trans. Alan Bass (Chicago: University of Chicago Press, 1981), 12, 41, 74–82.

47. Ludwig Wittgenstein, *Tractatus Logico-Philosophicus*, trans. D.F. Pears and B.F. McGuiness (London: Routledge and Kegan Paul, 1961), 151. James L. Marsh, Merold Westphal, and John Caputo, *Modernity and Its Discontents* (Bronx: Fordham University Press, 1992), 90–92, hereafter referred to as MAD.

48. Derrida, *Positions*, 12, 41.

49. MAD, 169–73, 199–200. Jacques Derrida, *The Post Card: From Socrates to Freud and Beyond*, trans. Alan Bass (Chicago: University of Chicago Press, 1981), 219.

50. Derrida, *Of Grammatology*, 3–93.

51. MAD, 89–91.

52. Ibid., 91–92.

53. Jacques Derrida, *Limited Incorporated*, ed. Gerald Graff (Evanston: Northwestern University Press, 1988). *Spectres of Marx*, trans. Peggy Kamuf (New York: Routledge & Kegan Paul, 1994). *The Other Heading*, trans. Pascale-Anne Brault and Michael B. Nass (Bloomington: Indiana University Press, 1992).

54. On the transition from Heidegger I to Heidegger II, see William Richardson, *Heidegger: Through Phenomenology to Thought*, 2nd ed. (The Hague: Martinus Nijhoff, 1967).

55. PCM, 143–57.

56. CAL, 64–74.

57. Ibid., 97–102.

58. MAD, 105–06.

59. Quotations from Derrida, *Writing and Difference*, trans. Alan Bass (Chicago: Chicago University Press, 1982), 21, 24. PCM, 118–22.

60. CAL, 219–34.

61. Ibid.

62. Gasché, *The Tain of the Mirror*, 177–251. *Positions*, 3–4, 14, 40, 46. *Margins of Philosophy*, 227.

63. Lonergan, *Insight*, 348–54. I will develop this idea of being as heuristic notion in the next chapter.

64. Ibid., 530–49. Gabriel Marcel, *Creative Fidelity*, trans. Robert Rosthal (New York: Noonday Press, 1964). Consider, 63–64, the following claim: "Whoever philosophizes *hic* and *nunc*, is, it may be said, a prey of reality; he will never become completely accustomed to the fact of existing; existence is inseparable from a certain astonishment . . . Personally I am inclined to deny that any work is philosophical if we cannot discern in it what may be called the sting of reality."

65. PCM, 112–14. CAL, 75–86.

66. Heidegger, "What is Metaphysics?," 356–61. Lonergan, *Insight*, 387–88. CAL, 44.

67. PCM, 23–29, 45–72, 125–57, 160–80, 183–97, 200–30. CAL, 17–45, 132–33, 174–76, 179–86.

68. See PCM, 166, and CAL, 32–33, for an account of the criterion or canon of comprehensiveness.

69. Alfred North Whitehead, *Process and Reality*, eds. David Ray Griffin and Donald Sherburne (New York: Free Press, 1978), 35.

70. When I use "church" here, I will be referring to the three main churches in the United States—Protestantism, Catholicism, and Jewish. When I intend a more specific referent, I will so indicate in the text.

71. See Whitehead, *Process and Reality*, 342–43, in which he talks about "Caesar conquering" in the existing religious practice not only of Christianity but also of Judaism and Eastern religion. Thus, very early we see how metaphysics has a political, critical, liberating function.

72. For Lonergan's formulation of authenticity as self-transcendence, see *Method in Theology*, 104–5. For "exteriority," see Enrique Dussel, *Philosophy of Liberation*, trans. Aquilina Martinez and Christine Morkovsky (Marynoll, N.Y.: Orbis Books, 1985), 39–49.

Chapter Two

1. Kant, *Critique of Pure Reason*, 17–37.

2. Lonergan, *Insight*, xvii–xxx.

3. PCM, 109–14.

4. Ibid.

5. Lonergan, *Insight*, 250–54.

6. See my critique of this position in PCM, 160–80.

7. CAL, 192–98.

8. See my critique of structuralism and poststructuralism in CAL, 17–45; and of Descartes in PCM, 6–13.

9. PCM, 13–24, 54–72.

10. Heidegger, *The Question Concerning Technology and Other Essays*, 115–54. Lonergan, *Insight*, 372, 412–16.

11. Lonergan, *Insight*, 348–57.

12. PCM, 109.

13. Lonergan, *Insight*, 348–50.

14. Ibid., 484–85.

15. Ibid., 391–92.

16. Ibid., 392.

17. Ibid.

18. Ibid., 399–400.

19. Ibid.

20. Ibid., 392–93.

21. PCM, 178–79. CAL, 3–16.

22. PCM, 45–54. CAL, 265–89.

23. Lonergan, *Insight*, 393.

24. Ibid., 431–32.

25. Ibid., 432.

26. Ibid., 434–37.

27. Ibid., 271–78, 499–592.

28. Ibid., 484–85.

29. Ibid., 125–26, 484–85.

30. Ibid., 118–19.

31. Ibid., 451–52, 458–60.

32. Ibid.

33. CAL, 198–205.

34. Lonergan, *Insight*, 444–47.

35. Ibid., 445–48.

36. Ibid., 447. CAL, 205–18.

37. Lonergan, *Insight.*, 459.

38. Ibid., 451–52. CAL, 205–18.

39. CAL, 192–98. *Insight*, 452–53.

40. Lonergan, *Insight*, 453–54.

41. Ibid., 461–62.

42. Ibid., 463–67. CAL, 22–23. Thomas Kuhn, *The Structure of Scientific Revolutions* (Chicago: University of Chicago Press, 1962), 10–22. Lonergan, *Method in Theology*, 27–29. Sigmund Freud, *A General Introduction to Psychoanalysis*, trans. Joan Riviere (New York: Pocket Books, 1953), 25–27, 32–43, 331–34.

43. Lonergan, *Insight*, 460–61.

44. Ibid., 463–65.

45. Ibid., 467–69.

46. PCM, 112–14. CAL, 4–7, 174–76.

47. Lonergan, *Insight*, 470–72. CAL, 54–56.

48. Lonergan, *Insight*, 473–74.

49. Ibid., 475. Quotation from St. Augustine, *The Confessions of St. Augustine*, trans. John Ryan (New York: Image Books, 1960), 194.

50. PCM, 112–14. CAL, 22–27, 174–76, 192–218.

51. PCM, 212–30. CAL, 219–34, 265–89.

52. Whitehead, *Process and Reality*, 211.

53. PCM, 112–30.

54. See CAL, 174–76, for a discussion of radical political conversion as an expression of intellectual and existential authenticity. See CAL, 64–67, 77–89, 109–14, for an initial discussion of intellectual conversion.

55. CAL, 175–76.

56. Herbert Marcuse, *One-Dimensional Man* (Boston: Beacon Press, 1964), 1–19. The alert reader may have noticed a similarity to Levinas for whom metaphysics is also ethical-political. I confess to being inspired by Levinas; indeed I have already used his notion of the other in CAL, 174–76, 179–86. But I lift up his postmodern or quasi-postmodern insight into the context of a critical modernist hermeneutics, ethics, critical theory, and metaphysics giving explicit, mediated, normative content to a phenomenological sense of the other that otherwise, in Levinas's hands, remains too immediate and indeterminate. The real other is the concrete other, excluded, marginalized, and exploited by late capitalism and known as such in the light of normative ethics and neo-Marxist hermeneutics and metaphysics. I do not find the problem that Levinas has with the phenomenological accessibility of the other; indeed I have given my own account of that issue in PCM, 128–33. His valid description of the other, therefore, needs to be complemented by an explicit universalistic, normative ethics, hermeneutics, and metaphysics. Also my metaphysical sense of ethical otherness is derived and sublated, not proper. The proper account of the ethical other occurs in CAL on the level of objective spirit. Moreover, ethical exteriority is not outside of being properly conceived but only outside being conceived by ontologies and forms of metaphysics defending and reflecting an oppressive political center. Moreover, I do not think that Levinas adequately distinguishes between a perceptual and an ethical sense of the other. Well-heeled New Yorkers on a subway train have no problem perceiving the other; they just ignore her or him ethically because they have a different ethic and hermeneutic. This is the reason that, against Levinas, I insist on the mediated ethical knowing of the other. For his account of the other, see *Totality and Infinity*, trans. Alphonso Lingis (Pittsburgh: Dusquene University Press, 1969), 187–219.

57. Marcuse, *One-Dimensional Man*, 1–19.

58. Heidegger, *The Question Concerning Technology*, 36–49.

59. PCM, 200–230. CAL, 166–72, 265–89, 313–55. G.W.F. Hegel, *Hegel's Philosophy of Right*, trans. T. M. Knox (London: Oxford University Press, 1967), 13.

Chapter Three

1. See John Courtney Murray, *The Problem of God* (New Haven: Yale University Press, 1964), 119–21.

2. Friedrich Nietzsche, *Thus Spake Zarathustra*, in *The Portable Nietzsche*, trans. Walter Kaufmann (New York: Viking Press, 1954), 124–25, 137–39, 171, 305,

308–9, 399. *Twilight of the Idols* in *The Portable Nietzsche*, 481–83. *Geneology of Morals and Ecce Homo*, 147–48. *Beyond Good and Evil*, 202–6. Quotation from *Thus Spoke Zarathustra*, 125.

    3. Jean-Paul Sartre, *Being and Nothingness*, 418. See lviii–lix. I am using this argument from Sartre's existentialist period because it is the clearest statement of his atheism and because he does not seem to have altered his position later on sufficiently to change his mind about God. On this question of the ambiguous, inconsistent, and not totally convincing move of the later Sartre to a more receptive, limited freedom, see Wilfrid Desan, *The Marxism of Jean-Paul Sartre* (Garden City, N.Y.: Anchor Books, 1966), 265–68.

    4. Jean-Paul Sartre, *Being and Nothingness*, 228–78.

    5. Ibid., 266, 397–99. *Existentialism and Human Emotions*, trans. Bernard Frechtman and Hazel E. Barnes (New York: Wisdom Library, 1957), 12–17.

    6. Jean-Paul Sartre, "Consciousness of Self and Knowledge of Self," *Readings in Existential Phenomenology*, ed. Nathanial Lawrence and Daniel O'Connor (Englewood Cliffs, N.J.: Prentice-Hall, 1967), 126–33.

    7. Charles Hartshorne, *Divine Relativity* (New Haven: Yale University Press, 1948), 110–15.

    8. David Hume, *Dialogues Concerning Natural Religion* (New York: Hafner Publishing Company, 1966), 66–70. See my discussion of Marcel and mystery in chapter 5.

    9. Whitehead, *Process and Reality*. Hartshorne, *Creative Synthesis and Philosophic Method* (LaSalle, Ill.: Open Court, 1967). Hegel, *Phenomenology of Spirit*, trans. A. V. Miller (London: Clarendon Press, 1977). For a reading of Hegel as a process metaphysician of spirit and defending a notion of God as process and as spirit, see Quentin Lauer, *Hegel's Concept of God* (Albany: State University of New York Press, 1982).

    10. Whitehead, *Process and Reality*, 351.

    11. Hartshorne, *Creative Synthesis and Philosophic Method*, 99–130.

    12. On this notion of God as supremely relative, see Hartshorne, *The Divine Relativity*, 1–59. Marcel, *Creative Fidelity*, 38–57.

    13. Hartshorne, *The Divine Relativity*, 1–59.

    14. Ibid., 32–33.

    15. Hartshorne, *Omnipotence and Other Mistakes* (Albany: SUNY Press, 1984), 26–27.

    16. Ibid., 17–18.

    17. Ibid., 44–49.

    18. Ibid., 69–86. Hartshorne, *Divine Relativity*, 23–24.

    19. Lonergan, *Insight*, 636–38.

    20. Ibid., 642–44.

    21. Ibid., 644. Hartshorne, *Omnipotence and Other Mistakes*, 26–27.

    22. Lonergan, *Insight*, 657–59.

    23. Ibid., 659–64. Hartshorne, *Omnipotence and Other Mistakes*, 119–26.

    24. Hartshorne, *Omnipotence and Other Mistakes*, 10–26, 69–72, 80–83. *Divine Relativity*, 137–42. Lonergan, *Insight*, 657–61.

    25. Hartshorne, *Omnipotence and Other Mistakes*, 10–26. *Divine Relativity*, 134–42.

26. Hartshorne, *Omnipotence and Other Mistakes*, 26–27.

27. Hartshorne, *Divine Relativity*, 19–22.

28. Ibid., 44–45, 120.

29. Ibid., 21–22. Hartshorne, *Omnipotence and Other Mistakes*, 121–26.

30. Gerard Manley Hopkins, "God's Grandeur," in *A Hopkins Reader*, ed. W.H. Gardner and N.M. McKenzie (New York: Oxford University Press, 1970), 66.

31. PCM, 148–55. Marcel, *Creative Fidelity*, 70–72.

32. Dorothy Sölle, *The Window of Vulnerability*, trans. Linda M. Moloney (Minneapolis: Fortress Press, 1990), 70–74.

33. Hartshorne, *Omnipotence and Other Mistakes*, 10–18. *Divine Relativity*, 148–49. Whitehead, *Process and Reality*, 342–43.

Chapter Four

1. Marcel, *Creative Fidelity*, 58–80. Heidegger, *The Question Concerning Technology*, 155–82.

2. PCM, 220–30. CAL, 265–89.

3. PCM, 45–72. CAL, 243–47. Susan Muto and Adrian Van Kaam, *Formation for Becoming Spiritually Mature* (Pittsburgh: Epiphany Association, 1991), 166–71. Lonergan, *Insight*, 451–52, 471–72. On indirect communication, see Kierkegaard, *Concluding Unscientific Postscript*, trans. David F. Swenson and Walter Lowrie (Princeton: Princeton University Press, 1968), 68–74. On second naivete, see Paul Ricoeur, *Freedom and Nature*, trans. Brazim Kohik (Evanston: Northwestern University Press, 1966), 466–73. *Symbolism of Evil*, trans. Emerson Buchanan (New York: Harper & Row, 1967), 348–57.

4. Heidegger, "What is Metaphysics," 356–61.

5. CAL, 60. A.J. Ayer, *Language, Truth, and Logic* (New York: Dover, 1950), 1–19.

6. Lonergan, *Insight*, 671.

7. Ibid., 671–72.

8. Ibid., 685. Kant, *The Critique of Pure Reason*, 298–303, 362, 627.

9. Lonergan, *Insight*, 339–42.

10. Jean-Luc Marion, *God Without Being: Hors Texte*, trans. Thomas Carlson (Chicago: University of Chicago Press, 1991).

11. Lonergan, *Insight*, 671–72. Charles Hartshorne, *Anselm's Discovery* (LaSalle, Ill.: Open Court, 1965), 83, 115, 163.

12. See my discussion of this point in Marsh, Caputo, and Westphal, MAD, 99–105.

13. PCM, 163–69. Gadamer, *Truth and Method*, 325–41.

14. CAL, 70–71, 97–109.

15. Lonergan, *Insight*, 276–77. *Method*, 6, 94, 305, 352–53.

16. Lonergan, *Insight*, 651–52.

17. Ibid., 652–53.

18. Ibid., 19–25, 666–69.

19. Ibid., 653–55.

20. Ibid., 655–57.

21. Ibid., 672–74.

22. Friederich Nietzsche, *The AntiChrist*, in *The Portable Nietzsche*, ed. and trans. Walter Kaufmann (New York: Penguin, 1954), 631–32.

23. The quotation about the "lonely island" is taken from Lonergan, *Insight*, 400. He was talking about Thomism; in my text I am talking about a phenomenologically and hermeneutically based theism. The quotation from Shakespeare is from *Hamlet*, in *William Shakespeare: The Complete Works* (London: Collins, 1951), Act I, scene 5, lines 166–67, 1038.

24. Marcel, *Creative Fidelity*, 38–57.

25. The quotation is from Shakespeare, *Macbeth*, in *The Complete Works*, Act V, scene 5, lines 26–28, 1025.

Chapter Five

1. See PCM, 45–182, for my development of receptivity on perceptual, intellectual, volitional, social, and hermeneutical levels; CAL, 59–74, 113–76, for discussions of receptivity on the levels of communicative praxis and morality.

2. Gabriel Marcel, *The Philosophy of Existentialism*, trans. Manya Harari (3rd ed.; New York: Citadel Press, 1963), 82–83. *Creative Fidelity*, 27–29, 88–92. *Reflection and Mystery*, vol. 1 of *The Mystery of Being* (2 vols.; Chicago: Henry Regnery & Co., 1960), 79, 83–85. PCM, 96–99.

3. Marcel, *Creative Fidelity*, 33. PCM, 143–57.

4. Marcel, *Creative Fidelity*, 32–35.

5. Ibid., 40, 51–52. PCM, 148–57.

6. Marcel, *Creative Fidelity*, 54. *Homo Viator*, trans. Emma Crawford (New York: Harper & Row, 1962), 18–19. PCM, 242–43. CAL, 278–79.

7. Marcel, *Creative Fidelity*, 50–51.

8. Marcel, *Homo Viator*, 15–19.

9. Marcel, *Creative Fidelity*, 47–49.

10. Ibid., 49.

11. Marcel, *Homo Viator*, 24–25.

12. Ibid. *Creative Fidelity*, 91–92.

13. Marcel, *The Philosophy of Existentialism*, 23–25, 33–36. *Creative Fidelity*, 70. *Tragic Wisdom and Beyond*, trans. Stephen John and Peter McCormick (Evanston, Ill.: Northwestern University Press, 1973), 118–19. *Reflection and Mystery*, 162. PCM, 212–30, 247–50.

14. Marcel, *Homo Viator*, 19–26. *Creative Fidelity*, 45–47.

15. Gabriel Marcel, *Being and Having* (New York: Harper Torchbooks, 1965), 131–32, 172–73.

16. Marcel, *Creative Fidelity*, 22–23, 68–71. *Tragic Wisdom and Beyond*, 235.

17. Marcel, *Tragic Wisdom and Beyond*, 6–7.

18. Quotation from Marcel, *Creative Fidelity*, 63–64. *The Existential Background of Human Dignity* (Cambridge: Harvard University Press, 1963), 7–12.

19. Marcel, *Tragic Wisdom and Beyond*, 11–15.

20. Marcel, *Creative Fidelity*, 28–29, 91.

21. Ibid., 36–37, 51. *Being and Having*, 22, 96–97. *Faith and Reality*, vol. II of *Mystery of Being*, 119–20.

22. Marcel, *Creative Fidelity*, 67, 99–100. *Reflection and Mystery*, 186–89.

23. Marcel, *Creative Fidelity*, 99–101.

24. Ibid., 145–46. *Faith and Reality*, 97–98. Quotation from *Being and Having*, 69.

25. Marcel, *Being and Having*, 123. *Reflection and Mystery*, 210–15. *Faith and Reality*, 97–98, 117–18.

26. Marcel, *Creative Fidelity*, 147–67.

27. Marcel, *Homo Viator*, 46.

28. Ibid., 48.

29. Marcel, *Faith and Reality*, 112–17.

30. Marcel, *Being and Having*, 125. *Creative Fidelity*, 68–69, 145.

31. Marcel, *Creative Fidelity*, 174–83.

32. Lonergan, *Method in Theology*, 104–17.

Chapter Six

1. PCM, 200–58. CAL, 173–76, 265–312.

2. Wayne Hudson, *The Marxist Philosophy of Ernst Bloch* (London: Macmillan, 1982). Russell Kleinbach, *Marx via Process* (Washington, D.C.: University Press of America, 1982).

3. Whitehead, *Process and Reality*, 18–30.

4. Karl Marx and Friedrich Engels, *The German Ideology*, ed. C.J. Arthur (New York: International Publishers, 1970), 39–95. Marx, *Grundrisse*, trans. Martin Nicolaus (New York: Vintage Books, 1973), 155–65. Carol Gould, *Marx's Social Ontology* (Cambridge, Mass.: MIT Press, 1978), 3–39.

5. Whitehead, *Process and Reality*, 290; see 310.

6. Marx, *Economic and Philosophical Manuscripts of 1844* ed. Dirk Stuick, trans. Martin Milligan (New York: International Publishers, 1964), 137.

7. Whitehead, *Process and Reality*, 166–67; Marx, *Grundrisse*, 158, 162.

8. Whitehead, *Process and Reality*, 284; Karl Marx, *18th Brumaire* (New York: International Publishers, 1963), 15.

9. Whitehead, *Process and Reality*, 43–46; Marx, *Economic and Philosophical Manuscripts*, 106–19; see PCM, 92–106 for my reflection on motivated freedom.

10. Whitehead, *Process and Reality*, 222.

11. Ibid., 22–23, 232–33. See also William Christian, *An Interpretation of Whitehead's Metaphysics* (New Haven: Yale University Press, 1959), 49–50.

12. Whitehead, *The Function of Reason* (Boston: Beacon Press, 1966), 8–9, 80–90.

13. Marx, *Grundrisse*, 298–99, 408–9, quotation from 409. See also Gould, *Marx's Social Ontology*, 40–68.

14. Marx, *Economic and Philosophical Manuscripts*, 134. With reference to Whitehead's thought noted above in the beginning of this paragraph, see *Process and Reality*, 175–80.

15. Christian, *An Interpretation of Whitehead's Metaphysics*, 119.

16. Marx, *Economic and Philosophical Manuscripts*, 106–19, 170–93. See my account of objectification in PCM, 75–89.

17. Whitehead, *Process and Reality*, quotation from 212; see 178–79, 186–87.

18. Marx, *Economic and Philosophical Manuscripts*, 139; see the whole of the argument which extends from 138–41.

19. Ibid., 140–42, 147–48, 165–69.

20. Whitehead, *Process and Reality*, 28. See also *Adventures in Ideas* (New York: Philosophical Library, 1947), 129; and Christian, *An Interpretation of Whitehead's Metaphysics*, 161, 207–8, 246.

21. Marx, *Grundrisse*, 304–18. Bertell Ollman, *Alienation: Marx's Conception of Man in Capitalist Society* (Cambridge: University Press, 1971), 27–42.

22. Whitehead, *Process and Reality*, 341.

23. Marx, *Grundrisse*, 155–65, 471–514.

24. Whitehead, *Process and Reality*, 47, 246–47, 283; Christian, *An Interpretation of Whitehead's Metaphysics*, 376–77. See my chapters 3 and 4 for my own systematic development of these points.

25. Whitehead, *Process and Reality*, 351.

26. Marx, *Economic and Philosophical Manuscripts*, 144–46.

27. Herbert Marcuse, *One-Dimensional Man* (Boston: Beacon Press, 1964), 1–18. See also Jürgen Habermas, *Towards a Rational Society*, trans. Jeremy Shapiro (Boston: Beacon Press, 1970), 90–122.

28. Gould, *Marx's Social Ontology*, 129–78. See also Marx, *Grundrisse*, 155–65. "On the Jewish Question," in *Karl Marx: Early Writings*, trans. and ed. T.B. Bottomore (New York: McGraw Hill, 1963), 13–14.

29. Jürgen Habermas, *Legitimation Crisis*, trans. Thomas McCarthy (Boston: Beacon Press, 1975), x–xxiv.

30. Whitehead, *Process and Reality*, 40, 44–45. See also Christian, *An Interpretation of Whitehead's Metaphysics*, 198–207. I am certainly not unmindful here of Whitehead's complaints about the philosophical inadequacy of the terms *particular* and *universal*. While agreeing with his criticisms, I employ these objectionable terms both here and later in the book, however, to best fit the historical context of my subject matter.

31. Marcuse, *One-Dimensional Man*, 215–16. Whitehead, *Process and Reality*, 101–2. On surplus value and reduction or substitution of living to dead labor, see *Grundrisse*, 304–10, 333–54, 690–95. I am indebted to my student, friend, and colleague, Anne Pomeroy, for her insights into the relation between the organic and inorganic and capitalism, and her linking of surplus value in Marx with creative novelty in Whitehead; her dissertation on Marx and Whitehead develops these notions in an extremely fruitful manner. In the meantime, consult her "Dissertation Proposal: Marx and Whitehead: A Process Reading of Capitalism."

32. The necessary interrelationship of freedom and necessity shows how much Whitehead has in common with the dialectical tradition of modern philosophy running from Hegel through Marx to twentieth-century critical social theory. This affinity thus highlights from another perspective why Whitehead framed his own philosophy as a deliberate alternative to that of Kant and makes it all the more unfortunate that the former was so unfamiliar with that of Hegel.

33. Marx, *Grundrisse*, 83–85. See also Gould, *Marx's Social Ontology*, 13–30. See my development of this point in PCM, 239–58.

34. Whitehead, *Process and Reality*, 7; see *Science and the Modern World* (New York: Mentor Books, 1925), 72–90; *The Function of Reason* (Boston: Beacon Press, 1929), 43–44.

35. Whitehead, *The Aims of Education* (New York: Mentor Books, 1929), 13–26, 52–68.

36. Samuel Bowles and Herbert Gintis, *Schooling in Capitalist America* (New York: Basic Books, 1976). See also Michael Apple, *Ideology and Curriculum* (London: Routledge & Kegan Paul, 1979).

37. The notion of a "political metaphysics" is, to some extent, influenced and inspired by political theology in Europe, and liberation philosophy and theology in Latin America. For representative examples of each, see Johann Baptist Metz, *Faith in History and Society: Towards a Practical, Fundamental Theology*, trans. David Smith (New York: Seabury Press, 1980); Enrique Dussel, *Ethics and the Theology of Liberation*, trans. Bernard F. McWilliams (Maryknoll, N.Y.: Orbis Books, 1978).

38. PCM, 45–72, 92–122. CAL, 180–86.

39. CAL, 277–78, 319–20. Quotation from Hopkins, "The Grandeur of God," 66.

40. PCM, 182–230. CAL, 235–63.

41. On this issue of the link between capitalism and utility, see Marx, *The German Ideology*, 109–14.

42. Whitehead, *Process and Reality*, 18–19, 21, 29, 35–36, 103–9.

43. Ibid., 89–92, 103–9.

44. Ibid., 18–19, 42.

45. Ibid., 57–60.

46. PCM, 51–52.

47. An initial version of this essay co-authored with William Hamrick appeared in *Philosophy Today*, vol. 28 (Fall 1984): 191–202.

Chapter Seven

1.. Karl Rahner, *Hearers of the Word*, trans. Michael Richards (New York: Herder & Herder, 1969), 106–8.

2. Ibid., quotation from 108.

3. Ibid., 107.

4. Gabriel Marcel, *Creative Fidelity*, 68–69.

5. Lonergan, *Method in Theology*, 115.

6. Rahner, *Hearers of the Word*, 80–91.

7. Lonergan, *Insight*, 69–70.

8. Ibid., 623–24.

9. Herbert Marcuse, with Barrington Moore and Robert Paul Wolff, *A Critique of Pure Tolerance* (Boston: Beacon Press, 1965), 81–109.

10. Lonergan, *Insight*, 631–32.

11. Ibid., 696–703.

12. PCM, 160–80.

13. Ibid., 6. Lonergan, *Insight*, 707–18. Gadamer, *Truth and Method*, 235–74.

14. Lonergan, *Insight*, 718–20. PCM, 99–106. Kierkegaard, *Concluding Unscientific Postscript*, 30–35.

15. Lonergan, *Method in Theology*, 104–5.

16. Lonergan, *Insight*, 721–29.

17. Paul Ricoeur, *Symbolism of Evil*, trans. Emerson Buchanon (New York: Harper & Row, 1967), 347–57. *Interpretation Theory: Discourse and the Surplus of Meaning* (Fort Worth: Texas Christianity Press, 1976), 94–95. CAL, 30–31. PCM, 161–69.

18. See my discussion of decision as motivated lead in PCM, 92–106. On such massive evidence for a historicity of the New Testament, see Gerald O'Collins, *Christology: A Biblical Historical and Systematic Study of Jesus* (New York: Oxford University Press, 1995). Edward Schillebeeckx, *Jesus, an Experiment in Christology*, trans. Hubert Hoskins (New York: Crossroads, 1995). James D.G. Dunn, *The Evidence for Jesus* (Philadelphia: Westminster Press, 1985). Michael L. Cook, *The Historical Jesus* (Chicago: Thomas More Press, 1986). Hugo A. Meynell, *Is Christianity True?* (Washington, D.C.: Catholic University Press, 1994.

There are, of course, issues that need discussing in this claim about the historicity of the New Testament. All the above authors are unanimous in accepting the results of historical-critical research, which includes form criticism and source criticism, of the last 150 years. Among the conclusions that must be accepted is the rejection of any simple one-to-one correspondence between events or sayings of Jesus as recorded in the New Testament and actual historical fact. Sometimes the events and sayings are ascribed to Jesus in the oral traditions and New Testament writings that emerged after his death.

Nonetheless, all these authors are unanimous in claiming that there are many events and sayings that seem to have occurred as they have been recorded. Others, if they do not refer to actual historical fact, express actually the spirit of Jesus and his self-understanding and the way the community understood him. Some incidents that are recorded differently by two or more authors reflect a difference of emphasis in the writers' interpretation, but nonetheless, do not cast serious doubt on the reality of the event as it occurred. Such, for example, is the case with the healing of the centurion's servant in Matthew 8:5–13 and Luke 7:1–10; see Dunn, *The Evidence for Jesus*, 13–18.

Many of the deeds or sayings of Jesus claiming or implying divinity are in John's Gospel, which is much more theological and less historical than the synoptic gospels—Matthew, Mark, and Luke. Many of the deeds and sayings, therefore, may not have actually occurred as they are recorded, but they do seem to reflect Jesus' self-understanding and that of the community. On this point Schillebeeckx stresses the way in which the beloved disciple, John, was a disciple of Jesus but not one of the twelve disciples, that John's Gospel is rooted in a tradition of Greek-speaking, Jewish-Christians going all the way back to Jesus, that a good deal of John's Gospel is based on the synoptic gospels, and that John's Gospel is a great deal more historically accurate about the events in Jerusalem and Sumaria than the synoptic gospels. See Schillebeeckx, *Christ: The Experience of Jesus as Lord*, trans. John Bowden (New York: Crossroads Books, 1993), 344–45.

The appropriate kind of faith, therefore, is not a naive, dogmatic faith based on the immediate historical presence of the "already out there now real" but a postcritical faith that has absorbed all that historical-reflection has taught us about the New Testament but still affirms the reality and significance of the historical Jesus. Indeed it is hard not to agree with Schillebeeckx when he says that "we are led to conclude that the New Testament, not in spite of its diverse kerygmatic projects but because of them, gives us substantial information about Jesus of Nazareth, at least as reliably as any other serious secular book in the period" (*Jesus*, 437).

Finally, Schillebeeckx lists five criteria of historical authenticity in the New Testament. First, when an evangelist records something that goes against his theological bent, for example, when a gospel rails against *teos aner* Christianity—Jesus as the divine miracle man—yet nonetheless records miracles, then there is good reason to regard these as authentic. Second, there is the criterion of dual irreducibility. We can affirm as authentic what is reducible neither to Judaism nor to the practices of Christianity coming after Jesus—for example, Jesus submitting to John the Baptist's baptism.

Third, we note the principle of the cross-section: that a saying or deed occurs in different gospels or forms, parables, catacheses, liturgical passages, or miracle stories. Jesus dealing with publicans and sinners, for example, is recorded in no less than four different literary traditions. Consistency of content is also a criterion—for example, consistency of content between different sayings or between actions and sayings having to do with the importance of humility, poverty of spirit, and love. If Jesus were found in a certain episode to be seeking praise or fame, wealth or his own selfish ends, that episode would probably not be authentic. Finally, there is the execution criterion. Sayings and actions of Jesus that would very likely enrage authorities and lead up to his execution and death are likely to be authentic. Such criteria allow us to distinguish between sayings and actions in Jesus' life that occurred as they are described in the gospels, elements in Jesus' life so infused with a current ecclesiastical viewpoint that one can only say of them in general terms that a central core derives from Jesus and hence that historically authentic reminiscences manifestly do have a part to play in them, and sayings and acts probably performed by the earthly Jesus, in which nonetheless, the community, by attributing them to him, gives expression to what the Lord alive in its midst concretely signifies for it in the recollection of his life or death; hence, Jesus functions as the norm and criterion for authenticity and truth. *Jesus*, 91–98.

Finally, I note that recent scholarship has affirmed the untenability of the very sharp contrast between the supposedly historical gospels devoted to the earthly Jesus, and the supposedly unhistorical, theological Gospel of John devoted to Christ as God. There are not a few "Johanine" passages in the synoptics, and some of these come from very early strata of the synoptic tradition such as the reciprocal knowledge of Father and Son (Matthew 11:27; Luke 10:22); and, as remarks made above indicate, there is much historical material and continuity with very early oral traditions, and more evidence for single authorship in John than was previously thought. We conclude that the traditional conception of Jesus as God is not only not undermined by historical-critical inquiry into the New Testament, but is supported by such criticism, especially by much of the later criticism of the last 30 to 40 years. On this point, see Hugo Meynell, *Is Christianity True?*, 68–78.

19. The version of the New Testament that I am using here is *The New Testament*, Revised Edition (New York: Catholic Book Publishing Company, 1986).

20. O'Collins, *Christology*, 113–15. Dunn, *The Evidence for Jesus*, 30–52. Meynell, *Is Christianity True?*, 79–80.

21. O'Collins, *Christology*, 142–43, 320–21. The version of the Old Testament that I am using here is *The Old Testament* (New York: Guild Press). See also Elizabeth Johnson's *She Who Is* (New York: Crossroads, 1992), 76–103, in which she shows that in both Old and New Testaments numerous references to God as spirit, sophia, and mother, all with feminine denotations and connotations, occur.

22. Søren Kierkegaard, *Concluding Unscientific Postscript*, 352–53. *Fear and Trembling*, 103, 146–47, 213, and *Sickness Unto Death*, trans. Walter Lowrie (Garden City, N.Y.: Doubleday Anchor, 1954). Here I concur with David Tracy's cautions and reservations about any attempts to recover the historical Jesus independent of or outside of the New Testament and the original apostolic witness. Any attempts at a more immediate account have to be given up; the revelation of Jesus and Christ is one given through the New Testament and apostolic witness, see Tracy's *The Analogical Imagination*, 233–41, footnotes 20–23, 245.

Tracy does not deny the legitimacy of inquiry into what historians can tell us about Jesus on strictly historical grounds. Historical-critical inquiry has another role to play insofar as it serves as a critical, purifying inquiry into the New Testament itself. Tracy argues that both uses of historical-critical inquiry are important, but that the first is not necessary for belief and that the Christian tradition is the major constitutive mediating factor.

The point is that either form of historical-critical inquiry is richly mediated; none gives us the historical Jesus in any immediate sense. My procedure in this and following chapters is to blend the two when I use or draw on historical-critical method, but primarily in its second role of purifying, criticizing, and giving us deeper insight into Jesus as revealed in the New Testament and original apostolic witness. Here I agree with Tracy that the main point of such inquiry is to recover Jesus as a dangerous memory.

23. PCM, 32–39, 133–43.

24. Cook, *The Historical Jesus*, 65–108. Paul Ricoeur, *Time and Narrative*, I; trans. Kathleen McLaughlin and David Pellauer (Chicago: University of Chicago Press, 1984), 3–87.

25. St. John of the Cross, "Sayings of Light and Love," in *The Collected Works of St. John of the Cross*, trans. Kieran Kavanaugh and Otilio Rodriguez (Washington, D.C.: Institute of Carmelite Studies, ICS Publications, 1991), 97. Kierkegaard, *Concluding Unscientific Postscript*, 23–25. Rudolf Bultmann, *Jesus Christ and Mythology* (New York: Charles Scribner's Sons, 1958).

26. Lonergan, *Method in Theology*, 23–25.

27. Jon Sobrino, *Spirituality of Liberation: Toward Political Holiness*, trans. Robert R. Barr (Maryknoll, N.Y.: Orbis Books, 1985).

28. Hans Urs von Balthasar, *Prayer*, trans. A.V. Littledale (New York: Sheed & Ward, 1961), 11–31. Rahner, *Hearers of the Word*, 94–108.

29. Merold Westphal, *God, Guilt, and Death* (Bloomington: Indiana University Press, 1984), 122–59.

30. Ibid., 4–137.

31. Hegel, *Phenomenology of Spirit*, 453–93. Kierkegaard, *Concluding Unscientific Postscript*, 176–206.

32. CAL, 114–17. Schillebeeckx, *Jesus*, 575–612.

33. Obviously this issue of the relationship of Christianity and other religions is too big to receive adequate treatment here. I can only indicate to the reader what resources I think I have in my own account to begin to answer the question. For further bibliographical resources, see Westphal, *God, Guilt, and Death* and Meynell, *Is Christianity True?* Also the point about the ecumenical openness, dialogue, and willingness to learn from other religions is crucial. Here one example is Thomas Merton's profound sympathy with Buddhist, Muslim, and Sufist sources of revelation. See his *Witness to Freedom: Letters in Times of Crisis*, ed. William Shannon (New York: Farrar, Strauss, Giroux, 1996), 261–340.

Chapter Eight

1. Merold Westphal, *Suspicion and Faith: The Religious Uses of Modern Atheism* (Grand Rapids: William B. Eerdman, 1993), 229; hereafter referred to as SF.

2. Ibid., 13–14.

3. Ibid., 13.

4. Gerard Colby and Charlotte Dennett, *Thy Will Be Done: The Conquest of the Amazon: Nelson Rockefeller and Evangelism in the Age of Oil* (New York: Harper Collins, 1995). Jack Nelson-Pallmeyer, *Brave New World Order* (Maryknoll, N.Y.: Orbis Books, 1992), 133–57. Douglas Kellner, *The Persian Gulf T.V. War* (Boulder: Westview Press, 1992), 279–80, n. 15. Bush is quoted by Kellner as praying at Camp David before ordering the war. As he described this incident before a Baptist convention on June 6, 1991, Bush wiped tears away from his eyes. Bush here is acting similarly to McKinley before the Spanish-American War, and I will go into McKinley's "wrestling with God" later in this chapter.

5. SF, 283–89.

6. Ibid., 3–6. Karl Barth, *The Epistle to the Romans*, trans. Edwyn C. Hoskyns (New York: Oxford University Press, 1933), 389.

7. Sigmund Freud, *The Standard Edition of the Complete Psychological Works of Sigmund Freud*, ed. and trans. James Strachey (London: Hogarth, 1953–74), 21: 74. Hereafter in referring to the *Standard Edition*, I will be giving merely the name of the author, volume number, and page numbers. SF, 38.

8. PCM, 215–16, 226–27. CAL, 17–45, 60.

9. Freud, 21:31,33.

10. Freud, 21:81–85. SF, 54–56. Ricoeur, *Freud and Philosophy*, trans. David Savage (New Haven: Yale University Press, 1970), 234–35.

11. Freud, 21:5–20, 21, 30, 33, 72–74. SF, 53.

12. Freud, 22:76–77; 19: 23, 25, 53. SF, 36–37.

13. Freud, 22:80; 21: 76; 2: 351. SF, 37.

14. PCM, 182–83. Freud, *A General Introduction to Psychoanalysis*, 25–27, 32–43, 58–62, 331–34.

15. Freud, 5:608; 4:160. SF, 43–45.

16. Freud, 4:106–21. SF, 45–47.

17. Freud, 4:106–21. SF, 44–46.

18. Freud, 3:162, 49–79; 9:117; quotation is from 3:79. SF, 85–86.

19. Freud, 9:118–27. SF, 96–98.

20. Freud, 13:31–79. SF, 103–8.

21. Freud, 13:75–79. SF, 108–9.

22. *The Collected Works of St. John of the Cross*, 295–389.

23. Daniel Berrigan, *The Nightmare of God* (Portland: Sunburst Press, 1983), 3–4.

24. SF, 110.

25. Thomas Merton, *Contemplative Prayer* (Garden City, N.Y.: Image Books, 1971), 25.

26. SF, 229–30.

27. See PCM, 76–81; MAD, 11–21, 87–109, 197–215; CAL, 61–64, 75–86, 128–33, 222–24, 291–312, 328–29.

28. PCM, 76–81. Nietzsche, *On the Genealogy of Morals and Ecce Homo*, 77–79, 118–19, 136–39, 150–51.

29. SF, 223–24. Friedrich Nietzsche, *Human, All Too Human*, trans. Marion Faber (Lincoln: University of Nebraska Press, 1984), 96.

30. Nietzsche, *Genealogy of Morals*, 15–23, 25–33. SF, 221–22.

31. Nietzsche, *The Gay Science*, trans. Walter Kaufmann (New York: Vintage Books, 1974), 194. *The Antichrist*, 631–32.

32. Nietzsche, *Human, All Too Human*, 47.

33. Nietzsche, *Beyond Good and Evil*, 214–15. SF, 232–34.

34. Nietzsche, *Genealogy of Morals*, 33–34, 36–46, 54–55. SF, 232–37. *Beyond Good and Evil*, 202–6.

35. Nietzsche, *Genealogy of Morals*, 31–35, 88–96. 97–98, 125–28. SF, 238–44.

36. Nietzsche, *Genealogy of Morals*, 44–48. SF, 246–47.

37. T.S. Eliot, "The Love Song of J. Alfred Prufrock." *The Waste Land and Other Poems* (New York: Harvest Books, 1962), 7.

38. Quotation from Nietzsche, *Thus Spake Zarathustra*, 212. *Genealogy of Morals*, 46–48, 121–25. SF, 252–55.

39. Quotation from Gilles Deleuze and Felix Guattari, *Anti-Oedipus: Capitalism and Schizophrenia*, trans. Robert Hurley, Mark Seem, and Helen R. Lane (Minneapolis: University of Minnesota Press, 1983), xiii. Nietzsche, *Genealogy of Morals*, 73–76. *Thus Spake Zarathustra*, 205–8. SF, 256–58.

40. Mumia Abu Jamal, *Live from Death Row* (New York: Addison-Wesley, 1995). Noam Chomsky, "Rollback Part II," *Z Magazine*, vol. 8 (Feb. 1995): 20–31.

41. Nietzsche, *Geneaolgy of Morals*, 124. SF, 258–62. *Thus Spake Zarathustra*, 352–56, 375–79.

42. *Thus Spake Zarathustra*, 133–35, 183–86.

43. SF, 268–69.

44. Ibid., 275–76.

45. Ibid., 279–80, quotation from 180.

46. Ibid., 248–51. PCM, 110–14. CAL, 4–7, 113–76, 376–79, n. 52; and 389–90, n. 40.

47. Nietzsche, *Thus Spake Zarathustra*, 395, 153; quotation from 153.

48. Paulo Freire, *Pedagogy of the Oppressed*, trans. Myra Bergman Ramos (New York: Herder & Herder, 1972), 75–118.

49. PCM, 200–258. CAL, 173–74, 265–312, 392–94, n. 8. Michael Parenti, *Land of Idols* (New York: St. Martin's Press, 1994), 75, 78–79.

50. Carol Gould, *Marx's Social Ontology*. Rodney Peffer, *Marxism, Morality, and Justice* (Princeton: Princeton University Press, 1990). Ollman, *Alienation*. Michael Harrington, *The Twilight of Capitalism* (New York: Simon & Schuster, 1976). Melvin Rader, *Marx's Interpretation of History* (New York: Oxford University Press, 1972). Michael Novak, *Will It Liberate? Questions for Liberation Theology* (New York: Paulist Press, 1986), 145–50, 174–75. *The Spirit of Democratic Capitalism* (New York: Simon & Schuster, 1982), 189–206.

51. CAL, 172–76, 210–13, 260, 314.

52. Ludwig Feuerbach, *The Essence of Christianity*, trans. George Eliot (New York: Harper & Row, 1957), 6–14, 32, 73, 120, 153, 204. SF, 127–32.

53. SF, 134–40.

54. *Karl Marx: Selected Writings*, ed. David McLellan (New York: Oxford University Press, 1977), 64.

55. Ibid.

56. Ibid., 134–40.

57. *Karl Marx: Selected Writings*, 45.

58. Quoted by Reinhold Neibhur, *Moral Man and Immoral Society* (New York: Charles Scribner's Sons, 1960), 102.

59. SF, 147–53. I had one bracing encounter with the Pro-Life Movement as ideology when I appeared on a television program in St. Louis as a liberal-radical critic of the Pro-Life Movement during October, Pro-Life Month. When I argued that the Pro-Life Movement functioned as an expression and legitimation of late capitalism, I was met by outraged stares and comments by my two conservative interlocutors and put my yet-to-come tenure at a local Catholic university at severe risk.

60. Quotation from *Karl Marx: Selected Writings*, 176. Kellner, *The Persian Gulf T.V. War*, 59–60.

61. *Karl Marx: Selected Writings*, 167–68. SF, 159–60.

62. SF, 174–79.

63. Ibid., 180–81.

64. Ibid., 186–88.

65. Gustavo Gutiérrez, *A Theology of Liberation*, trans. Sister Caridad Inda and John Eagleson (Maryknoll, N.Y.: Orbis Books, 1973), 37.

66. SF, 195.

67. Ibid., 10–12, 205–7, quotation from 205.

68. SF, 206–7, and note 4–5, 207.

69. Ibid., 210–12; and 211, n. 5. Westphal notes other places in Amos where he considers the plight of the poor, such as 2:6–8; 3:9–10; 4:1; 5:7, 10–12, 15; 6:12; 8:4–6; and the luxury of the rich, such as 2:8; 3:10–11, 15; 4:1; 5:11; 6:1–8.

70. SF, 214–15. For the generic call, see Psalms 40:6–8; 15: 8; Ecclesiastes 5:1; Isaiah 66:1–4; Jeremiah 6:16–21; 7:21–23; 14:10–12; Hosea 8:11–13. On sacrifice as unnaceptable to God when there is injustice to the poor, see Proverbs 21:3; Michea 6:6–8; Isaiah 1, the temple sermon from Jeremiah 7, the whole book of Amos, Isaiah 38.

71. SF, 199–204.

72. Ibid., 212–16.

73. See *Economic Justice for All* (Washington, D.C.: National Conference of Catholic Bishops, 1986), 45–46, for one formulation of "the Option for the Poor."

74. Gutiérrez, *A Theology of Liberation*, 237–39.

Chapter Nine

1. Gutiérrez, *A Theology of Liberation*, 27–37. PCM, 195–97. CAL, footnote 52, 376–79; footnote 40, 389–90. Deleuze and Guattari, *Anti-Oedipus*, xv–xxiv. Nietzsche, *The Gay Science*. Herbert Marcuse, *Eros and Civilization* (New York: Vintage Books, 1961).

2. PCM, 200–230. CAL, 265–89.

3. For a sampling of this literature, consult Shlomo Avineri, *The Social and Political Thought of Karl Marx* (Cambridge: Cambridge University Press, 1970). Ollman, *Alienation*. Rader, *Marx's Interpretation of History*. Roslyn Wallach Bologh, *Dialectical Phenomenology: Marx's Method* (London: Routledge & Kegan Paul, 1979).

4. For one example of all three forms of critical transcendence, see Marx, *The Economic and Philosophical Manuscripts*.

5. Gutiérrez, *A Theology of Liberation*, 9–10, 29–30, 27–75, 284, footnote 51. Arthur F. McGovern, *Liberation Theology and Its Critics* (Maryknoll: Orbis Books, 1989), 140–55, 160–64.

6. McGovern, *Liberation Theology and Its Critics*, 140–55, 160–64. PCM, 200–230. CAL, 265–89.

7. Tony Smith, *Technology and Social Form: A Critique of Lean Production* (unpublished).

8. Michael Novak, *Will It Liberate?*

9. CAL, 162–76.

10. Gutiérrez, *A Theology of Liberation*, 21–37. Noam Chomsky, *Turning the Tide* (Boston: South End Press, 1985), 37, 39f., 45f., 58, 96f.

11. Noam Chomsky, *World Orders Old and New* (New York: Columbia University Press, 1994), 83–188, esp. 178–88.

12. Ibid. Larry Everest, "The Selling of Peru," *Z Magazine*, vol. 7 (Sept. 1994): 35–36.

13. Gutiérrez, *A Theology of Liberation*, 3–15.

14. Jon Sobrino, *Christology at the Crossroads*, trans. John Drury (Maryknoll, N.Y.: Orbis Books, 1979), 115–39.

15. Gutiérrez, *A Theology of Liberation*, 153–57. Jürgen Moltmann, *A Theology of Hope*, trans. James Leitch (New York: Harper & Row, 1967), 103–6, 116–20.

16. Moltmann, *A Theology of Hope*, 161–65.

17. CAL, 277–78, 295–99. Gutiérrez, *A Theology of Liberation*, 157–60.

18. Gutiérrez, *A Theology of Liberation*, 160–68. Moltmann, *A Theology of Hope*, 149–61, 189–229.

19. Sobrino, *Christology at the Crossroads*, 45. See Dean Brackley's *Divine Revolution* (Maryknoll, N.Y.: Orbis Books, 1996) for a discussion of salvation as integral liberation in all three senses.

20. Ibid., 47–48.

21. Ibid., 50–54.

22. Ibid., 55.

23. Leonardo Boff, *Passion of Christ, Passion of the World*, trans. Robert Barr (Maryknoll, N.Y.: Orbis Books, 1987), 20–21.

24. Ibid., 17–18.

25. Boff, *Jesus Christ, Liberator*, 91–92.

26. Sobrino, *Christology at the Crossroads*, 211–17. Gutiérrez, *A Theology of Liberation*, 226–32.

27. Gutiérrez, *A Theology of Liberation*, 276. Sobrino, *Christology at the Crossroads*, 115–39. McGovern, *Liberation Theology and Its Critics*, 21–22.

28. Daniel Berrigan, *Steadfastness of the Saints* (Maryknoll, N.Y.: Orbis Books, 1985). Bill Wylie Kellermann, *Seasons of Faith and Conscience* (Maryknoll, N.Y.: Orbis Books, 1991). CAL, 96–97, 350–51.

29. Sobrino, *Christology at the Crossroads*, 201–5. Boff, *Jesus Christ, Liberator*, 100–120.

30. Sobrino, *Christology at the Crossroads*, 221–24. Boff, *Jesus Christ, Liberator*, 118–19.

31. Sobrino, *Christology at the Crossroads*, 336–72, 376–77.

32. Ibid., 379–80.

33. Ibid., 292–99. Moltmann, *A Theology of Hope*, 216–29.

34. St. Catherine of Siena, *The Dialogue*, trans. Suzanne Noffke (New York: Paulist Press, 1980), 29–47, 64, 65. Suzanne Noffke, *Catherine of Siena: Vision through a Distant Eye* (Collegeville, Minn.: Liturgical Press, 1996), 11–37.

35. Johann Baptist Metz, *The Emergent Church* (London: SCM Press, 1981), 1–16. Leonardo Boff, *Church, Charism, and Power*, trans. John W. Diercksmeier (New York: Crossroads, 1985), 32–46, 108–24.

36. PCM, 169–80.

37. Johann Metz, *The Emergent Church. Faith in History and Society*, 88–91. PCM, 172–73. CAL, 107–9. Daniel Berrigan, *Minor Prophets, Major Themes* (Marion, S.D.: Fordkamp Books, 1995).

38. Metz, *The Emergent Church*, 1–16.

39. Ibid., 1–16, 82–94. Boff, *Church, Charism, and Power*, 32–46, 65–88, 108–24.

40. Metz, *The Emergent Church*, 82–94. Boff, *Ecclesiogenesis*, 23–33.

41. Metz, *The Emergent Church*, 82–106.

Chapter Ten

1. PCM, 45–72, 75–89, 111–14. I should note that I do not in these places explicitly describe self-appropriation in terms of intellectual conversion, but the basic content is there.

2. CAL, 174–76.

3. Ibid., 125–31.

4. Ibid., 132–39.

5. Ibid., 139–47.

6. Ibid., 162–63.

7. Ibid., 166–73.

8. Ibid., 174–76.

9. Lonergan, *Method in Theology*, 237–38.

10. Ibid., 20, 267–69.

11. Ibid., 243.

12. Quotation from Ibid., 238. CAL, 27–31, 39–40, 43–45. PCM, 62–72, 75–89, 110–14.

13. Lonergan, *Insight*, 271–75, 423–30. CAL, 37–40, 43–45.

14. Marx, *Grundrisse*, 459–524.

15. Marx, *Capital*, vol. 1, trans. Ben Fowkes (New York: Vintage Books, 1977), 125–31.

16. Ibid., 165.

17. Stuart Ewen, *Captains of Consciousness* (New York: McGraw Hill, 1976). John Kenneth Galbraith, *The Affluent Society* (New York: Mentor Books, 1958), 114–23.

18. Marx, *Grundrisse*, 266–75, 281–89.

19. Ibid., 163; Lukacs, *History and Class Consciousness*, trans. Rodney Livingstone (Cambridge, Mass.: MIT Press, 1971), 83–222. Max Horkheimer, *Critique of Instrumental Reason*, trans. Matthew J. O'Connell and others (New York: Herder & Herder, 1972), vii–x.

20. T.S. Eliot, *The Waste Land and Other Poems* (New York: Harvest Books, 1962), 8. Jürgen Habermas, *Towards a Rational Society*, trans. Jeremy Shapiro (Boston: Beacon Press, 1970), 90–122.

21. Marx, *Grundrisse*, 228–37, 239–64; *Capital*, I, 254. PCM, 212–30.

22. Marx, *Capital*, I, 429–38, 492–639; PCM, 223–34.

23. Marcuse, *One-Dimensional Man* (Boston: Beacon Press, 1964), 1–18. Habermas, *Towards a Rational Society*, 120–22. PCM, 224–28.

24. Bernard Tyrrell, *Bernard Lonergan's Philosophy of God* (Notre Dame: University of Notre Dame Press, 1974), 39. Plato, *The Republic*, trans. Paul Shorey, in *Plato: The Collected Dialogues*, eds. Edith Hamilton and Huntington Cairns (Princeton: Princeton University Press, 1961), 747–52.

25. Guy Debord, *Society of the Spectacle* (Detroit: Black and Red, 1983), paragraphs 12, 34.

26. Martin Heidegger, *Introduction to Metaphysics*, trans. Ralph Mannheim (Garden City: Anchor Books, 1961), 40–41; Lonergan, *Insight*, 225–34.

27. Lonergan, *Method in Theology*, 35–41, 241–42.

28. Lonergan, *Insight*, 596–604.

29. Ibid., 191–96, 218–236. *Method in Theology*, 240–42.

30. Lonergan, *Insight*, 79–80, quotation from 80.

31. Ibid., 79–81.

32. Max Horkheimer, *Critical Theory: Selected Essays*, trans. Matthew J. O'Connell and others (New York: Herder & Herder, 1972), 188–243. Ernst Bloch, *The Principle of Hope*, vol. 1, trans. Neville Plaice, Stephen Plaice, and Paul Knight (Cambridge, Mass.: MIT Press, 1986), 1–18. CAL, 351–54.

33. CAL, 332–36.

34. Marx, *Capital*, I, 280.

35. Marx, *Grundrisse*, 459–71.

36. U.S. Catholic Bishops, *Economic Justice for All*, 15.

37. Ibid., 65–165; Marx, *Economic and Philosophical Manuscripts*, 106–19. Harry Braverman, *Labor and Monopoly Capital: The Degradation of Work in the Twentieth Century* (New York: Monthly Review Press, 1974). CAL, 265–89.

38. Habermas, *Legitimation Crisis*, 111–14. U.S. Catholic Bishops, *Economic Justice for All*, 145–62.

39. William Domhoff, *Who Rules America?* (Englewood Cliffs, N.J.: Prentice-Hall, 1967). Charles Lindbloom, *Politics and Markets* (New York: Basic Books, 1977), 161–233. E.E. Schattschneider, *The Semisovereign People* (New York: Holt, Rinehart, and Winston, 1960). Habermas, *Towards a Rational Society*, 90–122. PCM, 228–30.

40. Lindbloom, *Politics and Markets*, 237–309. Andrew Arato, "Critical Sociology and Authoritarian State Socialism," in *Habermas: Critical Debates*, ed. John B. Thompson and David Held (Cambridge: MIT Press, 1982), 196–218. John Stuart Mill, *Utilitarianism and Other Writings*, ed. Mary Warnock (New York: Meridian Books, 1970), 126–83.

41. Michael Waltzer, *Spheres of Justice* (New York: Basic Books, 1983), 295–303. CAL, 168.

42. Kai Nielsen, *Equality and Liberty: A Defense of Radical Egalitarianism* (Totowa, N.J.: Rowman & Allenheld, 1985), 46–61, 78–99. CAL, 162–72.

43. Nielsen, *Equality and Liberty*, 191–277. CAL, 149–76. As I indicate in CAL, equality is complex, not simple or numerical. The implication of such a notion is that my model of socialism and justice allows for legitimate forms of inequality; see my fourth principle of justice, which is a modified version of Rawls's difference principle. Complex equality is preserved in my notion of justice and socialism in at least six ways, described on 163–64 of CAL.

1. We prohibit the illegitimate imposition of inequalities of one sphere of endeavor on another; one is not, for example, entitled to hold political office or exercise political influence just because one is wealthy.

2. Everyone has an equal right to negative freedom from state interference, infringements on privacy, and so on.

3. Everyone has an equal opportunity for holding office, participating in the basic social, economic, and political decisions affecting life, and finding meaningful work.

4. Everyone has an equal right to basic subsistence and security.

5. Everyone has a right to equal self-respect and worth of liberty—that is, the ability to effectively exercise and realize formally guaranteed freedom and equal opportunity, and this right is and should be compatible with legitimate difference.

6. Benefit to the least advantaged is a criterion for the legitimacy of difference. Equality here is complex and lies in the right of the least advantaged in a society to have one's own voice heard. Does this difference benefit one? If not, then the difference is not allowable.

44. Walter Lafeber, *Inevitable Revolutions: The United States in Central America* (New York: W.W. Norton, 1983). William Appleman Williams, *Empire as a Way of Life* (New York: Oxford University Press, 1980).

45. Gabriel Marcel, *Creative Fidelity*, 88–91. Lonergan, *Method in Theology*, 104–7, 240–42.

46. Lonergan, *Method in Theology*, 104–7. Quotation from p. 105.

47. U.S. Catholic Bishops, *Economic Justice for All*, 28. Gustavo Gutiérrez, *The Power of the Poor in History*, trans. Robert R. Barr (Maryknoll, N.Y.: Orbis Books, 1984).

48. U.S. Catholic Bishops, *Economic Justice for All*, 55–92. Holly Sklar, "Who's Who: The Truly Greedy III, " *Z Magazine*, vol. 4 (June 1991): 10–12. Francis Fox Piven and Richard Cloward, *The New Class War* (New York: Pantheon, 1982).

49. Quotation from Marx, *Capital*, I, 798. See CAL, 270–74 for a fuller development of the link between capitalism and poverty.

50. Robert Lekachman, *Greed is Not Enough* (New York: Pantheon Books, 1982). Piven and Cloward, *The New Class War* .

51. Lonergan, *Method in Theology*, 101–9.

52. U.S. Catholic Bishops, *Economic Justice for All*.

53. See also James L. Marsh, "Interiority and Revolution," *Philosophy Today*, 29: 191–202. CAL, 43–45, 174–76.

Chapter Eleven

1. Robert M. Doran, *Theology and the Dialectics of History* (Toronto: University of Toronto Press, 1989), 387–417. Ronald Hall, *Word and Spirit: A Kierkegaardian Critique of the Modern Age* (Bloomington: Indiana University Press, 1993), 1–14.

2. Martin Jay, *Marxism and Totality: The Adventures of a Concept from Lukacs to Habermas* (Berkeley: University of California Press, 1984). Strictly speaking, Western Marxism also includes thinkers such as Merleau-Ponty, Sartre, Raymond Williams, and Althusser, but I am stressing the resources of critical theory here and its immediate historical antecedents and influences.

3. Karl Marx, *Economic and Philosophical Manuscripts*, 106–10.

4. Ibid., 110–12. Karl Marx, *Capital*, I, 492–639, quotation from 367.

5. Marx, *Economic and Philosophical Manuscripts*, 112–19.

6. Marx, *Capital*, I, 247–57. See Dussel, *Ethics and Community*, 112–69, for a development of the imperialistic implications of capitalism.

7. Marx, *Capital*, I, 125–77. *Grundrisse*, 401–16. Marcuse, *One-Dimensional Man*, 1–54.

8. Marx, *Capital*, I, 725–34. PCM, 212–30. CAL, 265–89.

9. Marx, *Grundrisse*, 163.

10. Ibid., 161–62. Stuart Ewen, *Captains of Consciousness: Advertising and the Roots of Consumer Culture* (New York: McGraw Hill, 1976). See my development of these points in CAL, 293–312.

11. Marx, *Economic and Philosophical Manuscripts*, 132–46.

12. Marx, *Grundrisse*, 161–62. See my developed argument in CAL, 166–76, 313–30.

13. For a fuller development of these ideas, see James Marsh, "The Corsair Affair: Kierkegaard and Critical Social Theory," in Robert Perkins, ed., *International Kierkegaard Commentary: The Corsair Affair* (Macon: Mercer University Press, 1990), 63–83. Søren Kierkegaard, *The Corsair Affair and Articles Related to the Writings*, ed. and trans. Howard V. Hong and Edna H. Hong (Princeton: Princeton University Press, 1982), 159.

14. Kierkegaard, *The Corsair Affair*, 172.

15. Ibid., 28.

16. Ibid., 170, 179, 189.

17. Quotation from T.S. Eliot, "The Four Quartets," in *The Complete Poems and Plays* (New York: Harcourt, Brace, and World, 1952), 120. Søren Kierkegaard, *Two Ages: The Age of Revolution and the Present Age. A Literary Review*, trans. Howard V. Hong and Edna H. Hong (Princeton: Princeton University Press, 1978), 90–104.

18. Soren Kierkegaard, *Two Ages*, 74–76, 88–89, 94–95, 104–5.

19. Ibid., 89–90.

20. Ibid., 84–91.

21. See Antonio Gramsci, *Selections from the Prison Notebooks*, ed. and trans. Quintin Hoare and Geoffrey Nowell Smith (New York: International Publishers, 1971) and Jürgen Habermas, *Communication and the Evolution of Society*, trans. Thomas McCarthy (Boston: Beacon Press, 1979), for their own rendering of the political.

22. Habermas, *Communication and the Evolution of Society*, 95–176. *Toward a Rational Society*, 81–122, *The Theory of Communicative Action*, I. *Reason and the Rationalization of Society*, trans. Thomas McCarthy (Boston: Beacon Press, 1984), 1–42, 216–42, 273–77, hereafter referred to as RRS; II: *Lifeworld and System: A Critique of Functionalist Reason*, trans. Thomas McCarthy (Boston: Beacon Press, 1987), 343–56, hereafter referred to as CFR. Lindbloom, *Politics and Markets*. See my own discussion in CAL, 192–34.

23. Habermas, *Toward a Rational Society*, 81–122. CFR, 332–73. Noam Chomsky, *Manufacturing Consent* (New York: Pantheon, 1988), 1–35.

24. Kierkegaard, *Stages of Life's Way*, trans. Howard V. Hong and Edna H. Hong (Princeton: Princeton University Press, 1988).

25. Habermas, *Lifeworld and System*, 1–111.

26. Kierkegaard, *Kierkegaard's Attack on Christendom 1854–55*, trans. Walter Lowrie (Princeton: Princeton University Press, 1944). *The Corsair Affair*.

27. Theodore Adorno, *Minima Moralia*, trans. E.F. Jephcott (London: New Left, 1974), 18.

28. Gary Wills, *Reagan's America: Innocents at Home* (Garden City, N.Y.: Doubleday, 1987).

29. Theodore Adorno and Max Horkheimer, *The Dialectic of Enlightenment*, trans. John Cumming (New York: Seabury, 1972), 120–67. Kellner, *The Persian Gulf T.V. War*, 11, 59–60, 115–16, 177–78. CAL, 293–312.

30. Noam Chomsky, *Year 501: The Conquest Continues* (Boston: South End Press, 1993), 155–95. *Manufacturing Consent*, 37–142. Michael Parenti, *Inventing Reality* (New York: St. Martin's Press, 1992). Walter Benjamin, *Passagen-Werk*, I, ed. Rolf Tiedmann (Frankfurt: Surhkamp, 1982), 60–61, 63–64, 76–77.

31. Marx, *Capital*, I, 163–77. Benjamin, *Passagen-Werk*, 435–36. Ewen, *Captains of Consciousness*. Michael Parenti, *Make-Believe Media: The Politics of Entertainment* (New York: St. Martin's Press, 1992).

32. Jean Baudrillard, *Selected Writings*, ed. Mark Poster (Stanford: Stanford University Press, 1988), 119–47. Douglas Kellner, *Jean Baudrillard: From Marxism to Postmodernism and Beyond* (Stanford: Stanford University Press, 1989), 60–121. Benjamin, *Passagen-Werk*, 495–96, 573–74. See my critique of and alternative to Baudrillard in CAL, 291–312.

33. See John Caputo, *Radical Hermeneutics* (Bloomington: Indiana University Press, 1987), 11–25, for a reading of Kierkegaard as postmodernist. See Mark Taylor, *Kierkegaard's Pseudonymous Authorship: A Study of Time and the Self* (Princeton: Princeton University Press, 1975); John Elrod, *Being and Existence in Kierkegaard's Pseudonymous Works* (Princeton: Princeton University Press, 1975); and Stephen Dunning, *Kierkegaard's Dialectic of Inwardness: A Structural Analysis of the Theory of Stages* (Princeton: Princeton University Press, 1985); for Kierkegaard's stances on the self, normativity, dialectical rationality, and critique. Quotations are from *Two Ages*, 91, 93, 106.

34. Kierkegaard, *Two Ages*, 94.

35. See Marcuse, *One-Dimensional Man*, 3, for a critique of American capitalist society as totalitarian.

36. Marx, *Economic and Philosophical Manuscripts*, 143–46. *Selected Writings*, 39–74, 159–91.

37. Kierkegaard, *Practice in Christianity*, trans. Howard V. Hong and Edna H. Hong (Princeton: Princeton University Press, 1991), 12–15, 38, quotation from 13. *Kierkegaard's Attack on Christendom 1854–55*, trans. Walter Lowrie (Princeton: Princeton University Press, 1944).

38. Kierkegaard, *Concluding Unscientific Postscript*, 352–53.

39. Kierkegaard, *Two Ages*; *The Corsair Affair*; *Kierkegaard's Attack on Christendom*.

40. PCM, 200–58.

41. See CAL, 174–76, for an earlier development of this idea of radical political conversion.

Chapter Twelve

1. Habermas, CFR, 46–53, 77–78, 83–84, 88–93, 106–111, 228.

2. Husserl, *Formal and Transcendental Logic*, 278.

3. Habermas, RRS, 273–399. Elsewhere Habermas talks about a fourth and even a fifth validity claim; see 123, where he mentions adequacy of standards of aesthetic value and comprehensability of symbolic constructs. Truth, sincerity, and rightness are privileged because they are the basis for fundamental kinds of speech acts in a way that other validity claims are not.

4. RRS, 256. Habermas, *Legitimation Crisis*, 107–8. Jürgen Habermas and Niklas Luhmann, *Theorie der Gesellschaft oder Socialtechnologie* (Frankfurt: Suhrkamp Verlag, 1971), 101–41.

5. RRS, 295–319.

6. Ibid., 28–95.

7. See Habermas, *Communication and the Evolution of Society*, 95, for a definition of his Marxism as "reconstructed."

8. Hannah Arendt, *The Recovery of the Public World*, ed. Melvin Hill (New York: St. Martin's Press, 1979), 303–15. Tracy, *The Analogical Imagination*, 285–87, 390–98. Adorno, *Minima Moralia*, 155–57, quotation taken from 157. Talcott Parsons, "Paradigm of the Human Condition," in *Action, Theory, and the Human Condition* (New York: 1978), 356

9. RRS, 332–34. Hannah Arendt, *The Life of the Mind*, ed. Mary McCarthy (New York: Harcourt, Brace, and Jovanovich, 1978). See my discussion of the contemplative domain in CAL, 47–58.

10. CFR, 71–76, 96–111. Lonergan, *Method in Theology*, 238–43. Kierkegaard, *Stages on Life's Way*, trans. Walter Lowrie (New York: Schocken Books, 1967).

11. Michael McCarthy, *The Crisis of Philosophy* (Albany: SUNY Press, 1990), 245–47. RRS, 366–99. Habermas, *The Philosophical Discourse of Modernity*, trans. Frederick Lawrence (Cambridge, Mass.: MIT Press, 1987), 131–60. Husserl, *The Crisis of European Sciences*. Alfred Schutz, *The Phenomenology of the Social World*, trans. George Walsh and Frederick Lehnert (Evanston: Northwestern University Press, 1967). See my own phenomenological account of intersubjectivity in PCM, 125–59. Robert Sokolowski, *Moral Action: A Phenomenological Study* (Bloomington: Indiana University Press, 1985).

12. Lonergan, *Insight*, 636–86. Kierkegaard, *Concluding Unscientific Postscript*, 177–83. Habermas, *Knowledge and Human Interests*, trans. Jeremy Shapiro (Boston: Beacon Press, 1971), 71–90.

13. Helmut Peukert, *Science, Action, and Fundamental Theology*, trans. James Bohman (Cambridge, Mass.: MIT Press, 1984), 182–245, quotation from 235.

14. Thomas McCarthy, *Ideals and Illusions: Reconstruction and Deconstruction in Contemporary Critical Theory* (Cambridge: MIT Press, 1991), 210–15.

15. See endnote 1.

16. RRS, 113–97, 216–42, 332–73. CFR, 119–52.

17. CFR, 147–48, 332–73. See my expanded discussion of such differentiation in CAL, 179–263.

18. Habermas, *The Philosophical Discourse of Modernity*, 83–210, 283–93. Alasdair MacIntyre, *After Virtue* (Notre Dame: University of Notre Dame Press, 1984). Marx, *Grundrisse*, 156–65. Habermas, *Communication and the Evolution of Society*, 182–88.

19. Charles Taylor, *Sources of the Self* (Cambridge: Harvard University Press, 1989), 355–57, 398–401, 449–55.

20. Talcott Parsons, *The Evolution of Societies*, ed. Jackson Toby (Englewood Cliffs, N.J.: Prentice-Hall, 1977), 182–214. John Courtney Murray, *We Hold These Truths* (Garden City, NY: Image Books, 1964).

21. See endnote 1.

22. Kierkegaard, *Concluding Unscientific Postscript*. Moltmann, *Theology of Hope*. Gutiérrez, *A Theology of Liberation*. Daniel Berrigan, *To Dwell In Peace* (New York: Harper & Row, 1987). It is finally my judgment that Habermas's Marxism is

much too limited in its backing off from the critique of capitalism as intrinsically unjust, from democratic socialism as an alternative, and from value theory. On this point, see CAL, 166–76, 265–312, and endnote 8, 392–94.

23. Caputo, *Radical Hermeneutics*, 257–94. Nancy Fraser, *Unruly Practices* (Minneapolis: University of Minnesota Press, 1989). Marx, *Capital*, I, 762–870. Peter Henriot, *Opting for the Poor: A Challenge for North Americans* (Washington, D.C.: Center of Concern, 1990). Dussel, *Ethics and Community*, 124–34.

24. Lonergan, *Insight*, 339–43. Kierkegaard, *Concluding Unscientific Postscript*, 99–108. Dussel, *Ethics and Community*, 124–34. Metz, *Faith in History and Society*, 22–57. David Tracy, *Blessed Rage for Order* (New York: The Seabury Press, 1978), 43–56.

25. Metz, *Faith in History and Society*, 88–89. St. Matthew, 25:31–45; St. Mark, 10:17–31; St. Luke, 10:17–31; *The New Testament*.

26. Rosemary Ruether, *Womanguides: Readings Toward a Feminist Theology* (Boston: Beacon Press, 1985). Boff, *Church, Charism, and Power*. Tracy, *The Analogical Imagination*, 390–98.

27. Habermas, *Communication and the Evolution of Society*, 130–77. RRS, 8–42, 216–42. See my development of these points in CAL, 87–112, 179–263.

28. Marcuse, *One-Dimensional Man*, 1–120. Habermas, *Legitimation Crisis*, 33–41, 57–58.

29. Habermas, *Legitimation Crisis*, 61–68.

30. Ibid., 68–75. CFS, 343–56.

31. Habermas, *Legitimation Crisis*, 75–92. See my development of these crisis tendencies in CAL, 231–33.

32. On this issue of formalism and motivation in Habermas, see Agnes Heller, "Habermas and Marxism," in *Habermas: Critical Debates*, ed. John Thompson and David Held (Cambridge: MIT Press, 1982), 22–41.

33. Tracy, *The Analogical Imagination*, 47–83, 371–98.

34. Boff, *Jesus Christ Liberator*. Sobrino, *Christianity at the Crossroads*. Ricoeur, *The Philosophy of Paul Ricoeur*, 213–22.

35. Westphal, *Kierkegaard's Critique of Reason and Society* (Macon: Mercer University Press, 1987.

36. Berrigan, *To Dwell In Peace*. Kierkegaard, *Two Ages*. Merold Westphal, "Kierkegaard's Sociology," and James Marsh, "Marx and Kierkegaard on Alienation," *International Kierkegaard Commentary: Two Ages*, ed. Robert Perkins (Macon: Mercer University Press, 1984), 133–74. Lonergan, *Method in Theology*, 104–5.

37. On this issue of fallibilism, see Habermas, *The Philosophical Discourse of Modernity*, 408–9, footnote 28, where he defends claims that are universal and fallible, against postmodernists like Derrida.

38. Marx, *Selected Writings*, 179–82. CFR, 391–96.

39. CFR, 391–96. Habermas, *Legitimation Crisis*, 33–41. Claus Offe, *Strukturprobleme des kapitalistischen Staates* (Frankfurt: Suhrkamp Verlag, 1972). See my discussion of social movements in CAL, 343–55.

40. CFR, 332–72. For an earlier version of colonization, although he does not call it by that name, see Marx, *Economic and Philosophical Manuscripts*, 165–69. Rather, he describes the rule of money in spheres whose intrinsic logic is alien to that

of money. Thus, for example, an ugly man who happens to be wealthy can buy himself the most beautiful of women.

41. CFR, 192. Ernst Mandel, *Late Capitalism*, trans. Joris De Bres (London: New Left Books, 1972), 108–46, 438–89. David Harvey, *The Condition of Post-Modernity* (Oxford: Basil Blackwell, 1989), 141–97. See my discussion of this issue in CAL, 145–55.

42. CFR, 393–94.

43. Lonergan, *Method in Theology*, 104–7.

Chapter Thirteen

1. Novak, *The Spirit of Democratic Capitalism*. Francis Fukayama, *The End of History and the Last Man* (New York: Free Press, 1992).

2. PCM, 200–258. CAL, 265–312.

3. Nelson-Pallmeyer, *Brave New World Order*, 4–5.

4. Derrida, *Specters of Marx*, 81–84.

5. Ibid., 85.

6. Ibid., 13, 87–92. On the role of the radical intellectual, see also Edward Said's *Representations of the Intellectual* (New York: Pantheon Books, 1994).

7. Chomsky, *Turning the Tide*, 37–42. In this chapter I am focusing on and using most of my examples from Central and Latin America, but the third world includes large parts of the Middle East, Africa, and Asia as well.

8. Everest, "The Selling of Peru," 35–36.

9. McGovern, *Liberation Theology and Its Critics*, 6–11. Gutiérrez, *A Theology of Liberation*, 211–37.

10. Kant, *Groundwork of the Metaphysic of Morals*, trans. H.J. Paton (New York: Harper Torchbooks, 1964), 95–98. Marx, *Economic and Philosophic Manuscripts*, 106–19.

11. Novak, *The Spirit of Democratic Capitalism*, 31–67. Chomsky, *Turning the Tide*, 157–59, quotation from 47. *Deterring Democracy*, 1–64, 351–401. CAL, 265–89.

12. McGovern, *Liberation Theology and Its Critics*, 152–53. Novak, *But Will It Liberate?*, 3–4, 49, 79, 82, 139. André Gunder Frank, *Latin America: Underdevelopment or Revolution* (New York: Monthly Review Press, 1964).

13. Novak, *The Spirit of Democratic Capitalism*, 301.

14. McGovern, *Liberation Theology and Its Critics*, 163–69. Fernande Henrique Cardozo and Enzo Faletto, *Dependency and Development in Latin America* (Berkeley: University of California Press, 1979).

15. McGovern, *Liberation Theology and Its Critics*, 106–17, 169.

16. Ibid., 117–31. Dussel, *Philosophy of Liberation*, 1–15. Marx, *Capital*, I, 340–416, 492–639.

17. McGovern, *Liberation Theology and Its Critics*, 113–14.

18. Ibid., 14–16. Williams, *Empire as a Way of Life*, 78–110.

19. McGovern, *Liberation Theology and Its Critics*, 114–17. Chomsky, *Year 501*, 172–75, 189–91, 197–219. *Turning the Tide*, 160–61, 154–57, 164, 127–46. One might

hesitate at my use of Haiti as a successful example of deterring democracy. Did not Clinton restore Aristide to power in 1994? In a sense that happened, but with so many constraints on him that Aristide's aims and hopes for his people will not be achieved, and such nonachievement is the intention of U.S. foreign policy. The issues here are complex hermeneutically, but the following seems clear and verifiable. First, Haiti had been the object for over a century of U.S. policies intending to render it a means to FW wellbeing. Second, over the last 60 to 70 years we have kept in power dictators like the Duvaliers to serve our interests and to keep the majority of their people in incredible poverty. Third, when Aristide ran for office in 1990, the U.S. financially and through media publicity supported the more conservative candidate, who, it was thought, would do our bidding. Fourth, the original arrangement in 1992–93 was to return a severely constrained and inhibited Aristide to power, unable to carry out his proposed reforms for the people, who would then not run for reelection a few years later. An apparent counter-instance to my interpretation turns out to be another verifying instance of that interpretation. On this point, see Chomsky, *Year 501*, 197–219. "Foreign Policy; Democracy Enhancement II: Haiti," *Z Magazine*, vol. 7 (July-August 1994): 49–61. "Democracy Restored," *Z Magazine*, vol. 7 (November 1994): 49–61. Paul Farmer, *Inside Haiti: U.S. Policy and the Plight of a Nation* (Westfield, N.J.: Open Magazine Pamphlet Series, 1994).

20. McGovern, *Liberation Theology and Its Critics*, 14.

21. Ibid., 119, 166.

22. Ibid., 172.

23. Novak, *Will It Liberate?*, 28, 114, 203–4. Dennis McCann, *Christian Realism and Liberation Theology* (Maryknoll, N.Y.: Orbis, 1981), 25–50, 118. Robert Cornelison, *The Christian Realism of Reinhold Niebuhr and The Political Theology of Jürgen Moltmann in Dialogue* (San Francisco: Mellon Research University Press, 1992), 2–13. Niebuhr, *Moral Man and Immoral Society* .

24. CAL, 332–41.

25. Marx and Engels, *The German Ideology*, 39–57, 60–64, 119–20. *Marx: Selected Writings*, 240–42, 243–45. CAL, 313–55.

26. Novak, *The Spirit of Democratic Capitalism*, 72–77. *Will It Liberate?*, 108, 202–4, 216, 238. For earlier books influenced by Lonergan, see *Belief and Unbelief* (New York: Macmillan, 1965) and *Experience of Nothingness* (New York: Harper & Row, 1970).

27. See, for example, Marcuse, *One-Dimensional Man*, 218–22. *Counter-Revolution and Revolt* (Boston: Beacon Press, 1972), 1–57; see esp. 42–57. On triumphalistic versus critical modernism, see MAD, 89.

28. Enrique Dussel, *Ethics and Community*, 139. I will be referring to this book often in the next several pages because it is in English, but we should also note three other magnificent interpretations of Marx in Spanish by Dussel, in which he expands Marxist theory into a theory of neoimperialism and dependence: *La Produción Teórica de Marx: Un Commentario a los Grundrisse* (Mexico City: Siglo Veintiuno editores, 1985), esp. 371–413; *Hacia un Marx Desconocido: Un Commentario de los Manuscritos del 61–63* (Mexico City: Siglo Veintiuno editores, 1988), esp. 313–61; *El Último Marx (1863–1882) y la liberación Latinoamericana* (Mexico City: Siglo 21, 1990), 295–49. These volumes in their thoroughness, originality, and insight are at least the equal of anything in English on Marx.

29. CAL, 267. PCM, 220–21. Moishe Postone, *Time, Labor, and Social Domination* (New York: Cambridge University Press, 1993), 72–83.

30. Dussel, *Ethics and Community*, 136–37.

31. Ibid., 139–40. Karl Marx, *Capital*, vol. III, trans. David Fernbach (New York: Penguin Books, 1991), 118, 133–42, 244–45, 251, 311.

32. Dussel, *Ethics and Community*, 141.

33. Ibid., 149–50.

34. Ibid., 149.

35. Ibid., 151.

36. Ibid., 152–56. Noam Chomsky, *World Orders Old and New* (New York: Columbia University Press, 1994), 180.

37. Dussel, *Ethics and Community*, 156.

38. Ibid., 158–63. Karl Marx, *Capital*, vol. II, trans. David Fernbach (New York: Penguin, 1978), 180–99.

39. Dussel, *Ethics and Community*, 164–69.

40. Rosemary Radford Reuther, *Sexism and God-Talk: Toward a Feminist Theology* (Boston: Beacon Press, 1983), 68–71, 85–92.

41. Chomsky and Herman, *Manufacturing Consent*, 1–35. Kellner, *The Persian Gulf TV War*, 62–76.

42. Chomsky, *World Orders Old and New*, 178–88.

43. Ibid., 113–18. Chomsky, *Year 501*, 1–21.

44. CAL, 293–312. David Harvey, *The Condition of Post-Modernity* (Oxford: Basil Blackwell, 1989), 121–97.

45. CAL, 33. Harvey, *The Condition of Post-Modernity*, 125–40.

46. CAL, 175–76.

47. PCM, 165–69. CAL, 31–36.

48. See Lonergan, *Insight*, 377–79, for a distinction between upper and lower blades.

49. Williams, *Empire as a Way of Life*.

50. CAL, 265–89.

51. Habermas, *The Past as Future*, ed. and trans. Max Pensky (Lincoln: University of Nebraska Press, 1994), 5–31. Nelson-Pallmeyer, *Brave New World Order*, 80.

52. Derrida, *The Other Heading* trans. Pascale-Anne Brault and Michael B. Nass (Bloomington: Indiana University Press, 1992), 77–79.

53. Allen Nairn, "Murder as Policy," *The Nation*, vol. 260 (April 24, 1995): 547–48. Anthony Arnove, "Criminal Habits: An Interview with Allen Nairn," *Z Magazine*, vol. 8 (June 1995): 22–99.

54. Nelson-Pallmeyer, *Brave New World Order*, 9–17, quotation from 12.

55. Ibid., 81–85. Ramsay Clark and Others, *War Crimes: A Report on United States War Crimes Against Iraq* (Washington, D.C.: Maisonneuve Press, 1992), 9–24.

56. Nelson-Pallmeyer, *Brave New World Order*, 80.

57. Kellner, *The Persian Gulf TV War*, 30–37.

58. Nelson-Pallmeyer, *Brave New World Order*, 85–93. Chomsky, *World Orders Old and New*, 189–272. Edward Said, *The Politics of Dispossession: The Struggle for Palestinian Self-Determination, 1969–1994* (New York: Pantheon Books, 1994), 413–20.

59. Kellner, *The Persian Gulf TV War*, 109–40.

60. Novak, *Will It Liberate?*, 82–95.

61. Chomsky, *Year 501*, 141–54.

62. CAL, 317–18.

63. Chomsky, *Year 501*, 157–70. *Turning the Tide*, 39–42, 82–84.

64. Chomsky, *Turning the Tide*, 62–63.

65. Nelson-Pallmeyer, *Brave New World Order*, 101. E.F. Schumacher, *Small is Beautiful* (New York: Perennial Library, 1973), 171–90.

Chapter Fourteen

1. U.S. Catholic Bishops, *Economic Justice for All*, 37–38, 69–76, 83–92. Chomsky, *World Orders Old and New*, 139–48.

2. Plato, *The Republic*, 605–30, 676–88.

3. Hegel, *Hegel's Phenomenology of Spirit*, 111–19.

4. Dussel, *Philosophy of Liberation*, 1–15.

5. Ibid.

6. Ibid., 8–9. Attentive readers of my work will note the return here to the theme of overcoming Cartesianism in PCM, esp. 1–39, 200–230, 239–58.

7. Ibid., 51–52, quotation from 52.

8. Ibid., 54–56.

9. Ibid., 53.

10. Ibid., 58–64.

11. Ibid., 64–66, quotation from 66.

12. Deluze and Guttari, *Anti-Oedipus: Capitalism and Schizophrenia*, xi–xiv.

13. Harry Braverman, *Labor and Monopoly Capital*, 293–356.

14. CAL, 301–8.

15. Marcuse, *One Dimensional Man*, 48–55. Habermas, *Legitimation Crisis*, 33–41.

16. Habermas, *Legitimation Crisis*, 45–50, 68–75.

17. Lindbloom, *Politics and Markets*, 170–88, quotation from 181.

18. Ibid., 170–88.

19. Habermas, *Toward a Rational Society*, 90–122.

20. Ibid., 112–113.

21. Habermas, *Legitimation Crisis*, 68–92.

22. Richard Parker, *The Myth of the Middle Class* (New York: Harper Colophon, 1972). Andrew Levinson, *The Working Class Majority* (New York: Coward, McCann, Geoghan, 1974). Gabriel Kolko, *Wealth and Power in America* (New York: Prager, 1962), 55–69.

23. CAL, 254–61, 291–312.

24. Chomsky, *The Year 501*, 141–95.

25. McGovern, *Liberation Theology and Its Critics*, 105–75.

26. Williams, *Empire as a Way of Life*. Chomsky, *The Year 501*, 197–219.

27. Guy Debord, *The Society of the Spectacle* (New York: Zone Books, 1994).

28. CAL, 331–55.

29. CAL, 291–312. William Kunstler, *My Life As a Radical Lawyer* (New York: Birch Lane Press, 1994). Noam Chomsky, "Rollback II," 20–31.

30. CAL, 301–8. Habermas, *Legitimation Crisis*, 45–50.

31. Jeremy Brecher and Primitivo Rodriguez, "On the House at the Global Casino," *Z Magazine*, vol. 8 (April 1995): 44–48.

32. CAL, 293–308. Harvey, *The Condition of Post-Modernity*, 141–72.

33. Chomsky, *World Orders Old and New*, 178–88.

34. Chomsky, "Rollback II," 20–31. "Rollback III," *Z Magazine*, vol. 8 (April 1995): 17–24.

35. Ibid. James O'Connor, *Accumulation Crisis* (New York: Basil Blackwell, 1984). Samuel Bowles, David Gordon, and Thomas E. Weiskopf, *Beyond the Wasteland* (New York: Anchor Books, 1983). Chomsky, *World Orders Old and New*, 139–48.

36. Chomsky, "Rollback II," 20–31; "Rollback III," 17–24; *World Orders Old and New*, 139–48. Bennett Harrison and Barry Bluestone, *The Great U-Turn* (New York: Basic Books, 1989).

37. Harrison and Bluestone, *The Great U-Turn*, 139–68. Chomsky, *World Orders Old and New*, 139–48.

38. Chomsky, "Rollback III," 17–24. Neil deMause, "Live Welfare Free or Die," *Z Magazine*, vol. 8 (April 1995): 29–32.

39. Nelson Pallmeyer, *Brave New World Order*, 94–113. CAL, 272, 273–74, 277–78, 279–80. Habermas, *Legitimation Crisis*, 41–44.

40. Habermas, *Legitimation Crisis*, 92–94. Nelson Pallmeyer, *Brave New World Order*, 20–22. Chomsky, "Rollback II,": 20–31.

41. CAL, 282–88, 341–53.

42. Chomsky, "Rollback III," 17–24. deMause, "Live Welfare Free or Die," 29–32.

43. CAL, 341–53. The quotation is from Marx, *Capital, I*, 353.

44. CAL, 348–49. Gramsci, *The Prison Notebooks*, 130–33, 418. Dussel, *Ethics and Community*, 78–87.

45. CAL, 348–49.

46. CAL, 257, 349–50. Gramsci, *The Prison Notebooks*, 5–23. Habermas, *The Structural Transformation of the Public Sphere*, trans. Thomas Burger with Frederick Lawrence (Cambridge: MIT Press, 1989), 1–26.

47. Derrida, *Specters of Marx*, 85–86.

48. CAL, 351–52.

49. Chad Meyers, *Who Will Roll Away the Stone?: Discipleship Inquiries for First World Christians* (Maryknoll, N.Y.: Orbis Books, 1994). An important source for my reflection on indigenous peoples, traditions, and religions is Mark Taylor's "Ghosts of American Lands: A Spirituality of Revolutionary Protest," unpublished.

50. Daniel Berrigan, *Ten Commandments for the Long Haul* (Nashville: Abingdon, 1981), 24–27, 52–55, 62–71.

Bibliography

Adorno, Theodore, and Max Horkheimer. *The Dialectic of Enlightenment.* Trans. John Cumming. New York: Seabury, 1972.

———. *Minima Moralia.* Trans. E.F. Jephcott. London: New Left, 1974.

Appel, Michael. *Ideology and Curriculum.* London: Routledge & Kegan Paul, 1979.

Arato, Andrew. "Critical Sociology and Authoritarian State Socialism." *Habermas Critical Debates.* Ed. John B. Thompson and David Held. Cambridge: MIT Press, 1982.

Arendt, Hannah. *The Life of the Mind.* Ed. Mary McCarthy. New York: Harcourt, Brace, and Jovanovich, 1978.

———. *The Recovery of the Public World.* Ed. Melvin Hill. New York: St. Martin's Press, 1979.

Arnove, Anthony. "Criminal Habits: An Interview with Allen Nairn." *Z Magazine*, volume 8 (June 1995): 22–99.

Augustine, St. *The Confessions of St. Augustine.* Trans. John Ryan. New York: Image Books, 1960.

Ayer, A.J. *Language, Truth, and Logic.* New York: Dover, 1950.

Barth, Karl. *The Epistle to the Romans.* Trans. Edwyn C. Hoskyns. New York: Oxford University Press, 1933.

Baudrillard, Jean. *Selected Writings.* Ed. Mark Poster. Stanford: Stanford University Press, 1988.

Benjamin, Walter. *Passagen-Werk.* I. Ed. Rolf Tiedmann. Frankfurt: Suhrkamp, 1982.

Berrigan, Daniel. *Minor Prophets, Major Themes.* Marion, SD: Fortkamp Books, 1995.

———. *The Nightmare of God.* Portland: Sunburst Press, 1983.

———. *Steadfastness of Saints.* Maryknoll, N.Y.: Orbis Books, 1985.

———. *Ten Commandments for the Long Haul.* Nashville: Abingdon Press, 1981.

————. *To Dwell in Peace.* New York: Harper & Row, 1987.

Bloch, Ernst. *The Principle of Hope.* Vol. I. Trans. Neville Plaice, Stephen Plaice, and Paul Knight. Cambridge: MIT Press, 1986.

Boff, Leonardo. *Church, Charism, and Power.* Trans. John Diercksmeier. New York: Crossroads, 1985.

————. *Ecclesiogenesis.* Trans. Robert Barr. Maryknoll, N.Y.: Orbis Books, 1977.

————. *Jesus Christ Liberator.* Trans. Patrick Hoches. Maryknoll, N.Y.: Orbis Books, 1978.

————. *Passion of Christ, Passion of the World.* Trans. Robert Barr. Maryknoll, N.Y.: Orbis Books, 1987.

Bologh, Roslyn Wallach. *Dialectical Phenomenology: Marx's Method.* London: Routledge & Kegan Paul, 1979.

Bowles, Samuel, David Gordon, and Thomas E. Weiskopf. *Beyond the Wasteland.* New York: Anchor Books, 1983.

———— and Herbert Gintis. *Schooling in Capitalist America.* New York: Basic Books, 1976.

Brackley, Dean. *Divine Revolution: Salvation and Liberation in Catholic Thought.* Maryknoll, N.Y.: Orbis Books, 1996.

Braverman, Harry. *Labor and Monopoly Capital: The Degradation of Work in the Twentieth Century.* New York: Monthly Review Press, 1974.

Brecher, Jeremy, and Primitivo Rodriguez. "On the House at the Global Casino." *Z Magazine,* volume 8 (April 1995): 44–48.

Bultmann, Rudolf. *Jesus Christ and Mythology.* New York: Charles Scribner's Sons, 1958.

Cardozo, Fernande Henrique, and Enzo Faletto. *Dependency and Deveopment in Latin America.* Berkeley: University of California Press, 1979.

Catherine of Siena, St. *The Dialogue.* Trans. Suzanne Noffke. New York: Paulist Press, 1980.

Chomsky, Noam. "Democracy Restored." *Z Magazine,* volume 7 (November 1994): 49–61.

————. *Deterring Democracy.* New York: Verso Books, 1991.

————. "Foreign Policy; Democracy Enhancement II: Haiti." *Z Magazine,* volume 7 (July–August 1994): 49–61.

———— and Edward Herman. *Manufacturing Consent.* New York: Pantheon, 1988.

————. "Rollback II." *Z Magazine,* vol. 8 (February 1995): 20–31.

————. "Rollback III." *Z Magazine,* vol. 8 (April 1995): 17–24.

————. *Turning the Tide.* Boston: South End Press, 1985.

————. *World Orders Old and New.* New York: Columbia University Press, 1994.

————. *Year 501: The Conquest Continues.* Boston: South End Press, 1993.

Christian, William. *An Interpretation of Whitehead's Metaphysics.* New Haven: Yale University Press, 1959.

Clark, Ramsay, and others. *War Crimes: A Report on United States War Crimes Against Iraq.* Washington, D.C.: Maisonneuve Press, 1992.

Colby, Gerard, and Charlotte Dennett. *Thy Will Be Done: The Conquest of the Amazon: Nelson Rockefeller and Evangelism in the Age of Oil.* New York: Harper Collins, 1995.

Cook, Michael L. *The Historical Jesus*. Chicago: Thomas More Press, 1986.

Cornelison, Robert. *The Christian Realism of Reinhold Niebuhr and The Political Theology of Jürgen Moltmann in Dialogue*. San Francisco: Mellon Research University Press, 1992.

DeBord, Guy. *Society of the Spectacle*. Detroit: Black and Red, 1983.

Deleuze, Gilles, and Felix Guattari. *Anti-Oedipus: Capitalism and Schizophrenia*. Trans. Robert Hurley, Mark Seem, and Helen R. Lane. Minneapolis: University of Minnesota Press, 1983.

deMause, Neil. "Live Welfare Free or Die." *Z Magazine*, volume 8 (April 1995): 29–32.

Derrida, Jacques. *Margins of Philosophy*. Trans. Alan Bass. Chicago: University of Chicago Press, 1982.

———. *Of Grammatology*. Trans. Gayatri Chakravorty Spivak. Baltimore: Johns Hopkins University Press, 1976.

———. *The Other Heading*. Trans. Pascale-Anne Brault and Michael B. Nass. Bloomington: Indiana University Press, 1992.

———. *Positions*. Trans. Alan Bass. Chicago: University of Chicago Press, 1981.

———. *The Post Card: From Socrates to Freud and Beyond*. Trans. Alan Bass. Chicago: Univerisity of Chicago Press, 1981.

———. *Spectres of Marx*. Trans. Peggy Kamuf. New York: Routledge and Kegal Paul, 1994.

———. *Writing and Difference*. Trans. Alan Bass. Chicago: University of Chicago Press, 1982.

Desan, Wilfrid. *The Marxism of Jean-Paul Sartre*. Garden City, N.Y.: Anchor Books, 1966.

Domhoff, William. *Who Rules America?* Englewood Cliffs, N.J.: Prentice-Hall, 1967.

Doran, Robert M. *Theology and the Dialectics of History*. Toronto: University of Toronto Press, 1989.

Dunn, James D.G. *The Evidence for Jesus*. Philadelphia: Westminster Press, 1985.

Dunning, Stephen. *Kierkegaard's Dialectic of Inwardness: A Structural Analysis of the Theory of Stages*. Princeton: Princeton University Press, 1985.

Dussel, Enrique. *Ethics and the Theology of Liberation*. Trans. Bernard F. McWilliams. Maryknoll, N.Y.: Orbis Books, 1978.

———. *Hacia un Marx Desconcido: Un Commentario de los Manuscritos del 61–63*. Mexico City: Signo Veintiuno editores, 1988.

———. *Philosophy of Liberation*. Trans. Aquilina Martinez and Christine Morkovsky. Maryknoll, N.Y.: Orbis Books, 1985.

———. *La Producción Teórica de Marx: Un Commentario a los Grundriße*. Mexico City: Siglo Veintiuno editores, 1985.

———. *El Último Marx (1863–1882) y la Liberación Latinoamericana*. Mexico City: Siglo Veintiuno, 1990.

Economic Justice For All. Washington, DC: National Conference of Catholic Bishops, 1986.

Eliot, T. S. *The Complete Poems and Plays*. New York: Harcourt, Brace, and World, 1952.

———. *The Waste Land and Other Poems*. New York: Harvest, 1962.

Elrod, John. *Being and Existence in Kierkegaard's Pseudonymous Works*. Princeton: Princeton University Press, 1975.

Everest, Larry. "The Selling of Peru." *Z Magazine*, volume 7 (September 1994): 35–36.

Ewen, Stuart. *Captains of Consciousness: Advertising and the Roots of Consumer Culture*. New York: McGraw Hill, 1976.

Farmer, Paul. *Inside Haiti: U.S. Policy and the Plight of a Nation*. Westfield, N.J.: Open Magazine Pamphlet Series, 1994.

Feuerbach, Ludwig. *The Essence of Christianity*. Trans. George Eliot. New York: Harper & Row, 1957.

Frank, André Gunder. *Latin America: Underdevelopment or Revolution*. New York: Monthly Review Press, 1964.

Fraser, Nancy. *Unruly Practices*. Minneapolis: University of Minnesota Press, 1989.

Freud, Sigmund. *The Ego and the Id*. Ed. James Strachey. Trans. Joan Riviere. New York: Norton, 1962.

———. *A General Introduction to Psychoanalysis*. Trans. Joan Riviere. New York: Pocket Books, 1953.

———. *The Standard Edition of the Complete Psychological Works of Sigmund Freud*. Ed. and trans. James Strachey. London: Hogarth, 1953–74.

Friere, Paolo. *Pedagogy of the Oppressed*. Trans. Myra Bergman Ramos. New York: Herder & Herder, 1972.

Fukayama, Francis. *The End of History and the Last Man*. New York: Free Press, 1992.

Gadamer, Hans-Georg. *Philosophical Hermeneutics*. Trans. David Linge. Berkeley: University of California Press, 1976.

———. *Truth and Method*. Trans. Garrett Barden and John Cumming. New York: Seabury Press, 1978.

Gasché, Rodolphe. *The Tain and the Mirror: Derrida and the Philosophy of Reflection*. Cambridge: Harvard University Press, 1986.

Gould, Carol. *Marx's Social Ontology*. Cambridge: MIT Press, 1978.

Gramsci, Antonio. *Selections from the Prison Notebooks*. Ed. and trans. Quintin Hoare and Geoffrey Nowell Smith. New York: International Publishers, 1971.

Gutiérrez, Gustavo. *The Power of the Poor in History*. Trans. Robert R. Barr. Maryknoll, N.Y.: Orbis Books, 1984.

———. *A Theology of Liberation*. Trans. Sister Caridad Inda and John Eagleson. Maryknoll, N.Y.: Orbis Books, 1973.

Habermas, Jürgen. *Communication and the Evolution of Society*. Trans. Thomas McCarthy. Boston: Beacon Press, 1979.

———. *Knowledge and Human Interests*. Trans. Jeremy Shapiro. Boston: Beacon Press, 1971.

———. *Legitimation Crisis*. Trans. Thomas McCarthy. Boston: Beacon Press, 1975.

———. *The Past as Future*. Ed. and trans. Max Pensky. Lincoln: University of Nebraska Press, 1994.

———. *The Philosophical Discourse of Modernity*. Trans. Frederick Lawrence. Cambridge: MIT Press, 1987.

———. *The Structural Transformation of the Public Sphere*. Trans. Thomas Burger with Frederick Lawrence. Cambridge: MIT Press, 1989.

————. *Theory of Communicative Action*. Volume I. *Reason and the Rationalization of Society*. Trans. Thomas McCarthy. Boston: Beacon Press, 1984.

————. *Theory of Communicative Action*. Volume II. *Life-World and System: The Critique of Functionalist Reason*. Trans. Thomas McCarthy. Boston: Beacon Press, 1987.

————. *Towards a Rational Society*. Trans. Jeremy Shapiro. Boston: Beacon Press, 1970.

———— and Niklas Luhmann. *Theorie der Gesellschaft oder Socialtechnologie*. Frankfurt: Suhrkamp Verlag, 1971.

Hall, Ronald. *Word and Spirit: A Kierkegaardian Critique of the Modern Age*. Bloomington: Indiana University Press, 1993.

Harrington, Michael. *The Twilight of Capitalism*. New York: Simon & Schuster, 1976.

Harrison, Bennett, and Barry Bluestone. *The Great U-Turn*. New York: Basic Books, 1989.

Hartshorne, Charles. *Anselm's Discovery*. LaSalle, Ill.: Open Court, 1965.

————. *Creative Synthesis and Philosophic Method*. LaSalle, Ill.: Open Court, 1967.

————. *Divine Relativity*. New Haven: Yale University Press, 1948.

————. *Omnipotence and Other Mistakes*. Albany: SUNY Press, 1984.

Harvey, David. *The Condition of Post-Modernity*. Oxford: Basil Blackwell, 1989.

Hegel, G.W.F. *Hegel's Phenomenology of Spirit*. Trans. A. V. Miller. London: Clarendon Press, 1977.

————. *Hegel's Philosophy of Right*. Trans. T. M. Knox. London: Oxford Univresity Press, 1967.

Heidegger, Martin. *Being and Time*. Trans. John Macquarrie and Edward Robinson. New York: Harper & Row, 1962.

————. *Discourse on Thinking*. Trans. John Anderson and F. Hans Freund. New York: Harper & Row, 1966.

————. *Introduction to Metaphysics*. Trans. Ralph Mannheim. Garden City, N.Y.: Anchor Books, 1961.

————. *On the Way to Language*. Trans. Peter D. Hertz. New York: Harper & Row, 1971.

————. *The Piety of Thinking*. Trans. James C. Hart and John C. Maraldo. Bloomington: Indiana University Press, 1976.

————. *The Question Concerning Technology and Other Essays*. Trans. William Lovitt. New York: Harper & Row, 1977.

————. *What is Called Thinking*. Trans. J. Glenn Gray and Fred Wieck. New York: Harper & Row, 1968.

————. "What is Metaphysics?" Trans. F.F.C. Hull and Alan Crick. In *Existence and Being*. Chicago: Henry Regnery Company, 1949.

Henriot, Peter. *Opting for the Poor: A Challenge for North Americans*. Washington, D.C.: Center of Concern, 1990.

Hopkins, Gerard Manley. "God's Grandeur." *A Hopkins Reader*. Ed. W.H. Gardner and N.M. McKenzie. New York: Oxford University Press, 1970.

Horkheimer, Max. *Critical Theory: Selected Essays*. Trans. Matthew J. O'Connell and others. New York: Herder & Herder, 1972.

Hudson, Wayne. *The Marxist Philosophy of Ernst Bloch*. London: Macmillan, 1982.

Hume, David. *A Treatise on Human Nature.* Ed. L.A. Shelby-Bigge. London: Clarendon Press, 1967.

———. *Dialogues Concerning Natural Religion.* New York: Hafner Publishing Company, 1966.

Husserl, Edmund. *The Crisis of European Sciences and Transcendental Phenomenology.* Trans. David Carr. Evanston: Northwestern University Press, 1985.

———. *Formal and Transcendental Logic.* Trans. Dorion Cairns. The Hague: Martinhus Nijhoff, 1969.

Jamal, Mumia Abu. *Live From Death Row.* New York: Addison Wesley, 1995.

Jay, Martin. *Marxism and Totality: The Adventures of a Concept from Lukacs to Habermas.* Berkeley: University of California Press, 1984.

John of the Cross, St. "Sayings of Light and Love." *The Collected Works of St. John of the Cross.* Trans. Kieran Kavanaugh and Otilio Rodriguez. Washington, D.C.: Institute of Carmelite Studies, ICS Publications, 1991.

Johnson, Elizabeth. *She Who Is.* New York: Crossroads, 1992.

Kant, Immanuel. *Critique of Pure Reason.* Trans. Norman Kemp Smith. New York: St. Martin's Press, 1965.

———. *Groundwork of the Metaphysics of Morals.* Trans. H.J. Paton. New York: Harper Torchbooks, 1964.

Kavanaugh, John. *Following Christ in a Consumer Society.* 2nd Edition. Maryknoll, N.Y.: Orbis Books, 1991.

Kellermann, Bill Wylie. *Seasons of Faith and Consciousness.* Maryknoll, N.Y.: Orbis Books, 1991.

Kellner, Douglas. *Jean Baudrillard: From Marxism to Postmodernism and Beyond.* Stanford: Stanford University Press, 1989.

———. *The Persian Gulf T.V. War.* Boulder: Westview Press, 1992.

Kierkegaard, Søren. *Concluding Unscientific Postscript.* Trans. David Swenson and Walter Lowrie. Princeton: Princeton University Press, 1968.

———. *The Corsair Affair and Articles Related to the Writings.* Ed. and Trans. Howard V. Hong and Edna H. Hong. Princeton: Princeton University Press, 1982.

———. *Fear and Trembling and Sickness Unto Death.* Trans. Walter Lowrie. Garden City, NY: Doubleday Anchor, 1954.

———. *Kierkegaard's Attack on Christendom 1854–55.* Trans. Walter Lowrie. Princeton: Princeton University Press, 1944.

———. *Practice in Christianity.* Trans. Howard V. Hong and Edna H. Hong. Princeton: Princeton University Press, 1991.

———. *Stages on Life's Way.* Trans. Howard V. Hong and Edna H. Hong. Princeton: Princeton University Press, 1988.

———. *Stages on Life's Way.* Trans. Walter Lowrie. New York: Schocken Books, 1967.

———. *Two Ages: The Age of Revolution and the Present Age. A Literary Review.* Trans. Howard V. Hong and Edna H. Hong. Princeton: Princeton University Press, 1978.

Kleinbach, Russell. *Marx Via Process.* Washington, D.C.: University Press of America, 1982.

Kolko, Gabriel. *Wealth and Power in America.* New York: Praeger, 1962.

Kuhn, Thomas. *The Structure of Scientific Revolutions*. Chicago: University of Chicago Press, 1962.

Kunstler, William. *My Life as a Radical Lawyer*. New York: Birch Lane Press, 1994.

Lafeber, Walter. *Inevitable Revolutions: The United States in Central America*. New York: W.W. Norton, 1983.

Lauer, Quentin. *Hegel's Concept of God*. Albany: SUNY Press, 1982.

Lekachman, Robert. *Greed is Not Enough*. New York: Pantheon Books, 1982.

Levinas, Emmanuel. *Totality and Infinity*. Trans. Alfonso Lingis. Pittsburgh: Dusquene University Press, 1969.

Levinson, Andrew. *The Working Class Majority*. New York: Coward, McGann, Geoghan, 1974.

Lindbloom, Charles. *Politics and Markets*. New York: Basic Books, 1977.

Lonergan, Bernard. *Insight: A Study of Human Understanding*. New York: Longman's Green and Co., 1957.

———. *Method in Theology*. New York: Herder & Herder, 1972.

MacIntyre, Alisdair. *After Virtue*. Notre Dame: University of Notre Dame Press, 1984.

Mandel, Ernst. *Late Capitalism*. Trans. Joris DeBres. London: New Left, 1972.

Marcel, Gabriel. *Being and Having*. New York: Harper Torchbooks, 1965.

———. *Creative Fidelity*. Trans. Robert Rosthal. New York: Noonday Press, 1964.

———. *The Existential Background of Human Dignity*. Cambridge: Harvard University Press, 1963.

———. *The Mystery of Being*. 2 Volumes. Chicago: Henry Regnery & Co., 1960.

———. *The Philosophy of Existentialism*. Trans. Manya Harari. 3rd Edition; New York: Citadel Press, 1963.

———. *Tragic Wisdom and Beyond*. Trans. Stephen John and Peter McCormick. Evanston, Ill.: Northwestern University Press, 1973.

Marcuse, Herbert. With Barrington Moore and Robert Paul Wolff. *A Critique of Pure Tolerance*. Boston: Beacon Press, 1965.

———. *Counter-Revolution and Revolt*. Boston: Beacon Press, 1972.

———. *One-Dimensional Man*. Boston: Beacon Press, 1964.

Marion, Jean-Luc. *God Without Being: Hors Texte*. Trans. Thomas Carlson. Chicago: Univeristy of Chicago Press, 1991.

Marsh, James L. "The Corsair Affair: Kierkegaard and Critical Social Theory." In Robert Perkins Ed. *International Kierkegaard Commentary: The Corsair Affair*. Macon: Mercer University Press, 1990.

———. *Critique, Action, and Liberation*. Albany: SUNY Press, 1994.

———. "Interiority and Revolution." *Philosophy Today*. 29: 191–202.

———. "Marx and Kierkegaard on Alienation." *International Kierkegaard Commentary: Two Ages*. Ed. Robert Perkins. Macon: Mercer University Press, 1984.

———, Merold Westphal, and John Caputo. *Modernity and Its Discontents*. Bronx: Fordham University Press, 1992.

———. *Post-Cartesian Meditations*. New York: Fordham University Press, 1988.

Marx, Karl. *Capital*. Volume I. Trans. Ben Fowkes. New York: Vintage, 1977.

———. *Capital*. Volume II. Trans. David Fernbach. New York: Penguin, 1978.

———. *Capital*. Volume III. Trans. David Fernbach. New York: Penguin Books, 1991.

———. *The Economic and Philosophical Maniscripts of 1844*. Ed. Dirk Struick. Trans. Martin Milligan. New York: International Publishers, 1964.

———. *18th Brumaire*. New York: International Publishers, 1963.

———. *Grundrisse*. Trans. Martin Nicholaus. New York: Vintage Books, 1973.

———. *Karl Marx: Selected Writings*. Ed. David McLellan. New York: Oxford University Press, 1977.

———. "On the Jewish Question." *Karl Marx: Early Writings*. Trans and Ed. T.B. Bottomore. New York: McGraw Hill, 1963.

——— and Friedrich Engels. *The German Ideology*. Ed. C.J. Arthur. New York: International Publishers, 1970.

McCann, Dennis. *Christian Realism and Liberation Theology*. Maryknoll, N.Y.: Orbis Books, 1981.

McCarthy, Thomas. *Ideals and Illusions: Reconstruction and Deconstruction in Contemporary Critical Theory*. Cambridge: MIT Press, 1991.

McCarthy, Michael. *The Crisis of Philosophy*. Albany: SUNY Press, 1990.

McGovern, Arthur F. *Liberation Theology and its Critics*. Maryknoll: Orbis Books, 1989.

Merton, Thomas. *Contemplative Prayer*. Garden City, N.Y.: Image Books, 1971.

———. *Witness to Freedom: Letters in Times of Crisis*. Ed. William Shannon. New York: Farrar, Strauss, Giroux, 1996.

Metz, Johann Baptist. *The Emergent Church*. London: SCM Press, 1981.

———. *Faith in History and Society: Towards a Practical, Fundamental Theology*. Trans. David Smith. New York: Seabury Press, 1980.

Meyers, Chad. *Who Will Roll Away the Stone: Discipleship Inquiries for First World Christians*. Maryknoll, N.Y.: Orbis Books, 1994.

Meynell, Hugo A. *Is Christianity True?* Washington, D.C.: Catholic University Press, 1994.

Mill, John Stuart. *Utilitarianism and Other Writings*. Ed. Mary Warnock. New York: Meridian Books, 1970.

Moltmann, Jürgen. *A Theology of Hope*. Trans. James Leitch. New York: Harper & Row, 1967.

Murray, John Courtney. *The Problem of God*. New Haven: Yale University Press, 1964.

———. *We Hold These Truths*. Garden City, N.Y.: Image Books, 1964.

Muto, Susan, and Adrian Van Kaam. *Formation for Becoming Spiritually Mature*. Pittsburgh: Epiphany Association, 1991.

Nairn, Allen. "Murder as Policy." *The Nation*. Volume 260 (April 24, 1995): 547–48.

Neibhur, Reinhold. *Moral Man and Immoral Society*. New York: Charles Scribner's Sons, 1960.

Nelson-Pallmeyer, Jack. *Brave New World Order*. Maryknoll, N.Y.: Orbis Books, 1992.

The New Testament. Revised Edition. New York: Catholic Book Publishing Company, 1986.

Nielsen, Kai. *Equality and Liberty: A Defense of Radical Egalitarianism*. Totowa, N.J.: Rowman & Allenheld, 1985.

Nietzsche, Friedrich. *The AntiChrist*. In *The Portable Nietzsche*. Ed. and trans. Walter Kaufmann. New York: Penguin, 1954.

———. *The Gay Science*. Trans. Walter Kaufmann. New York: Vintage Books, 1974.

————. *Human, All Too Human*. Trans. Marion Faber. Lincoln: University of Nebraska Press, 1984.

————. *On the Genealogy of Morals and Ecce Homo*. Trans. Walter Kaufmann. New York: Vintage, 1967.

————. *Thus Spake Zarathustra*. In *The Portable Nietzsche*. Trans. Walter Kaufmann. New York: Viking Press, 1954.

Noffke, Suzanne. *Catherine of Siena: Vision through a Distant Eye*. Collegeville, Mn.: Liturgical Press, 1996.

Novak, Michael. *Experience of Nothingness*. New York: Harper & Row, 1970.

————. *The Spirit of Democratic Capitalism*. New York: Simon & Schuster, 1982.

————. *Will It Liberate? Questions for Liberation Theology*. New York: Paulist Press, 1986.

Oakes, Edward T. *Patterns of Redemption: The Theology of Hans Urs Von Balthasar*. New York: Continuum, 1994.

O'Collins, Gerald. *Christology: A Biblical Historical and Systematic Study of Jesus*. New York: Oxford University Press, 1995.

O'Connor, James. *Accumulation Crisis*. New York: Basil Blackwell, 1984.

Offe, Claus. *Strukturprobleme des kapitalistischen Staates*. Frankfurt: Suhrkamp Verlag, 1972.

The Old Testament. New York: Guild Press.

Ollman, Bertell. *Alienation: Marx's Conception of Man in Capitalist Society*. Cambridge: Cambridge University Press, 1971.

Parenti, Michael. *Against Empire*. San Francisco: City Lights Books, 1995.

————. *Inventing Reality*. New York: St. Martin's Press, 1992.

————. *Land of Idols*. New York: St. Martin's Press, 1994.

————. *Make-Believe Media: The Politics of Entertainment*. New York: St. Martin's Press, 1992.

Parker, Richard. *The Myth of the Middle Class*. New York: Harper Colophon, 1972.

Parsons, Talcott. *The Evolution of Societies*. Ed. Jackson Toby. Englewood Cliffs, N.J.: Prentice-Hall, 1977.

————. "Paradigm of the Human Condition." *Action, Theory, and the Human Condition*. New York: 1978.

Peffer, Rodney. *Marxism, Morality, and Justice*. Princeton: Princeton University Press, 1990.

Peukert, Helmut, *Science, Action, and Fundamental Theology*. Trans. James Bohman. Cambridge: MIT Press, 1984.

Piven, Francis Fox, and Richard Cloward. *The New Class War*. New York: Pantheon, 1982.

Plato. *The Republic*. Trans. Paul Shorey. In *Plato: The Collected Dialogues*. Eds. Edith Hamilton and Huntington Cairns. Princeton: Princeton University Press, 1961.

Postone, Moishe. *Time, Labor, and Social Domination*. New York: Cambridge University Press, 1993.

Rader, Melvin. *Marx's Interpretation of History*. New York: Oxford University Press, 1972.

Rahner, Karl. *Hearers of the Word*. Trans. Michael Richards. New York: Herder & Herder, 1969.

Richardson, William. *Heidegger: Through Phenomenology to Thought.* 2nd Edition. The Hague: Martinus Nijhoff, 1967.

Ricoeur, Paul. *Freedom and Nature.* Trans. Erazim Kohik. Evanston: Northwestern University Press, 1966.

———. *Freud and Philosophy.* Trans. David Savage. New Haven: Yale University Press, 1970.

———. *Hermeneutics and the Human Sciences.* Ed. John B. Thompson. Cambridge: Cambridge University Press, 1981.

———. *Interpretation Theory: Discourse and the Surplus of Meaning.* Fort Worth: Texas Christianity Press, 1976.

———. *The Philosophy of Paul Ricoeur.* Eds. Charles Reagan and David Stewart. Boston: Beacon Press, 1978.

———. *The Rule of Metaphor.* Trans. Robert Czerny, with Kathleen McLaughlin and John Costello. Toronto: University Press, 1977.

———. *Symbolism of Evil.* Trans. Emerson Buchanan. New York: Harper & Row, 1967.

———. *Time and Narrative.* Volume I. Trans. Kathleen McLaughlin and David Pellauer. Chicago: University of Chicago Press, 1984.

Ruether, Rosemary R. *Sexism and God-Talk: Toward a Feminist Theology.* Boston: Beacon Press, 1983.

———. *Womanguides: Readings Toward a Feminist Theology.* Boston: Beacon Press, 1985.

Said, Edward. *The Politics of Dispossession: The Struggle for Palestinian Self-Determination, 1969–1994.* New York: Pantheon Books, 1994.

———. *Representations of the Intellectual.* New York: Pantheon Books, 1994.

Sartre, Jean-Paul. *Being and Nothingness.* Trans. Hazel Barnes. New York: Citadel Press, 1964.

———. "Consciousness of Self and Knowledge of Self." *Readings in Existential Phenomenology.* Ed. Nathaniel Lawrence and Daniel O'Connor. Englewood Cliffs, N.J.: Prentice-Hall, 1967.

———. *Existentialism and Human Emotions.* Trans. Bernard Frechtman and Hazel E. Barnes. New York: Wisdom Library, 1957.

Schattschneider, E.E. *The Semisovereign People.* New York: Holt, Rinehart, and Winston, 1960.

Schillebeeckx, Edward. *Christ: The Experience of Jesus as Lord.* Trans. John Bowden. New York: Crossroads Books, 1993.

———. *Jesus, an Experiment in Christology.* Trans. Hubert Hoskins. New York; Crossroads, 1995.

Schumacher, E.F. *Small Is Beautiful.* New York: Perennial Library, 1973.

Schutz, Alfred. *The Phenomenology of the Social World.* Trans. George Walsh and Frederick Lehnert. Evanston: Northwestern University Press, 1967.

Shakespeare, William. *Shakespeare: The Complete Works.* London: Collins, 1951.

Sklar, Holly. "Who's Who: The Truly Greedy III." *Z Magazine.* Volume 4 (June 1991):10–12.

Smith, Tony. *Technology and Social Form: A Critique of Lean Production* (unpublished).

Sobrino, Jon. *Christology at the Crossroads.* Trans. John Drury. Maryknoll, N.Y.: Orbis Books, 1979.

———. *Spirituality of Liberation: Toward Political Holiness.* Trans. Robert R. Barr. Maryknoll, N.Y.: Orbis Books, 1985.

Sokolowski, Robert. *Moral Action: A Phenomenological Study.* Bloomington: Indiana University Press, 1985.

Sölle, Dorothy. *The Window of Vulnerability.* Trans. Linda M. Moloney. Minneapolis: Fortress Press, 1990.

T.S. Eliot. "The Four Quartets." *The Complete Poems and Plays.* New York: Harcourt, Brace, and World, 1952.

Taylor, Charles. *Sources of the Self.* Cambridge: Harvard University Press, 1989.

Taylor, Mark. "Ghosts of American Lands: A Spirituality of Revolutionary Protest" (unpublished).

Taylor, Mark. *Kierkegaard's Pseudonymous Authorship: A Study of Time and the Self.* Princeton: Princeton University Press, 1975.

Tracy, David. *The Analogical Imagination.* New York: Crossroads, 1981.

———. *Blessed Rage for Order.* New York: Seabury Press, 1978.

Tyrell, Bernard. *Bernard Lonergan's Philosophy of God.* Notre Dame: University of Notre Dame Press, 1974.

Von Balthasar, Hans Urs. *Prayer.* Trans. A.V. Littledale. New York: Sheed & Ward, 1961.

Waltzer, Michael. *Spheres of Justice.* New York: Basic Books, 1983.

Westphal, Merold. *God, Guilt, and Death.* Bloomington: Indiana University Press, 1984.

———. "Kierkegaard's Sociology." *International Kierkegaard Commentary: Two Ages.* Ed. Robert Perkins. Macon: Mercer University Press, 1984.

———. *Kierkegaard's Critique of Reason and Society.* Macon: Mercer University Press, 1987.

———. *Suspicion and Faith: The Religious Uses of Modern Atheism.* Grand Rapids: William B. Eerdman, 1993.

Whitehead, Alfred North. *Adventures in Ideas.* New York: Philosophical Library, 1947.

———. *The Function of Reason.* Boston: Beacon Press, 1966.

———. *Process and Reality.* Eds. David Ray Griffin and Donald Sherburne. New York: Free Press, 1978.

Williams, William Appleman. *Empire as a Way of Life.* New York: Oxford University Press, 1980.

Wills, Gary. *Reagan's America: Innocents at Home.* Garden City, N.Y.: Doubleday, 1987.

Wittgenstein, Ludwig. *Tractatus Logico-Philosophicus.* Trans. D.F. Pears and B.F. McGuiness. London: Routledge & Kegan Paul, 1961.

Index

B

being: aspects of notion of, 36–37; as completely intelligible, 88–93; notion of, 32–37; notion of as heuristic, 32; as object of the pure desire to know, 44; as process, 45–54; as somewhat intelligible not making any sense, 89; as structure, 37–45

Berrigan, Daniel: xiii, 151, 171, 192, 244, 256, 259, 262, 318; book as dedicated to, v; as a Catholic organic intellectual, 316; his concept of linking work for institutional change with living in radical community as basic sanity, 319; as playing, in his critique of U. S. Society, a role analogous to Kierkegaard in his critique of Danish Christendom, 260; as witnessing to religious joy in the midst of suffering, 164–65

C

capitalism: commodification and commodity fetishism in, 216–17; definition of, 215; as an economy of death, 280–81; as essentially producing poverty, 227; as having a logic, 232–33; as instantiating Plato's parable of the Cave, 218; instrumental rationality in, 216–17; as internally contradictory, 220–21; purposive rational action in, 217; role of consciousness industry in, 239–40; stages of, 217; as in tension with contemplation, 227; as in tension with democracy, 221–26; as unjust, 212–13, 223

Christianity: preferential option for the poor as essential to, 225–26; radical interpretation of as more faithful to the Gospel than either conservative or liberal versions of, 189–90, 228

conversion: as discussed in other volumes of mine, 210–13; as intellectual, 214–18; as moral, 218–24; as political, fruit of intellectual c., 215–18; fruit of moral c., 220–24; fruit of religious c., 225–28; as religious, 224–28; as useful for social change, 228–29

the mystery of evil, 66, 71, 89–91; as illumining problem of divine foreknowledge and human freedom, 65–66; inadequacy of classical version of, 63–64; positive content of, 67–76; processive version of, 63–67, 71–76

God, reality of: argument for, 93–97; argument for as contextualized in and flowing from a process of inquiry, 80–81; argument for as intellectualistic and existential, not merely conceptual and ratiocinative, 79; argument for as part of hermeneutical circle, 79–81; causality as pertaining to the argument for, 87–93; ontological argument for criticized, 84–85; scandal of the argument for, 77–78; scandal of the argument for, overcome, 78–85

H

Habermas, Jürgen: account of communicative action, 248–50; account of modernity, 254–55; aspects of his rethinking of the economic in relation to the political, 236–37; different lines of relationship to religious belief, 262–63; as excluding illegitimately the metaphysical-religious level from his account of communicative action, 250–54; from his account of modernity, 254–55; from his account of crisis theory, 259–60; from his account of social movements, 262; as having the most developed account of the political in the Marxist tradition, 236; interpretation of crisis theory, 257–59

Heidegger, Martin: attempt to overcome metaphysics, 10–19; deficient phenomenology of objectivity in, 13–16; positive value of his account of *Denken*, 16–17; positive value of his insights, 16, 26, 27

I

ideology: ways in which religion functions as, 182–84

ideology critique: Scripture functioning as, 184–89

J

Jamal, Mumia Abu: imprisonment of as an instance of the injustice of the prison-industrial complex, 172–73

Jesus Christ: belief in as both historical and existential, 150–52; belief in as dialectical and phenomenological, 156–57; belief in as involving a legitimate overcoming of metaphysics, 135; as both "masculine" and "feminine," 149–50; characteristics of, 147–50; contemplative dimension of belief in, 152–54; as fulfillment and term of dialectical phenomenology, 155–57; reasons for a revelation of, 135–36, 152; steps in coming to believe in, 144–50; as a unity of opposites, 147; as universal and particular, 156

Jesus Christ, Liberator: aspects and qualities of, 199–206; as not on a power trip, lordly, triumphalistic, 204; as preaching not Himself but the kingdom of God, 199; as presenting a call to discipleship, 201–206; as siding with the poor and oppressed, 202–203; as suffering, 204

K

Kant, Immanuel: account of knowing the external world, 4–6; attempt to overcome metaphysics, 3–9; critique of his account of knowing God, 7–9; as a disillusioned naive realist, 5–6;

N